from news
to
newsprint

from news to newsprint

Producing A Student Newspaper

second edition

Robert Bohle

Virginia Commonwealth University

Prentice Hall
Englewood Cliffs, New Jersey 07632

Library of Congress Cataloging-in-Publication Data

BOHLE, ROBERT,
    From news to newsprint : producing a student newspaper / Robert
Bohle. — 2nd ed.
       p.   cm.
    Includes bibliographical references and index.
    ISBN 0-13-325325-2
    1. Student newspapers and periodicals—United States. I. Title.
LB3621.B58 1992   91-13048
371.8'974—dc20   CIP

© 1992, 1984 by Prentice-Hall, Inc.
a Simon & Schuster Company
Englewood Cliffs, New Jersey 07632

Printed in the United States of America

10 9 8 7 6 5 4 3 2 1

P. 244, Code of Ethics of the Associated Press Managing Editors, reprinted by
permission. P. 245, Code of Ethics of the Society of Professional Journalists,
Sigma Delta Chi, reprinted by permission. P. 246, Statement of Principles of
the American Society of Newspaper Editors, reprinted by permission.
Statement by James K. Batten, reprinted with permission of James K. Batten.

Acquistion editor: Steve Dalphin
Page make-up: Judith Winthrop
Cover design: Franklyn Graphics
Prepress buyer: Kelly Behr
Manufacturing buyer: Mary Ann Gloriande
Copy editor: Rene Lynch
Editorial assistant: Caffie Risher

ISBN 0-13-325325-2

PRENTICE-HALL INTERNATIONAL (UK) LIMITED, *London*
PRENTICE-HALL OF AUSTRALIA PTY. LIMITED, *Sydney*
PRENTICE-HALL CANADA INC., *Toronto*
PRENTICE-HALL HISPANOAMERICANA, S.A., *Mexico*
PRENTICE-HALL OF INDIA PRIVATE LIMITED, *New Delhi*
PRENTICE-HALL OF JAPAN, INC., *Tokyo*
SIMON & SCHUSTER ASIA PTE. LTD., *Singapore*
EDITORA PRENTICE-HALL DO BRASIL, LTDA., *Rio de Janeiro*

For Suzanne

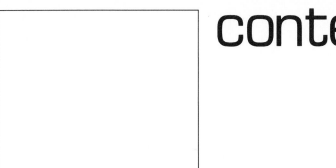

contents

preface

Most of the 18,000 high schools and 3,200 post-secondary schools in the United States have newspapers. The papers range from dailies at large universities to once- or twice-a-month papers at small high schools. But no matter what the size of the school, a sometimes small, always dedicated group of students keeps the rest of the campus informed and entertained with a regular publication.

Producing these newspapers takes an incredible array of skills. Students must plan issues, write stories and take photos, edit and proofread, design pages, sell and design ads, and often paste up and even print the paper. Because school-newspaper readers expect issues of the paper from the very beginning of the school year, there is little time for new staff members to become acquainted with the newspaper-production process.

Although there are many fine books and periodicals—several of which are listed in the chapter-by-chapter bibliography at the end of the book—there is usually too much information and perhaps too much detail in them for the beginning student to digest and use effectively.

This book is a guide, a handbook that offers basic instruction in all facets of producing a newspaper, whether it is a daily, a weekly, or a monthly. After this introduction, a student may study further in a given area by seeking out the books and periodicals in the bibliography. In many programs the first half of the book—the introductory and the writing chapters—could be used in a beginning course and the production chapters in an advanced course.

The stylebook is brief, including only those matters of style that would appear most frequently in a student paper. Each newspaper should also devise a booklet for styles unique to the school (a blank page has been left in the stylebook for additional rules) and select a professional stylebook (the Associated Press is the newspaper standard) as the standard for the staff.

Each chapter ends with a vocabulary list from that chapter. The glossary at the end of the book includes all the vocabulary lists, plus more newspaper or communications terms that the student or adviser might need to look up.

Professional and educational organizations for students and for advisers are listed and annotated in the appendix.

Each chapter has a list of suggested projects (a few also have exercises) so that students can reinforce and examine principles learned in that chapter.

I have tried to avoid sexism in this text. Occasional *he* or *she* references had to be made for clarity. But I am well aware that the majority of mass communications majors today are female.

I hope that this introductory text will help beginning students enter the complex world of producing a newspaper more easily and that it will inspire them to continue to study newspapering in even greater detail later.

Although my name is the only one on the cover of this book, I did not produce it alone. Without the help, inspiration, and advice of many people, I could never have completed the project. I cannot thank everyone, but I would like to list a few who helped me along the way.

Paul D. Wright, an experienced student publications manager, gave me invaluable advice throughout and helped write the photography chapter. Steve Dalphin, the Prentice-Hall editor for both my book projects, showed great understanding of the market and allowed me much flexibility with deadlines. Tom Kramer and Tom Pasqua, both valued colleagues in California community college journalism, gave me advice, friendship, and simply themselves: worthy professional and teaching examples to aim for. One day I hope to hit that high. I appreciate the time working professionals gave me so I could share their insights with students. Finally, I thank the students and faculty advisers who shared their enthusiasm and their work with me.

Individuals who provided photographs, artwork, and written information or who allowed me to interview them for the book also deserve thanks: James K. Batten, Paul Buys, Felicia Campbell, Stan Denny, Dave Ellis, Roger F. Fidler, Ron Fimrite, Robert Foster, Sam Goldman, Nancy Green, Michael Messing, Ron Osborne, Mike Penn, Faith Revell, Tom Rolnicki, Tim Rutten, Edmund J. Sullivan, Lee Terkelsen, Ana Veciana-Suarez, Dana Warren, Laura Wilcoxson and Ron Wills. The many professional journalists, college journalists, and college publication advisers who took the time to send me samples deserve a special thanks. I know how hard it is to find extra time in a day as full as yours.

The Prentice-Hall folks were especially kind this time around: Steve Dalphin, my long-suffering editor, and Judy Winthrop, who led the production this time around, after assisting on the first edition. That this edition makes sense and has order and logic to it is because of their guidance, not because I was able to do it myself.

Finally, I have to thank the three most important people in the creation of the second edition—the ones who truly helped me the most. First are my two sons, Cameron and Christopher. Their help around the house and good-natured acceptance of the time I spent staring at my Macintosh screen make me look good as a parent. I could not have completed even the relatively easy revision process without their help. Thanks, guys. Then there's Suzanne. At the risk of getting maudlin, I must say that her loving care for me during the past two years has made all the difference. Without that, nothing would have happened. And I mean **nothing.** A simple thanks is hardly enough, but perhaps a **THANKS** will come closer.

Robert Bohle

Richmond, VA

from news
to
newsprint

introduction to newspapering

Newspapers today are an integral part of our society. It is as hard to imagine a world without newspapers as it is a world without streets or telephones or houses. Newspapers are a part of the mass communications industry, which also includes magazines, books, films, radio, and television. These mass media make up a vast network of information suppliers that serve society in many ways. Without them, much of our way of life would change drastically.

Newspapers, like the other mass media, serve society in four ways: They inform, entertain, influence, and contribute to the economic system.

The information function of newspapers is the most obvious one. "News," as commonly defined, is something that happens in the community, state, nation, or world that is of some interest or importance to the reader. Newspapers tell us what we need to know as citizens about our government. They tell us what laws mean and when they go into effect. They tell us of good news and bad, big news and small. Without newspapers, we know only about what we actually experience and what we hear from family members and gossipy neighbors.

Newspapers also entertain us with human interest stories, features about interesting people, comic strips, crossword puzzles, and astrological forecasts. In fact, newspapers seem to be turning more and more to entertainment features as they try to fight stagnating circulation and decreasing market penetration. Television, VCRs, and films have taken up time that people used to spend reading newspapers.

Another important function of newspapers is to express opinion. Through its editorials a newspaper can try to influence a person or group to take action or support a philosophical stance that the newspaper believes is right. A vigorous newspaper can bring about many changes in a community—or on campus for that matter—by exerting pressure through its editorials and news coverage.

Most newspapers also have what is often called an "op-ed" page (*opposite* the *ed*itorial page), which is devoted to opinions from individuals other than the newspapers' editors. Good newspapers try to provide as wide a variety of opinions and topics as possible to help readers get the information they need to make up their minds and learn what others think about the crucial issues of the day.

The last major function of a newspaper may well be its most important: contributing to the economic system. A newspaper plays a vital role in the community's economy, and not just because it hires a number of people.

A paper sells space on its pages to local and national firms so that the firms' messages can reach the consumer. Without advertising, readers wouldn't know about sales, about items they need and the best places to buy them, about services for their homes or offices, and about items for sale by other readers of the paper through the classified ad section.

Without advertising stimulating the local economy, many jobs might be lost and the community itself would not be as financially healthy. Millions of dollars nationwide are spent on newspaper advertising. It's this last aspect of newspapers—the business side—that many people forget. A professional newspaper is, on the bottom line, a business—a money-making venture by its owner and publisher. But to get local businesses to advertise and to get people to buy and read, the newspaper has to perform well in the other three areas: information, entertainment, and opinions. It can't exist solely as an ad sheet.

With these important functions, it's hard to believe that newspapers haven't been around since the beginning of history. But they have existed for only 300 years.

History

Newspapers began in Europe, in the late 1600s, to fill an increasing need in society—a need for information. But information then didn't concern the general news of the community. Those were the days of increasing trade with the new world. Ships were returning daily, their holds bulging with exotic goods from far-off places. The growing merchant class that dealt in these goods was eager to know about arriving ships, their cargoes, and the prices.

Enterprising printers began publishing "broadsheets," so-called because they were one sheet of paper printed on both sides. These early newspapers contained shipping information and other tidbits gathered from sailors returning from foreign ports. Broadsheets were generally available only in the new "coffee houses," where merchants came to drink the newly discovered black brew, smoke their pipes, and make deals.

Newspapers in America also began as merchant papers, but soon printers began to take sides and print their views of political battles before, during, and after the Revolutionary War.

The average citizen still didn't read a paper, for two reasons. First the expense. Weekly newspapers cost about a dollar a year, but the average salary then was less than $10 per month. Papers were therefore passed among friends and families. Thus paid-circulation figures were much lower than the numbers of actual readers. In 1765, approximately 5 percent of all white families in the Colonies received a newspaper, although more actually read a paper.

The other reason the average Colonist didn't read newspapers was that he or she couldn't. The growth of newspapers and of society's thirst for information about the community roughly parallels the growth of literacy.

The first newspaper published in the United States was *Publick Occurrences Bothe Foreign and Domestick*, which appeared on September 25, 1690. But because that first issue irked the Massachusetts governor, it was also the last issue. The first newspaper to publish continuously for any length of time (72 years) was the *Boston News-Letter* (Fig. 1–1), a weekly paper. It began on April 24, 1704, and continued until 1776.

The first daily, the *Pennsylvania Evening Post*, began in May of 1783. It lasted one month. In those days just about anybody who had a printing press or access to one could print a newspaper. And just about everybody did. By 1800, there were approximately 200 papers in the United States. By 1900, there were nearly 14,000, including 1,960 dailies. Newspapers had become an integral part of daily life.

Today more newspapers are failing than are being started. There are only about 1,650 dailies and 9,000 weeklies, bimonthlies, and monthlies. Fewer daily newspapers compete for readers in major cities than in the 1960s, even though the total number of newspapers has remained about the same for the past 20 years.

The total circulation of daily newspapers in 1990 was about 64 million—down slightly from the year before but still a very large number considering that

Figure 1–1. The *Boston News-Letter*, a weekly, was the first U.S. paper to publish continuously.

REAGAN TAKES OATH AS 40TH PRESIDENT; PROMISES AN 'ERA OF NATIONAL RENEWAL'
MINUTES LATER, 52 U.S. HOSTAGES IN IRAN FLY TO FREEDOM AFTER 444-DAY ORDEAL

Figure 1–2. The *New York Times* is one of the great papers in this country. Its motto is "All the News That's Fit to Print." (© 1981 by The New York Times Company. Reprinted by permission)

Figure 1–3. The *Tryon* (N.C.) *Daily Bulletin* is the nation's—and perhaps the world's—smallest daily newspaper. Even in the 8½-by 11-inch format, however, this paper can meet the needs of its readers. Reprinted with permission.

the total U.S. population was 250 million. Few towns or villages are too small to support a newspaper. American newspapers range from giants like the *New York Times* (Fig. 1–2) to the *Tryon* (N.C.) *Daily Bulletin* (Fig. 1–3).

Even with the advent of electronic newspapers, sent to the home via cable and read on a computer terminal video screen, newspapers—whatever their form—are here to stay. They are too much a part of our daily lives ever to die out. That's one of the benefits of studying journalism: A need will always exist for good journalists and other professional communicators.

Scholastic newspapers developed along the same lines as professional papers, and today they are just as integral a part of modern schools as professional papers are a part of our society.

School Newspapers

The earliest known school paper can be traced to Revolutionary War days, according to Edmund J. Sullivan of the Columbia Scholastic Press Association, based at Columbia University in New York City. *The Students Gazette,* produced by students of the William Penn Charter School in Pennsylvania, was first published in June 1777. Because *The Students Gazette* was published during the British occupation, the first student newspaper in this country can be considered an "underground" paper!

As did professional papers, scholastic papers grew as school populations grew and as the school community wanted to know more about what was going on in its world. Today, according to Sullivan, there are approximately 18,000 junior high and high school newspapers, and 2,400 two-year and four-year college newspapers. These papers, from daily to once-a-month publications, range in size from small mimeographed high school papers, such as the award-winning *The Redbird* of Loudonville High School in Ohio (Fig. 1–4), to major university and

Figure 1–4. *The Redbird,* an award-winning newspaper from Loudonville High School in Ohio, is typical of a high-quality publication produced by a small number of students.

Figure 1–5. This front page of the Kansas State *Collegian* exhibits a good mix of important news and features.

Figure 1–6. The October, 1989, earthquake in the San Francisco Bay area gave the staff of the excellent community college newspaper, *The Advocate,* Contra Costa College, a real-life opportunity for a special coverage front page.

Figure 1–7. This tabloid front from the Loyola (New Orleans) University *Maroon* uses the four-column format—a good one for a tabloid.

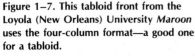

college dailies, such as Kansas State's *Collegian* (Fig. 1–5), Contra Costa College's *The Advocate* (Fig. 1–6), Loyola University's *Maroon* (Fig. 1–7), Tulane's *Hullabaloo* (Fig. 1–8), and UCLA's *Daily Bruin* (Fig. 1–9).

Good scholastic papers differ only slightly from good professional papers. The larger papers, such as *The Daily Bruin,* may include wire service stories and may cover national and international news events. On the other hand, *The Redbird,* though much smaller than *The Daily Bruin,* also covers stories of importance outside the school (see the photo of Jack Anderson in Fig. 1–4) as well as crucial issues on campus, such as costly school vandalism. Good papers cover their communities and their issues whether the community is a town or city, a large university campus or a small college or high school campus.

The scholastic newspaper has a special relationship with its community. The paper is produced by students for students, but its audience also includes faculty, staff, other members of the local community, and sometimes night-school students, who may be different demographically from day students. Trying to meet the needs of these diverse groups is comparable to trying to meet the needs of a city filled with large groups of people with differing ethnic or educational backgrounds.

What a newspaper staff should remember is that not all readers have the same backgrounds and interests that they do. The paper should meet the needs of the readers, not the egos of the editors. Just because an editor finds something boring or unimportant is no reason to kill the story. The questions to ask are: Is this important or interesting to all or even part of our readers? What do *they* want or need to know?

Figure 1–8. The Tulane *Hullabaloo* uses
full-color photography printed on a white
paper stock to add visual snap to its pages.

Figure 1–9. Another tabloid, The UCLA
Daily Bruin increases its story count on
page 1 by running briefs the length of the
first column.

So regardless of whether a newspaper is small or large, professional or
scholastic, its four major functions are the same: informing, entertaining, influencing, and contributing to the economic system.

Suggested Projects

1. Check your school library for copies or microfilm of early issues of the school
   paper. How has the look of the paper changed? How has the content
   changed?

2. Visit your local community paper or look in the library for old copies. When
   was the first issue published? How has the newspaper adapted to meet the
   needs of the community?

3. Find out more about your readers. Gather available information from the
   registrar. Try a small survey to find out who reads the paper and, more
   importantly, who doesn't and why.

4. Write a story about the history of your school paper and publish it. How
   many issues have been published? Who was the first editor? If that person is
   still around, arrange an interview to elicit some comments about the paper,
   then and now. Plan the story for National Newspaper Week.

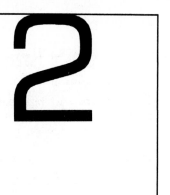

the nature
and language
of news

Defining the nature of news is as tough as trying to predict next year's news. Journalists nevertheless have been trying to nail down a definition for years. "What is news?" seems to be a question with an answer that changes, chameleonlike, with the needs of the newspaper's audience and the decisions of its editors.

News can be good or bad, big or small, from next door or far away. It can be what the readers believe they need to know about their world, or it can be what the newspaper believes they ought to know. It can concern the reader directly or it can concern events halfway around the world.

One post–Civil War journalist in New York, John B. Bogart, defined news as "When a dog bites a man, that is not news; when a man bites a dog, that's news." Charles A. Dana of the old New York *Sun* defined news as "anything that makes people talk." Arthur McEwan, one of William Randolph Hearst's editors at the *San Francisco Examiner,* said that news was "anything that makes a reader say 'Gee whiz!'" One of my journalism students, who shall remain unnamed, said that news is "whatever you send me out to get."

As Tulare (Calif.) *Advance-Register* editor Dave Ellis discusses in the sidebar to this chapter, two major aspects of defining news for the readers are (1) giving readers what they *ought* to know and (2) giving them what they *want* to know. Giving readers only what they *ought* to know would probably lead to a rather dull and dry account of the day's events, along with some commentary, opinion, and analysis of the more important events, such as city council meetings or new state business laws. But giving readers only what they *want* to know might lead to an abundance of entertainment pieces, crossword puzzles, comic pages, and personals in the classified ads. The best package combines the two.

A successful newspaper understands the character of its audience and the kind of information that is important to it. The *Advance-Register,* located in one of the richest agricultural counties in the United States, runs more farm news than does the *Washington Post.* Many newspapers are paying market research firms to go into the community and determine just what kinds of information are needed or desired by readers. This is smart, not only for the editors and reporters but also for the comptroller. Giving the readers a package of information that they want is just good business.

The reporter or editor should not make news judgments based on personal feelings about the importance of an event; he or she should make decisions based on a perception of *reader* needs and wants. If enough members of the community are interested in an event or an issue, then the paper should cover it, no matter how little importance the reporter or editor believes the event or issue has.

A school newspaper can gauge the college community's interests by having a market research or public relations class run a survey as a class project. Or it can

What is news?

David L. Ellis

Former editor, Tulare Advance-Register

Most beginning reporters are shocked and dismayed when a seasoned news executive tells them that the first obligation of a newspaper is to make a profit. And where does that dream about saving society, fighting evil, and protecting the innocent fit into this picture?

While this seemingly jaded attitude smacks of selling out, the truth of it is self-evident. Unless a newspaper remains financially stable, it can't continue to comfort the afflicted and afflict the comfortable. Without the black ink on the profit-and-loss statement, the newspaper will one day collapse into financial ruin, leaving forever unfulfilled those dreams that crusty old editors and young reporters have in common.

The reaction to the profit motive isn't surprising, considering that most beginning reporters are most interested in gathering the news and least interested in the monetary maneuverings that supply the filthy lucre needed to buy paper and ink—and pay their salaries. However, the nature of news is inescapably connected to the profit motive, and reporters should be experts on the nature of news, particularly young reporters who begin their careers at smaller newspapers where they may be called upon to exercise a great deal of independent judgment on their beats. Editors can't stand over a reporter's shoulder at an out-of-town, day-long meeting to nudge him or her periodically and say, "Write that down; that's news."

So I am surprised when beginning reporters aren't aware that news, by my definition and the definition of any journalist still in business, is something that interests the greatest number of people. Some entry-level reporters have indicated that news is something that people *should* be told, not something they necessarily want to know. That attitude carried to the extreme would spell death to a newspaper just as quickly as ignoring the need to make a profit.

Without readers, there would be no newspaper.

A friend who edits a daily newspaper in the Los Angeles area once picked up a copy of his publication while I was visiting his office and pointed out the front page to me. "Just look at that," he said with a smile on his face. I assumed he was going to pat himself on the back.

"Every story on that page is significant," he added, "and the entire package is boring as hell."

He was right—on that particular day. But his newspaper is successful, among other reasons, because he is aware that news has to grab readers' attention.

Certainly, the best newspapers are a mixture of the significant, the merely interesting, and the entertaining. It's all necessary for the health of the entire package. The trick is to make the significant stories interesting to the reader. It's not enough for a newspaper to display an article on page 1 and say in effect, "You should read this." It has to be written in a way that will relate the subject to the living, breathing daily life of that reader so that the worth of the story becomes self-evident to the reader.

The limiting factor on news, when it is defined in terms of reader interest, is that elusive quality: good taste. There are undoubtedly many things that people want to know but that mainstream newspapers are not willing to print. For example, there are many ways to justify printing a news story about a rape without the name of the victim, but the lurid details fall within that gray area that is usually ignored by responsible publications.

When that young, previously mentioned reporter is working a beat without benefit of immediate supervision, there are several questions that should routinely be part of the self-examination that screens news from non-news.

First on the list is the most important: Who are my readers? In other words, what are the particular interests of the group of people who read this newspaper? The interests

will vary, but there will be some common denominators, such as geography, life style, and financial benefit or loss (the so-called pocketbook stories).

Once the reporter has identified his or her readers, the next step is to decide which events unfolding on the beat will have the greatest impact on the greatest number of these readers. And impact is not limited to significance, as already mentioned. The seemingly frivolous story that holds the interest of a great number of readers by evoking their astonishment or tickling their funny bone is a worthwhile addition to the news columns. Reporters who take themselves and/or their beats too seriously can generate a great deal of deadly dull copy if not watched closely.

In the quest for the significant, the news with conversational value is too often neglected—or an angle with conversational interest is too often overlooked. One weekly editor who taught me which end of a typewriter to use continually admonished me to seek out news stories that readers would discuss in the coffee shop the next morning.

In earlier years, commonplace advice from editors to reporters was, "Write it the way you would tell it to the wife" (today we'd change that to "spouse"). On many occasions while I was working a news desk, reporters would relate something that happened on the beat the previous day, and the tale would be told with great warmth, animation, and excitement. The story, however, when filed, would bear little resemblance to the original telling. All the life had been drained out of it in an effort to be "objective," "meaningful," "committed," or "serious."

If a news story is objective, it will preserve a spark of the lively nature that was contained in the original event. If a reporter can preserve the excitement in the significant events while realizing that the exciting fragments of life have significance in their own way, then that reporter will be responsibly performing the duties that will help keep a newspaper alive.

hire a professional firm to do a survey. The University of Illinois *The Daily Illini* hires an outside firm to do an unbiased market evaluation to help the paper know its advertising market as well as its readership's wants and needs.

Some newspapers may even set policies on the newsworthiness of certain events. For instance, if the publisher of a paper in a small town is interested in keeping out developers who want fast growth for the community, he or she could send notices to the newsroom that prodevelopment stories should not be run or should be hidden inside the paper, and that antidevelopment stories should be given page-1 play. This rare and highly unethical action could mean that the news the community receives may be substantially different from what is actually going on.

So the interpretation of the nature of news is nearly always an individual decision. In fact, most news stories result from several different individual decisions. First, at an event the reporter must select from a sometimes huge body of facts those relatively few he or she believes are most important. Some of these facts may have to be arbitrarily cut while the reporter writes the story. The editor, because of space restrictions, may cut even more. On the final page paste-up, the editor may have to cut yet a few more, so the reader ends up with only 12 or 13 facts out of many that were deemed important on that day by a reporter, an editor, and a copydesk person. On a different day, with more space and another editor, the story may have come out entirely different.

Thus news depends, to a great extent, on whom you are writing for and whom you are working for. Over the years, however, certain standard attributes of news have been taught to all journalists. Besides these attributes, most newspaper staffs can, and should, devise categories of news that fit their unique readership.

News Values

Common attributes of news, or *news values*, are timeliness, proximity, consequence, conflict, change, prominence, and human interest.

Timeliness is perhaps the most obvious of news values. If it's *new*, it must be *news*. A story about a tax increase or an increase in activities fees on campus is worthy of coverage only if it just happened or if it is about to happen. A tax or fee increase that was imposed seven years ago is hardly worth covering today. Events that have happened recently or will happen become events that a newspaper should cover.

Stories that are based on events or issues occurring close to the reader represent the *proximity* news value. Although stories about earthquakes in Ecuador appear in newspapers, a story about an earthquake in the next county would certainly have more interest for the reader. The nearer something happens to the paper's circulation area, the more news value it will have for the reader. A story about fee increases for out-of-state students at Brigham Young University, for example, may have some news value for students at a Texas high school because a percentage of students, though small, may plan to attend BYU. But a story about fee increases at the University of Texas would have greater news value because of its closer proximity to the high school reader.

The earthquake in the next county will not mean much to readers unless it directly affects them, unless some *consequence* of the earthquake changes their lives. If the story merely discusses the damage to persons and their belongings, then the story is likely to have only mild interest (unless the reader knows someone mentioned in the story). But if the story describes how a weakened dam will mean a lowering of the water level and therefore water rationing for a five-county area for the next three months, then the reader's interest will increase dramatically. So if the consequence of an event has personal ramifications, then the event's news value increases.

On a campus, for instance, if art majors will have to pay increased fees for art supplies next year, the overall consequence to the campus will be minimal, although art majors may be incensed. But if *every* student will have to pay higher tuition or activities fees, then the relative news value of that event becomes much greater. It's probably the difference between a front-page story and a story on an inside page.

A news value that many reporters and editors seem to give too much importance is *conflict*. But whenever there are two or more people, groups, political parties, cities, or governments in conflict, there is interest in the ultimate outcome. The consequence of the conflict and its proximity to the reader might make the story even more worthy of coverage. Conflict, however, should not be considered such an important news value that other considerations are left behind. Small conflicts should not be blown out of proportion.

Conflicts on a campus seem to fall largely in the area of school governance, as when the faculty wants a 12 percent pay raise for next year and the school offers six, or when the student senate wants a longer time period to make up incompletes and the faculty senate refuses, or when John Doe wants his history grade changed and the instructor disagrees.

Conflicts often bring about *change,* another important news value. The change can be something that has already occurred, but sometimes an observant reporter can do a story in the midst of a change or point out beforehand what change is going to occur. The examples given could result in a story on how the faculty and administration agreed on a 9 percent pay increase, or how the faculty senate agreed to a committee study on the incomplete-grading policy, or why John Doe accepted the academic review board's decision not to change his grade. Conflict and the resulting change are news values that often occur together in a story.

Prominence is a news value that probably gets too much play in the media. The media often judge a story on that one news value alone. Thus we read that President George Bush hates broccoli, a story of questionable importance. Student editors should be sure that prominence isn't the *only* news value they consider when working on a story assignment.

Human interest is the broadest category of news values, but it's also probably, well . . . the most interesting. Readers are curious about nearly everything that happens to another human being. It can be sad, inspiring, terrifying, humorous, incredible, or humbling, but if it happened to someone, it can be made into a story that someone else would be interested in reading.

Student-newspaper editors occasionally fall into the trap of thinking that only instructors or administrators have enough human-interest news value to deserve stories. In fact, probably hundreds of students on every campus have a story to tell that would interest readers. It is the task of journalists to find those people and tell those stories.

The nature of news on campus is only slightly different from that of news found in a professional newspaper, but the difference does deserve a few words. The front pages of professional newspapers are often filled with stories about crime, disasters, and crises. Fortunately, campus newspapers have few of these stories to print. So news editors of scholastic papers have to look for other stories that meet their news criteria.

News can be divided into *hard news* and *soft news* (Fig. 2–1, 2–2). Hard news might also be described as event-oriented, or news of high importance and

Figure 2–1. A fire is an example of a news event or of *hard news*. The fire itself is an event, but a reporter may use the event as a way to dig into *news issues* that lay beneath the event—for example, arson or ignored fire-safety regulations in student housing. (Photo by Ron Osborne)

Figure 2–2. While a meeting itself is an obvious source of news, many times a curious reporter can find several stories that are not so obvious, such as why the board skipped so lightly over item 5 on the agenda. Or a reporter may know from premeeting research that item 4 was a hot issue several years ago and may probe that area in questions before and after the meeting. (Photo by Ron Osborne)

Figure 2–3. Nonevent-oriented news (*soft news*) should also be covered. Readers are not interested just in the big story. (Photo by Ron Osborne)

timeliness. Examples of hard-news stories are the regular weekly meeting of the student government, a press conference held by the college president to announce increased fees for next year, and the arrest of the football team's star player, who is charged with possession of stolen property. These items have a certain immediacy because they all happened "today." They all involve a specific event: a meeting, a press conference, an arrest. Because they can be so easily defined and categorized, they are called hard news, in the sense of the phrase: "A hard and fast rule."

Soft news (Fig. 2–3) is less easily defined. It refers to those events that are not narrowly defined as happening "today" or as coming from a specific event. Instead, soft news might be based on a series of happenings in recent weeks or months, such as the low-attendance records of certain student senators at senate meetings. Features and humorous stories or columns could also be considered soft news. Some humor columns, however, appear on the opinion or op-ed page.

Sometimes a news story, instead of being based on a specific event (the president's press conference on increasing fees), could cover the *news issue* behind the event (the effect of inflation on attending school). With a little thought, student editors can find several issues behind every news event that occurs on campus. For instance, besides stories on the specific effects of inflation on students, stories could also be based on the difference in cost between private and public schools, the effect that the increased fees may have on enrollment next year, the budget of the school (with detailed accounting of income and expenditures), the value of an education versus an entry-level job, and the various financial aid programs available to students. So any news event is just the tip of the news iceberg. For every story that can be easily found on campus, several more lurk beneath the surface, and they are often the better stories in the paper because they are the most interesting and helpful to the reader (Fig. 2–4, 2–5).

The news value that requires special attention from student editors and reporters is proximity. News that happens on campus is nearly always worth printing in the campus paper. But news that happens in the community near the college doesn't always deserve coverage. When it does (Fig. 2–6), it warrants a different angle than the city newspaper gives it.

Figure 2–4. Sports events are news, too. Some readers read only sports news and features. And serious issues often lurk beneath sports stories. (Photo by Ron Osborne)

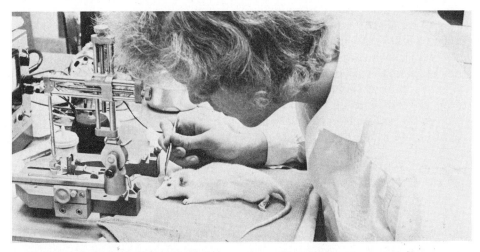

Figure 2–5. Occasionally a normal classroom activity can lead to an interesting story. Where do the lab animals in the science classes come from? What is the history of the rat or mouse as the classic lab animal? What reactions do students have to performing their first dissection? What about "animal rights" in scientific studies? (Photo by Michael Messing)

Figure 2–6. Even a noncampus event should be considered news if the event happened near campus or if a student was involved in the event. (Photo by Mike Penn)

When covering any story, but especially an off-campus story, reporters need to tie the story to the needs and interests of the readers of the campus paper. Because the majority of readers are students, news-value decisions must be made with their interests in mind. If, for example, the city decides to close all libraries on weekends and most weeknights because of increasing operating costs and a recent library tax cut, student reporters should not approach the story the same way the city press would. A student reporter should find out how the closings will affect students by talking to them, their instructors, and librarians who may be able to comment on student usage.

When a news event or issue happens in the community, student reporters must *localize* the story to their particular audience, just as professional papers do with national news. Find out how local events and issues will affect your readers, then write the story to show those effects, not necessarily the effects on city residents.

Newspaper Language

Journalism, like any other specialization, has a vocabulary all its own. An outsider overhearing two journalists talking shop will know as little about what is being discussed as if he or she were listening to two astrophysicists. But this special vocabulary exists for a reason: It makes talking about the specific tasks or items easier, quicker, and more precise.

While each chapter in this book has its own vocabulary list, the glossary is the best place to start to learn the terms special to newspapers. You should begin looking at the glossary right now and keep studying it page by page so that when terms come up later in the book, you will already know them.

But to get things started, let's listen in on a telephone conversation between a reporter and a news editor.

Hey, Chief, this is Mary. I just got out of the Planning Commission meeting. I think I've got a good **angle** *for a page-1 story with a* **sidebar.**

Oh yeah? What's the **slant**?

Turns out that the street map they've okayed for the south side is the same one that a citizens group sued the city over last year. Hard to say what they're thinking about.

Yeah, well, who ever said those commissioners think? Okay, give me about 20 inches and not a **graf** *more.*

C'mon, Chief, what's going on? You got a small **news hole** *today or something? It deserves more* **play** *than that. This is the best story to come off this* **beat** *in months. I've got a great* **lead** *all thought out, and I can give you 30 inches without* **padding** *a bit.*

Thirty inches plus a sidebar? You're not a **stringer** *for some gonzo magazine, you know. You'll be lucky if I give you a* **byline** *on this one.*

Okay, you old **curmudgeon**, *I know you're kidding now. Listen, who's sitting* **slot** *on the copy desk today?*

Why?

See if he'll check the **morgue** *for a* **mug** *of Schneider. He figures pretty heavily in the story. And tell him I can give him a listing of the street-name changes that he can put in* **agate.**

Should I also suggest that he drop the **flag,** *give you a* **skyline** *on the main story and a full page inside for the sidebar with art?*

Definitions

angle: part of a story that is emphasized

sidebar: a story, usually a feature, that accompanies a main story

slant: same as angle, as used here. Can also mean a bias, as in *editorialize*

graf: short for paragraph

news hole: the space left in a paper after the ads have been placed on the page

play: handling of a news story; its relative length and positioning in the paper. Good ''play'' would be on page 1

beat: a person or an office that is contacted regularly for news and story ideas

lead: the opening section of a story; sometimes refers to just the first graf

padding: adding unnecessary information to a story to make it longer

stringer: someone hired by a newspaper on a story-by-story basis

byline: the reporter's name above the story

curmudgeon: a surly, cantankerous person; often used to refer to editors

slot: the center of a traditional newsroom's copy desk, normally U-shaped. The slot person lays out pages and gives stories to edit to the persons on the *rim*. The terms are frequently still used in the modern VDT newsroom

morgue: the newspaper library of clippings of stories and photos

mug: a photo of the head or head and shoulders

agate: 5½-point type used for sports summaries, stock market figures, tabular material

flag: the name of the newspaper on page 1. Section names are also called flags

skyline: a headline above the flag that goes across the page

All right, all right, I'll back off. It just seems like a pretty hot story that'll break even hotter when that citizens group gets wind of what's in the works. I'm going to call them before I write the story.

*Now don't get all excited and **editorialize** on this one. I know this is a sensitive area for you.*

*I'll watch it. What kind of **deadline** can you give me? I don't know if I can get both stories in until about eight.*

*Great gadfries, we don't run a weekly here! Get them both in by six. We're short two people on the **rim** and one of the **VDT**s is on the fritz, so we need it as early as we can get it.*

*I'll see what I can do. One more question: What **style** do you want on the new assistant commissioner titles?*

*Let's **cap** them, just like the commissioner titles.*

*Okay, that's a **30** then, Chief.*

Cut the Jimmy Olson stuff, Mary, and start writing. You've got only three hours.

editorialize: to slant the story one way instead of presenting the facts objectively

deadline: not when stories or photos are due, as is commonly thought, but the absolute last minute they can be accepted at all. Even one minute after deadline should be considered too late

rim: portion of the copy desk around the slot person. Rim persons edit stories and write heads

VDT: *V*ideo *d*isplay *t*erminal, an electronic word-processing unit.

style: a standardization of capitalization, abbreviation, punctuation, and so on, throughout a newspaper

cap: uppercase letters; capitals

30: journalism term for "the end." Used to indicate end of story

Figure 2–7. News doesn't happen on schedule. A photographer without his or her camera will often miss fast-breaking events. (Photo by Michael Messing)

Suggested Projects

1. Devise a list of news values unique to your school publication. Discuss ways to find, write, and edit stories using your new criteria.

2. Clip stories from past issues of your school paper, and find examples of the different news values. Were there some that in retrospect you would have given more or better play? Why?

3. Search through past issues of your school paper for stories about news events that represent only the tip of the iceberg of a news issue. What other kinds of news stories could have been written about those events?

4. By looking back through past years' issues of your school paper, you can find events that happen yearly or cyclically. Are there any issues behind those events that you can develop a story around? Make a list and tack it to the newsroom wall for quick reference. Cover those issues in the paper this year.

5. Invite an experienced local journalist to discuss news values with your staff. Find out if his or her ideas about the nature of news have changed over the years.

Vocabulary

hard news
localize
news issue
news values
soft news

Exercises

Based on the standard news values described in the chapter and on ones that fit the needs of your campus, rank the items in the following lists from most to least important. For exercise A, all news comes from your campus. For exercise B, your paper also gets stories from a wire service. Explain your rankings.

A

1. The county chess champion, who comes from your school, won a tournament last weekend in your city.
2. The Sigma Nu fraternity wins the campus blood drive.
3. The projected school budget for next year means that $500,000 in financial aid will have to be cut.
4. A bike-theft ring on campus is broken when five bikes are found in the garage of a house near campus.
5. A local parent group wants to outlaw drug paraphernalia sold in several record shops near campus.
6. A former art student opens a tattoo parlor near campus, saying tattoos are for everyone.
7. The state college governing body discusses raising tuition next year by 35 percent.

B

1. The student government declares war on free faculty parking privileges. The associated student government wants faculty to pay because students have to.
2. Tomorrow is Chinese New Year and you have a sizable group of students of Chinese heritage on campus who have a celebration planned.
3. A bomb hurled in an assassination attempt on the leader of a military junta in Chile fails to go off and no one is hurt.
4. Administrators prohibit the distribution of an underground magazine published by a campus antinuclear group because the material would disrupt classes. The antinuke group cries censorship.
5. A swimmer from your school sets the state record in the 400-yard freestyle at yesterday's meet in another part of the state.
6. Campus utility bills have doubled in the past three years, and trustees are considering lowering thermostats this winter to 60° in all classrooms.

staff organization and copy flow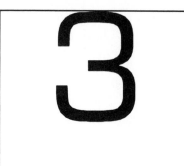

Meticulous organization is important for any newspaper, and it is especially important for student publications. Professional newspaper production is organized even to specific minutes for page plate-making to assure that the paper will be in the news rack or on the front step on time. If a student-newspaper staff starts out the year with a fuzzy idea of who is supposed to do what and when, then chances are those same questions will still need to be answered months later. Organization should come first—down to every seemingly small task that needs to be done—before anyone even begins to think about what stories should be in the first issue.

A look at professional newspapers and their organizations can help a student staff find one to model. Most professional newspapers are organized into three major departments: business, mechanical, and editorial.

The business department handles the advertising, both *display* and *classified*, and the circulation of the newspaper. Display ads come from specific stores or companies (local or national) and can be found throughout the paper. Classified ads run together in a special section and are placed mainly by individuals trying to sell or buy items from other individuals. The circulation department is responsible for making sure that papers get to homes, stores, and news racks every day. Other employees not directly involved with the production of the newspaper—secretaries, phone operators, janitors—are also considered part of the business department.

The mechanical department takes care of the physical production of the paper. Included here are typesetters, paste-up persons, proofreaders, press persons, and other technicians who help during all aspects of the paper's production. On most large newspapers, computer operators are part of the staff.

The editorial department consists of everyone who has anything to do with the writing, photography, and editing of the paper: reporters, sports writers, copy carriers, editors, artists, and photographers. The number of editors as well as the size of the staff depends, of course, on the size and coverage of the paper. On larger newspapers, managing editors rarely take part in the day-to-day work, but on many smaller ones, the M.E. must put in some editing and headline-writing time as well as perform management duties. A daily paper, for instance, may have different editors for city, state, national, and international news (Fig. 3–1). Under each editor are staff members who assist in the copy-reading and editing each day. On a small weekly paper, one editor and an assistant may cover everything except sports. The sports section is usually like a miniature newspaper: It sometimes has a separate editor and includes sports news, sports features, and sports opinion pieces. Large papers even have a letters-to-the-sports-editor section. No matter how large or small, every professional newspaper has a highly organized staff of specialists who work together to produce the final package.

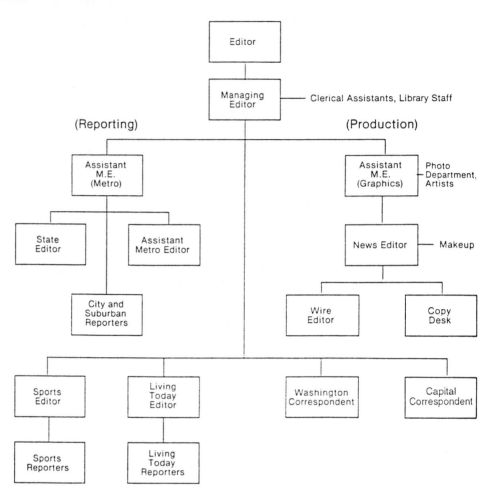

Figure 3–1. Organization of the newsroom of a mid-size daily.

School Newspapers

Every school newspaper should have the same basic organization as a professional paper. As with small professional papers, small student-newspaper staffs often double up on duties that might be performed by two persons on a larger staff. Nevertheless, as many student-newspaper staffs have proved, a quality product can be produced no matter what size the staff. One attribute that successful staffs, both small and large, share is effective organization.

Small Staff

A small newspaper staff covers most of the same events a large staff does, but with fewer people. Schools of all sizes have student-government elections, homecoming dances, athletic events, organization meetings, entertainment calendars, new class offerings, interesting personalities, and all the other important school events and issues. The newspaper should report on these people and events. A newspaper with 10 members (not including those who only take photos) might organize itself along the lines shown in Figure 3–2.

Editor. The position of editor, managing editor, or editor-in-chief—the name used varies from school to school—should be filled by a student who has the time to perform both the normal writing and editing tasks and the leadership duties of the head of a newspaper. The faculty newspaper adviser is just that—an adviser and no more. All work, including important decision making, should and must be done by the students. On a small staff, the editor should write almost all the editorials (as well as handle the other opinion functions of the paper—letters,

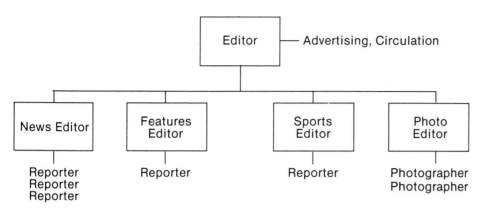

Figure 3–2. Suggested organization for a small student-newspaper staff.

opinion columns, and so on). He or she should represent the paper at important meetings, usually those of the student government and governing board. As the top executive of the paper, the editor also should maintain a good relationship with the school's chief administrative officer and the president of the faculty senate. Good language skills as a copy-reader are a must; often all copy on a small staff is edited by the editor.

The most important function of the editor, however, is providing leadership for the staff. No group operates well without a strong leader who is willing to make tough decisions. The editor is ultimately responsible for the newspaper and its staff. If the staff is functioning well together and producing good work, then the editor doesn't have to do much more than congratulate them and make sure the quality stays high. If the staff is not working well, the editor must find out what is wrong. The editor's responsibility is to produce a quality product through conscientious leadership.

News editor.   The news editor—sometimes called the city editor—probably has the most difficult and time-consuming position on the staff because of the large number of news events and issues on any campus. To cover these many events, the majority of reporters work under the news editor, or on *news side.* Reporting of news is the prime function of a newspaper. Comment, sports, and entertainment are important, but secondary, functions. The news editor should be in charge of the staff *beat* system, that is, he or she should identify the persons, groups, or places to be checked regularly in search of news. Common beats on a school newspaper often include the administration, student government, counseling services, library, faculty organizations, divisions or departments, clubs, fraternities and sororities, and campus police. Along with those common beats, the news editor should set up a system of other, less obvious, beats to check for news. The editor should be sure to get all the press releases from the college public-information officer by stopping by the office regularly. The PIO can be an important source of on- and off-the-record news items and tips. A good PIO knows what's going to happen well before it becomes public knowledge. Befriending this person can lead to a never-ending font of story ideas. The news editor should also get on the mailing lists of organizations that would be relevant to the students: city hall, such entertainment centers as local movie houses and concert halls, and other local colleges. It is the news editor's job to make sure that readers have access to all the information they need for all facets of their lives, not just their lives on campus. Although on-campus news should be of primary importance to the paper, off-campus news should not be ignored. Students spend a great deal of time away from campus. A good newspaper should include localized stories about important community and regional news in its coverage.

Features editor.   The features editor oversees not only feature stories about people on campus, but also entertainment coverage and calendars, reviews, personality features, features about new programs at the school, and photo essays (planned with the photo editor). Whereas the news editor should be aware of all the more "normal" aspects of the school and community—the regular events that should always be covered—the features editor looks for the unusual: the oil wells outside town painted to look like cartoon characters, a new program for deaf children at a local elementary school, the campus dog. Besides looking for the unique, the features editor should actively recruit students to write book, record, and film reviews and humorous stories or columns. This editor should work closely with the staff artist or art classes for illustrations. He or she should stay on top of local entertainment news to make students aware of spare-time activities in the community. The features editor works on a different schedule than the rest of the staff. Good feature stories are not typed up on deadline or even overnight. A feature story takes a long time to get and longer to write. While the rest of the editors plan for the next issue, the features editor is planning and making assignments at least two issues ahead so the writer has time to research, conduct interviews, and write and polish the story, and so the photographer or artist can be creative.

Sports editor.   The sports editor's job is fairly obvious: Cover all the campus sports events. But this is an oversimplification. The sports editor is also in charge of sports features and comments regularly on the sports program through a column. In essence, the sports section is a small replica of the entire paper, with its own news, features, and comments.

The sports editor should remember that the sports fan who reads the section has a higher level of interest in certain sports than the average reader. Coverage should be thorough and include detailed statistics and game summaries. Coverage must also be relevant to the publication date. Papers that publish weekly or less often have to deal with game stories differently than would a daily paper. It is rather silly to write a "news" story about a football game that took place 5 to 15 days before publication. Because most fans at the school will know from the local press who won and who lost, the weekly paper should concentrate on a feature of the old game story and an advance on the upcoming game. The feature angle, including quotes from the players and the coach, has special appeal to student fans because the local press rarely interviews players. The local press also rarely previews an upcoming game closely. Because the upcoming game is much more important than the previous game by press time, it should get more coverage than the game that has become history.

The sports editor should also generate features on outstanding athletes, male and female, intercollegiate and intramural. The increase in women's athletics has given the sports editor more teams to cover, but it has also made that section more interesting and appealing to a wider variety of people. A good sports editor should not slip into all-too-common sports sexism by giving male sports and athletes better coverage. The best teams and athletes, whether male or female, should receive the most attention.

Through a regular column a sports editor can comment on aspects of sports life on campus much in the same way that the editorial editor uses the editorial page to comment on the school as a whole. Sometimes the sports column can feature in a few paragraphs those individuals who deserve some mention but not an entire story. Letters to the sports editor can also be published in the column. A sports section without a column is incomplete.

Photo editor.   The photo editor gathers photo ideas during the regular editor's meeting and assigns them to staff photographers. The photo editor (or head photographer) works closely with the editor on photo assignments and photo selection.

He or she should also be in charge of the darkroom, the photo filing system, and supplies. Because photo filing systems can be a logistical nightmare, a photo editor needs good organizational skills. Negatives, proof sheets, published prints, and unpublished prints need to be filed and indexed for immediate location. The photo editor should also make sure that the darkroom is neat, clean, and well stocked.

The photo editor can help other editors both in assigning photos and in selecting them for publication. During the planning meeting for upcoming issues, he or she can suggest photo ideas for each story or, in fact, story ideas for the rest of the paper. A good photo editor is a part of the team making decisions for the whole paper, not just a service person for the other editors. After the section editor and the photo editor agree on the kind of photograph needed, the section editor writes out an assignment form. The photo editor then hands out the assignments and discusses each one with the photographers.

Large Staff

The larger a staff, the larger and more comprehensive its coverage can be. The number of pages in a paper is, of course, limited by printing facilities and budget. Figure 3–3 shows one way of organizing a staff of 20 (excluding photographers). Another alternative is a pool of staff reporters who can write any kind of story. Editors assign them different types of stories week to week. Because writers usually exhibit a flair for either news or features, however, editors should, if possible, allow each writer to stick to a chosen area. The best organization for any staff is the one that works.

Editor.   Although the editor has the same basic job whether the paper is large or small, the organizational aspect of the job is much more important on a large paper. The larger the number of students involved with the newspaper, the harder it is to get everyone together for meetings, and the easier it is for foul-ups or missed assignments to occur. The editor should ensure that lines of communication are open among all members of the staff (especially the editors), that photo assignments are made on time, that deadlines are met, and that the adviser is aware of any problems. The editor should meet with the entire staff as well as with the editors. He or she should check constantly with every staff member about deadlines, meet regularly with the adviser, and, perhaps most important, make sure that the staff is working together effectively and efficiently. The editor should foster the feeling of high *esprit de corps* and good teamwork that characterizes top newspaper staffs.

The functions of the remainder of the editorial positions are basically the same whatever size the staff, but usually more and better coverage can be achieved with a larger staff.

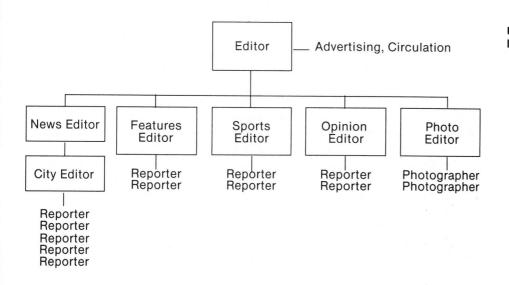

Figure 3–3. Suggested organization for a large student-newspaper staff.

News. On a large paper the duties of news editor can be successfully divided into two positions: off-campus and on-campus. The on-campus news editor (or city editor) handles the beat system and anything that has to do with campus activities. The off-campus news editor should be in charge of community events that concern the school and important stories from a wire service.

Features. The features editor of a large paper can assign such items as the entertainment calendar, consumer news, or entertainment review to an editorial assistant.

Opinion. A large staff allows a paper more opportunity to comment on news events as well as report them. An opinion editor manages the editorials, editorial cartoons, opinion articles, and letters to the editor.

Photo. A large photo staff must have a photo editor to hand out photo assignments to the staff, keep track of photo deadlines, set up a good negative filing system, and account for supplies. A library of mug shots of important campus persons is another responsibility of the photo editor.

Advertising and circulation. Two important positions on both a small and a large staff are the advertising manager and the circulation manager.

A person with a good business sense and a flair for selling should be selected for advertising manager. Such a person can often be recruited from salesmanship or advertising classes, which instruct students on the psychology and techniques of selling. (Journalism students rarely make good advertising managers.) The ad manager should not only sell, help design, and bill for the ads, but also lay out the ads on the pages. The layout should be done early so that editors can begin to fill that issue's *news hole*, the space left after the ads have been laid out on the page.

The circulation manager controls on-time delivery of the paper to the campus news racks and around-town displays. This person also mails the paper to other schools and files papers that are received. Sometimes the circulation manager keeps a clip file (*morgue* or library of stories about persons, events, and programs).

These two positions—advertising manager and circulation manager—usually receive pay: a straight salary for the circulation manager, a percentage commission for the advertising manager. On many larger papers, editors receive a salary as well.

Editor Selection

Because editors perform important functions on a newspaper, selection of these editors involves crucial decisions. On a student paper, because editors may be on staff for only a year or two, selection becomes even more critical.

Editor selection should be done by both the adviser and previous editors. This combination will help in making the right selection. At many schools an application form is used. The applicant indicates the position desired, his or her class schedule and work schedule next term, and past experience in journalism. Because the paper often takes more than 20 hours per week, an editor, even for a weekly paper, should not have a heavy class or work schedule.

Many schools include editor-selection policies and job descriptions in a staff manual. Job descriptions make it easy for prospective applicants to understand the nature of the position (Fig. 3–4). Including this information and other information that is used every term in a manual saves a staff from having to reinvent the wheel at every change of command.

Editors sometimes must be fired. Some process for removal of incompetent editors should be in the manual. Such a removal can be loaded with tension and emotion; a set procedure will help to defuse high emotions.

Figure 3–4. Job descriptions from *La Voz* staff handbook (*on pages 21–22*) (*De Anza College, Cupertino, Calif.*).

La Voz Staff Duties

Editor-in-Chief

General Duties:
1. Assumes final responsibility, in the name of the editorial board, for entire editorial and advertising production and content of each issue.
2. Acts as liaison between the staff and adviser, the staff and other groups: student body, faculty, administration, community.

Specific duties (may be delegated, but retains responsibility):
1. Organizes staff, with aid from adviser.
2. Assumes general charge of the editorial staff: news, sports, photo.
3. Conducts regular and special staff meetings and meetings of the editorial board.
4. Represents La Voz at student meetings and other conferences.
5. Answers correspondence and performs other duties as official La Voz student representative, with advice and cooperation from the adviser.
6. Checks periodically with ad manager and adviser on La Voz financial affairs; responsible for holding down expenses incurred by news-side personnel.
7. Has final approval authority on individual pages.
8. Submits to adviser within one week after the last edition of each quarter a report containing a discussion of procedures, suggestions for improvement, evaluation of staff performance (with aid from other editors).

City Editor

General Duties:
1. Is the direct editorial board contact with reporting staff; is responsible for assigning, covering, writing all news and feature copy (includes art, see Photo Editor), working closely with other editors.
2. Keeps future book of all upcoming, current, follow-up events and coverage.

Specific Duties (may be delegated but retains responsibility):
1. Supervises news beats, other assignments.
2. Checks all available sources (Grapevine, Faculty Newsletter, future tips, files, Office of Community Services, etc.) Seeks out and assigns news, plus features and photos through other editors as necessary.
3. Submits to adviser a weekly report on staff performance, indicating high spots and problem areas, using report form provided.
4. Checks coverage of news for omissions, under-and over-emphasis, excessive play to one person or group.
5. Provides all pertinent information available when assigning stories; assigns follow-ups; alerts reporters to feature or photo possibilities.
6. Reports at editorial board meetings on coverage errors, omissions, high points.

7. Assists reporters with rewriting as necessary.
8. Helps check proofs.
9. Submits to adviser a report, within one week after last edition of each quarter: discussion of procedures, suggestions for improvement; evaluation of writing staff performance, in conjunction with copy editor.

Feature Editor
(or assistant city editor)

1. Is a producing writer of features.
2. Assigns all features (working with photo and city editors).
3. Maintains list of feature ideas, checking all available sources.
4. Checks all features assigned by or to him, rewriting as necessary, before submitting them to city editor and/or copy editor.
5. Checks with city editor to exploit all feature possibilities, sidebars or tie-ins with news copy; avoids duplication of effort but seeks appropriate development of story-and-art situations.
6. Oversees production of columns and reviews.
7. Checks exchange papers for feature possibilities.

News Editor

General Duties
1. Primary responsibility for page dummying and pasteup (physical appearance).
2. In absence of editor, may decide story play, headline and page makeup.

Specific Duties (may be delegated but retains responsibility):
1. Plans and supervises makeup of the paper.
2. Is La Voz' expert on dummying, pasteup, preparation for printer.
3. Makes tentative dummy from copy editor and city editor run sheets (schedules), posting headline and story slug, art sizes and content.
4. Double checks photo cropping: is responsible for cutlines (with others).
5. Keys all copy and makes up final pasteup dummy.
6. Double checks all copy before it goes to typesetter and printer for size, heads, boxes, and special handling required.
7. Supervises or assists with pasteup.
8. Assists copy editor with assigning and writing headlines.

Copy Editor

General Duties
1. Primary responsibility is to assure smooth copy flow from reporters (through city editor) to typesetter (through news editor).
2. Assumes responsibility for copyediting operation.

Specific Duties
1. Is La Voz' expert on copyediting, style, good writing.
2. In charge of copyediting procedure:
a. corrects errors in punctuation, grammar, spelling, style.
b. checks for inaccuracies, untruths, distortions, omissions, policy violations.
c. marks copy directions for typesetter (with news editor).
d. dispenses copy for rewriting, further checking.
e. helps news editor with headline writing, using available staff.
f. holds copyreaders to strict deadlines, helping out as necessary.
3. Maintains run sheet (schedule), posting information necessary to enable news editor to make up tentative dummy.
4. Turns over to typesetter all copy in typewritten, corrected form.

Sports Editor

General Duties:
Responsible for production and display of all athletic news, features, photos.

Specific Duties (may be delegated but retains responsibility):
1. Makes assignments to sports reporters to assure adequate and accurate coverage of all sports activities; varsity, intramural, men's and women's.
2. Maintains own Sports Futures Book, file, references; checks all sources to assure comprehensive news, feature, photo coverage.
3. Dummies sports pages, assigns or writes headlines and cutlines.
4. Copyreads all sports copy, rewriting as necessary. Submits edited copy to copy editor (upon request) or news editor before it goes to typesetter.
5. Bears responsibility for meeting printer deadlines.
6. Cooperates closely with campus sources: athletic director and coaching staff, athletic news writer (Community Services), intramural advisers.
7. Keeps adviser apprised of performance of staff sports writers.

Photo Editor

1. Is a producing photographer, who oversees work of the photo staff.
2. Checks with ad manager and other editors for assignments; originates individual and photo page assignments from own sources, builds up idea log.
3. Impresses photo staff with need for news quality in all news photos: candid, unposed, avoiding the stereotyped; strives for clever, original photos.

4. Makes photo assignments; emphasizes need for accurate/complete cutline information; stresses need for beating deadlines and meeting appointment times.
5. Responsible for getting finished product (photos, cutline or cutline information) to appropriate staffers and editors.
6. Works with lab assistant for smooth darkroom and equipment usage.
7. Keeps negative files and proof book numbering accurate and up-to-date.

Advertising Manager

1. Is a producing advertising salesman, who oversees work of the sales staff.
2. Keeps Ad Run Sheet current and accurate; requires contracts for all accounts and keeps these accurately filed.
3. Assigns ad accounts to salesmen, supervises their work, checks their copy before it is dummied or goes to the typesetter; reads proof on all ads.
4. Supplies editors with ad dummies of all pages in accordance with deadlines; checks with editors for page requirements, size of issues and changes of ad size.
5. Is official La Voz business representative; attends editorial board meetings.
6. Assumes responsibility for increased ad sales for special editions.
7. On days of publication (normally Fridays) mails to each advertiser a tear sheet on which the ad appears. These are mailed first class.
8. Works closely with adviser on billing and collection procedure; with adviser, originates and answers correspondence relative to La Voz advertising.
9. Also see "La Voz Advertising Procedures."

Other Editors

To meet the changing needs of La Voz and to keep the operation flexible, Editorial Board By-laws permit appointment of other editors as the need arises. However, an effort must be made to work within the framework outlined above, avoiding having "too many chiefs and not enough Indians." The editorial board must never become a clique, a cozy in-group, with all that implies.

NOTE: Every member of La Voz is an active contributor, regardless of title, tenure on the staff or personal inclinations and preferences. Reporters will be asked to cover a variety of events, read proof, write headlines, help with whatever is needed in production of La Voz—and so will editors.

Figure 3–4. *continued*

Copy Flow

One of the most troublesome aspects of any newspaper operation, whether student or professional, is setting up an efficient *copy flow*, the movement of the story from the reporter's typewriter, computer terminal, or VDT to final paste-up at an off-campus print shop or in the campus composition room. If this process is to take place quickly and easily, deadlines for certain operations must be set and met.

Each piece of copy should be looked over by at least two staff members. (Some student-press law experts say that it is better if the adviser does not read student copy before publication; see Chapter 5.) A reporter copy-reads and corrects his or her story before turning it over to an editor. The editor then reads the story carefully, looking for inaccuracies, flawed grammar, misspellings, and style inconsistencies. The editor marks the copy with the correct typesetting information, indicates what page it is intended for, and then sends it to be set in type. In many PC newsrooms, the editor can send a story directly to the printer after editing. A copy of the story (many schools use carbonless copy paper) goes to the copy desk and the headline writer. After the story is set in type, it must be proofread for typographical errors only. (This is not the time to continue the editing process!) In the PC newsroom, the proofreading and the editing process are really the same. This process of write, edit, and proofread should be done by three different staff members to avoid the "breeze-over" reading that comes with the familiarity of repeated readings.

A good copy-flow process differs with the size and skills of staff members and with the type of equipment they have. The adviser should help the staff work out an efficient process. On a small-staffed paper usually all copy goes to the editor before it is sent to the typesetter. On large papers section editors copy-read and edit their stories, then route all edited copy through a copy editor, who reviews the total package for consistency before it is set in type.

Deadlines

Deadlines are the backbone of the newspaper business. A reporter or photographer who cannot meet deadlines will not be successful, no matter how well that person writes stories or takes photos. A newspaper results from team effort. If one member of the team is consistently and/or flagrantly late, the whole newspaper staff is affected.

In setting up deadlines for a school paper (and a professional one), the staff should work backward from the time the paper is scheduled to hit the news racks. Questions need to be asked in this order:

- When should the paper be distributed for effective reading and coverage? Friday morning? Wednesday?
- How much time will the presswork take?
- How much time should be allowed for negative production and plate-making?
- How many hours will be needed for paste-up?
- How fast can copy be set and photos produced? The copy be proofread?
- What amount of time should be allocated for editing the paper, writing heads, laying out pages?
- How quickly can the reporter write the story after meeting with the news source?

Now the staff knows when the stories have to be assigned. If the above tasks add up to three and one-half days, then the staff knows when story and photo assignments have to be made and handed in. Deadlines for advertisements can be set this same way. The importance of setting realistic but effective deadlines and meeting them cannot be overemphasized.

DEADLINES

ASSIGNMENTS

News, sports, photos—posted after 2 p.m. Tuesday.
Editorial—posted after noon Thursday, one week before publication.
Features (including news, sports features), accompanying photos, staff columns—16 days before publication.
Staff members should check mailboxes daily for assignments, handouts.

COMPLETED COPY

Features, staff columns—11 a.m. Friday, one week before publication.
Sports editorials—11 a.m. Monday.
News—11 a.m. Monday, late news—11 a.m. Wednesday.

PHOTOS

"Caption" print of proof—11 a.m. Wednesday.
PMT—11 a.m. Thursday.

ADVERTISING

Space reservation—4 p.m. Monday.
Completed layouts, copy—11 a.m. Tuesday.

LAYOUTS, OTHER

All pages posted by 11 a.m. Wednesday.
Ads on pages by 11 a.m. Wednesday.
All headlines completed by 2 p.m. Wednesday.
All stories to typesetter by 4 p.m. Wednesday; all remaining copy (except corrections) to typesetter by 11 a.m. Thursday.
Press rolls 7:30 a.m. Friday.
Distribution by 10 a.m. Friday.

Figure 3–5. Deadlines for every task in the copy-flow process should be set—and met. This example is for a weekly paper.

After the staff decides on the organization of the copy-flow chart (the official written description of how copy will move from reporter to paste-up), it should decide on deadlines in cooperation with the printer (Fig. 3–5). Every potential deadline should be included in the list, even one for late-breaking news. The staff should realize—especially if the printer is an off-campus shop—that the school newspaper is not the most important project on the printer's job list. Some late news and sports can be accepted, but stories that have an early *news peg*—the event that is the basis for the story—should be handed in early. Notice in Figure 3–5 that all stories without a news peg, or *timeless stories*—opinions, editorials, features—have a much earlier deadline than sports and news stories. Spreading out the work this way assures that a bottleneck will not occur with the typesetter, page composition person, or even the final-read editor.

Planning the Issue

Whether the paper is daily, weekly, or monthly, editors should have regular planning sessions to decide the size and content of future issues. During these meetings, the managing editor and ad manager (and possibly the adviser) should determine the number of pages the paper should have based on the number of ads, the amount of expected news copy, and the amount of money remaining in the newspaper's budget.

Some student papers have a written policy that calls for a certain ad-to-copy ratio of, say, 40 percent ads to 60 percent copy (professional newspapers and large student papers that exist on their own profits go as high as 70 percent advertising). Because many student newspapers are meant to be primarily a learning experience for future journalists, ad content rarely exceeds 50 percent for a semester or a year. Some issues may have more than 50 percent ads and some less. But this ad-to-copy figure should be considered when planning the size of the issue.

EDITORIAL BOARD POLICY

A. General
   1. Editorial Board is a class. The advisers are the teachers. The chairperson is the Editor-in-Chief, Managing Editor or Opinion Editor, at the discretion of the Editor-in-Chief.
   2. At least one Roundup adviser must be present at Editorial Board meetings.
   3. Considerations of Editorial Board include:
      a. Discussion of editorials, columns and cartoons.
      b. Discussion of the general shape and content of the news and feature coverage in upcoming issues.
      c. Any problems or grievances from inside or outside The Roundup, and any problems or issues surrounding policy.

B. Membership
   1. The Editorial Board is composed of the Editor-in-Chief, Managing Editor, City Editor, Opinion Editor, Sports Editor, Photo Editor, Scene Editor, Focus Editor, Art Director, Copy Editor and cartoonists.
   2. The Editor-in-Chief shall appoint his Editorial Board in consultation with the advisers.
   3. The Editor-in-Chief may appoint a maximum of two staff members, other than editors, to Editoral Board. They will take on all responsibilities and rights of other Board members.
   4. Any non-members may attend Editorial Board meetings, with the Board's consent, for discussion of a problem or presentation of an editorial or just to sit in on the meeting, but that person shall not have a vote.

C. Responsibilities of Board Members
   1. Attendance at Editorial Board meetings is mandatory. It is the responsibility of the Board member to inform the Editorial Board chairperson of an anticipated absence. A penalty may be assessed for an unexcused absence.
   2. Members of student government may not be Board members.
   3. Board members must present editorial ideas.
   4. Board members shall keep the Opinion Editor supplied with copy. The Opinion Editor shall develop a column schedule for Board members and shall deliver copies of the schedule to the Board members and advisers.
   5. Board members must be fair and accurate, and must avoid printing personal expression of limited interest (ego trips).
   6. Coming into a meeting emotionally set on an opinion is not enough. Background information is essential.

Figure 3–6. This excerpt from the editorial-board policy of the Pierce College *Roundup* (Woodland Hills, Calif.) shows how detailed policy statements should be.

After issue size has been determined, story and photo assignments are made, and some basic decisions on story play and organization of the issue outlined. As discussed further in Chapter 13, this is also the time to plan the design of your front page and other special information display, such as maps, charts, or illustrations. The features and opinion editors should already have assigned stories. They then select among assigned stories and any features not published the previous issue.

The editors' meeting is often a good time to discuss editorial ideas and stances for future issues. Many papers have an editorial board of top editors that meets separately from the editors' planning sessions. This editorial board decides the paper's stand on specific issues, because editorials must represent the carefully thought out and delineated position of the newspaper as a whole, not the personal feelings of one or two editors. If an editorial board cannot agree on a stand, the board might present a pro/con column to highlight both sides of a controversial issue.

To avoid any problems that might occur within a staff or on campus, most school newspapers have a written editorial policy for the paper (Fig. 3–6. Also, see Chapter 5). This policy explains what the editorial board does, how it arrives at an editorial stance, and what the paper tries to include and to avoid in its coverage of the campus. If these policies are written, a problem can be solved before it balloons into a major uproar. The written editorial policy can be checked and a fair decision can be rendered.

Copy-Flow Forms

Because most staff members on a student newspaper cannot be in the newsroom all day long, five days a week to get assignments, many school papers have printed forms so that assignments and other information can be placed in a reporter's or photographer's mailbox (Fig. 3–7). Of course, reporters and photographers have to check their mailboxes frequently—between classes if possible—to keep up on the information they need to know.

Figure 3–7. Story- and-photo-assignment sheets used by the staff of *The Campus*. (College of the Sequoias, Visalia, Calif.)

the campus
story assignment

Writer: _____   Date Due: _____   Date Assn. _____

Story: _____

_____

_____

_____

_____

_____

_____

_____

Contact: _____

Length: _____   Assn. by _____

PUB 3

PHOTO REQUEST FORM

Photographer: _____   Date: _____

For:

( ) The Campus   ( ) Horizontal

( ) Koh-Kyo   ( ) Vertical

( ) Other: _____

Describe desired photo: _____

_____

_____

Person to contact: _____   Room/Phone ext.: _____

Proof sheet due: _____   Print needed by: _____

Assigned by: _____

WHITE: PHOTO EDITOR
YELLOW: INSTRUCTOR

Some efficient copy- and news-flow forms and story- and photo-assignment sheets are beat information sheets, page budgets, masters budgets, story idea sheets, headline requests, page dummies, and cutline (or caption) forms.

Story-assignment sheets explain to a reporter exactly what the assignment is, and suggest whom to contact, how long the story should be, what the deadline is, and so on. The photo-assignment sheet does much the same thing for the photographer. The sheets are filled out in duplicate in case the original is lost or to remind editors of stories and photos still out as the deadline approaches.

The beat information sheet is used by beat reporters for turning in information from their beats to editors, who use that information to make story assignments. *Page budgets* (each section editor completes one) tell page layout persons exactly what is planned for individual pages, how long stories are, and whether there is a photo with a story. The *master budget* lists everything that is to appear in the paper. It can be used by the copy editor or editor to check off each story, headline, photo, and cutline as it is placed on the paste-up flat or sent to the print shop. Idea sheets can be used by staff members to help editors find good story and photo ideas every week.

Although it is important to remember that effective staff organization, efficient copy flow, and deadlines are extremely important aspects of producing a good newspaper, each staff has to tailor its production system to its unique needs. Evaluate the organization of last year's paper; analyze the programs used at other schools. If your paper has no staff manual, perhaps one should be written.

But first a good organizational system must be established. However the problem of organization is approached, it must be faced early. Don't wait until midyear to get things set up properly. Get the staff in place, have the forms printed, and set the necessary deadlines. Then meet them.

— *Suggested Projects*

1. Ask a local editor to critique your staff's organization, copy-flow system, and deadlines. Especially discuss the planning of special packages or issues. How does the local paper work out the logistics of getting a complex job done on time each day?

2. Visit a local paper's newsroom to see how it set up the physical surroundings for efficient copy flow. Discuss the importance of deadlines with a reporter or editor.

3. Review your present organization. Can it be improved? Take suggestions from all staff members.

Vocabulary

beat
classified advertising
copy flow
display advertising
master budget
morgue
news hole
news peg
news side
page budget
timeless story

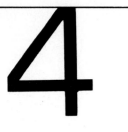 **4** gathering the news

The news must be gathered before the newspaper can be produced. Gathering news includes researching from documents and talking to people. If the reporter does not gather the correct information, the story will fail, no matter how well written it is.

The first step in gathering information for a news story is often document research in college or public libraries. The card catalog, electronic or paper, can direct the reporter to the appropriate documents. If the story is to be about abnormal psychology, for instance, the reporter would look up "psychology" in the subject/title section and would find the listing "abnormal psychology" as a subtopic. Those listings would guide the reporter to specific books. If the reporter needed information on a particular author, he or she would look in the author section of the catalog. Because most of the information in a book is, by nature, at least a year old, book research should be limited to subjects on which the reporter wants only general background information.

Recent information will be carried in magazines or newspapers in the periodicals section of the library, where periodical indexes are often placed near the stacks of magazines. The most common periodical index, the *Reader's Guide to Periodical Literature,* includes listings of articles from more than 100 magazines, but it does not include them all. *Playboy* and *Canoe,* for instance, are not listed, although they contain many valuable articles for a reporter. Other smaller indexes, such as *Access* or *Popular Periodicals Index* (which does include *Playboy*), cover magazines that *Reader's Guide* misses. Just as with the card catalog, the reporter can look up either a subject heading or a specific author or article title. *Reader's Guide* and the other indexes are kept up-to-date with monthly indexes that lag only about three months behind present issues.

Important regional papers such as the *New York Times* also have indexes. Because the *Times* is the nation's "newspaper of record," many topics of current national and international concern can be found in its pages. The *Times* usually comes to libraries on microfilm, and its index works the same way as the *Reader's Guide* index.

Other indexes list articles from magazines and journals that cover specific fields. Even the smallest library usually includes indexes specifically for fine arts, psychology and the social sciences, and the physical sciences.

The last major section of the library that the reporter needs to be familiar with is the reference room. This room holds encyclopedias, dictionaries, atlases, almanacs, record books, and some of the most outlandish accumulations of strange facts to be found between two book covers. These books can provide many original ideas for feature stories, as well as be helpful sources of information.

Reference books cannot be taken from the library, so some writers and newspapers purchase their own copies of the volumes they use most often. A few of the books that would be most valuable to a newspaper staff are:

- *Bartlett's Familiar Quotations*—the most famous quotations book (in the same vein, there are also several slang dictionaries that explain the meaning and background of dated and current slang words and phrases).
- *Columbia Encyclopedia*—a handy one-volume compendium of a wide range of information.
- *Current Biography*—a monthly issue of background information on prominent persons in the news. The monthly issues are bound into an annual volume.
- *Editorials on File*—editorials from newspapers around the country, listed by topic. A brief guide to different ideas from around the nation. Also an excellent place to study how editorials are written.
- *Facts on File*—a weekly file taken from newspapers and later collected into a large volume. An excellent starting point for research on current topics.
- *Famous First Facts*—lists of the first of nearly anything you can think of: the first airplane stowaway, the first skyscraper, and the inventor of the zipper.
- *The Guinness Book of World Records*—world records on nearly anything from goldfish swallowing to rolling-pin throwing. World bests in a myriad of serious categories, such as sports, largest ship, and largest city population.
- *Television News Index and Abstracts*—monthly summaries of the news broadcasts of the three major networks, compiled by Vanderbilt University since 1972.
- *Who's Who in America*—with *Current Biography* the most used reference work about people. There is an entire series of *Who's Who* books (by various publishers) on women, international persons, high school students, college and university students—even the deceased (*Who Was Who*).

Libraries, however, are not the only places to find facts. If a story is about a local matter, a reporter may have to go to a city or county office for information. County health departments have a wealth of information available to the public about local health concerns and facilities. The county law library may well be larger than the one available through the college or public library. The local chamber of commerce or tourist bureau also may have helpful information. Finally, the newspaper's own clip file or morgue should always be checked for stories written in the past (Fig. 4–1).

Good reporters know that information is available from many different sources, and they know how to get at it.

Figure 4–1. Checking the paper's clip file, whether in a file cabinet or on microfilm, is the first part of preparing for an interview or for covering a regular event. Knowing what has happened previously helps a reporter ask better questions. (Photo by Michael Messing)

Beat System

Although some news events happen without notice, many happen on a regular basis. To gather this kind of information, a newspaper staff sets up a beat system— persons, offices, or committees that have information or hold meetings on a regular basis. A *beat reporter* checks this source of news regularly and writes a story when needed. Beat reporters are rarely told when and what to write. They know what's happening on their beat and they talk over their story ideas with the editor. Usually 90 percent of their stories are unassigned.

Examples of beats on a professional newspaper include the courts, the police department, the state capitol, the city government, the county government, and the local schools. Examples of beats on a school paper might include student government, the school governing body (state agency or legislature), the board of trustees, the college president or chancellor, the faculty senate, the financial aid office, the academic divisions, and departments.

Because most beats generate news stories, the beat system is generally the responsibility of the news editor or city editor, who regulates the beats on campus, the reporters covering them, and when and how often that beat should be covered (daily, weekly, or less frequently). Beats in the fine arts or theater arts department may generate as many features as news stories and are therefore often given to the features editor. Regular sports beats could be supervised by the sports editor.

The duty of the beat reporter is, of course, to get the news that relates specifically to that beat. But the reporter should not have tunnel vision: Ideas for stories outside the beat should be passed along to editors for assignments to other reporters. The idea-gathering function is an often overlooked function of the beat system.

Beat reporters should set up regular and friendly dialogues with their contacts. Comfortable working relationships enable reporters to ask questions and dig below surface conversation for story ideas. Conscientious beat reporters also check their beat more frequently than the schedule calls for—just to look for those offbeat stories or for ideas for features or columns.

Here's an example. The beat reporter covering student government at Middle Valley College stops by the office a few days before the regular weekly meeting. The secretary looks troubled. The reporter finds out that the graduating class is having a hard time agreeing on a class gift. The beat reporter realizes that she's never before heard about a class gift. Then she remembers some brass plaques from classes from the 1950s and 1960s sunk in cement out by the statue in front of the college. Now she has an idea for a feature on all the class gifts the college has received over the 55 years it has been in existence. She's also going to look into the problem of this year's gift.

So story ideas can come at any time from a beat, not just during the editors' meeting. And if the beat reporter isn't interested in the story, at least the idea can be passed along so that someone else can write the story.

But the point of this example is that the reporter was listening, thinking, and observing what was going on around her. After researching her story idea in the newspaper clip file and at the library, she will engage in what may be the most important skill for a good reporter: interviewing.

Interviewing

Someone once said that interviewing—talking to people—is the real key to being a good reporter. If a reporter can interview someone well, then that reporter will probably have a good story. A bad interview will never lead to a good story. The best advice to give someone about how to interview is to act naturally. An interview does not have to happen in a formal, stilted atmosphere. Interviewing is just talking with someone about a specific topic. But, instead of merely hearing, the reporter is *listening* and writing down the pertinent details.

Preparation

Preparation is an important part of the good interview. If the reporter doesn't know enough about the subject or person to ask the right questions, then he or she will rarely receive or perceive good answers. Preparation will vary according to the length and depth of the story. A news story on the meeting of student government will require little more preparation than the gathering of background material on agenda items. Preparation for a story about increased student-activities fees or tuition or a feature story about a person take much more preparation.

Beginning reporters should prepare a list of questions—with space for answers—based on preliminary research. The questions should be arranged from general to specific. It is rarely advisable to start off with a "tough" question. Start with easy, sociable questions to relax the interviewee. Save the tough questions for later. But if the interview is short, or the interviewee hostile, ask the tough one right away. You don't want to miss it.

Don't rely too much on these prepared lists, however. Because the best interviews have the informality of a conversation, artificially structuring the interview around a list often impedes rather than enhances the interaction. Many experienced reporters prepare a list but use it only if the interview is slow or if the interviewee is not talking much. A good interview follows a natural order, not a preconceived one. A reporter who strictly follows a list may miss an interesting or crucial tangent that arises from the conversation. In other words, prepare a sequence of questions, but be ready to discard or amend the plan.

Taking Notes

A good interview can be wasted if the reporter can't record the answers accurately. Good note-taking, either by standard shorthand or by whatever method the reporter can devise, is crucial, but it is an acquired skill. Some kind of shorthand is a must. Few reporters use standard secretarial shorthand; most use some form of shortened writing, such as "w/o" for *without* or "inc" for *incomplete*. Initials can stand for persons and titles, and organization names can be given symbols. The reporter should set apart those statements to be used as direct quotes through circles, quotation marks, stars, or underlining.

Note-taking: an important skill

Lee Terkelsen

Lee Terkelsen spent time as the education-beat reporter for the Visalia (Calif.) Times-Delta, *and many years teaching high school journalism.*

Note-taking is, without doubt, one of the most important skills a reporter must acquire. It may even rank higher than being able to write well. After all, if a story the reporter writes is not accurate, then it doesn't really matter how well it is written. And accuracy depends on accurate notes.

Viewers of films or television newspaper programs rarely see reporters take notes. They apparently memorized everything their sources told them. That, of course, is pretty dangerous. An editor—not a reporter, mind you—once attempted to write a story based on his memory of a conversation. He used a tape recorder while interviewing the governor of the state of Washington, and when he returned to the newsroom, he discovered that the tape recorder had not worked properly. He filed the story, basing it on his memory of the conversation. To his surprise, the governor had also recorded the conversation. She protested that the story was inaccurate. The editor was suspended for 60 days.

Using a tape recorder is a pain, although I believe most reporters occasionally use one. There is no time to go back and forth on the tape to listen to a tape recording, especially if the story is due a few hours or minutes after the interview or meeting. I occasionally use a tape recorder, however, in conjunction with notes. I rely on my notes to write the story, but refer to sections of the tape recording when I am unsure of a point or a quote.

A tape recorder is also a valuable instrument when the reporter is also required to be the photographer. That has happened to me frequently. I'll simply turn on the tape recorder, put down my notepad, and concentrate for a few minutes on taking pictures. In that manner, I don't miss important items while I've got the camera in my hand. That isn't to say I always use the tape recorder when I take pictures; it's just a lot more convenient. I use the tape recorder, too, when I know I'll be interviewing a fast talker. There are a few of those on every beat. They simply talk too fast for me to take accurate notes.

Still, I cannot overemphasize that recorders are very time-consuming and should not be used on 95 percent of assignments.

There are about as many ways of taking notes as there are reporters. Each reporter develops his or her own system.

There are some general rules to follow, however. The most important one is to make certain that direct quotes are noted as such. I usually circle or put quote marks around direct quotes or quote phrases so I know they are quoted directly. Otherwise, I paraphrase or use the speaker's words without quotation marks.

I use a type of outline method to take notes when I know I'm going to write the story immediately after a meeting or interview. In that method, I rely on memory. I write key words that epitomize what the person is saying. When I later look at those key words, it helps me recall the person's statement or view.

I know one reporter who looks at his source directly during the entire interview. He writes without looking at his notepad. He admits he uses a lot of paper and doesn't stay between the lines. I've tried that, but I prefer looking at my pad when taking notes and looking at the source when asking questions.

In a meeting, the reporter has no control over what is said or the pace of the interview. In a one-on-one interview, however, the reporter does have some control. Occasionally, long after an interviewee has answered a question, I will still be taking notes on the response. In that case, I'll either ask the interviewee to clarify something or I'll ask an unimportant question to keep the conversation going while I finish my notes on the original question.

Some reporters use standard shorthand. They are the small minority. I don't think it's necessary. What is important is to develop your own note-taking system so that you can read your notes and guarantee their accuracy.

Another important note-taking skill concerns the handling of the notepad or tape recorder during the interview. Immediately flashing a notepad or pulling out and setting up a tape recorder may intimidate interviewees not accustomed to talking to the press. It is better to get out a notepad or tape recorder casually after friendly chatter. Sources who are interviewed often, however, may be more comfortable with note-taking or taping while they talk. Still, use caution and sensitivity. Don't shut off your source's flow of words.

Beginning reporters sometimes feel awkward bending down busily at their notepads while their sources talk. Though some reporters can develop note-taking skills to keep eye contact with sources while taking notes, beginners should remember that the source realizes the reporter is there to ask questions and record the answers. Sources are as interested in accuracy as the reporter is. They are more likely to get worried when no notes are taken at all than when the reporter is scribbling away. As a rule, sources used to talking to the press don't need eye contact, and sources who are new to or uncomfortable with the news-interview situation do need occasional eye contact as a reassurance.

Taking notes on only one side of the paper or pad makes their rearrangement back at the office to fit the story structure much easier. (Having to flip papers over and back is a waste of time and energy.) One reporter cuts the notes apart and reorganizes them before writing the story. That way she can concentrate on the structure and on writing and merely flip through the stack of notes.

Note-Taking Tips

1. Develop a shorthand or an abbreviated longhand. If you don't, you will be concentrating on your writing so much that you won't be listening.
2. Listen carefully. Don't note unimportant details.

Figure 4–2. Whenever possible, get the source away from the protected seat behind the desk and to an area where two people can talk more comfortably. At top, the desk physically interferes with a close relationship between reporter and source. At bottom, the setting is better, more like a conversation. (Photos by Michael Messing)

3. Ask for spellings on all names and titles that you are not sure of. It is better to ask now than to have to call back or—worse yet—get them wrong in the story. The source will usually appreciate your concern for accuracy.
4. Get direct quotations, especially on the main points.
5. Take lots of notes—more than you think you'll need—but don't write constantly.
6. Observe details about your source and surroundings, and write down your impressions.
7. Train your mind to remember details without taking notes.
8. Immediately after the interview review your notes and add to them. Make sure your notes are legible enough to reread later.
9. Arrange your notes in order of importance.
10. End the interview by making sure you can contact the source for further facts or clarification.

Tape Recorders

Many student-newspaper advisers are hesitant to allow their reporters to use tape recorders, calling them crutches. Most professionals do not like to rely on tape recorders, either, for two reasons: They are unreliable and there is usually not enough time to use them.

Too often a reporter relies solely on a tape recorder for an interview and the machine fails. There the poor reporter sits with a deadline an hour away and no tape and no notes. Reporters who use tape recorders should always back themselves up by taking notes as well. In their notes, the reporters should write the index number of the tape recorder's counter during important quotes. Then, to ensure accuracy, the reporter can quickly find that specific quote on the tape. If the recorder malfunctions, the reporter can still use notes to write the story.

Time is the greater reason reporters don't tape interviews, especially reporters on daily papers. If the reporter has an hour-long interview on tape, it will take several more hours to transcribe the tape into notes. Only then can story-writing begin. And more than a few hours to write a story is often a luxury that cannot be afforded. Also, a lot of information in an interview will not be used in the story. Transcribing the tape includes typing out those worthless sections as well as the important quotes.

But for very long personality interviews or for interviews on controversial topics, a tape recorder can be an excellent backup to ensure accuracy. The tapes, as well as the notes, can then be filed and referred to if the accuracy of the story is questioned after publication. Reporters should keep their notes and tapes on file for a year—longer for stories that may lead to further investigation or perhaps even to a courtroom.

Listening

Good listening skills seem such an obvious part of a good interview that many might ignore them. But there is a difference between hearing and listening. The ear hears many sounds daily and selectively screens them, assigning some to the category of "background noise" (cars passing by the library) and some to "important sounds" (the alarm clock or the assignment's due date). Important sounds require active mental participation from the listener. Only through this participation will the reporter pick up new ideas or story leads during an interview.

Observation

Another job for the interviewer—as if writing down accurate and complete notes isn't enough—is to observe sources and their surroundings, especially if the story is a personality feature. But even in a news-story interview, the reporter should notice *how* the source says something. An interviewee's hesitancy to answer a specific question, for instance, may help the reader understand the touchiness of that point.

Observation plays an important part in other areas of reporting, and not just the interview. Reporters covering a rally on campus will have different views of what happened depending on whom they talked to and where they were during the event. Reporters situated near the front, for example, may be standing among the supporters of the event, and it will seem that the entire crowd is animated and supportive. A reporter at the back of the crowd, however, may see little audience interest. People will be coming and going, and those who remain may make negative comments about the rally or not pay attention at all. Which story should the reader believe? Which one would be correct?

The good reporter observes from all angles, talks to sources on all sides of a story. If the reporter spends some time at the front of the rally crowd and some at the back, talking to people at both places, he or she will write a much more accurate story. As Joseph Pulitzer once told his reporters, the three most important rules of news reporting are accuracy! accuracy! and accuracy! And accuracy comes with *complete* newsgathering.

Off the Record

When to go off the record is always a tough decision for the reporter. Sometimes a reporter can be trapped by listening to off-the-record, or not-to-be-printed, information. If that reporter then hears that same information from a for-the-record source, printing it may jeopardize an important relationship with the first source. For this reason many reporters simply refuse to accept off-the-record comments at all. One editor would walk out on informal dinner meetings with government officials if someone wanted to make a statement off the record. Even though it was an informal—not on-the-job—situation, the editor didn't want to lose the opportunity to find out that information from someone else and use it.

> *Four Levels of Off-the-Record Material*
> 1. *Off the record.* The reporter cannot use it. Period.
> 2. *Not for attribution.* Reporters can use it, but they can't identify the source in any way.
> 3. *Background.* Reporters are given information so they can better understand a complex problem. The material should be used with general attribution. The reporter can write "A college official said," but nothing more specific.
> 4. *Deep background.* Highly sensitive material. Reporters may use it, but they cannot refer to any source at all.

Although a campus reporter will rarely get involved in background talks, off-the-record and not-for-attribution situations arise frequently if the newspaper is doing its job of digging into important news on campus. The problem here—as with the professional press—is that sources are not aware of the rules of the off-the-record game. Reporters are, however. The reporter should make sure that the source understands the ground rules before the interview begins—especially if the interview will cover sensitive areas.

Reporters can protect themselves by making sure the source understands that everything said is eligible for print unless the source specifies *beforehand* that a certain statement is off the record. Going back afterward and saying "Oh, that was off the record" is not fair. The reporter didn't get the chance to refuse to hear it. It is the responsibility of the reporter to make sure that this doesn't happen.

Another reason to set down the rules beforehand is that even among reporters there is no agreement as to what off-the-record means. Certainly sources will be a bit unsure. Reporters should be cautious when using these methods to gather information. Not naming sources decreases the credibility of a story and may put the reporter and the paper in a sticky situation. Plus the source may be lying to discredit someone. Reporters should use off-the-record material only when it is very important and cannot be gotten in any other way.

Investigative Reporting

Investigative reporting became a popular term in the mid-1970s, largely because of Carl Bernstein and Bob Woodward's book, *All the President's Men,* and the film based on it. By definition, investigative reporting deals with long-term and continuing research into a specific area. Bernstein himself, however, has said that he doesn't like the term because it implies that *all* reporting is not investigative in nature. A reporter who does not investigate is a stenographer, Bernstein says, not a reporter.

Student reporters, in their zeal to get that "big" story, can become more concerned with the story than with accuracy. Someone who wants to fight a battle in the paper—for instance, a teacher who has been denied tenure—can sometimes use the paper for a personal purpose. Reporters need to be very careful with such information when it comes from just one source.

So reporters need to be wary of "tips." Tips are not necessarily truth. They are just leads to be checked out carefully. And all possible sources must be checked. Don't get caught in the trap that a Washington, D.C., radio station did on a news tip that the mayor had been shot. The caller with the tip gave the station a number to call to verify the shooting. A station reporter did just that, but the number belonged to one of the caller's cronies. The friend verified the story and the station went on the air with it. It was a fabrication. If the reporter had called the mayor's office, it would have exposed the fabrication right away.

A good practice is to check facts at least twice. *Never* go with a story, especially a sensitive story, on the basis of information from one source. Don't be a stenographer for one side. The reporter's investigation may show that there is no actual conflict, only one person who is mad about something. Even though the story may then fall through, the experience might yield several other story ideas, such as how the press is used by single-interest groups.

Investigative reporting, stories about controversial areas, even exposés of persons or offices on campus are fine, but reporters and editors must guarantee accuracy and fairness. A good newspaper—whether student or professional— does not shy away from the tough story. A good newspaper *does*, however, make sure that the story is based on verifiable facts. A controversial story that is a result of solid investigation, good reporting, and careful writing can be defended—even in court. Shoddy work has no defense, even if the reporter is a rookie on a student paper.

— *Suggested Projects*

1. Take a guided tour of the library. Ask a librarian to compile a list of reference books in your library that would be helpful to reporters at your school.

2. Invite a beat reporter from a local newspaper to talk to your staff. Find out how a beat is covered, where story ideas come from, and how to take notes. Practice your craft by taking notes on the reporter's presentation and then writing a story about it. Compare your notes and story with those of other staff members. Are there differences? Why? Who was right? Send the stories to the beat reporter and have him or her critique them.

Vocabulary

beat reporter
clip file
investigative reporting
off the record

3. Use other classes to practice your note-taking. Imagine that you will be writing a story based on lectures in other classes. Observe mannerisms of the instructor and class members. Practice your listening and memory skills by writing down as much detail as you can after the class is over.

4. Invite several people who have been sources for stories in your paper to discuss the accuracy of the paper's version of an event or issue. Set up a panel among news sources and newspaper staff members to discuss how reporters gather news, how accurate notes are, and how close a news story can really get to the truth of a situation. Administrators probably would be interested in participating on the panel.

5. Invite an "investigative reporter" from a local paper to discuss investigative methods. Ask how many sources are needed to verify a fact and where to find certain information about local people or events. Perhaps the reporter can give you tips about specific stories you would like to work on.

legal and ethical issues

5

Because newspapers do not operate in a vacuum, problems occasionally arise. Sometimes they are legal problems: A politician believes the paper has ruined his reputation, or a local church group believes the investigative series on child pornography is itself obscene. Both may take the paper to court.

Sometimes they are ethical problems: The sports editor has been offered a free weekend trip to a new ski resort near town. Will a story based on this trip be considered, in essence, advertising not-paid-for?

School newspapers can have these problems and several more that are particular to a school press. All problems cannot be avoided—if a paper isn't raising a voice in protest once in a while, it's probably not doing its job. The challenge comes in knowing how to prevent major problems and how to deal with the minor ones.

Legal Issues

Legal issues that most often affect the student press of public schools and colleges are: (1) First Amendment rights and censorship, (2) libel and privacy, and (3) obscenity. Students in public schools enjoy more rights guaranteed by law than students in private schools. Private-school newspapers don't necessarily have First Amendment rights, for instance. Students in private schools need to achieve their own freedoms through negotiations with the administration of the school. Student, faculty, and outside professional organizations can help obtain a free press.

First Amendment Rights

This chapter will look at important concepts of First Amendment rights and other student press law issues that deserve attention and study. References to specific cases, some of which are outlined in Figure 5–1,* will be kept to a minimum.

The First Amendment rights of students generally come into question in three ways: (1) Do students have all the rights guaranteed in the U.S. Constitution, including freedom of expression and of the press, while they are on campus? (2) Is the board of trustees or school board the publisher of the paper and therefore able to decide content? (3) What are the rights and duties of the adviser to the paper, and what is his or her role in deciding content?

---

*References in the text are to case numbers in Figure 5–1. For more information, contact the Student Press Law Center (see appendix).

Figure 5–1. Summary of court cases referred to in text.

Important student press law cases

Descriptions followed by an asterisk are reprinted from the *Student Press Law Center Report*, printed by the Student Press Law Center. The others are based on Trager and Dickinson, *College Student Press Law.*

1. *Antonelli* v. *Hammond,* 308 F. Supp. 1329 (D. Mass. 1970). This case grants school administrators some power over content in a student publication if the publication would interfere with the educational process. The burden of proof is on the administrators, however, to show interference. The court wrote: "It would be inconsistent with basic assumptions of First Amendment freedoms to permit a campus newspaper to be simply a vehicle for ideas the state or college administration deems appropriate."

2. *Bayer* v. *Kinzler,* 383 F. Supp. 1164 (E.D. N.Y. 1974), *aff'd without opinion,* 515 F. 2d 504 (2nd Cir. 1975). The U.S. Court of Appeals affirmed a lower court's ruling that the seizure by the administration of "Sex-Information Supplement" to an official high school paper was unconstitutional. The supplement was "primarily composed of articles dealing with contraception and abortion" and was "serious in tone and obviously intended to convey biological information rather than appeal to prurient interests." The District Judge wrote: "It is extremely unlikely that distribution of the supplement will cause material and substantial interference with schoolwork and discipline."

3. *Bazaar* v. *Fortune,* 489 F. 2d 225 (5th Cir. 1973), *aff'd en banc with modification,* 476 F. 2d 570 (5th Cir. 1973), *cert. denied,* U.S. 995 (1974). This case involved a literary magazine at the University of Mississippi. Because an issue contained "earthy" language, a committee of deans decided that publication would be inappropriate. But the court found that the so-called earthy language was what the characters in the stories would normally use and that the language was not used in a pandering manner or in a sexual sense. The court further ruled that the university could not be considered the publisher of the magazine and thus could not censor it. The court wrote: "The University here is clearly an arm of the state and this single fact will always distinguish it from the purely private publisher as far as censorship rights are concerned."

4. *Calvin* v. *Rupp,* 471 F. 2d 1346 (8th Cir. 1973). The adviser of a high school paper refused to allow copy to be censored by school officials. The school board voted to withdraw the teacher's contract for the following year. The Court of Appeals upheld the school board, saying that the board may have been hasty or unwise, but that it had not deprived the teacher of his constitutional rights. The court did not feel that protecting students from censorship was a liberty protected by the Constitution.

5. *Channing Club* v. *Texas Tech University,* 317 F. Supp. 688 (N.D. Tex. 1971). The court ruled in this case that the "mere dissemination of ideas—no matter how offensive to good taste—on a state university campus may not be shut off in the name alone of 'conventions of decency.'"

6. *Dickey* v. *Alabama,* 273 F. Supp. 613 (M.D. Ala. 1967). A Federal District Court ruled unconstitutional a university's suspension of the editor of an official, school-sponsored newspaper for writing an editorial critical of state officials.

7. *Hazelwood School District* v. *Kuhlmeier,* 108 S. Ct. 562 (1988). This case, which dealt a serious blow to student press freedom when the U.S. Supreme Court handed it down on January 13, 1988, upheld the right of public high school administrators at Hazelwood East High School to censor stories concerning teen pregnancy and the effects of divorce on

Figure 5–1. *continued*

children. This decision includes a major change in how the determination of whether a newspaper is a "public forum" is made. This decision, according to the Student Press Law Center, applies only to school-sponsored student publications that are *not* public forums. Alternative high school publications and college and university publications are not affected by the decision.

8. *Jacobs* v. *Board of School Commissioners*, 349 F. Supp. 605 (S.D. Ind. 1972), *aff'd*, 490 F. 2d 601 (7th Cir. 1973), *vacated as moot*, 420 U.S. 128 (1975). The court ruled that materials do not lose their constitutional protection simply because they are disseminated under commercial auspices.

9. *Joyner* v. *Whiting*, 477 F. 2d 456 (4th Cir. 1973). The U.S. Court of Appeals upheld a District Court's decision that a college may not withdraw funding, fire editors, or in any way suppress a student publication merely because it dislikes or disagrees with the newspaper's editorial content.

10. *Korn* v. *Elkins*, 317 F. Supp. 138 (D. Md. 1970). At the University of Maryland, a student publication depicted a burning American flag on its cover. The university's president and the state attorney general believed the cover violated a state law, and they stopped publication. But a Federal District Court said that just because they feared prosecution, university officials could not apply a statute unconstitutionally.

11. *Lodestar* v. *Board of Education*, No. B-88-257 (D. Conn., March 10, 1989). In this case, the court said that the Hazelwood decision does not necessarily apply to all school-sponsored publications, pointing out that "public forum" status must be decided by school authorities before other actions take place.

12. *Milliner* v. *Turner*, 436 So. 2d 1300 (La. App. 1983). Following a libel suit filed by two faculty members against the school newspaper, the newspaper asked that the university be joined as a party to the suit. A trial court found both the newspaper and the university liable for damages. But the state appellate court disagreed, saying that because the First Amendment barred anything but advisory control over the content of the paper, the school was exempt from liability for the newspaper's libels.

13. *Nitzberg* v. *Parks*, 525 F. 2d 378 (4th Cir. 1975). A Federal Court of Appeals ruled that high school officials may read only non–school-sponsored or "underground" publications prior to distribution pursuant to existing rules. The rules must carefully specify the type of expression so that a reasonably intelligent student will know what is prohibited and what is not. All terms such as "disruption" and "interference" must be clearly defined by the rules. These rules must also contain procedures for appealing administrative decisions forbidding distribution of student material and must provide for timely appeals.

14. *Planned Parenthood of Southern Nevada* v. *Clark County School District*, 887 F. 2d 935 (9th Cir. 1989). The court said that as a matter of law, it first had to decide whether a publication was a public forum. In this case, the court upheld the school district's right to prohibit publication of pregnancy-related advertising, at least in part because it found the content controls established by the district meant that the publication in question was not a public forum. An important point in terms of the *Hazelwood* decision is that the court said that even if publications are not public forums, school restrictions must be "viewpoint neutral."

15. *Romano* v. *Harrington*, 725 F. Supp. 687 (E.D. N.Y. 1989) (denial of summary judgment motion). In this case, an adviser was removed from his position for allowing the student newspaper to run an editorial critical of

Figure 5–1. *continued*

the movement to make Martin Luther King, Jr.'s birthday a national holiday. The court said that publications produced outside the classroom and not for school credit are less limitable than what Hazelwood allows for "curricular" publications.

16. *Shanley* v. *Northeast Ind. Sch. Dist.*, 462 F. 2d 960 (5th Cir. 1972). A U.S. Court of Appeals ruled unconstitutional the suspension of five high school seniors for the publication of an underground newspaper that advocated review of marijuana laws and contained information on birth control and abortion. The Court ruled that "expression by high school students cannot be prohibited because other students, teachers, administrators, or parents may disagree with the content."

17. *Sinn* v. *The Daily Nebraskan*, 829 F. 2d 662 (8th Cir. 1987), aff'g 638 F. Supp. 143 (D. Neb. 1986). Two individuals wanted to place ads for roommates of a certain sexual orientation in the school newspaper. The editor rejected the ads claiming that they would discriminate against those who were not gay or lesbian. The suit, which claimed infringement of First Amendment rights, against the paper, the University of Nebraska, and its administrators was rejected. Two federal courts said that the First Amendment protects only against state agents, and the student editor, acting on his own accord, was not acting as an agent of the state. The editor's decision was protected by the First Amendment, the courts said. Thus, lack of school involvement in content decisions protected the school from legal action.

18. *Stanley* v. *Magrath*, 719 F. 2d 279 (8th Cir. 1983). This decision makes it more difficult for administrators to restrict funding to student publications, even when they claim the fund reductions are not because of disagreements with the content of the publication. Previously, attacks against the publication by administrators were not allowed as evidence. Universities have to be careful to show that fund reductions are solely because of financial reasons and are not an attempt to punish or control the publication.

19. *Tinker* v. *Des Moines*, 393 U.S. 503 (1969). The Tinker case is the landmark decision on First Amendment rights of students. The U.S. Supreme Court ruled that high school students may not be prohibited from expressing themselves, in this case by wearing black armbands to protest the Vietnam War, unless the school proves substantial disruption of or material interference with school functions.

20. *Trujillo* v. *Love*, 322 F. Supp. 1266 (D. Colo. 1971). A Federal District Court ruled that the labeling of a newspaper as a "teaching tool" by officials of a community college, when in reality the paper had functioned as a forum for student expression, did not permit censorship. The court decision reads, in part: "Having established a particular forum for expression, officials may not then place limitations on the use of that forum which interfere with protected speech."

21. *Vail* v. *Board of Education*, 354 F. Supp. 592 (D. N.H. 1973). A Federal District Court ruled that school officials may not impose a flat ban against all underground publications. The decision read: "The Board has the burden of telling students when, how, and where they may distribute materials, consistent with the basic premise that the only purpose of any restrictions on the distribution of literature is to promote the orderly administration of school activities by preventing disruption and not to stifle freedom of expression."

The first question is easily answered. In 1969, the United States Supreme Court extended all constitutional guarantees to both students and teachers in public schools (Fig. 5–1.19). Justice Abe Fortas said, "It can hardly be argued that either students or teachers shed their constitutional right to freedom of speech or of expression at the school house gate." So, under the Constitution, the student press is guaranteed freedom. Naturally, this right is not absolute. The factors that affect the basic freedom of expression are discussed below.

The second question, concerning the actual publisher of the paper, is more complex and less easily answered. The answer determines who controls the content of the paper and, perhaps more important, who is legally liable for what is printed should the paper break a law.

The most important student press law case in recent years covered exactly this point: the *Hazelwood School District* v. *Kuhlmeier* case (see citation in Figure 15–1.7), decided by the U.S. Supreme Court in January 1988. Basically, the decision upheld the right of high school administrators to censor stories concerning teen pregnancy and the effects of divorce from a school-sponsored newspaper. The decision had no effect on college and university publications.

Earlier Court decisions found that administrators could not censor because they disliked the content (Fig. 5–1.1), because they believed it would cause some disruption at the school (Fig. 5–1.5), or because the views expressed by the paper did not reflect the views of the majority (Fig. 5–1.5). Following *Hazelwood*, however, the restrictions on the high school press became much more strict.

Administrators may regulate time, place, and manner of distribution of student newspapers and magazines (Fig. 5–1.19). School officials may also restrain student expression if it will substantially interfere with the educational process (Fig. 5–1.6) or if the expression may lead to lawless action (Fig. 5–1.9). Courts have enforced the concept that the feared interference must be *substantial*, not just a minor disturbance.

The U.S. Supreme Court in the *Hazelwood* case said that if a publication is school sponsored, school officials will be allowed to censor when censorship is "reasonably related to legitimate pedagogical concerns." What "reasonably" means here is not clear, but it is a change in wording from the Tinker case, which said that only when the content would cause a "material and substantial disruption of school activities or an invasion of the rights of others" would censorship be allowed.

Guidelines covering time, place, and manner of distribution must be clearly written and posted or published so that all students are aware of the rules and the punishment for ignoring those rules. Courts have asked for specific guidelines because they fear that vague rules that apparently have nothing to do with content could be used to stifle expression. The basic principle behind student press freedom is not to see what the paper can get away with but to see that ideas, even those unpopular with the majority or opposed to by persons in administrative seats of power, have a chance to be expressed.

The court in one student press law case said that the proper remedy against censorship is restraint of the censor, not suppression of the press (Fig. 5–1.9). Rather than *restraint* of the censor—usually an administrator, but occasionally a faculty adviser—the remedy should perhaps be *education* of the censor. Schools are those places in our society where freedom of thought and of expression need to be nurtured, not curtailed. Administrators and others in a position to restrain student expression need to view student press freedom as a means for free and open inquiry and discussion of ideas. Student journalists also need to see these freedoms in the same light.

When administrators realize that they cannot control content, they frequently worry about legal liability should the student paper make an error that brings a lawsuit. The school believes that because it provides at least some of the financial support, a faculty member to advise the paper, and a room to produce the paper, it is the publisher. But courts have disagreed. No school press case has ever been decided in favor of the school having the right to control content because it was the publisher of the student paper.

These decisions have been based on what is called the "open forum theory" of the student press. Basically, the open forum theory states that if the student paper acts as an outlet for opinions of the campus community, and not just as a classroom exercise, then the paper is acting as an open or public *forum* for free expression. Thus the school is not the publisher in the same sense that a company or individual is a publisher of a privately owned newspaper.

Prior to the *Hazelwood* decision, the Student Press Law Center listed four key questions that need to be answered about whether a newspaper is an open or public forum:

1. Does the publication contain student expression on controversial matters in the form of news and editorials?
2. Is the publication open to free expression of ideas in editorial columns as well as in letters to the editor?
3. Is the publication distributed on campus, or is it simply produced as an uncirculated course exercise of the journalism department?
4. What is the history of the publication, why was it created, and how has its role in the school evolved?

Courts first must find whether the publication in question is a forum (Fig. 5–1.14). Then it can decide who has control over the content. If the school has established the student paper as an open forum, it cannot control content (Fig. 5–1.6; see also Figs. 5–1.11 and 5–1.14). In a case in which a student editor was expelled for writing an editorial critical of the governor of the state, a court ruled that the school was not legally obligated to operate a student newspaper. But because it had authorized the paper, it could not expel the editor for engaging in expression protected under the First Amendment (Fig. 5–1.6).

In another case, the court ruled that once a publication has been set up as a forum, a school cannot attempt to control content or punish for past content by withholding funds from that publication during the following year (Fig. 5–1.1). In other words, a school cannot use the power of the purse strings to close down a paper that publishes stories the school doesn't like. (See also Fig. 5–1.18.) Obviously, a school can decide to close down a publication, but it must be on grounds other than the content of the publication.

The most significant part of the *Hazelwood* decision was a change in how the Court determined whether a publication is a public forum. Since the forum status of a publication is a key to whether a school can exert control over content decision, this change is worth looking at.

The Court will now look at three different criteria to determine the forum status of a publication:

- Is it supervised by a faculty member?
- Was the publication designed to impart particular knowledge or skills to student participants or audiences?
- Does the publication use the school's name or resources?

If the answer to any of these three questions is yes, then the *Hazelwood* opinion suggests that the publication may be considered school sponsored and thus under school control of the content.

On the other hand, the majority of the Court wrote that a forum did not exist because the school had never explicitly labeled the newspaper as a forum and also because apparently the adviser had acted as the final authority over every aspect of the publication, including its content. So although the *Hazelwood* case was the first time that a court found a student newspaper *not* to be a public forum, a newspaper can still be considered a forum with First Amendment rights if it states explicitly that a newspaper is a forum and that an adviser does not have content control.

Again, remember that the *Hazelwood* decision applies to high school students in a public school. The courts have always allowed college students more freedom because college students are older and generally more mature than high school students. The intellectual atmosphere of a college campus also differs from that found in a high school.

Rights of the adviser.   An adviser to a school publication stands on shaky legal ground. Is the adviser an agent of the school? Should the adviser look out for the school's best interest? Or is the adviser a champion of student press freedom?

Student press case law has not solidified the adviser's ambiguous position. Courts have tended to uphold students' right to publish over the adviser's responsibility to control content. Decisions have depended on whether the paper was connected with an academic department and whether teaching (not just advising) was done by the faculty member connected with the paper.

According to Trager and Dickerson, *Trujillo* v. *Love* implies that if an adviser does not teach, and if the paper has been set up as a campus forum, no censorship of student expression will be allowed (Fig. 5–1.20).

Review boards that read news copy before publication have also been found unconstitutional (Fig. 5–1.1). The court in one case said that prior review to check for obscenity or for "responsible freedom of the press" may not be required by a school. Trager and Dickerson suggest that, by extension, a faculty adviser of the paper who previews stories could also be found unconstitutional.

Even fear of prosecution by a school is not reason enough for an adviser to censor student expression, according to another federal court decision (Fig. 5–1.10). So it seems that even if an administrator or adviser sees potentially libelous material in the paper, he or she cannot force the students to withdraw the story. An adviser can only advise.

If the school administration orders an adviser to censor student expression and the adviser refuses, he or she may be guilty of insubordination. On the other hand, if an adviser follows the order and censors students, he or she could be taken to court for infringing on the students' First Amendment rights.

Who Is Liable?

If the school cannot control content and the adviser cannot forcibly remove material from the paper, who is responsible if a lawsuit is brought against the paper? This question is frequently behind administrators' concern over the content of the school paper.

Although the law on this point is unclear, it seems that, under the forum theory of the student press, the students themselves are liable. The student staff of the paper may not have financial assets for which it may be sued, but it is still responsible for what it prints. As Trager and Dickerson say, the law does not state that free expression is limited only to those who can afford a court case.

The reasoning behind this position is simple. If a school does not have control over content, how can it be found liable for that content? Again, this has not been set out in these words in the law. Reading through various court cases that touch upon liability, however, leads one to believe that student liability would be upheld in a future court case.

Schools also need not worry that they are responsible because they help in distribution of the paper. In libel law, even distributors have some liability if a paper wrongfully ruins someone's reputation. But distributors can be absolved of responsibility if they can prove that they had no knowledge of the libel nor any reason to suspect a libel. Surely schools are in the same situation if the adviser (the representative of the school) *does not read copy before publication*. If the school is unaware of content prior to publication, it is less likely to be held responsible in a suit.

Freedom, Not License

Student press freedoms are not license to print anything student editors get a whim to write about. A court has ruled: "A college newspaper's freedom from censorship does not necessarily imply that its facilities are the editor's private domain. When a college paper receives subsidy from the state, there are strong arguments for insisting that its columns be open to the expression of contrary views and that its publication enhance, not inhibit, free speech" (Fig. 5–1.9).

The first item of business at a student paper is to be sure that it is set up as a forum in writing (Fig. 5–2, page 45) to protect the paper from arbitrary decisions by administrators. And administrators should be educated about the forum theory, the school's liability, and the present state of student press law.

The second and more important point is that student reporters must be aware of professional reporters' rights and responsibilities. The courts have given students the rights of professional reporters, and they have also given them the same responsibilities and legal liabilities. Students *must* know that once they decide to publish a newspaper they are no longer involved in a classroom exercise. They may be legally responsible for what they print. If the staff also understands the delicate situation of the adviser, few problems should arise. The staff is then free to perform all the functions of an active, vital newspaper on campus. Most legal cases are fought because the administration, the adviser, or the students are ignorant of student press law.

Libel, Privacy, and Obscenity

All student journalists should understand basic libel law. But when questions arise that an adviser or local professional journalist can't answer, a lawyer should be consulted before publication. What follows is a brief outline of libel law based on a Student Press Law Center report by Richard Weisman.

Libel involves published *defamation*, generally a false communication that damages someone's reputation. Slander is oral, or spoken, defamation. The six important elements of libel are (1) it must be false; (2) it must be communicated to a third party; (3) it must refer to a *specific* individual, business, or product, and the information must be relevant to that individual; (4) it must injure the person's reputation in the eyes of the community; (5) a reference to a private individual must have been made with negligence; and (6) a reference to a public figure must have been made with malice, that is, a deliberate disregard for the truth or knowledge of its falsity.

The best defense in a libel case is that the information about the subject is true. To be libelous, the information must be false. "True" here means that the information must be proved true under laws of evidence in court. Before you print something that is potentially libelous but that you know is true, make sure it can be proved true in court.

A libel cannot be committed unless it is communicated to a third party. Many journalists believe that a communication is libelous only if it is published in a paper. But as the publishers of the Alton (Ill.) *Telegraph* found out, libel cases can be brought on the basis of a confidential internal memo, not just a printed story. (In the *Telegraph* case, a local contractor sued the paper for a memo written by two reporters and sent to a Justice Department lawyer. The memo linked the contractor to organized crime.) Damages awarded may be limited, however, if few people see the libel.

Figure 5–2. Suggested policy guidelines for a student publication.
(Reprinted with permission of the Student Press Law Center)

SPLC Model Guidelines For Student Publications

I. STATEMENT OF POLICY

It is undeniable that students are protected in their exercise of freedom of expression by the First Amendment to the Constitution of the United States. Accordingly, it is the responsibility of school officials to insure the maximum freedom of expression to all students

It is the policy of the _____ Board of Education that ____(newspaper)____ , ____(yearbook)____ , and ____(literary magazine)____ , official, school-sponsored publications of _____ High School have been established as forums for student expression. As a forum, each publication should provide a full opportunity for students to inquire, question and exchange ideas. Content should reflect all areas of student interest, including topics about which there may be dissent or controversy.

It is the policy of the _____ Board of Education that student journalists shall have the ultimate and absolute right to determine the content of official student publications.

II. OFFICIAL SCHOOL PUBLICATIONS

A. Responsibilities of Student Journalists

Students who work on official student publications will:

1. Rewrite material, as required by the faculty advisers, to improve sentence structure, grammar, spelling and punctuation;

2. Check and verify all facts and verify the accuracy of all quotations;

3. In the case of editorials or letters to the editor concerning controversial issues, provide space for rebuttal comments and opinions;

4. Determine the content of the student publication.

B. Prohibited Material

1. Students cannot publish or distribute material which is "obscene as to minors". Obscene as to minors is defined as:

(a) the average person, applying contemporary community standards, would find that the publication, taken as a whole, appeals to a minor's prurient interest in sex; and

(b) the publication depicts or describes, in a patently offensive way, sexual conduct such as ultimate sexual acts (normal or perverted), masturbation, excretory functions, and lewd exhibition of the genitals; and

(c) the work, taken as a whole, lacks serious literary, artistic, political, or scientific value.

(d) "Minor" means any person under the age of eighteen.

2. Students cannot publish or distribute material which is "libelous", defined as a false and unprivileged statement about a specific individual which injures the individual's reputation in the community. If the allegedly libeled individual is a "public figure" or "public official" as defined below, then school officials must show that the false statement was published "with actual malice", i.e., that the student journalists knew that the statement was false, or that they published the statement with reckless disregard for the truth—without trying to verify the truthfulness of the statement.

(a) A public official is a person who holds an elected or appointed public office.

(b) A public figure is a person who either seeks the public's attention or is well known because of his achievements.

(c) School employees are to be considered public officials or public figures in articles concerning their school-related activities.

(d) When an allegedly libelous statement concerns a private individual, school officials must show that the false statement was published willfully or negligently, i.e., the student journalist has failed to exercise the care that a reasonably prudent person would exercise.

(e) Under the "fair comment rule" a student is free to express an *opinion* on matters of public interest. Specifically, a student enjoys a privilege to criticize the performance of teachers, administrators, school officials and other school employees.

3. Students cannot publish or distribute material which will cause "a material and substantial disruption of school activities."

(a) Disruption is defined as student rioting; unlawful seizures of property; destruction of property; widespread shouting or boisterous conduct; or substantial student participation in a school boycott, sit-in, stand-in, walk-out or other related form of activity. *Material that stimulates heated discussion or debate does not constitute the type of disruption prohibited.*

(b) In order for a student publication to be considered disruptive, there must exist specific facts upon which it would be reasonable to forecast that a clear and present likelihood of an immediate, substantial material disruption to normal school activity would occur if the material were distributed. Mere undifferentiated fear or apprehension of disturbance is not enough; school administrators must be able to affirmatively show substantial facts which reasonably support a forecast of likely disruption.

(c) In determining whether a student publication is disruptive, consideration must be given to the context of the distribution as well as the content of the material. In this regard, consideration should be given to past experience in the school with similar material, past experience in the school in dealing with and supervising the students in the subject school, current events influencing student attitudes and behavior, and whether or not there have been any instances of actual or threatened disruption prior to or contemporaneously with the dissemination of the student publication in question.

(d) School officials must act to protect the safety of advocates of unpopular viewpoints.

(e) "School activity"—means educational activity of students sponsored by the school and includes, by way of example and not by way of limitation, classroom work, library activities, physical education classes, individual decision time, official assemblies and other similar gatherings, school athletic contests, band concerts, school plays, and scheduled in-school lunch periods.

C. Legal Advice

1. If, in the opinion of the student editor, student editorial staff or faculty adviser, material proposed for publication may be "obscene", "libelous", or "cause a substantial disruption of school activities", the legal opinion of a practicing attorney should be sought. It is recommended that the services of the attorney for the local newspaper be used.

2. Legal fees charged in connection with this consultation will be paid by the board of education.

3. The final decision of whether the material is to be published will be left to the student editor or student editorial staff.

III. PROTECTED SPEECH

School officials cannot:

1. Ban the publication or distribution of birth control information in student publications;

2. Censor or punish the occasional use of vulgar or so-called "four-letter" words in student publications;

3. Prohibit criticism of school policies or practices;

4. Cut off funds to official student publications because of disagreement over editorial policy;

5. Ban speech which merely advocates illegal conduct without proving that such speech is directed toward and will actually cause imminent lawless action;

6. Ban the publication or distribution of material written by nonstudents;

7. Prohibit the school newspaper from accepting advertising.

IV. NONSCHOOL-SPONSORED PUBLICATIONS

School officials may not ban the distribution of nonschool-sponsored publications on school grounds. However, students who violate any rule listed under II.B. may be disciplined after distribution.

1. School officials may regulate the time, place and manner of distribution.

(a) Nonschool-sponsored publications will have the same rights of distribution as official school publications.

(b) "Distribution"—means dissemination of a publication to students at a time and place of normal school activity, or immediately prior or subsequent thereto, by means of handing out free copies, selling or offering copies for sale, accepting donations for copies of the publication, or displaying the student publication in areas of the school which are generally frequented by students.

2. School officials cannot:

(a) Prohibit the distribution of anonymous literature or require that literature bear the name of the sponsoring organization or author;

(b) Ban the distribution of literature because it contains advertising;

(c) Ban the sale of literature.

V. ADVISER JOB SECURITY

No teacher who advises a student publication will be fired, transferred or removed from the advisership for failure to exercise editorial control over the student publication or to otherwise suppress the rights of free expression of student journalists.

VI. PRIOR RESTRAINT

No student publication, whether nonschool-sponsored or official, will be reviewed by school administrators prior to distribution.

VII. CIRCULATION

These guidelines will be included in the handbook on student rights and responsibilities and circulated to all students in attendance.

Figure 5–2. *continued*

The libel must mention a specific individual, business, or product. The use of a name is not the only way to identify an individual; titles or obvious descriptions may identify as well. If you write about "a certain hardware store on Fifth Street" and there is only one on that street, you have identified that store. Large groups cannot be libeled. The statement "All chiropractors are quacks" is not libelous. But if you say that a specific chiropractor is a quack, you could be sued for damages.

The information must also be relevant to the reputation of a person, business, or product. If you say that a college custodian, for instance, cannot type, it has nothing to do with his reputation as a custodian. To make the same statement about a typing instructor might be libelous.

A person's reputation may be damaged in the eyes of a geographic community or of a "community" of peers. If an instructor's reputation is damaged through a libelous statement in a campus publication, the teaching community is the one considered. A teacher's reputation could also be damaged by publication to a statewide teacher's association (a community of peers).

In a 1974 case (*Gertz* v. *Welch*), the U.S. Supreme Court ruled that no one can be held responsible for "liability without fault." Whoever brings a libel suit must prove a libel was published without normal, prudent fact checking. Because states have differing laws as to what constitutes negligence, student editors should check with the laws in their state.

In the case of public officials, actual malice—defined by the Supreme Court as the knowledge or suspicion that a fact is false or a reckless disregard for its truth—must be proved. Actress Carol Burnett won a libel case against the *National Enquirer* in 1981 because, the jury said, an *Enquirer* reporter and the editors acted in "reckless disregard" for the truth of the report that Burnett was drunk in a restaurant. Testimony during the trial revealed that the *Enquirer* reporter did not attempt to confirm the story.

Because the standard of negligence differs from one of actual malice, a key question in many libel suits is whether the person defamed is a public figure or a private person. This delineation has changed over the years. Recent court decisions have often given private-citizen status to persons previously considered public figures. A *public official* is clearly a public figure. A politician carrying out the duties of office is more accountable to the public than is a private person. A *public figure* actively seeks publicity for his or her activities or assumes a role that can be expected to attract publicity, fame, or notoriety in the day-to-day affairs of society. In the Gertz case, the Supreme Court reasoned that a person may be a public figure in one part of his or her activities and a private citizen in others.

A journalist needs to be particularly careful in commenting on a private citizen or on the private life of a public figure or official. Public officials or public figures are fair game for criticism on their *public* activities, but their *private* lives fall under the guidelines for all private citizens.

It is unclear whether the courts assume that instructors or administrators are public figures. An Illinois court ruled that instructors do not *automatically* become public figures in the school community just by being instructors. But if two instructors were to become embroiled in a controversy covered in the student newspaper, then those two instructors would be public figures at that particular place and time.

Student journalists should be cautious whenever they write something that could damage another person's reputation. But if the information (1) can be proved true in court, (2) was said in a meeting protected by *privilege* (trials and legislative meetings are privileged because anything said in them is not open to libel action; some other meetings, such as school board meetings, are privileged under some state laws), or (3) was fair comment and criticism (without malice) of a public official or public figure, then journalists can feel legally secure. Still, court cases are not short, fun, or inexpensive, even if you know you are right. When in doubt, consult a lawyer before printing. Many local legal services have low initial-consultation fees. The American Civil Liberties Union has taken on student press cases for no fee.

Avoiding Libel

Knowledge of the law may help reporters avoid a libel. To avoid libel, be accurate and be careful. Make sure that all persons are fully and properly identified. Identify students by name, class, and hometown or major, and faculty members by academic rank and department. Nonstudents should be identified fully as well, including hometown, if possible. Photographers need written model releases from persons who are photographed at non-news events, for example, for a feature article or for an advertisement.

If an unintentional libel does occur, printing an immediate retraction can often mollify the libeled person. Because the readership of many student papers is limited, a retraction will probably reduce the damages if the case goes to court.

Take care in paste-up as well as in writing. Watch for switched captions under photos and for switched or incorrect headlines. Many libel suits have gone to court on the basis of a headline alone. Don't spend so much time worrying about whether a headline fits that you forget to check it for accuracy.

Privacy

Invasion-of-privacy suits are less frequent than libel suits, but student journalists should nonetheless be aware of the basic laws. There are four ways you can invade someone's privacy: (1) by intruding into a person's solitude, (2) by placing someone in a false light (as in libel), (3) by revealing embarrassing facts about someone (truth here is *not* a defense), and (4) by using a person's likeness or name in an advertisement without permission.

Photographers often come up against privacy problems. Is that photo of

Figure 5–3. Because student bodies change frequently, it is always a good idea to begin every year or term with a statement of policy on the editorial page to avoid later misunderstandings. (From *The Daily Illini*, Illini Publishing Company, Champaign, IL)

opinions
editorials represent the opinion of a majority of the editorial board

editorial
Our purpose and editorial policy

To mark the beginning of a new semester, The Daily Illini editorial board wishes to define the newspaper's purpose and editorial policy for its readership.

The Daily Illini is an independent student newspaper. It is neither owned by the University, nor is its content subject to University administrative approval. Its function is twofold—to inform the University community and to train students interested in the media. Any Universtiy student is eligible to become a member of The Daily Illini staff.

As a student newspaper, its news content is necessarily concentrated on campus issues and other matters of interest to its readership. Although The Daily Illini devotes space and attention to state, national and international issues, it places greater emphasis on the local sphere—an area where it possesses greater expertise and influence. Space limitations require coverage to be limited to that which is of the most interest to the greatest number of persons.

One of the requirements of a free press is public access to the media. The Daily Illini opinions page prints forums and letters to the editor written by readers. Forums are designed for statements which, to be communicated effectively, require a sizable amount of space; letters to the editor are briefer statements. Space limitation dictates that letters are more likely to be published than forums, but longer pieces are never-

theless encouraged if a forum length is necessary.

Because The Daily Illini inevitably receives more letters than can possibly be printed, some editorial judgment is used. Timeliness, clarity of thought and factual accuracy are the general criteria for choosing publishable letters.

The Daily Illini seeks to report the news as truthfully as possible. The newspaper's ethics code contains safeguards intended to eliminate some factors which may threaten a reporter's objectivity. Staffers must refuse gifts and "freebies" from persons or organizations The Daily Illini covers. Staffers are also prohibited from running for office, campaigning for or otherwise openly supporting any candidate. Its editorial views are intended for the opinions page and are distinct and separate from its news coverage.

The Daily Illini staff is dedicated to maintaining a free, independent, responsible student newspaper at the University; and to strengthening the newspaper and its reputation for the future.

editorial board

The editorial board, which decides Daily Illini policy and discusses editorial pieces each week, is composed of the executive and staff editors, salaried reporters and staff writers who have attended three consecutive editorial board meetings. Editorials reflect the opinion of a majority

of the board.

Members of the public are encouraged to address the board on specific issues but are asked to contact the opinions editor or editor-in-chief beforehand. The board normally meets at 7 p.m. Sundays.

Columns appearing on the opinions and sports pages reflect the opinions of the writers and are not necessarily the opinions of the editorial board.

letters policy

The Daily Illini welcomes letters representing all points of view in an attempt to make the Opinions section a forum for the many diverse views of the University community. We cannot, however, acknowledge or return unsolicited manuscripts. We ask writers to limit their letters to 300 words. All contributions MUST be typed and must include the writer's name and phone number. Names will be withheld upon request. The Daily Illini reserves the right to reject letters that are libelous and to edit as may be necessary for copyfitting, grammatical or spelling errors, and to make letters conform to DI style. Writers may expect a delay of several days before their replies to Daily Illini editorials, columns, reviews or news coverage are printed. All materials may be directed to the opinions editor. The Daily Illini, 620 E. John St., Champaign, IL, 61820.

the person sleeping in the library an invasion of privacy? Probably not, because the library is a public place. But don't shoot that kind of photo if it will show the person in a bad light—mouth agape, hair mussed up, glasses hung from one ear. The courts rarely hear privacy suits based on a photo taken at a bona fide news event, so if the event is newsworthy (which is probably why your photographer is there in the first place), you are probably safe.

Journalists also need to be careful about putting someone in a false light. For example, don't just use any file photo of a foreign student to illustrate a story about illegal aliens in your community.

Obscenity

Most so-called obscenity problems of the student press concern vulgar or lewd language, rather than actual obscenities. When a school acts to censor expression that is not obscene—and the school must be able to prove in court that the material is indeed obscene—it is violating students' First Amendment rights. Proving something is obscene is very difficult today. Because the student press rarely publishes nude photos or blatantly pornographic prose, questions of obscenity need not be covered in detail here.

The courts have ruled that the occasional use of common four-letter words, especially if they are a justifiable part of a story, cannot be restricted by school officials, even at the high school level. One court wrote that "although there is a difference in maturity and sophistication between students at a university and at a high school, we conclude that the occasional use of earthy words . . . cannot be found to be likely to cause substantial disruption of school activity or materially impair the accomplishment of educational objectives" (Fig. 5–1.8). The court also ruled that there was even less objection to earthy language in a college publication.

Unless the school can prove that *substantial* disruption of school activity would result from publication, or, following *Hazelwood*, if it fears "reasonable" problems, it cannot censor the publication. Student newspaper staffs would be wise, however, to think seriously about use of words that are bound to cause an adverse reaction at the school. If the language is necessary for the story to be accurate, then it should be printed. There is never a good reason to print vulgar language just to get a reaction.

Access

A more frequent legal problem faced by journalists is access to information. All journalists should know what they are allowed by law to see and what they may not see.

Student record files are open to the student, but not to the public. In most states, journalists are forbidden access to student or faculty personnel files. Public school budgets and salary schedules are, however, open information to the *public*, not just to journalists. Journalists have access as members of the public, not because they work for a newspaper.

School board meetings and most other school meetings are also open to the public, even though some administrators and faculty members may not want a mere "student" journalist to cover them. In some states, student government meetings fall under the law of meetings required to be open. Closed sessions of school board meetings are allowed in many states, however, to discuss personnel matters. But discussing a matter in closed session when it should be open to the public is against the law.

Journalists should also know the law concerning the actual running of meetings. If a meeting has been called illegally, no business conducted at that meeting is legal. Many states require public notice 7 to 10 days ahead of the meeting. Occasionally a decision by a governmental body is pushed through before the public is informed; as a representative of the public at a meeting, the journalist needs to help protect citizens' rights.

Beat reporters at student-government, faculty, and administration meetings need to understand the rules concerning the running of a meeting according to state and local school laws and regulations. If, for instance, the board of trustees acts on an item not listed on the agenda, it may have broken a law. Know the law and know your rights as a reporter.

Student reporters often find that because they are perceived as "only" student reporters, information open to professional reporters may be closed to them. In some cases this problem can be solved by pointing out that student reporters have the same First Amendment rights as professional reporters. Although news gathering has not been specifically granted First Amendment rights, the argument that student reporters have the same opportunity to gather news as professionals is valid. If negotiations fail, work with members of the local press to get the information you need. Most will be willing to help you either by sharing information or by talking to those who deny you access to information.

There are too many federal and state laws regarding access to information to be covered in this brief discussion. But the Freedom of Information Act and Government in the Sunshine Act are two federal laws that all student journalists should know about. Get copies of these laws for your newsroom.

The Freedom of Information Act declassified millions of government documents that had previously been classified as secret. This act may have provided access to interesting information about your local area. The Sunshine Act required policy-making boards to hold open meetings. Some states have laws that require non–policy-making committees to open their meetings if they suggest policy to the board. A Freedom of Information Center in Columbia, Missouri (P.O. Box 858, Columbia, Mo. 65205) collects and disseminates to the media facts about freedom of information and access.

Ethics

Journalists, like doctors and lawyers, have codes of ethical conduct to which most subscribe. The Society of Professional Journalists, the American Society of Newspaper Editors, and the Associated Press Managing Editors all have their own codes (see appendix). Student and faculty journalism associations also have codes for student journalists to follow.

Journalists follow these codes in different ways. Some follow them to the letter, regardless of personal hardship. Others adopt "situation ethics" and make decisions on individual cases. Daniel Schorr, a former CBS newsman, is an example of the former. He came into some information on the Central Intelligence Agency from a House Intelligence Committee meeting that was closed to the press. Schorr said that once he got this information, it was no longer a decision whether to reveal it to the public, even though revealing it might mean a contempt-of-Congress charge. He believed it was his job to pass along to the public whatever information he had. If he held some back, Schorr said, he would be acting as a censor. CBS refused to air the information, but the *Village Voice*, a newspaper in New York, did publish it, costing Schorr his job at CBS. A situation ethics practitioner might have decided in this instance to wait until the committee's information had been made public. You can't report information to the public if you are out of work.

Ethical Problems

Ethical problems for journalists usually concern (1) payola or "freebies," (2) deceitful identification, (3) conflicts of interests, or (4) as with Schorr, decisions regarding withholding information from the public.

Some newspapers limit the free gifts a reporter can accept. Others don't allow reporters to accept anything, not even a drink at a football game. In the past, professional sports teams would foot the entire bill for a reporter to accompany the team on a road trip. The team would give the paper a block of seats for home games and provide the working reporter in the press box with free admission, food, and drink. To foster objectivity, most newspapers today rarely allow a sports reporter to accept more than free access to the press box. Many movie reviewers and restaurant critics pay for their theater ticket or for their meal with expense money from their papers. The reporter thus feels freer to report an accurate assessment, positive or negative.

Stories abound about reporters disguising themselves to gain access to persons or places and then writing stories on the experience. Many of those same reporters win Pulitzer Prizes for those stories, after engaging in what many others believe is a deceitful practice. Those critics, both private citizens and other journalists, believe that journalists should always identify themselves. At least that's what the absolutists believe. But what if the information gained would save citizens thousands of dollars or hardship? Would the good results of the deception then outweigh the bad practice of deceiving the source?

Reporters may also be guilty of deceit when concealing the identity of a source. The use of the term "highly placed official" instead of the official's name is deceitful. Journalists justify the practice by claiming that valuable information outweighs the questionable ethics of not naming sources. Student newspapers may want to set guidelines for these situations.

Journalists also need to be concerned about conflicts of interest. A professional reporter who is a member of the local Kiwanis Club may be hard-pressed by

Figure 5–4. A statement of policy from the staff handbook of *Roundup*, Pierce College.

Los Angeles Pierce College Roundup Statement of Policy

The purposes of the Los Angeles Pierce College Roundup are primarily these:

1. To provide instruction in the discipline of journalism and to emphasize the professional as well as the academic approach to principles, rights and obligations of a free press in a free society.

2. To provide the college with a quality newspaper. A quality newspaper possesses at least the following:

Concern for its publics

The Roundup must be concerned with its publics (the student body, the faculty, the administration and the community at large) because a good newspaper reports, interprets and comments on those ideas and events that are of consequence and/or interest to its readers.

Meeting the needs of its publics should be the basic aim of the student-produced newspaper. That should be fundamental in the exercise of editorial judgment, in news play, content selection and editorial policy.

Readers should receive a newspaper that provides full and accurate coverage of campus life and exhibits sound judgment and reasoning in columns and editorials.

Readers deserve a newspaper that leads, informs, instructs and entertains with truth and accuracy foremost in the production of that newspaper.

Right to criticize

The Roundup reserves the right to criticize, to question and to evaluate, and assumes responsibility for the accuracy and completeness of that criticism.

Constructive criticism, thoughtfully prepared and respectfully presented, is basic to the freedom of the college press.

Responsibility

The Roundup realizes that the exercise of press freedom entails a heavy burden of responsibility.

That responsibility includes not only the right to print, but also the right not to print, for The Roundup realizes that, at least in part, the reputation of students, faculty and the institution, and the opinions of its readers, can be shaped by The Roundup.

The Roundup staff may make mistakes, but not without benefiting from those mistakes and not without full realization that it is responsible for those mistakes.

fellow members to conceal information that should be made public. To avoid this situation, many journalists do not join organizations they may have to cover. Student reporters often face conflicts of interest. The most obvious conflict is with the school itself—either the entire organization or a part of it, such as an athletic team. For example, a reporter who also works with the drama club should not be the beat reporter covering theater arts. A good student reporter is *always* objective when covering and writing a story. The reporter's job is to report, not to be a public relations agent for the college or team. Avoid conflicts when possible; when not, overcome them through professionalism.

Occasionally student reporters have trouble deciding whether to print some information. An example might be a story on an auto accident near campus involving a male faculty member who is married. The student reporter might see on the accident report that the other occupant of the faculty member's car was a young female student. Should the reporter mention this detail in the story? Or what if the college president has been arrested and charged with drunk driving and the local press has decided not to print a story unless there is a conviction? Should the student paper print the story anyway?

On other occasions a reporter may be asked to withhold publication of a fact until the administration has had time to investigate the problem or act on it. The classic example here is the Bay of Pigs invasion of Cuba in 1962. The *New York Times* found out about the invasion, but President John F. Kennedy asked the paper not to reveal it for fear that the invasion might be ruined. After the disastrous results of the invasion became known, Kennedy admitted that he wished the paper had gone ahead with the story. It may have saved the United States international embarrassment and the lives of the men who were killed.

Student reporters run into difficult situations, too. Absolutists in all ethical situations will always say: Print the story. But student journalists have to weigh many factors. Although they should be objective about the school's activities, they may need to exercise caution in some situations. If the school gets into a major problem brought on by a premature story in the school paper, everyone suffers—including the paper. Sometimes discretion is necessary. There are no easy solutions to ethical problems. That is why none are suggested here. Staffs should discuss each problem as it arises.

This chapter is only the barest summary of legal and ethical issues for student journalists. *No action should be taken based on the information given in this chapter; the author is not a lawyer.* This discussion is meant only to alert student journalists to important legal areas concerning their rights and responsibilities. For more general information, contact the Student Press Law Center. For a specific problem, consult a lawyer.

Suggested Projects

1. Ask a local reporter to discuss ethical problems faced by reporters. Find out what the local paper's policy is on accepting freebies.

2. Set up a roundtable discussion with several administrators and members of the faculty about the rights and responsibilities of the student press. Present them with some of the information from this chapter, and talk over some of the implications this information has for the newspaper at your school. See if they have any questions or complaints about the paper's operation or news coverage. Discussing possible problem areas ahead of time makes discussing specific problems when they occur much easier.

newswriting

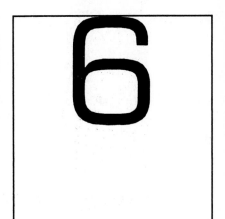

After returning to the newsroom with notes from the interview or meeting, the reporter must turn that information into a simple, yet complete telling of the important details. It's time to write the news story.

Writing a news account of an event or meeting is one of those apparently simple tasks that turns out to be difficult. But the difficulty in writing a news story disappears bit by bit with continued practice and experience. Newswriting experts have boiled down the complex skills needed to write a good news story into a small set of rules. Although many books have been written on how to write a news story, a look at those simple rules with illustrations of them should help you overcome any difficulty and enable you to write a good news story in a short time. After you learn the basic rules, it's a matter of practice.

Leads

News reports have not always been written the way they are today, with a beginning section (called a *lead*, pronounced "leed") that summarizes the main points of the event with details following. This method began, according to some historians, during the Civil War, when reporters from the North were having trouble getting their stories telegraphed back to the office. Sometimes their stories would be interrupted by more important military information or by Confederate soldiers who cut the wires. The stories would begin, but they were often interrupted before editors found out who won the battle. To combat this, editors instructed their reporters in the field to begin with the punch line, so to speak. Summarize the results of the battle first, they told their reporters, and then give us the supporting details. If the wire was then cut halfway through the story, the main points would have already been sent. This "end-result first" story structure is today called the *inverted pyramid* (Fig. 6–1), and it is used in the majority of news stories.

Because the inverted-pyramid structure provides the reader with the essential details in the first paragraph (or in the first few paragraphs of a more complex story), hurried readers can scan the lead to learn what the story is about and continue reading only if they are interested in the subject. Two other reasons for the inverted-pyramid structure are that (1) headlines can be written more easily because the copy desk person can read the first few grafs (paragraphs) and learn what the story is about and (2) the story's length can be cut more easily from the bottom, because those facts are the least important (Fig. 6–2).

Figure 6–1. The inverted pyramid represents how a news story should be structured. The most important point of the story should come first, with lesser details following in descending order of importance.

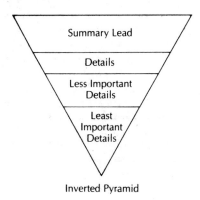

Inverted Pyramid

53

The first legal move has been made by the COS district in defense of a lawsuit filed against it by former basketball coach Kirby Mannon.

Robert P. Long, the attorney representing the district, said yesterday that he had been granted an extension of 30 days in which to file the defendant's response to Mannon's lawsuit.

Mannon is suing the district for $2.5 million, attorney's fees and an order that Mannon be reinstated as head men's basketball coach.

The lawsuit was delivered to the Board of Trustees Aug. 8, 1991. In the lawsuit, the district was given 30 days to respond. When that deadline passed this week and nothing had been placed on file in Tulare County Superior Court, Long said that Mannon's lawyer, J. Patrick Sullivan of Lindsay, had granted an extension over the phone.

"Mr. Mannon's attorney was gracious enough to allow us an extension," Long said.

"The lawsuit will be defended," he added. "We believe it to be without merit, but, as required, we will file the appropriate legal documents."

Long, however, declined further comment.

"We won't have anything further to say while litigations are going on in court," he said.

Long is a member of the Visalia firm of Hurlbutt, Clevenger, Long and Vortmann. The district's case was referred to the firm by James A. Davies, claim's agent of Fireman's Fund in Fresno, the district's insurance agency.

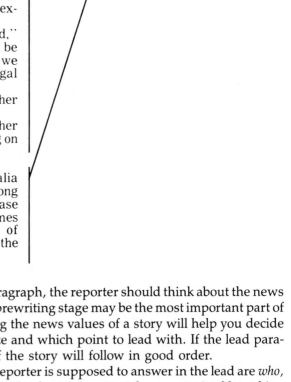

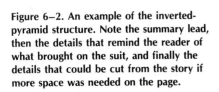

Figure 6–2. An example of the inverted-pyramid structure. Note the summary lead, then the details that remind the reader of what brought on the suit, and finally the details that could be cut from the story if more space was needed on the page.

Before writing the lead paragraph, the reporter should think about the news values of the story. In fact, this prewriting stage may be the most important part of writing a news story. Reviewing the news values of a story will help you decide which news value to emphasize and which point to lead with. If the lead paragraph is right, then the rest of the story will follow in good order.

The classic questions the reporter is supposed to answer in the lead are *who, what, where, when, why,* and *how.* Nearly any event can be summarized by asking these six questions. From the answers, the lead paragraph and the direction of the story can be fashioned.

Let's take a simple example.

- Who: Colleen Michaels, a student at Middle Valley College.
- What: Demanded reimbursement for articles stolen from her locker during a physical education class.
- Where: At a board of trustees meeting.

- When: Last night.
- Why: Michaels claimed that since the college required a physical education course, it should be responsible for running a theft-free locker room. She said her loss occurred because of negligence.

Sample lead paragraph:

A student who claimed that the college was responsible for items stolen from her PE locker told the board of trustees last night that the college should reimburse her for her loss.

Because the student is not a well-known figure, the "who" should not be emphasized. The "what" is the most important question to answer, as is true for most news stories. Although the "where" and the "when" should be mentioned in the lead, they rarely deserve being featured. In many lead paragraphs, the "when" is plugged in after the verb (Fig. 6–3).

The "why" and "how" are not generally in the lead. The answers to these simple questions often take several paragraphs and should come after the event has been described.

Each story needs its own special organization and lead. If the facts call for a "who" or "what" lead, then by all means write it that way. If the facts call for "when," "where," "why," or "how" leads, then they should be written that way.

Some stories are important because of the person involved (Fig. 6–4). Leads that name a person are usually about someone whose name alone will identify the person to the reader. There are very few of these persons in the country, much less on a campus, so a *blind lead* is often used (Fig. 6–5). A blind lead describes the person in the news event by some description other than a name: as a student (as in the PE theft example), a school employee, the president of a fraternity, a university professor, a local income-tax expert. Most "who" leads will be blind leads.

Some stories are so complex that these simple rules for leads just won't apply. The beginning portion of the story that summarizes the main points of the story may take two or more paragraphs. Student journalists should be reminded, however, that the term *lead*, although often used to refer to only the first paragraph of a story, really refers to the beginning section of a story, no matter how long it is.

Attribution

One more important item is usually found in the lead: *attribution*. News does not come directly from the reporter. The reporter is the conduit through which news passes from the event to the reader. Information comes from someone else, and the reporter should attribute the information to that someone—the earlier in the story, the better. Most news stories have attributions in the lead or at the beginning of a second paragraph.

This conduit function of the reporter is also the reason for writing in the third person (*he, she, him, her, it, they, them*) and not the first person (*I, me, we, our*). News reporters don't *make* news: they report it. The first person is acceptable only in clearly identified direct quotes, in which the source is talking about himself or herself. And reporters are supposed to report it *objectively;* that is, their reporting should be fair to all sides and free from bias.

Early and frequent attribution is especially important in crime stories. For instance, information in a story about an arrest should be attributed to police in the first graf and probably every graf thereafter. Although the attribution seems altogether too frequent when studied closely, readers are not slowed by the mentions and in fact probably appreciate knowing where the information originated (Fig. 6–6).

If the students of Middle Valley College were deciding the outcome of today's election, George Bush, Melissa Reid, and Frank McGuire would be the winners.

Academic suspensions may double this quarter, said Dr. Wilbur A. Tincher, dean of the office of student services.

June has been proclaimed "Honor Vietnam Veterans Month" at Cypress Gardens at the request of the Florida commanders of the American Legion, Disabled American Veterans, and Veterans of Foreign Wars.

Instructors choosing not to use plus or minus grading values are no longer required to notify students of this practice, as a result of action taken Tuesday by Middle Valley College's Faculty Senate.

MVC officials are expecting about 6 percent fewer incoming freshman and transfer students next fall, and at least one vice president is blaming the decline on the college's fiscal crisis.

Fear that small problems might snowball into major difficulties has prompted bookstore manager Dawn Fairbanks to request a full-time security patrol.

Figure 6–3. These sample lead paragraphs exhibit the many ways that a summary lead can be structured.

Lester Norris donated $2.5 million to Middle Valley College for the construction of a new sports complex, completing a center of facilities granted by Norris and his wife, Renée.

Figure 6–4. The "who" in this lead was important and well known enough to deserve mention in the opening paragraph.

Unearthing the remains of an abandoned city is dirty work. But the experience was very rewarding for two MVC students who last summer worked on an important archaeological dig in West Point, Mississippi.

Figure 6–5. When the "who" is not important or when the individuals are not well known, a "blind lead" that describes or identifies the individuals, but doesn't name them, should be used.

A Champaign man was stabbed in what police described as an attempted murder late Sunday night at the bar at the American Legion, 903 N. Fifth St., Champaign, *according to Champaign police reports.*

The victim, Oliver Jasper Jr., was reportedly involved in a fight with an unidentified man, *reports said.*

The fight ended when Jasper was stabbed by the other man, who fled from the bar, *according to the police.*

Jasper had been released Jan. 17 from the Champaign County Correctional Center, where he was being held on charges of driving on a suspended driver's license, *according to the Champaign County sheriff's office.*

Jasper was taken to Mercy Hospital, where he is listed in satisfactory condition.

Figure 6–6. Crime stories need more frequent attribution than other stories, as this example shows. (From *The Daily Illini*, Illini Publishing Company, Champaign, IL)

Now that we know what must appear in a lead, it's time to find out how to write one. Studies show that the summary and attribution should be done in one sentence of no more than 30 words (25 is better) for optimum readability. If the sentence is too long, the reader's comprehension suffers.

All other paragraphs, not just the lead, should be kept to one sentence as often as possible, though two short sentences are acceptable. Each graf should contain only one idea. These rules differ from the rules on paragraphing that you learned in your English composition classes. In fact, one-sentence paragraphs might get you in trouble in your comp class, but they will please your journalism instructor.

One-sentence grafs have two major functions in journalism, and neither has much to do with writing (except for the readability factor). Short grafs make it easier to cut a story that is too long. One or two fewer sentences may make the difference between a story fitting and it being too long. If paragraphs all contain several sentences, cutting one sentence may mean costly and time-consuming resetting of type.

Short grafs also look better on the page. A newspaper, by nature, is a series of long, narrow, vertical columns of gray type. Long paragraphs intensify this grayness, which is unpleasant to look at. Breaking the copy into paragraphs approximately every inch (four lines of type on a typewriter or PC screen, seven or eight lines of type in the paper) adds white space to the columns at graf beginnings and ends and breaks the monotony.

Quotations

Simple news stories, such as the one on the PE theft, rarely quote the source directly. Attribution is there, but the information is in the reporter's own words. Longer stories, however, gain from (and sometimes require) the immediacy of a direct quote from the speaker. Learning what to quote and how to use these quotations are important parts of learning to write a news story.

Even though an entire story may come from one or two sources, the reporter should summarize the basic facts for the reader. The source, in either *direct* or *indirect quotes,* can then illuminate or explain certain facts. The reporter does the play-by-play, so to speak, and the source adds the color commentary (Fig. 6–7).

Direct and indirect quotes differ in their closeness to the original speech of the source and in their structural uses within a story. Direct quotes should be very, very close to the source's precise words. Many journalists believe that direct quotes should be 100 percent accurate, but realistically, this perfection cannot always be achieved. People rarely speak in complete sentences, and sometimes words are not pronounced completely ("gonna" instead of *going to,* "sumpin'" instead of *something*). Unless poor grammar or slurring of speech is important to the story or to the source's personality, the reporter should correct the quote for the speaker.

In indirect quotes—close summaries or paraphrases of what the source said—the reporter may change or cut some words. Thus indirect quotes are not surrounded by quotation marks, whereas direct quotes are. Quotation marks indicate to the reader that what falls within them can be assumed to come directly from the source; indirect quotes are close to what the source said, but they have been run through the filter of the reporter.

Direct and indirect quotes are used differently in a story. The major function of an indirect quote is to pass along information, to give facts with slightly more credence than the summaries the reporter provides. Indirect quotes, therefore, can appear almost anywhere in a story. Direct quotes, on the other hand, explain or illuminate what has already been introduced. For that reason, direct quotes are always preceded by a summary paragraph from the reporter or an indirect quote from the source that sets the scene for the direct quote. Information has to be introduced to enable the source to expand on it (Fig. 6–7). For this reason direct-quote leads are not often used in news stories. The direct quote would have to be extraordinary to merit leading with it (Fig. 6–8).

Speech Tags

All quotes, direct or indirect, have what is called the "speech tag," or attribution of the quote. The speech tag is usually the name of the source or a pronoun followed by "said." "He said" is preferred over the "said he" inversion. Although speech tags may be found nearly anywhere in a quote, there are a few general rules.

Indirect quotes should begin with a speech tag and include the word "that" to introduce the quote.

- Fenwick said that the proposed bill would . . .
- She said that her reasons for quitting were . . .
- A University of Michigan humanities professor said that . . .

Occasionally, speech tags will appear in the middle or at the end of an indirect quote. The reporter has to decide whether the quote itself or the speaker is more important, and then lead with that. But speech tags are usually better at the beginning of indirect quotes.

Conversely, speech tags for direct quotes are usually better in the middle or at the end.

- "The flight was an exhilarating experience," the pilot said.
- "It is a tempting idea," she said, "but I'll never try that stunt again."
- "I've never seen anything like it before," he said. "It may even be a new species."

Notice that when the speech tag comes in the middle of a direct quote, it may be either in the middle of a sentence (as in the second example) or between two sentences (as in the third example). The reporter should make sure that the quote is punctuated correctly. If the speech tag comes after a clause, a comma should follow the speech tag because the quote continues (as in the second example). If the speech tag comes between two complete sentences, a period should follow the speech tag (as in the third example).

If a paragraph contains several short sentences of direct quotes, the speech tag should come no later than the end of the first sentence (Fig. 6–9). Also, in extended quotation in which the quote takes several paragraphs, the speech tag need not appear in every paragraph. If it is obvious that the same speaker is continuing, every other paragraph should include the speech tag. More than one speech tag per graf is rare.

Many beginning reporters get bored with using the verb "said" all the time in speech tags. They mistakenly believe that the reader notices the repetition and would like to see other words, such as *admitted, revealed, confessed, whispered, smiled, stuttered, grumbled, conceded,* and so on. But sometimes these words say more than the reporter intended. "Revealed," for instance, implies that what the source said had been hidden before the interview—which may not be true. "Confessed" and "admitted" also have connotations that may not be intended by the reporter or speaker. Many of the other words have problems, too. For instance, some writers use "she smiled" as a speech tag. But how do you "smile" something? When you smile, you can't talk at all. Perhaps the sources said something *with a smile,* or she said something and then smiled. Many adverbs or prepositional phrases may be added to "he said" ("he said *in a whisper*"). Sticking to "said" remains the best rule of thumb.

The state Journalism Hall of Fame will be housed at the Middle Valley College Department of Journalism library.

Director Mary Pat Michaels said that this was an important milestone for the department.

"Housing this will be an important connection with the professional media in the state," Dr. Michaels said. "This marks an important moment in the growth of journalism at MVC."

She said that the first nominations would be gathered in the spring.

"We hope to put out a call for nominations early during the spring semester," she said. "The induction ceremony will be later in the spring, probably in May."

Figure 6–7. In this example, the direct quotes expand upon ideas already introduced in the preceding indirect quote.

"We've never had this many students be in the state level," seemed to be the consensus of Michele McGuire and John Stoffel, who had eight music students qualify in the state music programs.

Figure 6–8. The direct quote should be important *and* colorful to merit the lead. This lead graf does not meet the requirement.

Figure 6–9. When a direct-quote paragraph consists of several sentences, the speech tag should come no later than the end of the first sentence.

"A lot of people don't realize how dangerous a false alarm can be," remarked O'Connor. "When I was in the Seattle Fire Department, somebody pulled a box on a street corner. On the way to the scene, two firemen were killed when the fire engine collided with a mail truck that had failed to hear the siren."

Structure

Now's the time to tie everything together in a meaningful sequence. As mentioned previously, the lead sets the structure for the rest of the story; if the lead is well thought out, the rest of the story comes together easily. Many reporters spend half their writing time on the lead alone. The guiding principle behind story organization is that the structure must help the reader to understand what you are writing about. The structure should lead the reader from idea to idea simply and clearly. The object is to give readers information, not to wow them with convoluted style.

Figure 6–10. In news stories, transitions are usually repeated words or phrases rather than the common "on the other hand," or "however." (From *The Daily Pennsylvanian*, University of Pennsylvania)

Minority Data Update To Delay Hiring Plan

By PETER CANELLOS

Implementation of the University's affirmative action plan has been delayed due to an updating of figures on the availability of minority and women candidates in the Philadelphia area.

University affirmative action officer Davida Ramey said yesterday that the updating will be completed "hopefully within two weeks," at which time the University will use the updated figures to find which areas are having trouble attracting minority and women applicants.

The updating of availability figures was greeted by leaders of campus minority and women's groups as "a significant step forward."

"I think the updating is a very good sign," Penn Women's Center Director Carol Tracy said yesterday. "Now our data will be more reflective of the current labor pool."

"I think President Hackney heard what we have been saying about the data needing revision and followed our advice," she added.

The University is currently using availability data collected in 1970, and affirmative action advocates have protested that availability of minority workers has grown significantly since then, making the University's computations misleading.

Although current data on the availability of minority workers in Philadelphia for specific jobs has not been collected, Ramey said she is able to estimate availability using a system designed by Regional Studies Professor Janice Madden.

"We are able to draw the data forward by combining current data on availability in specific jobs in the nation with data on general availability in Philadelphia," Madden said yesterday.

Madden, who has served as a pro-

fessional affirmative action consultant, added that a panel of affirmative action experts commissioned by the U.S. Department of Labor has recommended that her system be adopted by the Labor Department as a means of determining availability data for cities across the country.

"I suggested using this method to update the University's availability data two years ago but my suggestion was not accepted," Madden said. "At that time, the Labor Department had just announced it would review the University's affirmative action plan and people didn't want to complicate things."

"At the time, I think the administrators felt the review would be over quickly," she added. "Now that it is apparent that nothing will be decided quickly, they are suddenly willing to try it."

Although Ramey has said she will use the updated data for the University's affirmative action audit, Madden said Ramey is apprehensive about submitting the new data to the Labor Department."

"It hasn't been resolved yet whether the new data will given to the Labor Department," Madden said. "Right now, (she) is busy finishing the updating."

The audit, which will begin the implementation process, was originally scheduled to be performed on the week of March 2.

"The affirmative action task force met last week to finalize preparations for the audit," Ramey said. "As soon as the availability data is ready, we will begin."

With one-sentence paragraphs consisting of only one idea—*block paragraphs*—it would be easy for a story to appear as a series of statements without any smooth flow from one idea to the next. Block paragraphing makes the use of effective transitions important. *Transitions* are words or phrases that link two ideas, making the movement from one to the other clear and easy. Obvious transitional phrases are *thus, therefore, on the other hand, next, then,* and so on.

Short block paragraphs are used partly to make it easy to cut a story during paste-up. Using obvious transitions such as "on the other hand" makes it tougher to make those cuts. If the graf preceding "on the other hand" is cut, the idea the phrase refers to is gone. Cutting "on the other hand" then means resetting an entire paragraph.

Transitions in news stories are generally done by repeating a word or phrase or using a synonym for a key word in the preceding paragraph (Fig. 6–10). Think of block grafs as islands tied together with transitional bridges of repeated words or phrases.

There are nearly as many structures for news stories as there are stories. Each story calls for its own structure. But beginning reporters can use several basic formats and modify them to meet the needs of each story. The inverted-pyramid structure—a summary followed by the coverage of the details in descending order of importance—works for most stories. Two other simple structures are the summary-and-chronology format and the A and B format. These three basic formats are just skeletons or outlines of an organization for a news story and should not be followed to the letter for every story. The reporter must decide which is the best structure to use. Following these simple outlines frees the reporter to concentrate on plugging in facts creatively.

Inverted Pyramid

The inverted-pyramid story begins with the summary lead, usually focusing on "what" and "how" (Fig. 6–11). The points of the story are covered in a general-to-specific direction, with reporter summaries followed by indirect and direct quotes from sources. Each point is covered in a miniature inverted pyramid: The

Figure 6–11. This story covers the important points in descending order of importance. (From the *Auburn Plainsman,* Auburn University)

Suspensions may rise Winter due to switch in grade system

By Pete Mohney
Plainsman Staffwriter

Academic suspensions may double this quarter, said Dr. Wilbur A. Tincher, dean of the office of student services.

Five to six hundred students could be suspended after this quarter, Tincher said. The major factors in the rise are the switch to the four-point grade system and slightly increased standards for probation and suspension.

"A person who has any F's will have a lower GPA on a four-point system than on a three-point system," Tincher said.

D's and F's are equal on the three-point system, but they are not equal on the four point system. This will cause a few people to slip below the required number of grade points needed to avoid suspension, he said.

The changeover to the four-point system was approved by Auburn President Harry Philpott with the understanding that the Admissions Committee would not suspend anyone during Fall quarter and that they would be lenient with juniors and seniors with respect to suspensions after that.

The standards for suspension were raised from a maximum shortage of 21 grade points on the three-point system to a maximum shortage of 33 grade points on the four-point system, an increase of bout 15 percent.

Although Auburn's entrance requirements were stiffer than most Alabama universities, Auburn officials found that "other institutions similar to Auburn had higher academic standards than we did," Dr. Tincher said. It is harder to get into Auburn, but it is "a little easier to stay once you're here."

Appeals about academic suspensions can be made to the Admissions Committee. Suspension, which is a two-quarter absence from Auburn, could be reduced to probation, which is a warning, Tincher said.

point is first summarized and then details are discussed. If reporters remember the inverted pyramid when covering each point, the reader will be able to follow each idea easily.

Summary and Chronology

The summary-and-chronology format opens with a summary of the final or the most recent result of the event or issue (Fig. 6–12). After the reader has been told the most recent result, the reporter takes the reader back to the beginning and tells the story chronologically, always following the summary-before-details sequence. If room still remains after the major points of the story are made, the reporter can return to the beginning point and give more details, and/or go further back and discuss background leading up to the beginning of the issue. It's as if the reporter is making continuing sweeps through the story's fact bin, getting more and more minute facts with every sweep. The story then can end with a few grafs about what may happen next.

A-and-B Format

A-and-B format stories are those with two distinct parts or sources. Although A-and-B stories can lead with summary grafs and follow a chronological order in the body of the story, the main organizational factor is *opposing viewpoints*. For instance, you may be doing a story about the faculty's negotiations with the school for a new contract. Because the negotiations may concern several factors—say, a salary increase, new medical benefits, more faculty input in the hiring of administrators, and a shortened teaching calendar—it may be confusing for the reader to read the faculty side of the story early on and then switch to the school's side later in the story. Besides, if the story has to be cut from the bottom, it may appear biased and unbalanced.

The best way to structure the story is to introduce the major points of contention between the two groups in a summary lead and then discuss them

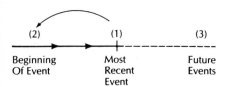

Figure 6–12. The summary-and-chronology story opens with a recent event, which is the reason the story was written. Then, moving back in time, the story covers the beginning and ensuing events to return the reader to the present. The story can also end by looking to future consequences.

Figure 6–13. This A-and-B-format story compares tuition and fees between Milwaukee Area Technical College (MATC) and the University of Wisconsin. (From *MATC Times*, Milwaukee Area Technical College)

Tuition likely to increase in 1981-82: Senate

By Susan Grittner

Student senate members are anticipating an increase in tuition for associate degree programs at MATC, according to indications received from state legislators.

The increase will be unlike the 22 percent tuition hike for the 1980-1981 school year. That increase was a result of inflation and increased instructional costs. There was no actual change in the formula for determining tuition.

Since 1976, tuition for technical programs has been figured at 9½ percent of what it costs MATC to run a particular program. The only exceptions to this are the college parallel courses, where tuition is based on 25 percent of statewide instructional costs.

Recent indications from legislators reveal that future tuition rates for associate degree courses could also be based on 25 percent of MATC's instructional costs. This type of change in the formula would result in an MATC student paying a much higher rate than students in the University of Wisconsin System.

Students within the UW System are currently paying 25 percent of the cost of their education in the form of tuition, so it might seem reasonable to expect MATC students to pay that same percentage. It might seem reasonable if the nature of the two educational systems were similar; however, they are not.

MATC is a technical college functioning with a ratio of approximately 20 students to every one instructor in many courses. This one to 20 student/teacher ratio is maintained in the various programs within the Service and Health Occupations Division, the Graphic and Applied Arts Division, the Industrial and Technical Divisions, and the Television Division. Student safety is assured in areas such as laboratories and machine shops with this student/teacher ratio.

The cost of instructional equipment utilized at MATC is another factor that must be considered when evaluating

instructional costs. A technical college requires a tremendous amount of money to operate the equipment used for instructional purposes. These expenses will be reflected in the cost of tuition.

The University of Wisconsin System is easy to contrast with MATC's needs for instructional equipment, since many UW classes require only a podium and a chalkboard.

The UW System further differs from MATC's educational system with lecture classes that have student/teacher ratios of anywhere between 1 to 30 and, in some instances, 1 to 300.

Annual tuition and fees for the UW System for the 1980-1981 school year range from $315 at UW — Superior to $516 at UW — Milwaukee for the full-time equivalency (FTE) student.

The most recent audited figures available for MATC instructional costs are for the 1978-1979 school year. In that year FTE students in the Service and Health Occupations Division would have paid $1,160 in tuition if it had been based on 25 percent of instructional costs.

FTE students in the Industrial, Technical, and Television Divisions would have paid in excess of $600 per year.

In fact, tuition in most divisions at MATC would have been substantially higher in the 1978-1979 school year when figured at the new formula than the current (1980-1981 school year) tuition rates in the UW System.

MATC college parallel courses differ from UWM in relation to tuition costs. Alidor Vanderport, dean of students, said that MATC is quite cost effective in this area. General Education instructors at MATC are required to instruct on a 15-hour class schedule instead of the nine-hour class schedule assigned to UW instructors.

Vanderport said that the costs of MATC college parallel courses are reduced because of this difference in class assignments. The UW instructors, however, are required

to do research. This research is not required of MATC instructors.

The hidden expenses of education are an area that should not be overlooked when evaluating tuition and educational costs. Hidden costs can be found when purchasing books, materials, supplies, and paying for room and board, transportation, and parking. As a technical college located in downtown Milwaukee, MATC challenges student pocketbooks with its hidden costs.

For example, an MATC FTE student studying in the Photography program pays the current annual tuition of $1,333 (including supplies and fees), books at $210, miscellaneous expenses at $800, daily lunches at $300, and room and board (at home) of about $1,300.

Transportation to and from MATC can range from $100 (if the student utilizes public transportation) to over $1,000 (if the student maintains a car and purchases parking in the downtown area). Total expenditures for this student would range from $4,043 to $4,943 depending on transportation needs.

A university student rarely pays the hidden costs that technical college students are confronted with. An FTE UW—Eau Claire student, for example, will pay $955 for one year's tuition. Included in this expense is textbook rental and course fees. An additional $1,450 will be paid for room and board, along with $800 in miscellaneous expenses.

After these expenditures, the monetary drain on the university student ceases. Transportation is not a problem because the student lives on campus and areas are readily accessible.

Students in all educational systems are in a financial bind, according to Vanderport. Educational costs are getting higher and the recent cutback in federal government aid programs leaves the student with less money to purchase an education.

point by point, first one side (A) and then the other (B), commenting in indirect and direct quotes (Fig. 6–13). This three-part sequence of summary, A quotes, and B quotes can be used throughout the story in miniature inverted pyramids within the overall inverted-pyramid structure.

The A-and-B format, by the way, actually appears in many news stories for the simple reason that one-source stories are usually avoided in the interest of fairness. The A-and-B format is one way to see that at least two sides get a chance to air their views to the public. More sources can be added when needed.

Remember that structure comes from the facts and how they need to be presented, not from some set of rules in a journalism book. Variations or combinations of these formats can and should be used as necessary. But if a format fits a story, then it acts like an outline, allowing a reporter to concentrate on getting the details down clearly without having to worry about where the story is going to go next.

Speeches and Meetings

What the person said is the most important aspect of the speech story, so something important from the speech should be in the lead. Many beginners come up with such speech-story leads as:

> Sen. Robert Dole (R-Kan.) gave a speech last night in the Little Theater.

This lead tells the reader nothing. A story that tells the reader of a speech next week or an *advance story* in which the reporter does not yet know what the speaker will say may use this kind of lead. If the title or the subject area of the speech is known, even the advance lead should have something besides the basics:

> Sen. Robert Dole (R-Kan.) will outline the U.S. Senate's committee structure in a speech at 8 tomorrow night in the Little Theater.

A good speech-story lead begins with something specific the speaker said. After all, the fact that something is being said is why the reporter is covering the event.

After listening to the speech, the reporter must present the ideas from that speech to the reader, not give the reader a verbatim transcript. Nor should the reporter write the story following the order of the speech. The reporter should listen to the speech, evaluate it, and structure the story in an inverted-pyramid format, giving the most important points at the top of the story (Figs. 6–14 and 6–15).

The chronology within the speech should not be disregarded. Important points could be covered and quoted in the order that the speaker said them. But the story should not necessarily follow the order of the entire speech from start to finish.

Good coverage of a speech also includes going beyond what the speaker said. The reporter's observation skills come into play here. How large was the audience? Was it quiet? Unruly? Responsive? Were there frequent interruptions for applause? Were there pickets or demonstrations outside? What were people talking about when they left the speech—the speech or the heat in the auditorium or the ice cream cone they were on their way to get? These questions all add up to good coverage of a speech. Remember that a reporter's job is to *be* at the speech for the reader.

A speech can be thought of as little more than a formal interview that is held in public. As with an interview, a speech story should be researched beforehand. The reporter should get biographical information on the speaker and look in recent periodicals to see if the speaker has given speeches recently on the same topic. Perhaps the speaker has changed an idea or a stand to fit a specific audience.

Locking up more and more criminals won't solve the current upsurge in crime rates, Howard Way, head of the California prison system, told students and faculty Friday.

"All we need to do in California and America is take a look at the record and you will see that prisons as they have been run throughout history were failures," Way said.

Guest speaker Way told the audience in the COS Theater that when criminals are put behind bars, they are exposed "to every sordid, deviant sex act known to man," not to mention a ready availability of drugs and alcohol. In other words, prisons are not favorable environments for rehabilitation.

"Remember, 95 to 96 percent of these people (prisoners) are going to come back to their communities—your communities—eventually," Way said.

Figure 6–14. This story uses a correct lead following a speech. The story structure does not follow the outline of the speech; instead, it covers the speech topics in order of importance. (From *The Campus*, College of the Sequoias)

Figure 6–15. The basic structure of a speech story.

Nuclear war is becoming more likely, largely because of the computerization of nuclear weapons, a former defense department official said yesterday.

Speaking to Concerned Students Against Nuclear Weapons, a Middle Valley College student group, John K. Doe said that computer chips fail nearly as often as human beings make errors of judgment.

"It's simply not true that computerization is safer because it avoids the possibility of accidental nuclear war caused by human error," he said. "We're in greater danger today because of mechanical failure than ever before."

Doe, who was head computer operations chief for the defense department from 1968 to 1981, told the packed audience in the auditorium that as computers get smaller, more difficulties in reliability arise.

"The reason behind this is simple," he said. . . .

Increased awareness on the part of the reporter leads to a better story and a better-informed reader.

Speech-Story Structure

Most speech stories can follow a set structure. One way to organize the story is to summarize in the lead either the content of the entire speech or a major point from the speech that the reporter believes should be emphasized. Following either lead, the remainder of the structure could be the same.

The reporter summarizes a main point in the first graf or paraphrases something the speaker said (never using a *direct* quote). The second graf should be an indirect quote that follows up the point made in the first, and the third graf should be a direct quote on the same subject (general to specific, introduction to explanation).

Following this miniature inverted pyramid, the fourth paragraph can act as the transition paragraph by providing information about the speaker, where the speech was given, audience composition, and so on, while moving into or summarizing the next point. Naturally, these graf-by-graf suggestions don't have to be followed precisely.

The remaining points can be covered in the usual indirect-quote-and-direct-quote, general-to-specific manner. The story could then end with a graf or two of biographical data on the speaker. This information is usually last because it is less important than what the speaker said in the speech and is therefore easily cut.

Another way to set up a speech story would be to lead with the usual summary of the speech but then to discuss the possible effects of the speech. Then return to the speech itself.

Let's say the president of the college delivers an annual speech to the faculty about next year's budget. Revenues for the college will be severely reduced, forcing tuition and fees to be raised 50 percent. Enrollment will probably decline for the first time in the school's history. The real story here is not so much the president's speech, but what the speech *means*. The reporter should discuss this first. The lead could summarize the main points, and then the story could discuss who is likely to be excluded next year, what effect the cuts on financial aid programs will have, and what the reasons are behind the budget cut. The story could then return to the speech for the president's explanation of the decision to cut back in these areas.

These are not the only ways to write speech stories; they are, however, structures that you can use for speech or meeting stories until you feel confident enough to devise unique structures of your own.

Meeting Stories

Meeting stories are similar to speech stories, except that there are usually many speakers in them, not just one. The rules, however, are basically the same. The most important item may not be listed first on the agenda, but it should be covered first in the story. In fact, the most important item is often scheduled last on the agenda so that the other items can be covered before the group gets locked into an involved debate over the hot topic of the day.

Meeting stories often follow the basic A-and-B format. The lead summarizes the points covered in the meeting in order of importance. The story then covers each point—in the same order as mentioned in the lead—using summaries and supporting quotes from each important speaker. The story should cover the main points before returning to make a second sweep through the secondary points (Fig. 6–16).

The exception to this rule is when one of the issues discussed in the meeting is of overriding importance. The important issue can be discussed in the opening graf, the other points can be briefly summarized in a "swing" graf, and the story

---

Scicon fees were increased and a new bid on a Scicon cabin was accepted during Wednesday's meeting of the Tulare County Board of Education.

Citing increased costs, the board voted to raise all fees for attendance at Scicon.

Weekly fees per student for county schools that have cabins will go from $45 to $48, county schools without cabins go from $47.50 to $50.50, out of county schools will go from $60 to $65 and private schools will go from $65 to $70.

Delano, even though it is in Kern County, pays the same as Tulare County schools because it has been in the program for a long time.

Dean Hall, associate superintendent, indicated that even with the increases the fees are lower than for similar programs in other areas.

Vetter & Vetter Construction Co. of Dinuba was awarded the contract to rebuild the Dinuba cabin. The firm's bid of $18,475 was the lowest of three submitted. Carter Construction of Visalia submitted a bid of $20,457 and Bow-Thorn Construction of Visalia bid $22,360.

The bid had been previously awarded to Vetter & Vetter at $17,000, but because one of the other companies felt that it had been an improper bid, the county counsel said that the bids should be reopened.

Vetter & Vetter had originally based its bid on a 90-day time table instead of 60, which the other companies used. The present bid is for 90 days.

After insurance the total cost of the rebuilding to the county will be $6,728. The cabin burned last October.

Figure 6–16. Meeting stories can use the same structure as speech stories, as this story shows.

can then return to the important issue, covering it exhaustively. The remaining issues can be reported afterward. In some stories, the reporter can cover the major issue in its entirely before even mentioning minor issues. Again, it is up to the reporter to judge the material and decide what structure it calls for.

This prewriting phase, or reporting phase, may well be the toughest part of being a journalist. Writing the story seems fairly cut-and-dried next to the difficult decision-making process that is part of reporting. The question-asking, note-taking, note-organizing, fact-selection, and outlining that go on before the first keyboard strokes are really the tough part of the reporter's job. But it is the reporter's responsibility to the facts and to the reader that makes journalism a creative and exciting field.

Daily versus Weekly

Most newswriting textbooks and many journalism instructors teach only one kind of newswriting—the daily newspaper. Students are taught to write a story as if it were going to be published the next day. The story is structured as if the event had just happened, even if the story is for a weekly paper and the event happened six days before. This is simply unrealistic.

Student reporters who write for weekly or less frequently published newspapers must change their writing habits to fit the needs of their publications and readers. Weekly-newspaper reporters would do well to discard the it-just-happened-folks approach and go for more analysis, summary, and preview. They should turn to *Time, Newsweek,* and *Sports Illustrated* for examples to follow.

This advice negates, to a certain extent, what we just covered about news-story structure. It may mean doing away with the standard summary-lead paragraph in favor of a magazine-style approach.

The story in Figure 6–17 won a William Randolph Hearst award for newswriting. The story does not follow a "standard" structure, but it works.

Newspaper Style

"Newspaper style" refers to a set of standards concerning writing mechanics that all newspaper reporters follow. There are standards in capitalization, abbreviation, punctuation, numbers, and other areas. By asking reporters to follow these standards, the paper achieves a consistency that is important to its credibility.

If one reporter writes about a meeting at "eight PM," and another announces a concert at "7:30 p.m.," and another informs the reader about a baseball game at "10:00 A.M.," the reader may become confused about all the different ways in which times of day are written. Even if readers are not confused by the

Figure 6–17. This award-winning story from the Cal State Long Beach *Daily Forty-Niner* does not follow the standard, inverted-pyramid format. That format may in fact be on the way out as newspapers must meet the needs of new readers. (Courtesy of the *Daily Forty-Niner*)

Resignation puzzles CSULB top administrators

By Charles Bevier
Daily Forty-Niner

Administrators at Cal State Long Beach were puzzled by Larry Reisbig's choice of words in his resignation as head 49er football coach, but praised him as a good competitor.

After all, some said, Reisbig was hampered in his coaching efforts by lack of funds and an injury-plagued season.

Reisbig, 48, handed his resignation to Athletic Director Corey Johnson at 11 a.m. Thursday. Johnson held a press conference in his office at 2 p.m. to announce the resignation. In Reisbig's letter he said, "We have been trying to fight with our hands tied behind our backs in many ways."

Reisbig refused to elaborate on the subject at the press conference.

President Curtis McCray said he did not know why Reisbig had made the remark regarding "tied hands."

"We've been rebuilding slowly . . . and I think in another three years we could have turned it around," McCray said. "Reisbig is a good man with high moral standards, with a great enthusiasm for the sport."

Reisbig took the helm of the football team three years ago, after being head coach at Pasadena City College for three years. This year the CSULB football team, plagued by weekly injuries to key players, has won three games out of 10. Reisbig has had 10 wins and 23 losses overall at CSULB.

Keith Polakoff, NCAA faculty representative for CSULB, said the football program has been hemorrhaging from lack of funds, which in turn has influenced the number and quality of potential recruits who consider CSULB.

"When Larry agreed to take the job, he knew what he was getting into but he had decided to make the best of what he had to deal with," said Polakoff, assistant vice president for Academic Affairs and dean of Graduate Studies.

"He was a great coach and an excellent role model, an excellent representative for the university," Polakoff said.

"But we clearly function at a competitive disadvantage from lack of scholarships for recruits and the fact that we don't have a home football stadium," he said.

"In terms of recruiting, it's going to make it hard for any head football coach to remedy those disadvantages. The lack of a stadium is a problem, but I think the biggest problem is our inability to fund scholarships."

To become competitive in National Collegiate Athletic Association Division I football, CSULB will have to increase the number of scholarships it bestows on its players, Polakoff said. The university currently offers approximately 75 scholarships, which is "20 to 25 less than what Fresno State or San Jose State offer," Polakoff said.

"The problem is the state does not fund athletic scholarships," he said. Scholarship funds have to come from outside sources or revenue raised in the programs itself, like ticket sales or other athletic programs.

---

20 Rules for good writing

1. Prefer the plain word to the fancy.
2. Prefer the familiar word to the unfamiliar.
3. Prefer the Saxon word to the Romance.
4. Prefer nouns and verbs to adjectives and adverbs.
5. Prefer picture nouns and action verbs.
6. Never use a long word when a short word will do as well.
7. Master the simple declarative sentence.
8. Prefer the simple sentence to the complicated.
9. Vary your sentence length.
10. Put the words you want to emphasize at the beginning or end of your sentence.
11. Use the active voice.
12. Put statements in a positive form.
13. Use short paragraphs.
14. Cut needless words, sentences, and paragraphs.
15. Use plain conversational language. Write like you talk.
16. Avoid imitation. Write in your own natural style.
17. Write clearly.
18. Avoid gobbledygook and jargon.
19. Write to be understood, not to impress.
20. Revise and rewrite. Improvement is always possible.

From the Writer's Digest School, a division of Writer's Digest magazine. Reprinted with permission.

variations, they may wonder about the reliability of the staff if the reporters can't agree on how to write what time something will happen.

So newspaper staffs agree on a style for certain items that are written about day after day. Large newspapers like the *New York Times*, the *Los Angeles Times*, and the *Washington Post* have developed their own style manuals. Most newspapers rely on the *Associated Press Stylebook* as their standard.

An occasional student complaint about newspaper style—which is admittedly picky at times, but absolutely necessary—is that it, along with all the other rules of journalism, hampers creativity. What complaining students are really saying is that they don't think style is important enough to spend their time worrying about. These are sometimes the same students who believe that spelling and correct comma and colon usage are unimportant. They usually don't last very long as writers.

Most writers are artisans. Just as a carver works with wood, a writer works with words. A good woodworker would never use the wrong tool for a job; the good writer would never use a comma instead of a semicolon or "imply" instead of "infer." Newspaper style is a set of tools for the craft of journalism. A student who expects to be a journalist accepts the rules of newspaper style, grammar, and spelling.

As mentioned, the basic rules of style can be divided into five categories: abbreviation, capitalization, numerals, punctuation, and miscellaneous. The stylebook in the appendix is a very simplified one that can be referred to quickly and easily. It does not, however, cover every rule. Each newspaper staff will have to add style rules as it tailors its style to its own campus and community. A blank page has been left for that purpose.

If each staff member can't get hold of a professional stylebook, at least a copy or two should be part of the newsroom library. The AP stylebook is probably the best because it also includes a good libel manual.

Look over this book's stylebook today. Now is the time to begin learning the fundamentals of style.

Copy Preparation

To make the handling of stories easier for the copy desk and the typesetter, reporters should prepare copy in a standard way. Minor differences may exist between newspapers, but the basic concepts are universal.

First, all copy should be typed. In many newsrooms, the reporter types directly into a computer and sometimes the story gets into the paper with little editing. Speed and accuracy in typing are definite assets. Stories should be double-spaced on white $8^{1}/_{2} \times 11$ bond paper. Flimsy erasable bond should not be used because type smudges easily on it. Corrections are made by printing in the space *above* the error. Type-overs and crossing out errors are taboo. Copy-editing marks (Fig. 6–18) should be used when adding to or deleting from a story.

Corrections that have to be read sideways up the margin of the page will slow down typesetting and should be avoided. Long corrections or additions should be typed on a separate sheet of paper and marked for insert or physically cut and pasted onto the page. Some typesetters don't like a page longer than 11 inches, and some don't mind. Check with yours to find out which is preferred.

Another way to help your editor and your typesetter is to avoid hyphenating words at the end of a line. If a complete word doesn't fit, start the next line with it. That way no one will have to guess whether the word really needs to be hyphenated or whether it is just split between lines.

Each page of a story should include certain information. In the upper left corner is the *slug*—the reporter's name, a few words describing the story (these words are also referred to as the *slug* or *slugline*), the date, and such other information as the section of the paper the story is intended for. This information should appear on *every* page of the story so that if stories are mixed together accidentally during typesetting, the pages can be put back in place easily.

Page 1 does not need a page number in the slug, but all other pages do. Some newspapers use *p.2, p.3, p.4* for ensuing pages, and others use *add 1, add 2, add 3*. ("Add 1" refers to the first *additional* page after page 1, and "add 2" is the second additional page.) Either method is fine, but every staff member should use the same method to avoid confusion.

If the story is longer than one page, paragraphs should not be split between pages. When a story does continue to another page, the reporter should type or write the word "more" at the right-hand bottom corner of the page to make sure that the editor and typesetter know that the story continues.

When the end of the story is reached, an end symbol—usually *30, #,* or just *"end"*—should be placed in the center of the page two lines beneath the last line of the story (not at the bottom of the page).

Extra white space should be left at the top of page 1 for typesetting instructions and headline-writing information. Usually one third to one half of the page should be left open for these instructions. Ensuing pages may begin a few lines beneath the slug.

One-inch margins should be left on each side and at the bottom of the page. Paragraph indentations should be five spaces. Because some copy-counting methods (which estimate how long the story will be set in type) rely on the number of characters or letters that fit into an inch of type, many newspaper staffs have paper with premarked margins to help the reporter and editor estimate story length (Fig. 6–19). If a small staff has only a few PCs to input stories, this approach may still be helpful.

These mechanical details of newspaper style and copy preparation are necessary to a good news story, but they certainly are not sufficient. Reporting the news in clear and concise writing is at the heart of newspapering. Learn first to be a good newswriter and the other types of writing will come easily and naturally.

COPYREADER'S SYMBOLS

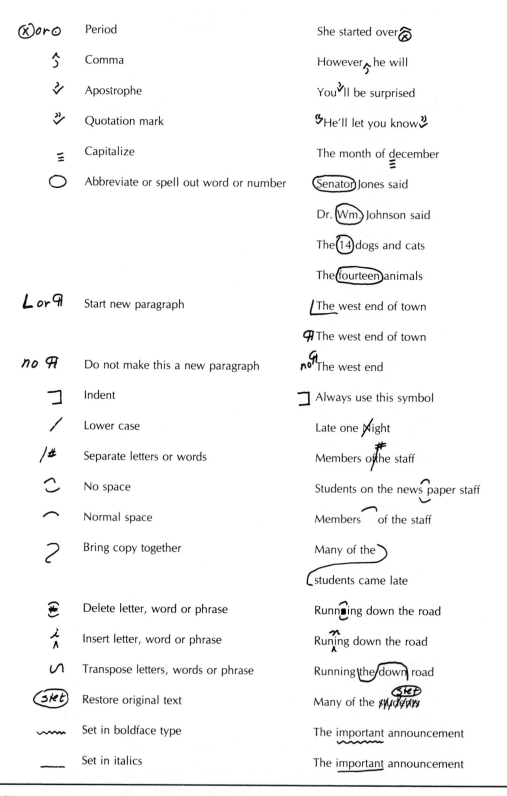

Symbol	Meaning	Example
ⓧ or ⊙	Period	She started over ⓧ
⌃	Comma	However ⌃ he will
⌄	Apostrophe	You⌄ll be surprised
⌄⌄	Quotation mark	⌄⌄He'll let you know⌄⌄
☰	Capitalize	The month of december
◯	Abbreviate or spell out word or number	⟨Senator⟩ Jones said
		Dr. ⟨Wm.⟩ Johnson said
		The ⟨14⟩ dogs and cats
		The ⟨fourteen⟩ animals
L or ⁋	Start new paragraph	⌐The west end of town
		⁋ The west end of town
no ⁋	Do not make this a new paragraph	no ⁋ The west end
⌐	Indent	⌐ Always use this symbol
/	Lower case	Late one Night
/#	Separate letters or words	Members of the staff
⌣	No space	Students on the news paper staff
⌢	Normal space	Members of the staff
∫	Bring copy together	Many of the students came late
⊘	Delete letter, word or phrase	Running down the road
⅄	Insert letter, word or phrase	Runing down the road
∿	Transpose letters, words or phrase	Running the down road
⟨stet⟩	Restore original text	Many of the students
∿∿∿	Set in boldface type	The important announcement
___	Set in italics	The important announcement

Figure 6–18. Copy-editing symbols are a shorthand to help the typesetter understand the corrections made by the reporter. Even in the computerized newsroom, marking "hard copies" with these symbols is still a frequent occurrence.

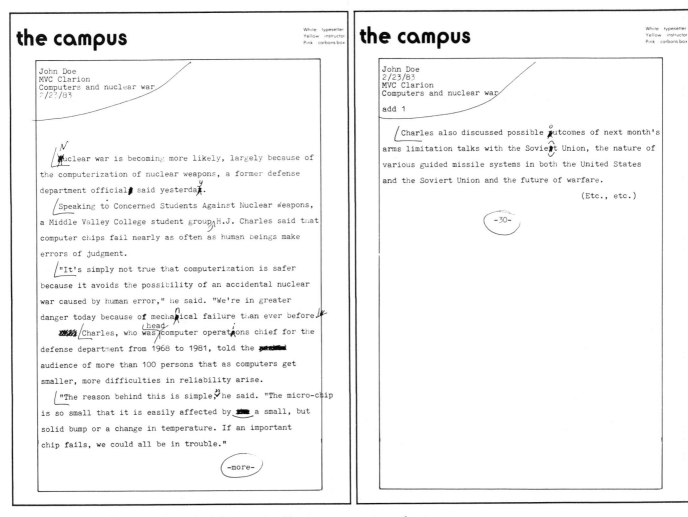

Figure 6–19. The information in the upper left corner should appear on every page of a story. Page 1 needs no number, but each additional page should be marked. Typing on the first page should begin low so that the editor has room for typesetting information. Ensuing pages may begin just below the slug.

Suggested Projects

1. Clip several stories from local papers that follow the structures discussed in the chapter. Did the writers select the proper structures for their stories?

2. Select two or three long professional news stories that you think are well done. List the aspects of the stories that the reporter handled well (lead, quotes, use of quotes, structure, clarity of writing, use of examples). Can your staff devise a list of attributes that all good news stories have in common? Post the list above every typewriter in the newsroom.

3. Attend a speech or a meeting that you know will be covered by a reporter from the local paper. Take notes, write a story, and compare yours with the local reporter's. Are your leads the same? Do you cover the same major points? How do your stories differ? Call the reporter and discuss your differences in perception of the event. Perhaps this could be a good class project. Perceptions of an event and ways of reporting it will probably vary widely. Which is the best story? The *right* story? How can you guarantee complete coverage, fairness, and accuracy to your readers?

Vocabulary

advance story
attribution
blind lead
block paragraph
direct quote
indirect quote
inverted pyramid
lead
objectivity
slug
slugline
30
transition

Exercises

1. Retype the following short news story in the correct format. Use the proper copy-editing symbols to correct minor typing errors.

The annual preview of Valley State University will be held on March 14 and 15 to give students the opportunity to receive a first-hand feeling for the university.

Joanna Northton, director of public relations for the university, said that students will visit residence halls, cafeterias, and classrooms. Students will also be able to meet with counselors, if they wish, she said.

"This is an excellent opportunity for students to see the quality education Valley State can give," Northton said.

Applications for the preview day, which will last from 9 a.m. to 4 p.m., are available in the counseling reception area of Holloway Hall.

2. Write lead paragraphs based on the jumbled facts below. Use correct journalism style.

A. In the Student Activities Office, on the north side of the gym, a camera will be set up. Photos for student I.D. cards will be taken. Next Monday and Tuesday. The time is from 8 until noon and 1 to 4.

B. From the campus police. Lt. Thomas O'Keefe is source. Canisters of mace are available from dept. office. Canisters are called "Paralyzer." Used to be given away free, now students who can justify need for one may purchase one for $2, their cost to dept.

Quote from O'Keefe: "At one time we furnished these canisters free of charge to faculty and students who had reason to believe they needed protection. These were furnished mostly to evening-division students and faculty." He said that recent price increases made it necessary to begin charging for the canisters.

C. It's time for that great annual school event, the fall drama production. The award-winning Middle Valley College drama department will present an old favorite beginning tonight at 8 and also tomorrow night at 8. The play, which was written by Thornton Wilder, won the playwright a Pulitzer Prize in 1942. It is a three-act comedy, *The Skin of Our Teeth*. Tickets are $3 for students with student body cards and $5 for non-student-body-card holders.

D. From Middle Valley College wrestling coach Adam Davids: The MVC wrestling team will wrestle against Woodlake Community College of Darbyville, Oregon, in a match next month. The match will begin at 8 p.m. on Nov. 9. Woodlake is the two-time national champion.

E. The city has begun a program of regular inspection of local taverns and restaurants with liquor licenses. According to the Fire Department's Chief Inspector, Stanley Williams, the inspection was prompted by a new package of building and safety codes that took effect the first of this month. The new codes were the result of a series of surprise inspections several months ago. A team of city building, fire, and safety inspectors found violations in 16 of 20 bars and restaurants near campus. The goal of the new inspection codes is to reduce fire hazard in businesses that sell liquor, according to Williams. The new codes allow inspectors to look at some areas that did not previously fall under the present safety codes. Inspectors can then demand that the violations be corrected within 60 days. So far, according to Williams, cooperation from businesses has been excellent. "We've had real good cooperation from the business people," he said.

F. Five members of the Sigma Chi fraternity chapter on campus—Edward Reynolds, Dave Greening, John Bird, L. T. Ogles, and Bob Walters—slashed the tires of 36 tour buses parked in a lot next to the 1992 World's Fair site here in town. The five were arrested by campus police, source for this information. They were arrested on May 5. Today, two months later to the day, the five were given two years probation by Judge J. T. Newberry of Criminal Court. They were fined $500 each and required to pay for the damages to the buses—a total of $3,765.49. All five are seniors at your school.

3. Put the following direct quotes in the correct style. Use "Smith said" as your speech tag for all quotes, and place the speech tag where indicated.

A. (*at end of sentence*) This program is the first of its kind in the nation.

B. (*in middle of sentence*) As far as I'm concerned, the administration hasn't made a reasonable offer yet.

C. (*in between first two sentences*) This could be one of the best wrestling matches of the decade. We have the best community college team in the nation coming in and we feel we're one of the better programs in the state. It'll be interesting to see how our state compares with the rest of the nation.

D. (*wherever you want*) It doesn't matter what they do, I refuse to be cowed by their actions. I think it's despicable. They don't know what they want. They are just muddling through this. It's hard to believe.

4. Write a story based on the speech by James K. Batten in Chapter 8.

7 features and reviews

Entertaining readers while providing them with news and information is an important function of a newspaper. Newspapers entertain readers in many ways: comic pages, crossword puzzles, horoscopes, and other noninformational regular columns and feature stories. Feature stories can be funny, sad, dramatic, touching, or terrifying. But they all must entertain the reader.

Most school papers do not have the space to provide comics, crossword puzzles, or the other feature material that is offered by feature *syndicate* services. Besides, staff-produced work always should be preferred over syndicated material. Any paper, no matter what the size or frequency of publication, can and should provide readers with ample entertainment through feature stories (Fig. 7–1).

Feature Coverage

Some newspaper staffs believe that feature ideas are more difficult to think up than news stories. After all, news stories are tied to easily found and definable events such as meetings and accidents. But feature stories are easy to find, too, if reporters are observant.

Every reporter should look constantly for story ideas and share those ideas with the rest of the staff. Some staffs have regular brainstorming sessions prior to official planning meetings to share story ideas.

As mentioned in Chapter 4, beats are good places to uncover feature stories. Where else do you look besides the beats? One place, according to Ruthe Stein, when a reporter for the *San Francisco Chronicle,* is personal experience. What would *you* like to know? If you are interested in something, other readers probably will be too.

What about that car you always see in the parking lot with the "Belly Dancing School" sign on the door? And those two people you passed in the hall who were discussing a friend who dances on *Soul Train?* Or those paintings on the wall in the PE instructor's office (they were signed by the instructor)? And how about that ecology instructor who lobbied long and hard with the city government to set up a recycling center—and won? Features are everywhere—if you pay attention. The trouble is not in finding them, but in finding time to write them.

A few points about features and feature coverage need to be discussed before we look at how to write a feature story. The first is the ratio between features on students and features on instructors. It is very easy to do a regular "teacher feature," because instructors always seem to be doing something interesting with their spare time. The English professor had some poems published, the PE instructor runs in marathons on the weekends, and the engineering instructor is designing a recumbent bicycle. These feature stories are good, but they are obvious and easy. Remember that students are still the largest portion of your audience, and they would like to read about other students, not just about faculty.

■ Rappers too much for Alexander City   B-3   ■ Avant-garde printmaking studio opening   B-5

Village Life

November 16, 1989   *The Auburn Plainsman*   Section B

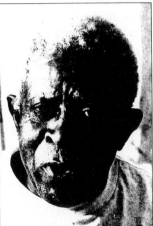

Jeff Snyder/staff

Innocence found in Mose T's world

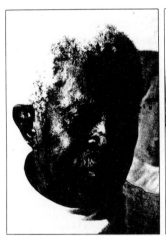

Jeff Snyder/staff

Mose T's collages are often biblical. He makes use of glitter, glue and matchsticks to accentuate this theme.

Michael Gordon
Assistant Village Life Editor

The primitive folk artist from Montgomery, Mose Tolliver, has the unique ability to perceive everyday items and topics from the small, sheltered world of a child.

Tolliver or "Mose T" is 70 years old, crippled and has a certain naivete that keeps him sheltered within his own world.

"I love to paint. I just get these ideas in my head, a bird, a cat, a rat, people, it doesn't matter. I just paint what I feel," he said.

Tolliver has been painting for 32 years. "I started decorating houses and then one day I just decided that I wanted to paint pictures...so I did," he said.

Most of his paintings are child-like in appearance. On a particular painting of a dancing girl, "a man came in here (his home) and asked me 'Why did you paint that woman with four legs?' I said those are just two legs and the sides of her dress," Tolliver said.

"A lot of people come in here (his home) and try to figure out my work, but it is just the way I paint. I don't think there is anything to figure out," he said.

Though he is black, Tolliver's paintings do not reflect a world solely

indigenous to a black man. His primitive paintings reflect a pure vision of everyone's world.

"I guess that is what so many people like about me," he said.

Tolliver lives in a small four room duplex, with varied numbers of his 12 children. "They come around and help for a while and then some of them go live their own life," he said.

His works received a modicum of notoriety, but it was not until 1986, when his works were exhibited by Nancy Reagan at the Cocoran Gallery in Washington, D.C., that he began to take off in the art world.

"I went to Washington and met Mrs. Reagan; now, some people say that she is mean, but she was very nice to me," Tolliver said.

"I was treated to a dinner at the White House with all these people, there must have been a million of them. After the dinner I went back to the dining room, and they were putting all the food into a big bag," Tolliver said.

The men who were clearing the table told Tolliver that they were going to put the food in the garbage. "Heck, give me some of that...I have got 12 kids," he said.

See **Mose**, B-8

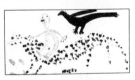

file

The primitive quality of his paintings is shown in "Man on Horse" (top) and "Self Portrait."

Supporting UPC events helps get better shows

OK Auburn, it's doing it. The UPC is bringing two excellent college bands, The Hoodoo Gurus and The Connells, but are we going to respond?

Well I should hope so. Students at the UPC bust their proverbial butts trying to please everyone with entertainment, and sometimes we just don't respond.

People on this campus have been complaining about major entertainment for quite some time. Yet, if they understood the logistics of getting a decent band they might appreciate the UPC more.

According to the UPC's coordinator

Shayne Bowman

Village Life Editor

Will Nance, the UPC has a total budget of $256,000 per year (all four quarters). Major entertainment is given $30,000 of that budget.

That's not a heck of a lot of money to work with considering the price of artists these days.

Nance said, "Entertainers' prices are unbelievable. Rod Stewart and Whitney Houston were about $110,000 and big comedians like Bill Cosby are $150,000. We're not trying to make any money by charging for acts. We're just trying to break even."

At this point, I don't think I'd want Will's job. How in the heck do you satisfy 20,000 demanding students with only $30,000?

The UPC tries to circumvent the money problem by charging a ticket price but then students start whining. I can hear them saying, "Ooooh didn't we already give you some money?"

On its latest adventure with the Hoodoos, the UPC spent $25,000. Whereas a fraternity could bring the same concert for $14,000, the UPC has added costs germane to the University. About $12,000 of this concert will go to production costs, security, catering and the list goes on.

Because of these added costs, the UPC has to raise the ticket price. Instead of $3 it's $5.

But if all this wasn't enough for Will and the gang, they have to second guess the most finicky consumer of them all, the Auburn student.

I ask you to support the UPC by

going to the Hoodoos show. Besides listening to some of the best college music around, it wouldn't hurt to put some security in the minds of people who bust their butts for you every week, the UPC.

Tempting Faith

To all those who didn't understand how a non-Christian could write about Christianity I say this: The majority of music critics were never musicians. If you're not a journalist, should you be allowed to critique *The Plainsman*? Of course, you have an opinion. .

Figure 7–1. This feature front has a main story and a staff column underneath. The painter's signature—MoseT—is in color, as is the line beneath the story. The two teasers above the section flag give the page, in a sense, four stories. (Courtesy of the *Auburn Plainsman*)

So good feature coverage means including a feature story about a student at least as often as one about an instructor. Don't get caught in the "star syndrome," however. The star quarterback, the star student, and the star lead in the next drama production are the easy stories; but they've been done so much that unless these persons are truly extraordinary, the story will read like the one last year and the year before that. How about the quiet fellow in the back of your history class? Did you know that he's the top player in the Computer Chess Club? Or the girl who always speaks out in your psychology class (she's a youth leader in the little known local Ku Klux Klan chapter)? *These* are the people and the stories that are unique.

Just because these students' involvements are off-campus does not make them off-limits. A good newspaper does not limit itself to covering only on-campus happenings, just as the local city paper doesn't cover only city events, ignoring county, state, national, and international news. On-campus news and features should be considered most important, but complete coverage includes anything of interest to the reader, regardless of the geographic location of the event.

A good features section includes regular information that will help readers find local entertainment. A calendar of events can tell readers what entertainment—movies, plays, dances, concerts, lectures—is happening on campus and off (Fig. 7–2). Ask to be put on the mailing lists of local convention centers, playhouses, theaters, and galleries. They send out press releases regularly to local

Figure 7–2. This calendar section lets students know what's happening on campus and off. (Courtesy of *The Tech Talk*)

THU

CONCERT: The Louisiana Tech Concert Association and the Louisiana Music Teacher's Association present pianist Nicolas Constantinidis in recital at 8 p.m. in Howard Auditorium, Center for the Performing Arts.

INTERNATIONAL: The International Wives Group will meet from 10 a.m. to noon every Thursday at the Presbyterian Westminster Center. For more information contact Sondra Clark at 255-0633.

CO-ED VOLLEYBALL: Co-ed Volleyball will be played at 5 p.m. at the Catholic Student Center.

PRAYER: Midday prayer is held at 12:30 p.m. on Thursdays at the Catholic Student Center.

FRI

DEBT MANAGEMENT: A debt management counseling session will be held from 11 a.m. to noon in Wyly Tower Auditorium, Room 244. Information on how to keep student loan obligation "under control" will be presented. For more information call 257-2641.

COWBOYS CHEERLEADERS: The Dallas Cowboys Cheerleaders will perform from 8-10 p.m. in Thomas Assembly Center. Admission is $1 for students and $5 for the general public.

MONSTER CONCERT: The Monster Concert will begin at 8:30 p.m. in Howard Auditorium, Center for the Performing Arts. This event is free to Tech students. For more information call 257-2930.

SAT

FALLFEST: Fallfest, a college day program, is scheduled to begin at 10 a.m. High school students will remain on campus for various programs until Tech's football game.

HALLOWEEN BALL: GO C.A.R.E., an AIDS-dedicated organization, will pre-

Trumps by Curt Brandao

sent "The Halloween Masquerade Ball" beginning at 9:30 p.m. at the Knights of Pythias Hall, 125 1/2 St. John St. in Monroe. Tickets are $7.50 in advance and $10 at the door. For more information contact David Sanborn at (318) 251-0692 or GO C.A.R.E. at (318) 325-1092.

SUN

HAUNTED TRAIL: Come visit the Haunted Trail from 7 p.m. to midnight through Halloween night at Hideaway Park.

KLPI: "The Police" will be the featured group on Dean's 10 o'clock Rock show on KLPI 89.1 FM.

UB MOVIE: "Field of Dreams" is the Union Board Sunday night movie at 7:30 p.m. in the Student Center.

MON

NEEDY DRIVE: The Student Government Association will sponsor a Needy Drive for people from now until Nov. 1 in the Student Center.

SEMINAR: Tech's Counseling Center presents part one of "Where There's a Will, There's an 'A'," at noon in Keeny Hall, Room 325. Part two will be at 4 p.m. the same day, and part three will be Tuesday at noon.

PHYSICS: The Society of Physics Students will meet at 6:30 p.m. in the Student Center to have pictures taken for the Lagniappe. Members will go to the Planetarium after pictures are taken.

MEETING: Adult Children of Alcoholics meetings are at 7 p.m. Mondays at the Catholic Student Center

library.

PHOTO EXHIBIT: The Art Gallery in Prescott Memorial Library, fifth floor Wyly Tower, will exhibit works by photographer and fiber artist Olga Perez from 9 a.m. to 4 p.m. Monday through Friday and 2-5 p.m. Sunday until Tuesday.

TUE

HALLOWEEN CARNIVAL: The Panhellenic Council will sponsor a Halloween Carnival free for the children and grandchildren of Tech's staff and faculty from 4-6 p.m. at the sorority lodges on Hestia Lane.

LECTURE SERIES: Tech's Student Government Association will sponsor a lecture series by Amnesty International at 2 p.m. in the main floor of the Student center. A seminar will be held afterward at 4:30 p.m. in the Student Center, Room 222.

TRICK OR TREATING: Adams Residence Hall will allow trick or treating at the front desk Tuesday night.

HAUNTED HOUSE: The department of Residential Life-Housing and the

Residence Hall Association will present Nightmare on Tech Drive, a haunted house, in the basement of Mitchell Residence Hall. The haunted house will start at 7 p.m. Admission is 50 cents.

AFRICAN ART: A collection of African

art will be shown from 1-5 p.m. Tuesday through Friday and 2-5 p.m. Saturday and Sunday until Nov. 19. The show will be held at Meadows Museum in Shreveport.

BIBLE STUDY: The Presbyterian Westminster Center will hold a Bible study every Tuesday at 6 p.m. For more information call Sondra Clark at 255-0633.

LUNCHEON: The Wesley Foundation will hold a luncheon and program from 11 a.m. to 1 p.m. every Tuesday.

SCULPTURES: The Stoner Arts Center in Shreveport will hold an exhibit of sculptures by Francois Degueurce and new paper casts by Michael Tichansky Tuesday through Sunday 1-5 p.m. until Nov. 11. For more information call (318) 222-1780

WED

CANTERBURY: The Canterbury Association meets each Wednesday at 6 p.m. in the Episcopal Church of the Redeemer located at 504 Tech Drive.

TECHSTERS VOLLEYBALL: The Lady Techsters Volleyball team will have matches at 3 p.m. and 7 p.m. against Centenary and Prairie View A&M.

MASS AND SOCIAL: There will be a Mass and social at 9 p.m. Wednesdays at the Catholic Student Center.

EXHIBIT: "American Printmaking: Selections from the La Grange National," an exhibit featuring 40 prints from the permanent collection of the Chattahoochee Valley Art Association will be on display from 9 a.m. to 4 p.m. Monday through Friday.

professional papers but often neglect school papers. Get information from off-campus sources, add on-campus events, and your listings will come together easily.

The review column helps the reader decide what is good and not so good in campus and local entertainment (Fig. 7–3). If local theaters cooperate by giving the features editor a schedule of movies to be shown soon the editor can plan a review to coincide closely with the opening date of the film or concert. Most film companies, such as 20th-Century Fox or Warner Bros., will send publicity photos and press releases about their films upon request. These can be used by the reviewer for background information. A publicity photo to run with a review can enhance coverage. Remember that a review should be available *before* an event; covering a movie after it has left town or a rock concert after it is over is rarely useful to the reader.

Another good idea for feature coverage is to include a regular self-help column written by a staff member or by guest columnists from on or off campus.

Figure 7–3. A review should help the reader understand or appreciate an event, not discuss what the reader missed because the event is over. (From *The Daily Texan,* University of Texas)

Many school papers have columns on nutrition for people who cook for themselves, the best place to buy clothes and food, dieting tips, students' legal rights, means of avoiding sunburning during spring break, tactics for buying a used car, study methods for final exams, bicycle tune-ups, and other such information of interest to students. These columns can provide a tremendous service for readers.

Figure 7–4. Sometimes feature fronts can be single-topic pages, with either a serious or more fun-filled focus. (Courtesy of the *Optimist*)

Many feature sections include a regular rotating column by the editor or a staff member (see Fig. 7–1). Newspapers run these "light" columns on the opinion or op-ed page or in the features section. If the staff has a resident comic, a column could be a popular feature. Make sure the writer is funny, though—there is nothing worse than something that is supposed to be funny and isn't. The column could also be a serial soap opera or romance/adventure story based on fictionalized local events and places. Remember that the feature section is supposed to *entertain*. Do that in whatever way you can, based on the talent of the staff.

Very few items should *not* be included in a feature section, but one exception is a gossip column. A column on what students, faculty, and alumni are doing or honors they have won, however, is permissible. In other words, a newspaper has room for legitimate information about people, but not for gossip, which can be unkind or malicious and which can lead to a lawsuit. Feature coverage can also include special sections with lengthy coverage on one person or issue.

October 26, 1989   The Tech Talk   1B

Figure 7–5. Tabloid-sized pages lend themselves more easily to the single-topic approach. (Courtesy of *The Tech Talk*)

Weekender

Masquerade ball to raise funds for AIDS

By AMY WYRICK
Staff Writer

Think Halloween, and three things should come to mind: masquerade costumes, non-stop music and an all-night party.

All these elements will be in abundance during the Halloween Masquerade Ball, a benefit to raise funds for AIDS victims, at Knights of Pythias Hall, 125 1/2 St. John St. at 9:30 p.m. Saturday in Monroe.

The Knights of Pythias Hall, a three-story building established early in the 20th century by a community organization called The Knights of Pythias, will cast a ghastly atmosphere for every witch and warlock throughout the evening.

Creeping and seeping through the walls of this eccentric hall will also be a wide variety of music. The first floor will house the bands God's Favorite Dog (a band that can only be defined as a cross between The Surfers and The Cramps), The Fields (a college, alternative band from Monroe) and The Lollipop Guild (the featured headline band that will play originals from its independent album due to be released in six weeks).

Doug Duffey, a rhythm-blues and jazz musician from New Orleans, will fire up a red hot taste of the jazz capital of the world on the second floor of the hall.

Rounding out the night on the third floor will be Spice, a group specializing in dance music. Tickets are $7.50 in advance and $10 at the door.

The masquerade ball will be presented by GO C.A.R.E., the Greater Ouachita Coalition Providing Aids Resources and Education, and will help fund services for AIDS victims such as free, confidential and anonymous HIV (Human Immunodeficiency Virus) testing for concerned individuals and free transportation to and from LSU Medical Center in New Orleans for HIV-positive individuals (those with the AIDS virus).

Jo Hale, project coordinator at GO C.A.R.E., said other services provided by the AIDS-dedicated organization are written materials by the Centers for Disease Control in Atlanta, physician referrals, and support groups for both HIV-positive individuals and their families.

"Many people are HIV-positive but are not showing the onset symptoms of the virus, which would mean they do have AIDS," Hale said.

For ticket information to the fundraiser call David Sanborn at 251-0692. Or contact The Orbit Exchange, The Crystal Heart (both in West Monroe), Cormier's Cajun Catering, The Pub & Eatery Gallery or Wesley Foundation of Northeast Louisiana University.

Contact GO C.A.R.E. for more information about AIDS.

Writing

Feature writing differs little from newswriting in that the story still has to be grounded in the basics. But features have more leeway in length, structure, and creativity. News stories are written to inform, to get the news to the reader as quickly and easily as possible. They accomplish this goal by using the inverted pyramid, a summary lead, short sentences, and a bare style.

Feature stories, though, from little brights to longer personality features, have a few attributes that are different. *Brights* are short stories that would be totally uninteresting were it not for a twist. For example,

> The U.S. Mail may go through "snow . . . rain . . . heat" and "gloom of night," but it does not always get through Lonsdale.
>
> Postal Carrier Billy Chesney told police yesterday he was returning to his delivery truck in the 900 block of College Street when he saw a man inside it. As Chesney approached the truck, the man fled with a bag of mail. The door to the truck had been pried open, police said.
>
> The bag contained mail for Knoxville College, Maynard School and several streets in the Lonsdale area, police said. No arrests were made.
>
> —*Knoxville News-Sentinel*

The angle of the bright, the little twist in the story that makes it interesting, is what the reporter must see before setting up the story. In this example, it's the irony between the statement on the U.S. Post Office building in Washington, D.C., and the stolen mailbag. Unlike news leads, most leads for brights hold back a fact or two so that the reader is drawn into the story. After the lead graf, the story is usually just a straightforward, chronological account: It more or less tells itself. Writing a bright isn't the tough part for reporters; recognizing the angle is what stumps them. But a reporter who is alert and creative can usually recognize the little incongruities of daily life.

By far the most common feature story is the "personality feature" or the *profile* (Fig. 7–6). People like to read about other people, their likes, dislikes, hobbies, interesting moments, and such. The success of *People* magazine and its clones is testimony to this fact.

Good personality features, like good news stories, begin with preparation. Preparation for a personality feature is much like preparation for a news story. Both must be thorough and complete. Questions such as "Now what is your title and how long have you been doing this?" should be answered through preliminary research.

The best way to prepare to interview someone is to (1) study the person's background from library or clip-file research and interviews with that person's superiors, (2) investigate what the person does (if the person builds ships in bottles, read about how it is done), (3) talk to the person's friends, relatives, and/or colleagues, (4) observe the person in action if possible, and (5) arrange to interview the person, perhaps even several times. By the time you reach step 5, coming up with questions—good questions—will be easy.

This method is rather like a spiral; you begin your research far away from the actual person—in documents, for instance—and slowly close in, getting more and more specific details as you get closer to your subject. With a student, you could begin with a faculty member the student works closely with—the basketball coach, an English professor. Then talk to family, friends, roommates. Observe the person in action. Go early to a game or a poetry reading, and follow the person through the advance preparation. Then finally interview the person after the event.

Mild-mannered Marchant peels to new personality

By Felicia Campbell
News editor

Jeff Marchant just doesn't seem the type for red sequins and roller skates.

Last fall, as the sometimes goalie of the COS water polo team, he usually remained aloof and apart from the locker room antics of the rest of the team.

Quiet and reserved. Conservative. Shy.

Yet there he was last Tuesday, clad in little more than a glorified G-string, bumping and grinding his way around a laughing, excited, eager bunch of women.

And he loved it.

Marchant is a male burlesque dancer. He performs two nights a week at one of the most popular night clubs in Fresno. And is having the time of his life while earning enough money to continue his education at COS.

But what turned a mild-mannered water polo player into a star of an incredibly popular, slightly risque striptease show?

It was his sister who first suggested he try out for the new show that was being planned at Birdie McTweet's Pawn Shop and Social Club, a Fresno night club.

Marchant's sister Julie was working at the club as a cocktail waitress when she heard about the show being planned. She suggested to her brother that he try out.

"My first reaction was 'No way,'" Marchant said. "I wasn't going to take my clothes off for anyone."

Julie, however, convinced him that he wouldn't have to take off all of his clothes (indeed, the dancers are never nude) and Marchant decided to try out.

"When Jeff first tried out, he didn't know any dancing," said Michael Seal, the show's producer and choreographer. "He really didn't know how to do much more than roll around on the floor."

But with the help of the show's two other choreographers, and more than 18 hours a week of rehearsals, Marchant is now doing intricate dance routines and production numbers.

Marchant said that the experience has given him a lot more confidence in almost all aspects of his life.

"I'll try anything once," Marchant said. "Doing the show has really opened me up."

It's not hard to tell that Marchant is a favorite with the audience at Birdie's; when he appears on the dance floor they scream, clap their hands and stomp their feet.

Marchant responds to their approval like a diabetic to cookies.

"The more they react," Marchant said, "the more I do."

As he runs from the stage after a performance, women reach out to touch him, not in a sexual way, but more of a tentative thing—almost as if to see if he's real.

Although he performs two nights a week—Tuesdays and Wednesdays—Marchant still carries a full academic load at COS.

His classes include such diverse subjects as political science, human sexuality, nutrition and weightlifting. Marchant said he hopes to continue his education and eventually earn a degree in physical education.

When he's not in school or doing a show, Marchant can sometimes be found at the Visalia Racquetball Club, where he works part-time.

Racquetball is one of his favorite hobbies, along with boxing. Part of the unusual decor in the house Marchant shares with fellow water poloist Dave Miller includes a punching bag that hangs in the living room.

"It's really good," Marchant said of the punching bag. "I can come in here and work off all of my aggressions."

The house also has an enormous backyard, a necessity since Marchant has an 80-pound black labrador and Miller owns a husky.

His busy life has taken its toll, however, and Marchant has had to give up one thing he really misses—sleep.

"With the show and everything else," Marchant said, "I just can't get as much sleep as I need.

"You want to know what I do with my spare time in the afternoons?" he said. "I come home and take a nap for about four hours."

Both the owners of Birdie's, Bruce Liotta and Stephen Anderson, and the producer Seal have high hopes for the act and for Marchant.

"He's great," Liotta said. "When he's out there he owns the stage."

There's a rumour that they may eventually take the act to Las Vegas. If the show does go on the road, Marchant would like to go with it.

"That could open up all kinds of possibilities," Marchant said. "I'd really like to travel around with the show.

"If a show business possibility came along, I'd go for it," he said.

But what about the shows that were cancelled in Visalia?

The negative reaction that came out in the newspaper, Marchant claimed, was probably from people that hadn't even seen the show.

Seal thinks the criticism of the show was unfair.

"I think it's a very classy show," Seal said. "We don't do anything lewd or obscene.

The dancers spend about 80 percent of the average six-minute routine dancing—with their clothes on. They only strip for the last minute or two of the performance.

"Once they take their clothes off," Seal said, "There's no reason for them to stay out there.

"It's a striptease," he said, "with an emphasis on the tease."

"The show drew a large crowd in Visalia," Marchant said. "The Holiday Inn had never done that kind of business on a Sunday night before.

"We'll be back," he said, with an air of confidence.

> "It's a striptease with an emphasis on the tease."
> —Seal

Figure 7–6. This story about a student at the college covers something he does off campus. What students—or faculty members—do off campus is sometimes much more interesting than what they do on campus. (From *The Campus,* College of the Sequoias)

Let's say you are to do a feature on the ecology instructor. The personnel office tells you he's taught at your school for 12 years and was department chairperson four years ago. By looking in the course catalog, you see that he received his BA and MA degrees from Ohio State University and his PhD from the University of North Carolina. By doing a little math, you guess that he got his job at your school right after finishing his doctoral studies. Later his department chairperson gives you other information about articles your teacher has written and speeches that he has given locally. The chairperson also mentions that his twin hobbies of astronomy and astrology are an odd coupling.

Now you skim a few books on those subjects in the library. A quick check through the *Reader's Guide to Periodical Literature* leads to articles on the two star-gazing hobbies that give you several great questions to ask.

You talk to students in his class and fellow instructors in his department. You even call his wife to try to find out what he's like when he's not behind the lectern. You sit in on one of his classes to get a feel for his teaching personality.

Finally, you set up an interview with him in his office on campus. He invites you to his house later that week for a peek through his new telescope. You find out that he ground and polished the telescope mirror himself.

So when you get to his office for the interview, you have a prepared list of questions. And they are good questions, not just the standard ones that any unprepared reporter could come up with. If you show an interest in, and a knowledge of, what the interviewee is involved with, he will probably be much more open with you and you will get better quotes.

Without your preparation, you could have opened the interview with, "Well, uh, just how long have you been a teacher?" Because you prepared, you can open with, "Today is the day that the moon moves into Aquarius. As a Pisces, how is this going to affect you?"

Which question do you think will lead to a good answer, a good interview, and a good story?

A story about a person should give the reader new insights into the person. A feature story about a professor's courses, years at school, degrees, and so forth is little more than a boring list. Your readers may already know these details. You want to show them what makes the person tick.

Telling details—what makes the person tick—can be gathered by observing your subject in action or at the interview. Listing specific details about a person can be fascinating if the details have been selected carefully. Merely writing that someone is 45 years old, five-four, 135 pounds, and likes cats is pretty boring. The details don't *mean* anything. But telling your reader that the college president has an unusually tall chair behind his desk and a soft couch that a visitor really sinks down into shows your reader something about the president, especially if you also find out from his wife that he's always been sensitive about his five-foot, four-inch height. Then the detail gives an insight into the president's personality.

Open-ended questions will also allow the interviewee to reveal telling details of his or her personality. Variations on the old who-would-you-like-to-be-stranded-with-on-a-desert-isle theme, if worked into the proper context, can work well. Ken Metzler, in his excellent text, *Creative Interviewing*, lists several good questions, such as: Who are your heroes? What's the sand in your oyster? What do you like to read for enjoyment? He also suggests observation techniques for the reporter during the interview. The "things" that surround a person at the office or at home can also be telling details.

The bottom line of these questions is that they are open-ended enough to allow the interviewee to answer in a wide variety of ways. The answers will no doubt tell you—and your readers—something new and interesting about the person. If asked at the wrong time or if the interviewee is not in the proper mood, they can sound awkward or corny. But these questions will often lead to interesting tangents not covered in your pre-interview preparation. Even though you are interviewing someone who has been written about frequently, if your story includes information that hasn't been printed before, it will be a good one.

Certain rules can be followed in organizing feature stories. Naturally, there are as many organizations for features as there are features. The story itself should dictate the structure. One structure, however, works in the majority of cases: the *Wall Street Journal formula*, perfected by that newspaper years ago.

The *Wall Street Journal* formula helps the reader understand someone better or a complex issue more easily by using a specific example in the lead (Fig. 7–7). The formula works best for stories about issues, but in modified versions it can work for almost any kind of feature.

The *Wall Street Journal* formula, as described by Brooks and others in *News Reporting and Writing*, is made up of four parts: (1) a "hook" that is an example or a narrative of an aspect of the big picture, (2) a transition that ties the hook to the main part of the story, (3) the main body of the story, and (4) an ending much like the opening or even a continuation of the opening that gives a final example of the issue.

If the story concerns the effects of reduced financial aid on low-income students, the opening might be:

> Cuts in federal aid to students may be devastating to lower-income students at Middle Valley College.

A *Wall Street Journal* formula narrative lead would hook the reader with:

> Jane Doe read the notice from the federal government one more time and slumped even deeper into the threadbare couch in her small studio apartment near campus.
>
> Tears appeared in her eyes as she explained the contents of the letter. Because of recent legislation, she would no longer be eligible for federal assistance to attend school.
>
> So now, with little more than one semester remaining in her two-year computer programming course, Doe will have to drop out of school and look for a job.

Then the story would turn from Jane Doe to the effects of reduced federal aid on all students. The end of the story would either return to Jane Doe or describe another individual just as affected by the cuts.

The formula works for news analysis or news features. If you plan to do a story about how your school's income is made up of state funds, two kinds of federal funds, local taxes, school bonds, tuition, fees, donations, and grants, the story may be very confusing. But if you boil all that down to the simplest, most specific terms (at least in the lead), the reader will be able to comprehend the story easily.

> If Middle Valley College could get through an entire year on $1, nearly 43 cents of that dollar would come from the state government.
>
> The remaining 57 cents would come from federal funding (17 cents), tuition (33 cents), grants and donations (3 cents), students fees (1 cent), and miscellaneous income (3 cents).
>
> But next year, according to college president Dr. Fenton T. Harper, state tax cuts are going to reduce the college's yearly allowance to 94 cents, or a budget 6 percent lower than this year.

Without going into complicated formulas and discussions of millions of dollars, the reader understands something about the college's budget.

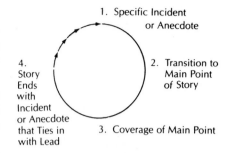

Figure 7–7. The *Wall Street Journal* formula opens with a specific incident, ties it into the "big picture," covers the picture, and ends with another specific incident—either one tied back into the opening or a new one.

Reviews

Good feature sections include regular reviews of movies, concerts, record albums, books, or whatever. Some papers have entire review (entertainment) sections as part of their regular coverage (Figs. 7–8 through 7–10). A good reviewer can help the reader not only by sharing opinions but also by preparing the reader for the event. Background information on the event and facts on how the event fits into a larger whole can make the experience much more enjoyable and rewarding.

Critic versus Reviewer

A critic differs from a reviewer in level of expertise. Almost anyone can be a reviewer, but it takes a specialist, a person knowledgeable in a given area, to be a critic.

Figure 7–8. Movies and records are not the only good subjects for reviews. (From *Spectator,* University of Wisconsin, Eau Claire)

Ballet brings touch of Glasnost to New Orleans

By Lisa Miller
Staff writer

To most, *glasnost* is purely a political term; one wouldn't normally think of it as a reference to ballet.

However, the New Orleans City Ballet has made it a major element in its repertoire. The Ballet will host the First Annual *Glasnost* Ballet Tour, featuring leading ballet stars from several Communist countries, for one performance only Nov. 5 at the Theatre of Performing Arts.

The Ballet revealed information about the performance at its season-opening press conference Monday.

Mickey Barthelemy, wife of New Orleans Mayor Sidney Barthelemy and a member of the Ballet's Board of Directors, made the announcement.

"Gold medal winners from Russia's Bolshoi Ballet will dance together for the first time with dancers from four other communist block countries," she said.

Dancers from Hungary, Czechoslovakia, Bulgaria, the People's Republic of China, the Soviet Union, Australia and the New Orleans Ballet will perform 10 selections from various ballets. They include pieces from *Sleeping Beauty, Le Corsaire, Santella, Romeo and Juliet* and *The Birds*.

Mrs. Barthelemy urged the city of New Orleans, especially the women, to support the performance.

"To all the wives in New Orleans, the New Orleans Saints don't have a game that night, so get your husbands to come along with you," she said.

Mayor Barthelemy was also on hand to lend his support to the New Orleans Ballet and the performance.

"It is really exciting for New Orleans to be a leader of *glasnost* ballet. It gives us an

"The language of the ballet is international and in the spirit of *glasnost* we are all dancing together for the first time. It is a great feeling," Kurova said.

"We are very happy to have the opportunity to represent our art in [the United States]," she said.

The performance will be a mixture of classical Russian ballet and contemporary interpretations of modern ballets, Kurova added.

> **"The language of the ballet is international and in the spirit of glasnost we are all dancing together for the first time. It is a great feeling... We are very happy to have the opportunity to represent our art in [the United States]."**
> **— Jana Kurova**

opportunity to show off our city. We can share our culture and our way of life with [the dancers]," he said.

Three of the dancers involved with the performance attended the press conference: Katalin Volf, a Hungarian native, Jana Kurova, from Czechoslovakia and Russian Vitaly Artiushkin.

Kurova expressed her delight with having the opportunity to dance in the United States.

Katalin and Vitaly echoed her sentiments, saying that they are glad that the first performance of the tour is in New Orleans.

"I would like to incorporate jazz into my choreography, and what better place to learn about jazz [than New Orleans]," Vitaly said.

Katalin shares Vitaly's love of jazz.

"I'm extremely happy to perform in New Orleans. I love jazz, and New Orleans

is such an exciting city for it," she said.

"It is a great celebration of friendship, with great food, just like home," Kurova said.

Introduced at the press conference was the Ballet's new general manager, Jon Teeuwissen, who comes to New Orleans from the critically acclaimed Dance Theatre in Harlem, where he was the company manager for three years.

"I had no idea I would consider leaving New York, but the artistic level of this company is great. I'm really looking forward to being here," he said.

The performance of two ballets, *Carmina Burana* and *Concerto*, Friday, Oct. 20 and Saturday, Oct. 21, will mark the opening of the Ballet's seventh season, Ruary O'Connell, president of the Ballet's Board of Directors, said.

She said that these performances will mark the first time the New Orleans Symphony Orchestra has performed with the city's ballet company.

Mayor Barthelemy took the opportunity at Monday's press conference to welcome Teeuwissen and comment on the future of the Ballet.

"I'd like to welcome Jon and say that with programs like [the *glasnost* ballet] and Jon's leadership, we are going to see the New Orleans City Ballet take off like a rocket," he said.

Production of 'Godot' makes wait pleasurable

By Cathy Baroco
Staff writer

Otherworldly, surrealistic — the atmosphere immediately sets the audience apart from the characters on the stage of Samuel Beckett's *Waiting for Godot*, allowing a perspective of distance necessary for the both serious and comic appreciation of the successful Loyola Theatre production playing Oct. 20-21 at 8 pm. in Marquette Theatre.

The audience is gently brought into both the setting and the outlook of the characters, Didi and Gogo. Both are portrayed as

Theater

female destitutes, waiting, and hoping, for another chance at life through a meeting with the seemingly ethereal Godot.

They spend their time talking, laughing, singing, crying, arguing, joking and screaming on a bare set [save for a few mounds of earth and a single tree] until diversions in the form of the lunatic Pozzo and her carrier, Lucky, pass through their little part of the universe.

Kathleen Eason, communications sophomore, plays the part of Didi, an older woman whose body has been torn by poverty, though her spirit remains clear and vital. Eason vividly expresses the mental maneuverings of her character.

Mary Clare Hartman, a UNO graduate who plays Gogo, physically portrays a woman who has been ravaged by time and humanity. Mentally, however, Hartman seems to be somewhat distant from the character she delineates.

Gogo's need for companionship and hope, though, are made obvious as she

runs back to the stronger Didi for support and acceptance.

Katherine French, drama/communications freshman who plays Pozzo, portrays her difficult character with a professionalism necessary to keep her character from becoming too obviously stereotypical.

Janet Ruli, drama/speech senior who plays Lucky, creates one of the most believable characters in the performance as the domineering Pozzo's carrier. Ruli becomes almost invisible onstage when her character is in the background, yet she astounds the audience with her acting ability when Lucky becomes a principal player in the women's afternoon.

Maggie Hennehan, playing the little girl, is difficult to hear at times, but offers some of the most mentally provocative lines in the play.

The all-female cast offers a slightly different perception of humanity than an all-male cast, but the women on the stage at Marquette work together to develop a scenario that involves the audience and encourages them to think about their own individual outlook.

The cast moves quickly at times, somewhat out of character for a group of older women, but falls back into the paces of humanity, fighting solitude, poverty and pain with companionship, laughter and hope.

The delicately balanced production is a well-orchestrated mix of intellectualism and comedy — a play that taken lightly proves much too dry, but taken too seriously proves to be mind-boggling and not much fun.

If, however, one enters the theater with an open mind, the production is pleasantly surprising.

Photo by Troy Blappert

Waiting is the hardest part — Lucky (Janet Ruli) chews anxiously on her whip as Pozzo (Katherine French) looks on in Loyola Theatre's *Waiting for Godot*.

Figure 7–9. Reviews of campus productions can help prepare attendees for a better understanding or appreciation of the event. (Courtesy of *Maroon*)

A review is not a discussion of whether the work was done well or poorly. It outlines the play performance for the playgoer or book plot for the reader and points out what the reviewer's reactions were. The reviewer makes no attempt to judge the worth of the performance or material.

A critical review, on the other hand, does judge the performance or material and compare it to other performances of the same play or treatments of the same plot, for instance. The reviewer merely comments on the performance, its merits, and its shortcomings based on personal opinion, not on a set of standards gleaned from years of study and hundreds of hours of experience.

ARTS

'Windwalker'—hackneyed Indian tale

By Frank Smoot

It is winter. Man is on death bed. Tells grandsons about his wife and their twin sons. The first-born was kidnapped by the enemy who killed his wife. Tells them how he left the second son to look for the first. How he never found him and has come back to die.

Man is buried, but the Wise One Above brings him back to see his sons reunited and the enemy defeated by the kidnapped son, who escaped from the enemy's gang (the enemy's life is spared, of course). Man can safely die now and walk the skies with his wife, instead of walking the earth with his enemy.

If you haven't seen stereotyped Indians plugged into a stock plot like this, go to "The Windwalker."

Not that the film doesn't have its good points. The strikingly beautiful Serene Hedin makes an enchanting screen debut as a shy, sexually-repressed Cheyenne girl who falls in love with young Windwalker. (The characterization is, by the way, realistic in the setting — Utah in the mid-1880s.) Director of photography Reed Smoot (no relation) strings together several hundred lovely views of Wasatch National Forest, and if you've never been there, the travelogue might be worth your ticket price. Doug Seus' bear portrayal, which shows a total lack of understanding of the behavior of a hibernating bear, is blessed at last with tremendous enthusiasm.

As a portrait of Cheyenne-Crow culture, the film lacks depth of detail — we only get impressions. Worse, these impressions are sometimes wrong.

The Crows are drawn in the movie as a gang of painted boogie men and sex-crazed stupid hoodlums. ("Nice little woman, that one. I will take her to my lodge." I expected the other Crows to wink and titter.)

Enemies of the Cheyennes, the Crows were, in reality, rarely violent toward them, considering it a higher honor to touch a Cheyenne with a weapon than to beat or kill him. They were also known for

giving children a free, easy life; in the film they are quite cruel to Windwalker's kidnapped child.

Furthermore, they characteristically made their raids on foot — so they could return on horses of their enemies. In "The Windwalker" they start on horseback. Small points, but still. . .

The Cheyennes receive fairer and more accurate treatment.

However, in real life, they almost never carried stone war clubs, here every cinematic Cheyenne has one. Also, the men never sat idle while their wives were birthing — they tended the fire and helped cook for the birthing attendants.

In the film's defense, the picture of young Cheyenne love is pretty accurate, and it's sort of gushy if you like that stuff. Overall, though, the film, under Keith Merrill's pedestrian direction, drags from one bit of padding to another, and Ray Goldrup's screenplay is vapid and stereotyped ("Let us circle until the sun sleeps.")

I could accept all those faults, but what really got me was the plot. It lacks just enough — or has just too much "legend" flavor to make it impossible to believe the supernatural element. The film comes off as a "trick."

Trevor Howard (in the title role), certainly a seasoned actor, is not an American Indian and seems to lack a feel for their culture and legendry. His half-Tecumesh (to mix tribes), half-Danny Thomas portrayal merely emphasizes this "trick." He wakes up on his burial scaffold and asks the Wise One Above, "Why are my feet so cold?" The scaffold collapses and he rolls into a pack of starving wolves, which he keeps at bay with a small stick. They force him to the edge of a cliff, and then off it.

He wakes up in a cave with a fully-grown belligerent brown bear. This plucky old guy beats the bear to death in seconds. If this isn't enough, he neatly skins it, tans the hide without the help of a

sharp instrument and heads to the second son's camp. Come on, the Wise One can only do so much.

"The Windwalker" is mainly in the Cheyenne and Crow tongues, which, while surely refreshing after the long run of "Yes, Kimosabe" Westerns we've suffered through, presents its own problems. Windwalker's (Howard's) internal dialogue is English, which is unrealistic (get this: a Cheyenne from the wilds of Utah, already old in 1850, who only speaks Cheyenne, thinks in English).

Furthermore, since the film is

geared toward young audiences, a lot of kids in the theater were too young to read; their mothers had to read the subtitles for them, which created a peachy echo, but didn't add to the film's impact.

If you're short of vacation money, have to entertain a 7 year old, want to see a rather touching treatment of young Cheyenne love, or like impressive horse stunts (a few), see "The Windwalker." If you want a believable plot, fresh dialogue and generally interesting characterizations, this is one to skip.

Figure 7–10. A review does not have to be filled with judgments to be good. The object is to prepare readers to enjoy the entertainment event by giving them a better understanding of what they will see and hear. (From *Spectator*, University of Wisconsin, Eau Claire)

Most reviews in a campus newspaper will not be *critical* reviews—"most" because a staff member may be an expert in the area reviewed. Because few students have the background to provide worthwhile criticism of artistic performances, criticism should be left to the experts.

Reviewing college plays, for instance, can be a sensitive issue for newspaper staffs. The students in the drama department often will not take negative comments very well, especially from other students. If the reviewer is hard on the student performances, the drama students may rightfully wonder about the reviewer's credentials.

So reviewers, unless they have a professional-level background, should compare school plays with past school productions, not with professional work. Don't be afraid to point out obvious weaknesses in a performance however, such as not being able to hear a particular performer. People are paying money to see the play. But keep a realistic level of expectation for student performance.

Writing

Paying attention to simple guidelines about coverage and structure will make nearly any reporter a competent reviewer. The most important rule is not to use the jargon of the art in the review. Many reviewers have an almost fanatical attachment to a certain art form. They review it to spend more time with their chosen art. This kind of reviewer tends to write to other fanatics of the art form, not to the general reader of a newspaper. Don't try to impress your reader with technical language and your knowledge of the field. Help the reader better understand and appreciate the work.

Also, don't like or dislike a work, or part of one, without telling readers why. The mere fact that a reviewer likes a work is rarely enough persuasion for readers.

In structuring a review, explain the background of the work and summarize it before going into specific details. Give your readers an idea of the context in which the work exists. If it's a farcical play, explain what a farce is and where it originated. If a book or painting is representative of a certain time period either in the life of an artist or in the genre, point that out. Set the scene, then show how the work fits in.

The reviewer should also point out to the reader what other critics have thought about the work. If it was very popular when it was written but has not been popular recently, the reader should know. Have critics cited the work as one of the best?

Specifically, the lead graf should summarize the reviewer's feeling toward the event, highlight an important feature of the event, or lead up to the beginning of the event (Fig. 7–11). The context the work fits into should come next. The plot of a play, movie, or book should be outlined in no more than three or four paragraphs.

Comments on the play should follow some kind of sequence that depends on the nature of the work being reviewed. The natural order of the play review should move from main actors and actresses through minor actors and actresses, cos-

Drama highly acclaimed

By Melinda Thiesen
Editor

When drama director Noble Johnson decided to perform Henrik Ibsen's biting play, "Hedda Gabler," he might have bitten off more than he could chew.

But he didn't.

It was obvious by Saturday's performance that the crew of "Hedda Gabler" is entirely capable of accepting such a challenge.

review

Donna Dickey does an outstanding and convincing job in her portrayal of the prima donna, Hedda Gabler.

Through the use of her posture, speech and expression, she communicates a sense of arrogance, spitefulness and general bitchiness to the audience. Similarly to the spell she casts over her supporting cast members, Dickey succeeds in manipulating audience emotion, forcing them to either love her or, more frequently, detest her.

Ken Jensen, does an effective job in his portrayal of the stupid, henpecked George Tesman. His kind ways and naivete in contrast to the cold abruptness of Dickey provides and intriguing, and often humorous, comparison.

The ineptness of Jensen's character becomes even more pronounced when Judge Brack is introduced into the story.

Judge Brack, portrayed by Patrick Tromborg, comes across as a conniving, selfish man, almost a match for Hedda — but not quite.

Throughout the play, Judge Brack pursues Hedda, in hopes of having an affair — on his terms, of course; blackmail not being beneath him. His pursuit of Hedda's affections go unrewarded, however, as she proves that she is not to be manipulated in the final, dramatic scene of the play.

The one person to whom Hedda directs even the slightest amount of affection is her former beau, Eilert Lovborg.

Jim Coxsey is the talented, yet foolish, budding writer, Eilert Lovborg. He effectively communicates the tragic vulnerability his character has to Hedda's spell.

Although he seeks love and friendship in Hedda, Eilert Lovberg fails to recognize these qualities in Mrs. Thea Elvsted.

Mrs. Elvsted is played by Toni Conway. She portrays her fluttery, unintelligent character effectively, almost causing the audience to cheer when Hedda threatens to burn her hair.

Supporting characters Jill Dudley as Aunt Julia Tesman and Cheryl Dixon as the maid, Berte , also give fine performances.

Dudley does an excellent job speaking with the accent adopted by the cast members while Dixon's sarcastic nature is appreciated by the audience.

The sets and lighting for the play were effective and did an exceptional job establishing the scene and general mood of the production. The illusion of the sun filtering through the leaves of a tree was a particularly nice effect.

Although on the long side, the consistent intensity of the play commanded the audience's attention. The excellent projection and diction of the actors' voices further aided interest in the very dramatic and symbolic play.

Performances at 8 p.m. tonight and tomorrow evening will mark the final production of "Hedda Gabler."

Tickets, available at the door, are $2.50 for adults, $2 for students and senior citizens and $1.50 for children under 12. Reserved tickets are available at the COS Theater box office and may be made by calling 734-5500.

Figure 7–11. The structure of a review is dependent on the event covered. Usually, however, a summary opening followed by comments on portions of the event in descending order of importance (or of like or dislike by the reviewer) works best. (From *The Campus,* College of the Sequoias)

tumes, lighting and sets, to audience reaction. Examples from the play should illustrate each of these items. Opinions without illustrating examples are virtually useless. Specifics help readers' awareness and appreciation when they attend the play. Information about admission prices and performance times can be included either at the end of the review or right after the lead. Reviews on other art forms—books, paintings, films, television shows, dance, photography, concerts, records—follow the same basic format.

Focus on people

Ana Veciana-Suarez was the Latin-community beat reporter for The Miami (Fla.) Herald *at the time of this interview. After graduating from the University of South Florida with a degree in journalism, she worked at the* Miami News *as a general-assignment reporter. She won a Women in Communications Clarion Award for a newspaper story about growing up in a Cuban family in Florida. She began working for the* Herald *in 1982.*

Q: What's the difference between a general-assignment reporter and a reporter who writes mostly features?

A: Because we are an afternoon paper, a lot of times we have to take a feature approach to a story because it has already been covered by the morning papers. We try to find another story that answers more of the "why" or "how." We usually try to humanize the news.

Let's say that there's a story about the president cutting Medicare benefits. We'll try to find a family that will be hit hard from the loss of benefits. That would be the first time we'd report it. We'd have all the same facts that the morning paper had, but we'd put it more in "people" terms. In other words, this is what it means to John Doe, this is what it means to you.

Feature stories are about people or even animals. The stories tend to hit you more in the gut than in the brain. When you read a news story, you read it for information. You also read a feature story for the information, but it's really for entertainment, to read about other people.

Q: Where do you get your story ideas?

A: I generate 100 percent of my ideas covering my beat. I do still get some from general assignment. I'm the person responsible for being the paper's eyes and ears in that community. So I'm responsible not only for the stories for tomorrow's paper, but for long-range ones as well.

As for generating ideas, I read a lot—other papers, weekly papers, those shoppers you find in a grocery store. I might even get an idea from the ads. I also watch television and listen to the Spanish-speaking radio station here. Many times they'll have a talk show that will prompt an idea. Just living in the city helps. I'll go to a restaurant and overhear a conversation that might lead to a good story. After you've been in the business a while, people will call you with story ideas. About 50 to 60 percent of the time, they are pretty good ideas. Most of these people, by the way, are people I've met while covering other stories.

Q: How do you prepare for an interview?

A: The most important thing is to do research before you go. That includes going to the newspaper's library, calling friends or even enemies of the person, talking to people who work with him or her. I like to know what type of person he or she is. The things other people tell me will prompt questions.

I also prepare a list of questions. I know that some reporters don't. I don't, either, on a short day-to-day story. But on a feature that's going to take a little more time and organizing, I always prepare the questions. They may be real brief, say 10 questions, but I know the direction I want to take or I know the essential questions. If you're interviewing someone, that

person may go off on a tangent. If you don't have the list of questions to look at, you'll end up having to call the person. A lot of times you have to call a person and that's okay. But if you end up asking a major question over the phone, it can be embarrassing.

Q: Do you have any favorite questions that you always ask during an interview for a personality story?

A: I do use one question a lot because it opens people up. People tend to like to talk about themselves. I always ask them, "Describe yourself in just three words." It always gets them thinking. And I find that people always enjoy it. That's not the first question I ask them. I try to reach some common ground first. My research may have shown that they have a hobby I'm interested in, for instance. First I want to get them to trust me, to get more relaxed when I'm there.

Q: How much time do you like to spend on an interview story, including research time and writing time? How long should a good "personality" interview be?

A: Ideally, the interview session should be an entire day. You should watch the person at work, watch him with relatives, see him in different situations. But in newspaper work you don't have that much time. So you have to keep your conversation concise, which hurts the interview. I would imagine that ideally the minimum you should spend on a newspaper profile would be three days. Spend one day for research, one day for the interview, and one day to write the story. Most of the time, however, I have to do a profile in one day, so everything is cut short.

Q: Do you use a tape recorder for interview stories?

A: I don't use one much because I find that people either put up an act or they are afraid of them. But if I am going to do a major project, I will use one, so that if I interview someone and he says, "Hey, I didn't say that," I have the tape. I do use a recorder in a case like that, but I take notes, too. On a normal basis, for just everyday stories, I use notes.

If I want to be sure I get a word-for-word quote, especially on a subject that could be controversial, I ask the interviewee to repeat it or I put an asterisk by it on my notes. At the end of the interview, I'll check those quotes by asking the source: "Is this what you mean?"

It's up to the individual, but I find that for a straight, day-to-day story, a tape recorder takes up too much time. Not only are you taking notes during the interview, you have to transcribe the tape and then write.

Q: How do you approach the actual writing of the story? Do you write with a specific reader in mind? Or do you write for your whole audience?

A: I always write for myself. There are stories every day that I just don't get the way I want because I didn't have the time or because I just didn't live up to my expectations. I think reporters know in the back of their minds if they've done a good story or a bad story. So if I had a recommendation, I would tell beginning reporters to write for themselves. Once you have your own set of values and standards for your work, you'll know when you've goofed the assignment.

In terms of the audience, I know I'm closer to a lot of the issues I cover. I read about them, I report them, I know about them in depth—a lot more so than readers. So I have to keep in mind that the people I'm writing for aren't that close to the issues, they don't know all the details. I have to explain a lot of things. Sometimes I think I'm wasting beautiful prose on explaining things I know so well. But I have to slow down. I think this is essential, though, especially in news-papers. Newspapers are primarily there to inform.

Q: To use one of your own ideas, can you describe a good feature writer in just three words?

A: I'll try! But then let me explain what I mean. *Inform, entertain, sensitivity. Inform:* I think that's why a newspaper is published. You're there to inform the public. *Entertain:* By the very fact that someone is reading a feature story that is longer than a news story, you have to *entertain* that person with your writing. Maybe the story has been given special play—a big picture, a special headline, or something graphic. These say, "Read this story. It's something special."

As for *sensitivity*, the stories I've enjoyed reading are the ones that make me *feel* for the person. I can say, "Boy, that guy's been through the worst of times, and I thought I had it bad." The point is that it brings out feelings in the reader. That's what you're going for. Again, it's the going for the gut that I mentioned earlier. You've got to hit the reader where it hurts.

Features and reviews are tougher to write than a simple news story, so the better writers on the staff should write these stories. A common complaint about student newspapers is that they are boring. This attitude can be changed by providing the reader with interesting stories, columns, and entertainment reviews in the features section.

Suggested Projects

1. Find feature stories you like in the local paper or in papers from other schools. Why do you like these stories? What could you use in your own stories?

2. Begin an idea file for feature stories, then fill it. It should grow thicker every week as staffers come up with ideas.

3. Find stories that use the *Wall Street Journal* formula. Outline them. How do the four parts fit together? Do you notice anything else about the structure of the story, such as whether there is an inverted-pyramid section or whether a chronological account is used?

4. Invite the reviewer from the local paper to share ideas with the staff about how to approach a review assignment. Attend a performance that you know the reviewer will attend. Write a review and compare yours to the reviewer's. Were your reactions the same? Should they have been?

5. Have the entire staff watch a dramatic production on television and review it. Compare the reviews. Which was the best? Why?

Vocabulary

bright
profile
syndicate
***Wall Street Journal* formula**

Exercises

1. Select a unique person on campus—a student or an instructor—and write a *Wall Street Journal*–formula lead based on that person.

2. Write a *Wall Street Journal*–type lead based on the facts below. You may embellish the facts slightly to fit your needs.

The Handicapped Student Services office has just released information showing that fully 7 percent of the students at your school use their services. Their study was done recently with the help of a grant from the federal government. Besides identifying the handicapped population at the school, the study looked at architectural barriers and other physical problems handicapped students face. Nonsighted students have the most problems because of cracked walkways.

Mike Lehan, a 19-year-old criminal justice major, is a blind student at your school. Walking around campus with his red-tipped white cane, Lehan has stumbled more than once. Recently he tripped over a section of sidewalk that had been lifted up by the root system of an elm tree and severely sprained his right ankle. "It's hard enough getting around here without the use of sight," he said, "but it's even harder with this limp. I sure wish something could be done to correct the situation."

3. Practice uncovering telling details by interviewing another staff member on the newspaper. Find as many details as you can through observation; then write a brief profile including the staff member's experience as a reporter on your paper.

editorials and opinion columns

OPINION

Guns a goofy idea

"Buy me a flute and a gun that shoots"
— Bob Dylan and The Band, The Basement Tapes

I'm not really sure what these song lyrics have to do with the recent uproar over the campus police and firearms, it's just a cool song. I do know that the campus police couldn't care less for a flute, and want guns that shoot.

I just find it extremely funny that they can't muster any support to allow the campus police to carry guns. The reason can be only one thing — nobody trusts them.

Why else would Student Congress, as well as the majority of the students, be so terribly against letting our good pals at the campus police station carry guns? Maybe because everyone feels that they're goofs.

Popular opinion about this issue must be that a gun would just be a new toy for them to play with. Rumor has it that when they first got patrol cars, they would drive around and play with the sirens. It got so bad that they had to have a rule that regulated how much they could use the sirens. What, then, would happen with guns?

I'd be speaking for myself, but I wouldn't particularly want to be shot for, say, playing street hockey illegally. I tend to think that it would ruin my day.

And it doesn't help their case very much that an officer said recently that he would refuse to go to a potentially hostile situation without a gun.

Hey, if they're going to arm the campus police, they might as well arm every Tom, Dick and maniac on campus. Would it be that much more unsafe if everybody was packing heat, as opposed to just the campus police?

What we need is more police walking through the Oak Grove and other potentially hazardous places late at night and on weekends. Just to be there for protection, and not there to bust the obligitory drunk people walking through. Protection without a gun — what an interesting thought.

Remember, we always have those amiable guys at Indiana Police Department here to protect us.

Gus Guenther *is sports editor of* **The Penn.**

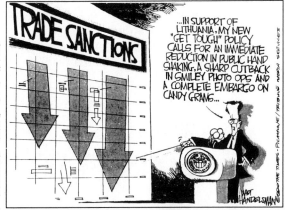

THE PENN
THE INDEPENDENT STUDENT VOICE OF IUP

Editor in Chief
Elizabeth M. Evans

News Editor Patrick O'Shea	**Assistant News Editor** Susan Hafler
Features Editor Tracy Trauger	**Assistant Features Editor** Ginny Perrine
Sports Editor Gus Guenther	**Assistant Sports Editor** Bill Kenny
Managing Editor Teresa Talarigo	**Photography Editor** Joe Wojcik
Classified Manager Heather Ockler	**Business Manager** Ted Hervol
Advertising Director Dawn Parker	**Production Manager** Joseph J. Lawley

Student Publications Director
Amy Casino

Editorials, unless otherwise indicated, are written by the Editor in Chief. Letters to the Editor represent the opinion of the writer. Opinions expressed in columns, letters, or cartoons are not necessarily those of **The Penn.** Opinions expressed in the Opinion section are not necessarily those of **The Penn,** the university, the Student Cooperative Association or the student body. **The Penn** is financially independent from the university.

Letters Policy

Letters intended for publication must not exceed one typed, double-spaced page and must contain the author's name (typed), signature, telephone number, and university affiliation, if any. **The Penn** will not honor requests to withhold names from letters without just cause. Letters not meeting these requirements will not be printed. **The Penn** reserves the right to edit all letters chosen for publication. Columns must have approval from the Editor in Chief before being submitted for publication. Unused letters will be returned to the author upon request. Letters can be mailed or personally delivered to:

Editor in Chief
**Room 220, Hadley Union Building
319 Pratt Drive
Indiana, Pa. 15701**

COPYRIGHT 1990 The Penn.

LETTERS TO THE EDITOR

Rally in the 'Grove

As most of you are probably aware, this is a contract negotiation year between faculty and the Chancellor, Dr. James He McCormick. Dr. McCormick is the advocate for SSHE and as such he is responsible for ensuring not only the maintenance, but the improvement of the State System of Higher Education.

It is clear to most of us that our buildings are deteriorating; equipment is in serious need of replacement; we need more faculty and that we no longer have a competitive salary scale. We are finding it increasingly difficult to attract new faculty because we cannot compete with the salary or workload of other institutions. The list goes on.

The point I am making here is that we need to demonstrate our needs to the Chancellor. On Wednesday, May 9th, at high noon, there will be a rally in the Oak Grove to urge the Chancellor and the Governor to provide adequate funding for SSHE.

We urge those of you who care about public higher education at the state universities to be present at the rally and to show your support for our position.

Incidentally, Dr. McCormick will be on campus this week.

**Anthony DeFurio, President
IUP APSCUF**

Davis demotion a disgrace

Regardless of your personal feelings about arming campus police, the ham-handed censorship of Sgt. Greg Davis by the IUPland administration is disgraceful, especially for an institution allegedly dedicated to the free exchange of viewpoints. I have known Sgt. Davis since he joined the force here. He is an honest, thorough, competent and respected professional. He is also apparently too articulate in expressing his beliefs. Unhappily, the same may not be said for those who sat in judgment of him.

I hope that someone higher up on the management food chain might stumble over the folly of this heavy-handed, light-minded censorship and turn that poor judgment into justice. My hope is not very strong, though, as our IUPland management has been consistent in its attitude of Just Us, rather than justice.

Whoops, just as I was about to really climb aboard my rhetorical soapbox, a lady from a nearby office asked me why I don't just go along, you know, and trust our managers. "They know what's best in the big picture, they're managers," she told me.

I think she is one of the ever-new sub-directors for the administrative manager of the Interglobal Institute for the Ego Advancement and Image Enhancement for Cultural Esperanto and Ethnic Diversity Research and Publication, or something like that, stuff that's really *in* around IUPland these days.

With my gas-pained smile I asked her if she had a few weeks to listen while I briefly outlined the reasons why I have serious trouble believing most any management explanation of most anything they say or do, up to and including that this is May of 1990. By the way, has anyone read

any newspaper ads from the other Indiana lately? Are there any openings for managers at our Ball State Branch?

J. David Truby

Bargaining with students

The possibility of a strike is a lot more realistic than many students believe. Pennsylvania ranks as one of the lowest states in the nation with regard to money allocation to state schools. It is because of this that many professors are leaving schools like IUP and going to higher paid, private universities.

The person responsible for this chain of events is Governor Casey. He seems content with the current situation and is continuing to leave higher education at the bottom of his budget priority list. There is something that can be done. Casey is up for re-election soon and he is very sensitive to public pressure.

Chancellor James McCormick, a representative of Casey, will be coming to IUP on Wednesday, May 9. A rally led by APSCUF, the teacher's union, will be held on that Wednesday in the Oak Grove from noon until 1 p.m.

Everyone, please think about this. A strike would hurt the students more than anyone else. The graduating seniors would probably suffer the most because they would not be able to get a jump into the job market. Juniors, sophomores and freshman: What kind of summer job would you be able to get if you started in late June or July? Do not let anyone use you as a bargaining chip for his or her problems. It is only a one-hour rally on the Reading Day. Take a study break; come to the Oak Grove and take charge of your future.

**Adam Goldstein
Vice President-elect, SC**

The science of choice

I would like to make a few comments concerning Lisa Metrik's letter to the editor about her Physical Science II professor. I had this very same professor and I thoroughly enjoyed the time I spent in his class. I found him to be an excellent professor and also one of the nicest faculty members on this campus.

Maybe Miss Metrik enjoys a professor who stands in front of the class and lectures straight from a book, but I like a professor who enjoys himself during class. I am grateful to have a professor who interacts with his students.

I did not find this professor's class to be any less challenging than other college level courses, and I have carried a perfect 4.0 for the three semesters I have been here.

As finals approach, I would think that Miss Metrik would have something better to do with her time (like studying for her finals in fine arts courses) than make unfounded statements with regard to a doctor of chemistry. I think Miss Metrik should be more concerned with her own classes than with the way a respected faculty member conducts his classes.

Donna Jean McAllister

Figure 8–1. Opinion pages, though not read by a majority of readers, are important places to add context to the news of the day and to take a stand on some of those issues. (Courtesy of *The Penn*)

87

Newspapers need to provide opinions as well as news and entertainment. They not only tell us what is going on in our world through their news columns, they also reserve a special section of the paper where they comment on and give their opinions on the news through editorials and columns. Opposing viewpoints usually appear on the op-ed, or opinion, page.

Editorials have been a part of newspapers since the early days of journalism. In colonial times, nearly everything in the paper was an editorial on how the government should be run. Objectivity in news reports was not yet the style.

After a long evolution of ideas on the composition and presentation of news, most newspapers now *editorialize* only on the editorial pages and keep news columns free from personal opinion and bias. But the newspaper still reserves the right to comment, both positively and negatively. The First Amendment to the U.S. Constitution guarantees this right.

Through its editorial columns, a newspaper may explain a difficult legislative act (Fig. 8–2), suggest that the readers vote for or against a bill or a person

Figure 8–2. Editorials can explain complex legislative bills or just dehydrate bloated bureaucratic language down to the important points so that readers can better understand what they need to know. (From *The Campus,* **College of the Sequoias)**

editorial
Consent not needed

Is encouraging openness between parents and their children regarding sex really a matter under congressional jurisdiction?

Pending legislation that would mandate parental permission for minors attempting to obtain prescription contraceptives from federally-funded family planning agencies will, in all probability, not achieve this purpose.

The Moral Majority and other political groups are behind this legislation because they say it will open up better communication in families about sex.

If this law passes, it will not succeed in opening up communications, but will only cause the number of teenage pregnancies to increase. The majority of young people aren't going to ask their parents' permission to use contraceptives, so they won't use the planning agencies' services. And teenagers aren't going to stop having sexual relationships.

The current law allows anyone to seek treatment and prevention at an agency, and the parents of the minor are not contacted.

The legislation would require that the parents of minors living at home be notified within 10 days by the agency after their child obtains prescription contraceptives. Each time the teenager wants the prescription filled, parental consent would be required.

The Campus does not believe that forcing family planning agencies to contact the parents will lead to more family communication. What the legislation is attempting is to cut federal spending in the area of family planning and to force certain religious beliefs on everyone.

Teenagers need to be able to talk with their parents about sex and birth control, but requiring parental consent for prescription contraceptives is not the answer.

editorial
Small change hurts

The storms that blew through town Monday night left leaves, twigs, branches and sometimes whole trees scattered about. Though we may have been fond of a certain tree that fell in the neighborhood, we know the storm left healthier trees and shrubs standing. We expect the storms of spring and summer, the havoc they wreak upon us. We expect, too, that new trees and shrubs will replace the old.

Yet, when we walk through Campustown and see that three merchants—the Campus Five Cent to $1 Store, Flynn's and Grunt's—have uprooted themselves, and that Bubby and Zadie's may soon join them, we find ourselves more than a little upset. Change is to be expected, but to have the stability of Campustown shattered in such a way affects us; it bothers us and makes us anxious—like last spring, when a number of fallen trees left gaping holes in the Quad. The new, smaller trees will not fully replace the old for quite some time.

There seems a trend, in these times of recession, to eliminate the small businessman, the small store. This is unfortunate, for compared to the large department stores with their corresponding volume sales these small stores offer personal service and a calm atmosphere. Atmosphere, however, is not the drawing incentive it used to be when compared to prices.

Likewise, atmosphere is not an adequate defense against rent increases.

Flynn's left for personal reasons. This is to be expected as part of the normal turnovers of business. Likewise, our capitalistic system dictates that some businesses survive and some don't. This too is to be expected. Yet, when substantial rent increases drive old busineses out—as in the case of the dime store and Grunt's—something is not right.

And so, in the face of these increases, a small general store with its charming sales help is replaced by a money-making business.

The new, small business we greet to Campustown is a pinball arcade, which will move into the spot left by the Campus Five Cent to $1 Store. There is little doubt the arcade will drastically alter Campustown's atmosphere.

The owner says the rent hike is justified, that the store had been there for 35 years on a generous lease, that it was time to bring the rent in line with others. He is right.

Yet, there are problems in this thinking. Stores charge more in Campustown for the convenience of nearby buying. The property, as such, is more valuable and the owners charge a higher rent. Prices soon rise to keep pace with rent, and vice versa.

Cost-push inflation. The black plague of our times.

The winds of change are firm; we are all a little poorer for the wear. Just as we await the results of the summer storms, we can expect our poverty to be more tangible when the rent increases show up on the cash register.

Figure 8–3. Opinion coverage should cover any on-campus or off-campus event or issue that might interest readers of the paper. (From *The Daily Illini*, Illini Publishing Company, Champaign, Il)

running for office, comment on the state of affairs (Fig. 8–3), or even poke fun at someone—or at itself.

The opinion function is more important than many school newspapers think. Some faculty and administrators wrongly believe that students have no right to comment on the activities and business of the school. But all journalists, student or professional, have a duty to help the readers of the paper discuss the important ideas and issues of the day, including those of the school.

To fulfill this duty in part, the newspaper comments through unsigned editorials that represent the opinion of a consensus of the editors, not of any particular person. Individuals also comment and analyze issues and ideas through signed opinion pieces. The public comments through printed letters to the editor and through guest-opinion columns. And artists comment through editorial cartoons.

Because the courts have upheld the rights of reporters and newspapers in public schools, editorial boards of school papers may comment on anything on campus or in the community that they feel deserves comment. Student editors, therefore, need not fear that saying something negative about an administrative action will result in suspension. If the opinion is based on fact, is logical, is presented clearly, and is not libelous or obscene, the Constitution protects the right of the newspaper to say what it believes is right.

The Auburn Plainsman

Serving Auburn University for 96 years

Paige Oliver	**Dan Lyke**
Editor	Business Manager
B. Bryan Bittle	**Mark Silvers**
Managing Editor	Creative Director

Matt Smith, News Editor	**Martha Cronk,** Copy Editor
Jennifer Allen, Sports Editor	**Jennifer Wynn,** Features Editor
Shayne Bowman, Village Life Editor	**Lee Ann Flynn,** Art Editor
Jennifer Stimson, Technical Editor	**Cliff Oliver,** Photo Editor

Editorial Assistant-Paul DeMarco; Assistant News Editors-Teresa Gaston and Emily Riggins; Assistant Sports Editors-Greg Klein and Deena Pettit; Assistant Village Life Editors-Michael Gordon and Stephanie Elsea; Assistant Technical Editor-Christi Borgquist; Assistant Copy Editors-Larisa Lambert and Owen Barnes; Assistant Features Editor-Juleigh Sewell; Assistant Photography Editor-Jeff Snyder

Production Artists-Louis Nequette, Lori West, Stephen Lohr, Isabel Sabillon and Chris Naylor; Advertising Representatives-Beth Ballard, Lisa Lunsford, Kristi Kirby, Kathleen Morgan and Beth Gault; PMT Specialist-Jamie Callen

Figure 8–4. Masthead from the *Auburn Plainsman*.

Figure 8–5. This editorial is topped by a small box explaining how the stance of the paper is decided—a terrific idea. (Courtesy of *The Graphic*)

The *Graphic* is published weekly by Pepperdine University's student publications. Unsigned editorials reflect the majority view of the Editorial Board.

Volunteerism prevails among Pep students

Pepperdine students are often accused of being spoiled and self- centered. Results of Monday's blood drive sponsored by the Red Cross, prove otherwise.

The spirit of volunteerism, which was publicly emerged through student organizations such as the Volunteer Center, SGA, and the Greeks, surfaced again as many students donated time and courage to give blood.

The students of Pepperdine should be proud of the results. The original 94 pint goal, set by the Red Cross, was surpassed by six pints. The significance, however lies not in the amount of blood donated but in the overwhelming student participation in the event.

Towards the end of the blood drive, Red Cross volunteers were forced to turn student donors away because they had more donors than could be accommodated.

Speculation implies that this surge of volunteerism was sparked by last months earthquake in San Francisco. It's inspiring to see students continue in their desire to help.

Although many students have family and friends in the Bay area, many who do not participated in the blood drive to aid those in need.

This effort adds to a sequence of car washes, food drives and other relief aids organized by Pepperdine students and staff.

The students here are aware of the world around them and they do care about people outside of their daily lives.

Although the recent earthquake may have served as the motivation behind this effort, the donated blood will be used wherever it is needed the most. It is believed that the biggest need is in the area affected by the earthquake.

Those who gave blood and worked to make this blood drive a success must be commended.

In a society of individualism let us hope that this wave of volunteerism will continue.

Opinion Coverage

The opinion editor works closely with the news editor to keep up on current events of reader interest. The opinion editor decides what issues deserve editorial comment (an expository editorial), a one-sided stance, or a pro/con format debate.

The editorial board, led by the opinion editor, selects one or two ideas for editorials that deserve immediate attention, discusses and votes on them, and then assigns a writer for each editorial.

The editorial board is usually listed in a staff box, or *masthead* (Fig. 8–4). The masthead, *always* on the editorial page, lists the editors for the paper (sometimes even the entire staff) and other pertinent information about the newspaper. This information may include the address and phone number of the newspaper; memberships in journalism associations and awards won through these organizations; brief statements of editorial, advertising, and letters policies; and subscription cost. Though some parts of a newspaper can be cut, advertising and the masthead are not among them.

Good opinion coverage includes not only campus events and issues—student-government actions, administrative actions, and anything else deserving comment, whether it has a news peg or not—but also local and national events and issues (Fig. 8–5).

Opinion coverage, just as with news coverage about national issues, must focus on local impact. A national story about cuts in state aid to the college should be written to show what those cuts will mean to local students. The opinion coverage should also focus locally and suggest a solution to the problem, not just speak out against the proposed state budget.

The opinion editor must select only a few topics from many to include in the section. The editor has to deliberate on current issues and engage in actual reporting to determine which topics need to be discussed. The space restrictions on the page also limit topic selection.

Writing

The best editorial, very simply, is one that communicates its ideas effectively. Editorials must follow the general journalistic rule of writing tightly—even more tightly than news stories. Editorials are probably the toughest type of story to write, mainly because of space limitations. The topic must be trimmed to only one point. If you have another argument to make, write another editorial. Editorials are never as long as news stories would be on the same subject, for two reasons. First, there is simply not enough space on the page. Editorial writers are limited to eight or nine paragraphs in which to make a point. Because an editorial often is a follow-up of an event or issue that has been covered in the news columns, space need not be given to a complete list of details—the reader may already know the facts. An editorial writer, however, is a reporter. New details not covered in the news story can give even greater credence to the opinion. All editorials should include at least a summary of the facts. The reader deserves more than an opinion not supported by fact.

One benefit of writing editorials is that it makes good writers. The restrictions of an editorial mean that you will have to use good grammar and word selection, clear thinking, and logical argumentation if you hope to get your point across. Learning how to write editorials can only help you become a better writer, even if you hope to spend your career in the sports department.

Many student journalists believe that they have to feel strongly about an issue before they can write an editorial. A strong belief may mean that you write a better editorial, but not feeling strongly shouldn't preclude you from writing one. If you are unable to stand on one side of the fence or the other, write an *expository editorial*, that is, one that explains and analyzes facts. This type of editorial actually may be of more service to your readers than an opinion piece, and the exercise of presenting both sides may help you come to a conclusion on your personal stance.

Editorials are usually written in the first person plural (*we, us, our*) because they represent the view of the newspaper as a whole, not the view of any individual. For this reason, editorials are always unsigned.

At a large metropolitan newspaper, a team of editorial writers meets every morning with the editorial-page editor to discuss ideas for the next day's editorials. After the writers share their ideas and discuss their viewpoints, several ideas are selected for the editor to present to the editorial board of the paper. The writers also attend the meeting with the board in case further explanation is needed. The ideas are then voted upon, and the writers return to their offices to compose the editorials. These writers' names never appear in the paper; the editorial is not meant to be their point of view but the view of the entire newspaper.

Structure

Although there is no one correct way to write an editorial, one structural setup works effectively when the paper is taking a stand on an issue. This three-part system is described well by Curtis MacDougall in *Principles of Editorial Writing*. First, begin the editorial by summarizing the news peg (remember that the editorial does not have to cover something in great detail). Second, outline the newspaper's reaction for or against the point. Third, explain why the reader should think, believe, or do what the editorial suggests. In the last graf of the editorial, summarize the argument and repeat the stance (Fig. 8–6). In some instances, this structure can be reversed after the opening graf (Fig. 8–7).

If you are trying to convince readers to believe more strongly in something they already slightly believe in, use the summary-outline-explanation structure and give the paper's stand before listing the reasons why. If, however, you believe that you have to change a lot of minds to get a majority of your readers to agree with your point, explain why the paper's stance is right before you come right out

Figure 8–6. To remind the reader of the paper's stance, an editorial can end with a brief summary. (From *The Campus*, College of the Sequoias)

I s it unconstitutional to exclude women from the military draft solely on the basis of sex? U.S. Supreme Court justices began deliberating on this question last Tuesday.

Their decision may affect women's role in the military — and in society.

The Campus believes that women should be included in the draft, as the current draft unfairly discriminates against men.

Last July a federal court in Philadelphia ruled that the current draft unconstitutionally discriminates against men and that women must be included.

Welcome G.I. Jane.

The ruling came three days before former president Carter's plan for draft registration was slated to begin. A flurry of legal maneuvers permitted registration to go as planned until the Court declares it unconstitutional.

The Campus believes it should.

Excluding women from the draft consigns 50 percent of the nation to second-class citizenship. In the words of a legal brief submitted to the Court by the National Organization for Women (NOW),

the draft "sanctions a continuing false view of women as weak and unfit to serve their country."

Feminists view the inclusion of women in a draft as an important step toward equality. NOW maintains that military service by blacks alongside whites was a key step toward racial integration and that service by 18-year-olds prompted legislation granting them the vote.

Currently, over 8 percent of our military manpower is female. These women aren't all file clerks and nurses — many are highly-trained technicians involved in support units vital to any defensive action. Defense department officials told Congress that during a military mobilization 650,000 draftees would be needed — including 80,000 women who can move quickly from civilian to non-combat jobs, freeing men for the front.

The Campus believes that the Supreme Court should find that women and men are equally suited for service. Any decision arrived at, however, won't resolve the issue of women in combat, but it will bring women closer to first-class citizenship.

Bell not to tune of Pierce

It is understandable that El Camino Real High School has an El Camino Bell. It is logical that El Camino Bells line El Camino Real.

But the Roundup doesn't understand why Ronnie Wald, Associated Student Body (ASB) president, wants an El Camino Bell for Pierce College; unless, perhaps, its ring would have a Piercing quality.

Wald plans to replace the wood sculpture, "Directions," which has been a fixture in the free speech area for more than five years, with an El Camino Bell.

What does an El Camino Bell have to do with Pierce College?

Ask El Camino Real High School what has happened to its El Camino Bells in the past. You'll hear that they have been stolen. An El Camino Bell is small and easily removed.

According to El Camino Real's plant manager, Edward Fluora, several bells were stolen when the school first opened. Subsequently, one was placed in an inside location and bolted to an 18-inch thick concrete wall, where it has remained since.

Wald says that an El Camino Bell would be donated to the college by the L.A. City Council. But is the the L.A. City Council going to bear the cost of replacing the bell when it is inevitably removed by pranksters or vandals?

The Roundup doesn't think so.

If "Directions" is to be removed, it should be replaced with a sculpture or other display that is relevant to Pierce College; something large, heavy and durable; something that will mean something to the student population.

Something that rings true to the Pierce image.

Figure 8–7. Sometimes the stand of the paper is mentioned only at the end. (From *Roundup*, Pierce College)

and say it. You are more or less "tricking" readers into reading your logic before showing them that the conclusion of this well-thought-out argument is the opposite of what they believe. Use these two structures whenever the paper takes a stand on an issue.

In contrast to partisan editorials, expository editorials read much like news stories. Although the writers are free to add comments as they relay facts in the editorial, they downplay the editorial stance (Fig. 8–8). The editorial writer can offer insights or comments on the facts to make a better story; the news writer cannot. When an issue is just breaking and few people are familiar with it, a paper can introduce it in an expository editorial. Instead of taking a stand, the editorial suggests that the problem be investigated further by the proper authorities. Later, after more study and news coverage, an editorial stand would be more justified.

Figure 8–8. Some editorials do not need a news peg or a strong editorial stance. A comment on a situation that deserves attention is enough. (From *The Ranger*, San Antonio College)

Students need second language

Although the foreign language requirement has been dropped for many degrees, students should take advantage of the opportunity to learn a second language.

Foreign language study not only teaches another language but also teaches the customs and cultures of another people, thereby helping the student to better understand others.

The nearly 50 percent decline in foreign language enrollment here since 1976 is alarming in view of international events which affect all countries and the growing trend in business of competing on the international level.

San Antonio, with its proximity to Mexico, provides a large bilingual population and culturally mixed atmosphere, which makes it practical and wise to avail oneself of the opportunity of learning a second language.

Students should enrich their education by taking advantage of the excellent foreign languages department here. It is a wonderful opportunity to enhance employable skills in the job market.

A bilingual or multilingual applicant would seem to have the inside track in high positions with business or government.

We live in a fast shrinking world which has been made so by sophisticated communication systems and rapidly expanding international commerce.

Knowledge of a second language helps the student understand the people of foreign countries and their cultures.

This knowledge has economic benefits and prepares the student to be a better neighbor and citizen of the world as well.

Op-Ed Pages

In the interest of giving readers as many viewpoints as possible, many papers have instituted an op-ed page (Fig. 8–9). This page may include syndicated columns, columns by staff members, opinion stories from local professional writers, opinions by members of the local community, and editorial cartoons. The topics for opinion columns can be political, social, or personal. Personal columns should make a point that most readers can identify with. They should not be merely stories. Unlike editorials, opinion pieces represent viewpoints of individ-

---

OCTOBER 20, 1989 • THE LOYOLA MAROON • 11

Figure 8–9. This page adds to a complete opinion section with letters from readers and two columns. (Courtesy of *Maroon*)

Letters to the Editor

Young is misguided

Editor:

In the Sept. 29 issue of *The Maroon* I was quite pleased to see on page three the Housing Now! article dealing with SGA funding. However, I was quite disturbed to read Amy Young's (Arts and Sciences representative) comments.

Miss Young said that "several people have approached me on campus saying they're opposed to [funding], so I was simply representing my constituency."

Miss Young is misdirected if she believes 30 people adequately represents her constituency. According to Charlie Brown, president of LUSSO, at least 300 student and faculty signatures were collected in support of Loyola representation at the march.

Miss Young also stated that she does not see how a march would produce concrete results.

A march focuses attention so that action may be taken to eradicate a problem on a local and federal level. Anyone remember the civil rights movement of the 1960s?

Moreover, does Miss Young see fit to define fetal life as more important an issue

to a Catholic university than the lives of more than 500,000 homeless children in America by suggesting that Loyola "donate to pro-life" instead?

I would argue that if "Catholicism has nothing to do with [homelessness]," then Catholicism has nothing to do with pro-life.

Stephanie A. Mumme
Elementary education senior

Headline offensive

Editor:

I was personally offended with something that appeared in "The Glance" section of *The Maroon* Oct. 6. *The Maroon* chose to head an announcement in bold print as "Christ, not another benefit concert."

Please don't misunderstand my intentions, I do not advocate censorship of *The Maroon*.

I simply found it incredulously ironic that a Jesuit university would remove *Campus Connections* from the shelves of their bookstore because of a condom advertisement and yet allow my god's name to be used in such a vain and inappropriate manner.

On page eight an advertisement for two homosexual bars appears, ironic in light of the condom ad situation. One of these bars is probably the oldest out-of-the-closet gay bars in the city. This bar sponsors an annual drag queen (female impersonator) beauty contest on Bourbon street in front of it every Mardi Gras.

Is Loyola ever sending mixed signals here!

Once again, I don't believe Loyola should be in the censorship business; however, if the university feels that they must, just don't do it halfway.

Rodney Conti
Psychology freshman

Maroon induces bile

Editor:

It brings bile to my mouth to read the unabashed childishness that comprises *The Maroon* (more popularly known as the Moron).

Grow up ye pagan Maroonians.

First of all, the somewhat weak cartoonist penned in a Greek in his Oct. 6 cartoon. The Greek was wearing the letters (what else?) ΔUM. That's right, "Dumb."

Oh, gee. Funny. Original. Gripping. You wackies keep me in stitches. Well, from what I understand, the Greeks as an organization have among the highest (if not *the* highest) grade point averages at Loyola. Why, then, is "dumb" appropriate? Coming from a paper that feigns social righteousness, this blatant prejudice is intolerable.

Then in the announcement section, a headline reads "Christ, not another benefit concert." Gee fellas, that's fantastic. Taking the Lord's name in vain to belittle philanthropy is journalistic ethics at its very finest.

These are just two examples of "Kommunication Krazies" that go on in *The Maroon*.

As the de facto leader of the quasi-underground Loyola Liberation Front (Lambda Lambda Phi for the zany cartoonist), I propose that *The Maroon* change its name to another color. I think *The Brown* would more closely represent what is written in this tabloid.

Have a nice day.

Tim O'Brien
Arts and Sciences Rep.
History sophomore

Loyola's oligarchy fails to give Christian example

The last few years have shown me a new understanding of what it means to be a Christian, not so much in what I believe is my true faith but in the way other people are treated or should be treated. Loyola's goals are to further and expand upon a Catholic ideal, and that is to better one's fellow man. Until now, however, I have seen little of that. Indeed, I do see the outstanding efforts of organizations such as LUCAP, LUSSO, and Housing Now! Loyola, but I fail to see any real efforts by the Jesuit oligarchy of the Rev. James C. Carter, S.J., university president, or by his assistant, Vincent P. Knipfing, vice presi-

dent for Student Affairs, to do anything for anyone outside of their realm.

Two weeks ago I sat in on one of Hous-

Viewpoint
Kye Vera

ing Now! Loyola's meetings and was warmed by a spirit of goodwill that 50 other students shared. Their vision was not apathetic. Their vision was to help and to

better their fellow man. They wanted to go to Washington D.C. and march with thousands like them for those less fortunate, representing their university in the process. Their problem was funding — at that point they had none. Nor did they have any support from the SGA or the administration. All they had was their good intentions. Since then, however, things have changed. The SGA has appropriated about $700 in order for them to defray the cost of the trip. Good move, SGA. Carter's office, however, has done nothing.

Loyola University should be an institution where social action should be one of

its main concerns along with the true education of the Christian spirit. Instead of glorifying in the attempted demise of such "rancid organizations that are a plague to the human spirit" such as that which they believe is Pi Kappa Theta. They should be involved instead in the uplifting of the society of the whole. One thing is to preach, and another is to practice what you have preached. Loyola's administration has done nothing for me, nor have they shown me what it means to be a "good Christian."

Kye Vera is a communications senior.

Chemical weapons bring out American hypocrisy

Gaseous warfare was undoubtedly among the worst offenses on humanity brought about by the first world war. The outlawing of the use of chemical weapons in 1925 was intended to purge the world of this horrid genre of conflict.

The last 65 or so years have been spent immunizing the world against the chemical threat. No one wants chemical warfare — just last year Washington threatened to bomb a suspected chemical weapons plant in Libya.

So it seems pretty surprising that our country is sitting on about 74 million pounds of undestroyed chemical weapons. Reagan spent $8 billion on nerve gas research during his presidency.

Talks in Geneva are progressing to the point that all the countries participating will have dismantled all of their weapons around the turn of the century. George Bush says America intends to cooperate.

But the Pentagon has different plans. Our military has been pushing for the go ahead on the production of a new chemical weapon: the egg laid in an $8 billion nest, a bomb codenamed Bigeye.

Bigeye is a binary bomb, one that combines two substances to create a deadly gas that may, depending on weather conditions, remain in the area, still toxic, for as

Stranger than Fiction
Henry Griffin

long as several weeks.

As the poison created by Bigeye, a nerve agent known as VX, permeates clothing and other materials, garments retrieved from the blast site remain lethal, causing paralysis and blocked breathing.

So why does the Pentagon propose production of Bigeye in 1992, if the assumption is that they will be dismantled scant years after their costly manufacture?

The justification is that, although all chemical warfare will presumably no longer exist in eight years, there is no excuse for the United States slacking off in the arms race. So new chemical weapons should be produced until it becomes no longer viable to prolong the grotesque mockery of war that chemical weapons offer.

An easy response would be that the taxpayers' dollars the Pentagon is pouring into chemical weapon production could be better spent on interests more vital to the liveli-

hood of our country, such as the homeless problem or the immense budget deficit.

Pragmatism intrudes, however. Any money not spent on Bigeye won't find its way out of the Pentagon. At least the money could be better spent on conventional weapons, maybe to defray the cost of the B-2 stealth bomber money pit the Defense Department is slowly digging for itself.

The obvious moral here is that chemical warfare has no place in a civilized world, and its expulsion from our global society cannot arrive soon enough.

War is for the soldiers, and chemical warfare, like its nuclear counterpart, is simply another easy way for the armies of the world to cut their conventional weapons. Poison gas saves money. How economical.

More importantly, what needs to be noticed in this debacle is the hypocrisy our government is espousing. Chemical weapons should be eliminated, they say, but we must keep making ours until they get rid of theirs. Such paranoia has no place in world government.

Henry Griffin, English junior, is Assistant Life and Times Editor for 'The Maroon.'

ual writers; editorials represent the viewpoint of the paper. Opinion pieces, therefore, are written in the first person singular (*I, me, my, mine*).

Though opinion pieces are usually longer than editorials, all the rules of good writing still apply. Many newspapers will purposely select columnists whose viewpoint is opposite the stance taken on the editorial page. The opinion page gives readers different ideas so they can come to intelligent decisions based on the facts and opinions they read. Running only one viewpoint through the editorial columns of the paper would not be the best service to the readers.

Take stands, give context

Tim Rutten is the editor of the Sunday opinion section of the Los Angeles Times. *He began his journalism career as a reporter at the* San Gabriel Valley Tribune, *where he worked for four years. In 1972, he joined the* Times *as news editor for the "View" section. Then he became an assistant editor of the op-ed pages and the managing editor of the opinion section before taking his present position.*

Q: What is the importance of the opinion function of a newspaper?

A: There are two points that are most important. First, we've had in the newspaper business a fairly dramatic expansion of what we believe news is. It is well established now that a newspaper has an obligation to present not only news in the sense of systematized facts but also the context in which these facts occur.

The context gives them meaning to the readers. Very often it is impossible to present this context without analyzing, and you can't analyze without having opinions. So to the extent that we have a responsibility to report the news, we also have a responsibility to provide our readers with the background, the context that gives them an ability to interpret and make use of that information.

The second is a little more nebulous. It is true that we have come to believe that newspapers also have an obligation for public discourse—toward the direction and the quality of public discourse. In other words, we have many, many issues in this society of which reasonable people can take a look at the facts and the context and still come up with different opinions. We've come to believe that we have an obligation to provide a place where readers—outside the normal process of gathering news—can make their opinions and interpretations felt.

Q: How does the newspaper's taking a stand on a public issue through its editorials fit into the opinion function?

A: Here we are on a little firmer ground because we have had a long journalistic tradition and history to draw on. There was a time when newspapers were nothing but editorials. But despite this evolution in the forum, newspapers as institutions are concerned with the news, with public issues, and they take upon themselves the responsibility for leading or directing public opinion. It's very straightforward. There are very few people who believe there should not be editorial pages.

Q: What makes an editorial a well-written one? Should the stance of the paper be mentioned first or saved as a conclusion?

A: The best editorials, just like the best articles, are the ones that work. It's easier to talk about principles than structure. Obviously they have to be clearly written. I don't really think there's much difference in whether you present your position up front or not. I think it will vary piece to piece as to which is right. So long as a writer argues clearly and with integrity with at least a minimum sense of style, I don't think it matters.

I think there are a few things that do matter a great deal. Most people believe that because editorials are short and because they are expressions of opinion, you don't have to report them or research them. Nothing can be further from the case. Editorials, in fact, require much more research and much more thought than the average news story, for several reasons: One, because the space is dramatically limited. The average editorial at the *Times* is less than a tenth of the length of a news story. So in a story where economy of expression is that much of an issue, you really have to know what it is you are going to say. Second, because in an editorial you, as a representative of a newspaper, have taken it upon yourself to tell people what they should do and what they should think, you have an obligation to make sure that you have as full and accurate a comprehension of the facts as possible. That takes a lot of time and research and a lot of hands-on reporting. Most people seem to have a perception of editorial writers—particularly on student newspapers—as in a kind of ivory tower. The editorial writer is someone who sits in his or her office and thinks great and lofty thoughts, and in isolation brings these pungent little essays to pass. Well, it's not the case. A good editorial writer works the phone, meets people, goes out and sees things, just as a reporter does. Very often you are trying to go beyond what the news stories can actually tell you, doing a lot of first-hand reporting.

In editorials, all the basics of style apply but more so, and so do these two other conditions: You not only have to be a good, clear, concise writer, but you also have to do a lot of advance thinking and a lot of reporting.

Q: Do you write editorials for the elite, the "opinion leader," and let the thought trickle down to the common man, or do you write an editorial for the common man?

A: Ideally you ought to construct an editorial that is written in such a way, argued in such a way, that an expert on the topic would read it and not feel patronized and that an absolute novice could read it and not feel shut out or mystified. It's tough to do. What it requires is this: If you've thought about the topic with enough rigor and you're skillful enough as a writer, you can plan in advance ways to slip in the necessary background information so that someone coming fresh to the issue picks it up as he goes along, yet the expert doesn't feel like he's being patronized

You ought not to be naive about who reads the editorial page, however. The reader of the editorial page of any newspaper is going to be in a minority among your readers. That's just the way it is. But you ought not run the thing like an insider's club and not make the editorial accessible to everyone. My position is that good writing and clear thinking make things accessible to everyone. You have an obligation to do that anyway. And the people who want to will be able to read and understand them.

Q: How do you decide what topics are important enough to merit editorials or opinion pieces?

A: There are two interests you want to balance here in about a 70 to 30 ratio. I'll talk about the larger one first, going back to what we were talking about originally—providing a context, providing a way of analyzing the most pressing news of the day or week. You sit down and look at the deadlines of when you are coming out next and say to yourself: "Between now and then, which events are going to be of the most interest and most importance to my readers?" It's a little easier for me than for a student editor. I am backstopped in my perceptions of the news by other institutions. I can pick up *The New York Times*, for example, and see the way they are playing a story and perhaps see that I have undervalued a story. Student editors don't have that. If they don't keep a clear grasp of what's going on in their world—the things in the community and the school issues that affect them—there is no one for them to draw on, so their position is a little more precarious.

The other interest—the 30 percent part—is harder, but it is really more interesting. You also have an obligation to dig a little deeper and ask yourself: "What is it that needs to be said about something? What issue or unnoticed point should the readers know about that they won't discover otherwise? What needs to be talked about that isn't talked about?" On a campus it might be housing discrimination in nearby apartments, or grade inflation—things that don't demand immediate attention. They don't jump up and bite you, but they may have a profound effect on the community.

A good op-ed page will often include two stories in a pro/con format. Pro/cons can clarify complex issues; according to the *Los Angeles Times* opinion-section editor Tim Rutten, they can sometimes be detrimental as well. "Newspapers can sometimes give the appearance of being fair without really being fair," he said of the pro/con format. "The person to whom you have the greatest obligation to be fair is the reader. And you are not being fair to the reader if you leave him totally at sea and just provide him with two screaming zealots. Where pro/cons work best are where basic facts are well known and not in dispute." Rutten also said that pro/cons should not be an easy way out for editors who don't want to come up with an editorial stance of their own. "The danger of pro/cons is that they often leave the reader not knowing what to think, what to believe," he said. "Editors ought not to use pro/cons to evade their own responsibility to think through issues, which is too frequently the case."

But Rutten is still a fan of the pro/con format. They can be used effectively if the editor selects the topic with care; if good, intelligent writers are selected who will argue from the same set of facts; and if the editor verifies the facts. Only then can the editor be sure that the pro/con is providing the reader with a true service.

Readers should be allowed to express themselves on the op-ed page. After all, the paper exists for *all* students to air their opinions. Put letter boxes at popular places, such as the student union, library, or snack bar, to make it easy for readers to get their thoughts to you. Because of the importance of student input, many papers give space priority to letters over other opinion pieces on the opinion page.

A letters policy should be part of the paper's series of policy statements. The policy should include how to accept letters from organizations rather than individuals, how to deal with chronic letter writers, and the use and nature of editor's notes.

$300 a month for the car, and $100 a month for the chauffeur to drive it around 'cause I can't find a parking place.

"Quick, Ronnie, we're losing altitude! Throw out some more of those little ones!"

Figure 8–10. Editorial cartoons encompass a wide variety of international, national, and on-campus topics. (By Robert Foster, from *The Campus,* College of the Sequoias)

The opinion editor should always check with an organization's president or faculty adviser whenever the paper receives a letter from a member of the organization. Many papers accept organization letters only if they are personally signed or authorized by the president of the group.

Dealing with chronic letter writers is a little more difficult. Your letters column is not a soapbox. On the other hand, some chronic letter writers call attention to important points and their views should be aired. Limit the discussion of any given topic to three issues.

Editor's notes must be employed with care if they rebut the *argument* of a letter. Then in essence the newspaper always gets the final word—an unfair practice that will only discourage future letters. An editor's note should be used, however, to correct errors or inconsistencies of *facts* in letters.

Remember that editing of letters is allowed and frequently appropriate. Editing can include a decision *not* to run a letter as well as a decision to shorten or clarify the writing. Just be fair. Run as many letters as seem reasonable. Have a set letters policy with guidelines for every possible situation, and stick to it. If chronic letter writers insist that their ideas are crucial to the good of mankind and that their ideas just *must* be in the paper, tell them to purchase ad space!

Editorial cartoons are important to an opinion page (Fig. 8–10). Often a point about a complex issue can be made more clearly in a cartoon than it can in writing. Thus, a good editorial cartoonist is necessary in an opinion department.

Although a cartoon's topic can coincide with an issue's editorial stance, it should not have to. The cartoonist is sharing an individual viewpoint on a topic and should be treated just like an opinion writer. The cartoonist can also illustrate opinion columns and pro/cons to make the ideas in those pieces easier to understand.

Guest columns by faculty members or experts on a particular topic can help the reader understand complex issues. But the editor should still select the writer carefully and check the facts.

Another item that many opinion sections include is a man-on-the-street column that displays the opinions of the public on a topic of current concern (Fig. 8–11). Each opinion is usually accompanied by a photo of the person interviewed. If handled poorly or frivolously, this feature adds little to the section. But readers' opinions are important; this feature may be the only way many readers get a chance to air their views. Use good questions in these reader polls. Avoid tired or silly questions. A good question may tie in with a topic discussed on the editorial or the opinion page, it can be an unrelated topic of public concern, or it can occasionally be lighthearted.

Figure 8–11. One good way to get readers' names and faces in your paper—always a worthy goal—is to ask them their opinions on important issues. (Courtesy of *Spectator*)

What role should the United States have played in the recent coup attempt in Panama?

Eugenio Pinero
assistant professor
history

"As far as the United States intervening militarily in Latin America, after 22 or 23 times of doing that and failing to have any success, it is obvious they shouldn't have. It is obvious.

"Why it is always the military solution there is beyond me. That suggests the diplomatic corps of the United States in Latin America is really sending the signal that they failed and that every time they failed, (the United States) used a military solution. That is up until Reagan, because Reagan didn't think of any other solution. He went for the military solution from the beginning. In my opinion it is really pointing to a diplomatic failure.

"My only opinion is that they shouldn't. It isn't working at all."

Bret Storck
freshman
business

"I think they should stay out of it first, but if they are going to do something then do it. It's none of our business really what happens there, but if they are going to do something, let's not do it halfway. Let's do it all the way.

"As of right now they haven't shown any effort to do anything, which is better than doing something halfway and losing.

"My point of view is if they are going to do something, do it all the way. If they are not going to do anything, keep their nose out of it."

Holly White
freshman
journalism

"I guess they shouldn't play any role. It should be (Panama's) prerogative. If they want to fight, let them fight. We should mind our own business."

Pete Loew
junior
geography

"I think they should have gone the road that they did. They didn't do anything really. I think they are right in staying out of (Panama's) business.

"I think ... they didn't react to (the attempted coup) because they screwed up in information. They didn't know what was going on so they didn't interfere, but I think if they would have (had ample intelligence information) they would have intervened. I think that they shouldn't though in the first place, and they were right that they didn't.

"If they would have intervened I would have said it was wrong, because if the Panamanians want a change in their government they are going to do it themselves without interference by the U.S."

Dean Duffing
junior
business management

"I feel that they need help down there, but I don't know if they should take a very noticeable role. I guess it should be kind of secretive because a lot of Americans don't really understand what is going on in Panama. ... They are against us getting involved in anything like that down there.

"I think it should be secretive because Americans as a whole ... are not for a direct involvement in Panama."

Theresa Manley
junior
political science

"I think if we played a role it should have been a limited one. I believe in the sovereignty of the country. I think that they are an individual country.

"I don't necessarily think that harboring some of the people who were involved is a bad thing, because we all know what would have happened if they hadn't been taken care of. I mean it would have been China all over. I think it is good we played the role of a safekeeper for those involved, but at the same time I think it is a role we have to watch carefully. Involvement isn't necessarily a good thing.

"I think too often the United States gets overinvolved in foreign countries. And this is a situation where there has to be a selective decision-making process as opposed to a rash decision that we should get involved, because this is communism attacking all continents."

Answers should be edited. Answers on opposing sides of a hot issue should be displayed in the approximate ratio that the total answers were given. If 20 persons were questioned on gun control laws and 15 spoke in favor of them, the answers should be laid out in the same three-to-one ratio. (If you had space for eight responses you would select six "for" and two "against.")

All these comments and opinions in the paper—editorials, opinion pieces, cartoons, letters, polls—are important facets of a good newspaper. Giving readers only news is unfair. The opinion section gives readers the context in which the news can be understood.

— Suggested Projects

Vocabulary

editorialize
expository editorial
masthead

1. Invite a local editorial writer to discuss how to research and write an editorial.

2. Compare several editorial pages of local papers. Which paper has the broadest editorial and opinion coverage?

3. Evaluate recent opinion pages in your paper. Have they provided ample "context" for your readers? How can you improve the opinion section?

4. Go to *Editorials on File,* a library reference book, and read all the editorials on one topic of interest to you. Compare the logic of the argument, the facts used, and the writing style. Which editorial is most effective? Why? Write several paragraphs explaining your selection.

Exercises

1. Write an opinion column and an editorial based on one of the following texts. Take any approach you wish. Take a stance or write an expository editorial.

A. The following is a chapter from *College Student Press Law,* by Robert Trager and Donna L. Dickerson.*

Adviser: Teacher or Censor?

The position of the newspaper adviser is common in journalism departments of both large and small universities. The adviser's responsibilities usually include overseeing the paper's financial and business affairs, being available to students for advice, guiding students in the production of an issue, suggesting story and features ideas, critiquing student work, acting as liaison between student staff and the rest of the university, and, above all, teaching students the duties and responsibilities of journalists. College Media Advisers, Inc., suggests that the "adviser serves primarily as a teacher whose chief responsibility is to give competent advice to staff members in the areas to be served, editorial and/or business. . . . "

Advisers are not strictly teachers; because they deal with management, finances, and personnel, they may also be considered administrators. This is where the problem—both ethical and legal—for advisers arises. They are expected not only to teach responsible journalism but also to administer the school newspaper in the college's behalf. The potential for conflict is quite obvious.

The case of Pat Endress at Brookdale Community College in New Jersey points out some pitfalls. A journalism instructor, she was teaching students about investigative reporting. On one assignment the students uncovered what appeared to be a deliberate steering of audio-visual equipment contracts to a firm in which the chairman of the Brookdale Board of Trustees had a family interest. The staff of the student paper asked that a nonstudent assistant working with Endress write the story because of his experience and

*Reprinted with permission of the College Media Advisers, Inc., formerly National Council of College Publications Advisers.

knowledge about investigative reporting. Endress wrote an accompanying editorial, which was approved by the newspaper staff. She was fired by the school president. In the meantime, documents proved not only that the chairman's tie with the audio-visual company was through family, but that he was a member of the firm's board of directors. Endress filed a libel suit against the trustees, claiming they made false statements about her and alleging breach of contract and violation of her rights of free speech and press. After a lengthy court battle, she was ordered reinstated with tenure and was awarded back pay and damages, including $2,500 in punitive damages against the Brookdale Community College president. The libel claim was settled before trial for $900 and was therefore not brought before the trial court.

Advisers may find themselves in one of two positions when censorship of the student paper is involved. They may be censors, acting on their own or the administrators' behalf to see that certain material is not published (e.g., Trujillo, 1971; Dickey, 1967; see Chapter 5 for case summaries). Or they may refuse to censor, upholding the students' rights to publish as long as there is no substantial or material disruption of campus order. In the first instance, the students may file suit alleging that the adviser, acting on behalf of the school, has deprived them of their constitutional rights under the First and Fourteenth Amendments. In the second, advisers who choose to protect students against censorship may find that their jobs are in jeopardy. Refusal to censor may be interpreted by the administration as insubordination and cause for dismissal.

Courts have recognized that teachers must be given maximum leeway in order to properly perform their function as teachers. As one justice wrote, "Teachers . . . must be exemplars of open-mindedness and free inquiry. They cannot carry out their noble task if the conditions for their practice of a responsible and critical mind are denied to them. . . . " Faculty members, like students, do not shed their constitutional rights at the school door (Tinker, 1969). In *Pickering* v. *Board of Education* (1965), the Supreme Court held that teachers could not be constitutionally forced to give up rights under the First Amendment that they would otherwise enjoy as citizens. Thus, teachers may speak and write freely about the schools in which they work as long as discipline and harmony are not disturbed, the teacher's performance is not impaired, and the statements are not knowingly false or reckless. The *Pickering* decision went far toward protecting teachers from arbitrary discipline by school officials when constitutional rights are being exercised.

Do advisers have a constitutional right to refuse to censor a paper? Or, stated another way, do advisers have any constitutional right to protect students from censorship? No such right has been specifically upheld by the courts.

One high school case points out the problem of the adviser as protector of students' constitutional rights. In *Calvin* v. *Rupp* (1973) the adviser of a high school newspaper refused to allow the news copy to be censored by school officials. The school board voted to withdraw Calvin's contract for the next year. The Court of Appeals upheld the school board, saying that the board may have been hasty or unwise but that "the school board's decision did not deprive [Calvin] of any of his rights under the due process clause of the Fourteenth Amendment." The court did not feel that the right to protect students from censorship was a liberty protected by the Constitution. Questions of tenure and teaching assignments may further confuse this issue.

On the other side, do advisers have the right as teachers to censor publication content because they feel the material is either irresponsible or against the best interests of their school? The answer has not been clearly given by the courts, since the degree to which a publication is connected to an academic department may cloud the situation. However, the scales seem to tip toward a negative answer.

The code of the College Media Advisers, Inc., reads:

> The adviser must guide rather than censor. . . . Student journalists must be free to exercise their craft with no restraints beyond the limitations of ethical and legal responsibility in matters of libel, obscenity and invasions of privacy.

The line between censoring and teaching, though, may be a very fine one for some advisers.

In 1970, the operation of the student newspaper at Southern Colorado State University was transferred from the student government to the Mass Communication Department. The *Arrow*, which had been operated as a campus newspaper and student forum, was to be used as an instructional tool; an adviser, Thomas McAvoy, was named. During the early fall, McAvoy ordered a page deleted from an upcoming issue. McAvoy felt that the material, a cartoon and a story about the president of the university, was irresponsible and libelous. A month later, managing editor Dorothy Trujillo submitted a column about the upcoming attorney general's race and an editorial criticizing a local judge. Again, the adviser felt the material was libelous and unethical, saying that the editorial needed to be rewritten. Before Trujillo revised the editorial, she was fired. The editorial was rewritten by McAvoy, and the column never appeared. Trujillo filed suit against various state officials, the University, and the adviser, seeking reinstatement to her position on the paper.

A federal District Court said that the faculty adviser's conduct had the effect of "reining in on the writings of Miss Trujillo" while leaving the work of other *Arrow* writers free. "We cannot uphold such conduct merely because it comes labeled as Teaching when in fact little or no teaching took place." The court also noted that the change in the operating policy of the paper had not been put into effect "with sufficient clarity and consistency" and that the *Arrow* continued to serve as a student forum. The implications of the Trujillo decision are (1) if there is no teaching by the adviser, only arbitrary censorship of individual copy, the student's rights will be upheld, and (2) if the newspaper is operated as a student or campus forum, censorship by the adviser will not be allowed (Trujillo, 1971).

The Fifth Circuit appeared to modify the Trujillo distinction between a student forum and a departmental teaching tool when it involved censorship. The court, speaking of a magazine published by the English Department to provide an outlet for the creative writing course and advised by a faculty member, said that "once a university recognizes a student activity which has elements of free expression, it can act to censor that expression only if it acts consistent with First Amendment constitutional guarantees" (Bazaar, 1973). Hence, whether a publication is a student forum or a departmental tool, the Fifth Circuit indicates that it is protected by the First Amendment against censorship. In this case, the adviser and the English Department had supported the publication of two articles using street language and "four letter" words. The case speaks only to censorship by administrators.

An argument may be made that in most instances advisers are the administration's representatives to the student publication, and when censorship is effected by an adviser, it is in fact the act of an administrator—the censorship is on the school's behalf. If that is the case, whatever court decisions may say concerning administrative censorship may apply equally to advisers.

In the landmark case on campus press rights, *Dickey* v. *Alabama State Board of Education* (1967), the federal District Court spoke directly to advisers and their activities. In *Dickey*, the adviser of the Troy State *Tropolitan* had refused to allow an editorial to be published which criticized the Alabama governor and legislature. After stating that free press and free expression could be restricted only where the exercise "materially and substantially interferes with requirements of appropriate discipline," the court said: "Boards of education, presidents of colleges, and faculty advisers are not excepted from the rule that protects students from unreasonable rules and regulations" (Dickey, 1967). The court appeared to be equating advisers with administrators, holding that advisers can censor only when there is "material or substantial interference."

Only one other case has spoken to the question of censorship by a nonadministrator. In *Antonelli* v. *Hammond* (1970), the president of Fitchburg State College became upset with the student newspaper for publishing a reprint of an Eldridge Cleaver article which used "four letter" words and "street language." After the particular publication was refused printing and distribution privileges, the president appointed an advisory board which was responsible for approving material before funds would be released to pay for publication.

A federal District Court said that "prior submission to the advisory board of material . . . [to] decide whether it complies with 'responsible freedom of the press' or is obscene, may not be constitutionally required." The advisory board is analogous to advisers in smaller schools; thus the *Antonelli* proscription against prior censorship could be read as applying to advisers as well.

Although the College Media Advisers, Inc., code allows restraints within the limits of libel, obscenity, and invasion of privacy, this must be understood as self-restraint by student journalists, not censorship by advisers. In *Korn* v. *Elkins* (1970), a federal District Court said that fear of prosecution alone is not sufficient reason to apply a statute unconstitutionally. In other words, if advisers see potentially libelous material, at least this federal court seems to argue that they can only give advice, that is, suggest its omission or correction, but they cannot actually prevent its publication. The Supreme Court language in *Near* v. *Minnesota* (1931) listing exceptions to the general rule against prior restraint, however, may speak to the contrary.*

B.   The following is a statement by James K. Batten, former group vice-president/news, Knight-Ridder Newspapers. Batten addressed the Senate Select Committee on Small Business, which was holding hearings on economic concentration in the newspaper industry.

As a Washington correspondent in the 1960s, I spent many fascinating days in Senate hearing rooms, but I must confess I never expected to be back in the role of witness. Nonetheless, I appreciate your invitation, and I am glad to help the committee explore some of the issues under discussion here.

You ought to know, by way of background, that my career has been spent basically as a reporter and editor, and that my present corporate responsibilities with Knight-Ridder continue to focus primarily on our news and editorial operations. I am less intimately involved, in a day-to-day way, with the business and financial affairs of our company.

My role, in a way, reflects the long-established separation of the editorial and business functions in our company. We are a business, to be sure, but a business with a difference. We are in business to make a profit, but we also have, in our free society, enormously important public service obligations. The dichotomy in our mission is reflected in our structural arrangements. We think it is vital that our editors be given a large measure of autonomy not only from corporate headquarters in Miami, but from their newspapers' local business-side management.

Within our profession—or industry, if you like—I think it is fair to say that Knight-Ridder is known as a company which traditionally has placed very high priority on editorial excellence. That tradition goes back to John S. Knight, who, with his brother Jim, built our company. Jack Knight, who held most of the titles at one time or another, likes to say that there is no higher title than editor. He won a Pulitzer prize for his personal column, "An Editor's Notebook," which he wrote for many years. Lee Hills, who recently stepped down as chairman of the board after a distinguished career which led from a variety of editorial chairs to the chief executive's post, won a Pulitzer for his own deadline reporting.

So our company has been shaped to an unusual degree by practicing journalists of considerable distinction. And this generation of leadership, under Alvah H. Chapman Jr., our president and chief executive officer, is deeply committed to the notion that Knight-Ridder will be second to none in journalistic excellence and service to our readers and our communities. We are serious people, and we have no intention of failing to meet that test.

The committee's interest, as I understand it, is in the growth of large newspaper groups. We are, unquestionably, one of those groups. Knight-Ridder owns 32 daily newspapers, ranging in size from big metropolitan dailies such as the *Philadelphia Inquirer, The Miami Herald* and the *Detroit Free Press* down to small-city papers such as the *Aberdeen American News* in South Dakota and the *Boca Raton News* in Florida.

Our daily circulation is around 3.5 million, which by that yardstick makes us the largest in the United States. We have approximately 16,000 full-time employees.

So, we are big; there is no question about that. The question, I suppose, is whether bigness per se is bad in newspaper publishing, as some critics tend to assume. It will come as no shock to you that my answer is an emphatic no.

I'd like to elaborate on the reasons why in just a minute. But first, I want to make it clear that I do not regard myself as an apologist for the group-newspaper phenomenon. While there are a number of groups which, as Knight-Ridder, are committed to editorial quality, there are others which are not committed to that ideal. I think such publishers, whether they publish dozens of newspapers or only one, are failing in their First Amendment obligations. They do a grave disservice to us all.

*NOTE: As the legal issues chapter details, the *Hazelwood* decision may have changed some of this. This is only an exercise, not legal advice.

In personal terms, I must confess there is a side to me which would prefer an idyllic world full of truly excellent, ruggedly independent, locally owned newspapers. But that, of course, is a world that never was, despite the critics' nostalgia.

There is no question that a fair number of American cities a generation or two ago were blessed with such newspapers—devoted to their communities, fearless in their integrity, sufficiently strong in economic terms to do a first-rate job for their readers.

But, sadly, that was never the dominant pattern. Large numbers of newspapers in this country were simply not very good, to put it gently. In some cases the deficits were in resources; there just wasn't enough money to do a first-class job. In other cases there was an appalling shortage of professionalism. And for still others, the problem was unwillingness to stand up to self-serving special interests. In many cases, all three problems were present—and inevitably reinforced one another.

I think the crucial fact that needs to be understood in this debate over group newspapering is that quality and public service are not at all functions of the *size* of a newspaper's owner nor of how many newspapers the company owns. They depend, instead, on the intentions, capabilities, and performance of the owners.

There are excellent newspapers owned by groups and excellent newspapers owned by local independents. And conversely, there are mediocre newspapers published by groups and mediocre newspapers published by local independent owners.

In the case of Knight-Ridder, our size and resources help us assure quality. Our reputation for improving newspapers is well known. Let me give you only a couple of many possible examples:

Under Knight-Ridder ownership, which commenced in 1969, the *Philadelphia Inquirer* has moved from mediocrity to distinction. There has been a massive effort to improve every part of the newspaper, and it has been remarkably successful. A few weeks ago, the *Inquirer* won its fifth Pulitzer prize in five years, an almost unprecedented record in American newspapering. Beyond the Pulitzers, the *Inquirer* has won more national journalism prizes over the last five years than any other newspaper in the United States. Prizes are not the only index of excellence—and not the most important one—but they do tend to reflect the tangible benefits a newspaper brings to its readers and to its community.

Another example, in a smaller city:

The *Lexington Herald* and the *Lexington Leader,* in the bluegrass country of Kentucky, became Knight-Ridder papers in 1973. Since that time, the news staff has increased by 50 percent. There are 20 percent more columns of news and 30 percent more local stories. We added full-color printing, Washington bureau coverage, increased state capitol coverage, *Parade* magazine on Sundays, a weekly television magazine, a sharp increase in letters to the editor, and on and on.

Another way we use our resources to serve readers better is through steps that enrich the material available to all our newspapers. In the last five years, for example, we have added six reporters and editors to our Washington bureau. Today, it is unquestionably among the best bureaus in this city.

At our annual shareholders' meeting last month, Alvah Chapman, our president and CEO, announced that in the next two years Knight-Ridder will be substantially increasing our foreign coverage. For many years, top reporters both from the Washington bureau and from individual papers have traveled and reported from abroad. We have had good results from that approach. For example, the *Philadelphia Inquirer's* Richard Ben Cramer won this year's Pulitzer prize for international reporting with his brilliant and sometimes dangerous work in the Middle East. And *The Miami Herald* has regularly produced first-class coverage of Latin America since the 1940s.

In discussions over the last year, however, we have concluded that we should provide more systematic foreign coverage for our readers. A number of U.S. news organizations have been retrenching in their foreign coverage in recent years. But we believe that foreign news, if anything, is even more important these days. Readers of the *San Jose Mercury-News* who are waiting in long gas lines understand that part of their frustration is traceable to events in Tehran.

So within the next 24 months, our plan is to open eight foreign bureaus in strategically located cities around the world. That will be an expensive project, but we think it's going to be good for our papers and good for our readers. We think it is in line with our obligations.

It is reasonable to ask why Knight-Ridder puts such high priority on improving its newspapers. There are two interlocking reasons. One is that the people who run our company believe there is a moral obligation to publish the best newspapers we know how. The press has very special responsibilities in our democratic system, and we take them seriously.

The other reason is that we believe good newspapers are good business—and that in the years ahead, stagnant, hold-the-line newspapering is not likely to succeed particularly well. One of the reasons is that the competition for people's time and attention is growing steadily more intense. Newspapers which fail to change and improve, in my opinion, are likely to see severe erosion of their place in readers' lives.

Let me take just a minute to underscore the intensity of the competition faced by newspapers. In Charlotte, for example, the largest city in North Carolina, Knight-Ridder owns the two daily newspapers—*The Charlotte Observer* and *The Charlotte News*. But in addition, Charlotte has two VHF and three UHF television stations, plus 16 radio stations and a twice-weekly community newspaper. And in the surrounding counties of the Piedmont Carolinas where the *Observer* has roughly half its circulation and has been the morning newspaper for many years, there are a large number of steadily improving afternoon newspapers which serve their communities well and are giving the *Observer* strong competition. Any newspaper which rests on its laurels in that sort of dynamic competitive environment is going to have trouble.

A more subtle form of competition for newspapers is the proliferation of specialized print media: books and magazines on very narrow subjects addressed to small but intensely interested audiences. If the amount of time and money people spend on information media of all kinds remains constant over time, as suggested by professor Max McCombs of the University of Texas, then these publications represent another very important kind of competition for all newspapers.

Finally, let me address a question that understandably concerns a number of critics of large newspaper groups. That is the danger of excessive centralized power over the dissemination of news and commentary in this country.

The first point to be made is that the day of the press lord in America is long gone. Anybody who tried to use a group of newspapers these days to propagate the owner's political or policy views wouldn't get very far. Today's readers are simply too sophisticated and skeptical to swallow such a thing.

In the newspaper groups that have grown up since World War II, the strong trend has been toward local autonomy in news and editorial decision-making. Significant departures from that pattern are so unusual—as in the case involving the Panax newspapers—that they make news and attract a great deal of flak, which is healthy.

In our company—and most others I am familiar with—nobody at the top dictates what goes into a local newspaper. The corporate role basically is to pick good people to edit our newspapers and then do everything we can to help them do their best work.

Newspapers by their very nature belong, in a real sense, to the communities they serve—and newspaper editing is an intensely local process. There is no other way to do it right. Any group-owned newspaper which carries a branch-office flavor will be distrusted and resented. And it should be.

There are, of course, no sure guarantees that we will have no bad newspaper groups, just as there are no sure guarantees under the First Amendment that society will never have to endure a bad or irresponsible individually owned newspaper. The Founding Fathers set out to protect free expression, not to assure the quality of that expression.

In a speech at the Yale Law School in 1974, Supreme Court Justice Potter Stewart pointed out that publishing is "the only organized private business that is given explicit constitutional protection." In our constitutional scheme, the press is specially designated to be independent of, and not beholden to, the government.

American newspapers today are fallible and human institutions. They make mistakes. Sometimes they are unfair, and occasionally even irresponsible. But overall, in my view, the press today is more principled and professional than at any time in our history—and is widely acknowledged as the best in the world. For all our blemishes, we are serving our country and our citizens vigorously and well. And newspapers owned by groups are a large part of that story.

9 sports

The fourth major section in a newspaper is really a combination of the other three, but with a specific focus—sports. A good sports section includes news about sports and recreation, features, opinion columns, schedules of coming events, and even letters to the (sports) editor.

It is easy for a sports editor to plan the section because, by and large, all the sports *events* of the year are lined out in schedules. Naturally, the section also needs to cover *issues* in sports—how much money should be allocated for women's sports or whether athletes really work at the jobs they receive as part of a financial aid package. Because game times are known far in advance, the sports editor can plan coverage for special events or important games more easily than can the news editor, whose coverage is not nearly so clear-cut or prescheduled.

Good sports coverage includes intercollegiate competitive sports for men and women, recreation and intramural activities, and physical-education classes. Intercollegiate sports belong in every sports section (Fig. 9–1). Fans at your school will want to know how each team and individual progresses throughout the season. Because the local professional press also covers at least the major sports at your school, however, the school's sports section should offer slightly different coverage: for example, in-depth interviews with players instead of just quoting the coach, behind-the-scenes looks at the various sports and athletes, and increased coverage of "minor" sports. Although your coverage, to a certain extent, should match the interest of your readers—football stories will be more popular than fencing stories—both sports deserve some coverage. And one place you can beat the local paper is in coverage of the minor sports (Fig. 9–2).

Although women's sports have achieved recognition in most newspapers, the stories are still sometimes forgotten, relegated to the bottom half of the page, or pushed to the back pages. Women's teams deserve the same coverage as men's (half your audience may well be female). And if the men's team is having a mediocre season and the women's is leading the league, the women deserve more coverage than the men. Temper your belief in what you think the readers *want* to read about with what you know from experience *should* deserve the most coverage.

On the other hand, sometimes losers provide better stories, especially if there has been a history of winning or if a team has had an incredible losing streak. Winners are sometimes guilty of spouting nothing but clichés, while losers, deep in self-analysis, can offer better quotes and stories. The bottom line is: Don't get caught in the same old sports coverage ruts. Look for the unique.

Along with major intercollegiate sports coverage, plan regular and consistent coverage of recreational and intramural sports. If your college has recreation majors, look to their department for news and features. If you have a skiing club or a rugby club, then cover them as well. There may be as much reader interest in the intramural basketball championships as in the cross-country team, even though

Figure 9–1. This sports front shows a wide range of coverage: major sports teams, recruiting successes, ladies' golf, and a sports column at the bottom. (Courtesy of the *Auburn Plainsman*)

Sports

November 16, 1989·   *The Auburn Plainsman*   Section C

West German team slam dunks Tigers

Jennifer Allen
Sports Editor

> What: Auburn vs. Bamberg
> Where: Memorial Coliseum
> Result: Bamberg 115, Auburn 96

In a game that was closer at times than the score indicated, the Auburn Tigers lost an exhibition game to TTL Bamberg of West Germany by a score of 115-96 Saturday night.

"We knew they were a good basketball team coming in here, and I think that's what we've got," Coach Tommy Joe Eagles said.

The Tigers' opponent Saturday was a pro team that participated in Germany's version of the Final Four last year. This game was the third of a 10-game U.S. tour.

The Tigers kept the game close in the first half, even leading with 9:57 to go in the period as John Caylor hit a layup to put the Tigers up 25-23.

That was to be Auburn's last lead of the game, however, as the West Germans had the lead 56-45 at halftime.

and they never relinquished it after that.

During the second half, the Tigers couldn't cut the lead to less than 12 points. At one point, Bamberg led Auburn by a margin of 24.

"We wanted to use this as an evaluation of where we are," Eagles said.

Derrick Dennison led the Tigers' offense with 22 total points. Caylor had 15, Ronnie Battle had 13 and Chris Brandt ended the game with 12.

"Chris Brandt played well tonight," Eagles said. "Derrick Dennison showed

See **Exhibition**, C-6

Basketball teams net 7 early

Greg Klein
Assistant Sports Editor

The Auburn men's and women's basketball teams signed a total of seven high school seniors to letters of intent to play basketball on the Plains next year during the early signing period.

The men's team announced the signing of four forwards last week: Jeffrey Belmer, Cameron Boozer, Robert Shannon and Aaron Swinson. The women's team announced

three signees Tuesday: guard Kim Mays, forward Bonita McFarland and forward Joy Berry.

Boozer averaged 26 points and 12 rebounds in his junior year at Lanett (Ala.) High School. He is the first player from the state of Alabama that new Auburn coach Tommy Joe Eagles has recruited.

Eagles had stated previously that signing Alabama state players was a high priority.

"We're delighted to have Boozer as

See **Signees**, C-6

Cliff Oliver/staff

Chris Brandt, no. 44, goes for a basket despite the West German defenders. Brandt led the Tigers with six rebounds and had 12 points in the game.

> Next Game
> What: Auburn vs. Georgia
> Where: Athens, Ga.
> When: 11:40 a.m. CST

Georgia

Bulldogs prepare for Tigers following upset over Gators

Greg Klein
Assistant Sports Editor

Another chapter in one of the longest running feuds in the country will take place Saturday when Auburn travels to Athens to play the Georgia Bulldogs.

It will be the 93rd time the two teams play. Last year the Tigers won 20-10 to take a one game lead 43-42-7.

"Any time Auburn and Georgia get together it's going to be exciting football," Auburn head coach Pat Dye said.

The Bulldogs are coming off a 17-10 win against Florida and have a record of 6-3, 4-2 in the SEC.

Since Ray Goff became head coach, the Bulldogs have changed their offensive style, according to Dye.

"It used to be that all you had to do to stop Georgia was stop their running game, but now they've got a balanced attack between the run and the pass," Dye said.

On offense the Bulldogs are led by quarterback Greg Talley, who has thrown for 1,186 and six touchdowns.

"Talley reminds me of (former Georgia quarterback) Reggie Campbell," Dye said. "He's not going to burn you for an 80-yard run, but he will run seven or eight yards for a first down to keep your defense honest."

Tight end Kirt Warner is the Bulldogs leading receiver with 311 yards on 24 receptions and one touchdown.

Running backs Rodney Hampton and Brian Cleveland are also targets for Talley out of the backfield.

Hampton is Georgia's leading rusher and the second overall in the SEC. He has rushed for 934 yards on 192 carries and scored 10 touchdowns.

"Hampton is the best runner we'll face all year, and that includes Emmit Smith and Reggie Cobb," Dye said.

Georgia kicker John Kasay is tied for first in the NCAA with 18 field goals.

On defense the Bulldogs will also have a different look than when Vince Dooley was coach.

"They are playing different schemes on defense, but they still look like Georgia in that you can move the ball on them, but the closer you get to the goal line the harder they play," Dye said.

Safety Ben Smith leads the SEC in interceptions with eight.

"If anyone deserves credit on their defense it's Smith," Dye said.

Turnovers will be the key to the

See **Georgia**, C-6

Lady Tiger golfers drive to rank 6th

Team receives national recognition during fall season after successful tournament play

Chris Stewart/staff

Jay Coulter
Staff Writer

Last year at the Lady Sun Devil Open in Tempe, Ariz., many of the top women's golf teams in the country were surprised when Auburn's team was second after the first round.

This year Bud Marsee's lady Tigers are one of those top teams.

The lady Tigers are currently ranked sixth in the country by the National Golf Coaches Association and third nationally by Florida Golf Week.

Marsee said he isn't surprised by his team's fast start.

"I thought we could be good, because we have a lot of solid players returning and also a lot of good new players coming along," Marsee said.

Following last season's first-place finish at the SEC Championship and 13th-place finish at the NCAA Championships, the lady Tigers have continued their successes this fall.

They have received solid performances by the whole team, especially from seniors Joal Rieder and Diane Rama.

Rieder, who was an All-American a

year ago, has had a big year, winning the individual title at the Lady Kat Invitational in Lexington, Ky., and finishing in the top 10 at The Tiger-Tide Intercollegiate and Dick Mcguire Invitational.

While winning the Lady Kat Invitational, she paced Auburn to the team championship as well. Rieder is currently ranked tenth in the NCAA individual rankings.

Marsee said the turning point for this team came last spring at the Arizona State Tournament.

"It was great," he said. "We were the only team east of the Mississippi playing in the tournament.

"We ended up finishing fourth overall, beating programs like UCLA and Stanford. Our kids realized they could play with anybody in the country.

Auburn's schedule doesn't slack up after the holidays. The lady Tigers travel to California in January to take on more Western powerhouses in the Yamaha Classic in Palm Desert.

The SEC Championship takes place May 5-7 in Greensboro, Ga., while the NCAA Championship is May 16-23 in Hilton Head, S.C.

Lectron continues Auburn running back tradition

Saturday marked the beginning of the "Electronic" era of Auburn football. Darrell "Lectron" Williams, the Alabama player of the year last year out of Vigor High School, made his presence known against Louisiana Tech scoring two touchdowns and rushing for 108 yards.

"I've always felt that if I could get in the game I could make something happen," Williams said.

Williams got the chance to show his stuff because of the injuries that have sidelined Stacy Danley and hampered James Joseph.

"He didn't disappoint anyone – cer-

Greg Klein
Assistant Sports Editor

tainly not the fans who have been waiting to see the athlete they have heard so much about. Williams was well known throughout the state after leading Vigor to two Alabama state championships.

When he decided to attend Auburn, he picked a school that has a history of

great running backs.

That tradition may have started with Monk Gafford who in 1942 helped the Tigers upset the Georgia Bulldogs 27-13. The Bulldogs were the top-ranked team in the nation at the time and were heading to the Rose Bowl.

The tradition continued into the '50s with Joe Childress and Fob James, who would later become the governor of Alabama.

Jimmy Sidle became the second Tiger back to rush for more than 1,000 yards in a season in 1963.

In the past two decades the number of outstanding backs to play for

Auburn is astonishing.

William Andrews began playing for the Tigers in 1976. That same year Joe Cribbs began playing for the Tigers and in 1977, so did James Brooks.

In five years the trio amassed more than 8,000 yards rushing.

As those three went on to distinguished NFL careers they were replaced by Lionel "Little Train" James in 1980 and Brent Fulwood and Tommy Agee in 1983. Each of them has also gone on to pro careers.

Then there was Bo.

Bo Jackson came to Auburn in 1982, and in his four years here he broke

almost every Auburn rushing record that existed on his way to becoming Auburn's second Heisman Trophy winner in 1985.

Included in Jackson's records were career scoring (274), rushing yards in a season (1,786) and rushing yards in a college career (4,303).

Since then runners like Curtis Stewart, James Joseph and Stacy Danley have continued the tradition.

Soon it will be Williams' turn for greatness, and it's likely that he will succeed.

And Saturday was just the beginning.

---

the cross-country team competes with other schools. Don't get trapped into thinking the only important sports involve interschool competition.

Physical-education classes also need to be covered in the sports section. Although few outright news stories come from PE classes—except for new instructors, classes, or the occasional accident—they are excellent places to look for features. A surge in badminton's popularity may, for instance, cause three classes to be added. That fact could tie into a feature on badminton, on its popularity worldwide, and maybe on tips from an expert. Sports features may cover *anything* that has to do with sports (Fig. 9–3).

Figure 9–2. This sports front also displays wide coverage, but the columnist is run down the first column. (Courtesy of *The Advocate*)

SPORTS The Advocate Friday, May 5, 1989 7

Michael Hughes

Off the record

Coach, heart work in Warriors favor

The Warriors swept and the Jazz wept. Having lost the last six games of the regular season, the Warriors entered their series against the Utah Jazz talking as if they had no more of a chance against the champions of the Midwestern Division than Manute Bol has of starting at point guard. Just when it appeared that the Warriors spell of magic had dried up, Don Nelson pulled another rabbit out of his hat.

After the Jazz were lulled to sleep by the Warriors, they experienced a terrible nightmare, and when they awoke they were groggy and utterly defenseless against the sneak tactics of the Warriors, which proved not to be a dream, but the real thing.

In fact, it seemed as if it were the Warriors who were dreaming, not a nightmare but the kind of dream they would be sorry to have interrupted by the light of day. The Warriors dreamed of conquering a foreign land behind their fearless general, who was dressed in shining armour and tennis shoes.

The Warriors didn't just defeat some scrappers, they beat the team that many of the experts said had the best chance of beating the mighty Lakers. The Jazz had the Mailman, the league's top assist-maker, the league's best sixth man, they play Eastern style slug it out low post basketball, they had the home court advantage, and they nearly made the NBA finals last year.

Warriors overmatched

Although it may be inaccurate to say the Warriors have no talent, as Nelson has been heard to say, it is safe to say that they should have been overmatched by the league's best defensive team. This is the team that gave the Lakers fits until the end of the seventh game last year was predicted to hold the prolific Warrior scorers down. In the games between the teams this year, the Warriors won the wide open high scoring affairs, but Utah prevailed in the games when the scoring was low.

Many people felt the Warriors had been winning with mirrors throughout the year. A good record against the Eastern Conference teams, which the Warriors rarely see, compared to the not-so-good record against western teams that are more familiar with Golden State's tactics were pointed to as proof of this theory. The logic was that Nelson could surprise a team for 48 minutes and win a ballgame, but over time, playing the same team over and over, the Warriors' deficiencies would show.

Sweep defied logic

According to that logic, the Warriors should have faded quickly in the playoffs. But never underestimate a Don Nelson team. Nelson had the Warriors push the pace, and he adjusted when Utah was successful at slowing it down.

In game one, the Warriors were successful running an up-tempo gameplan, which was the key to their regular season victories against the Jazz. They frustrated Karl Malone by constantly bumping him, making him work for every inch he didn't get. On offense they got the ball to the big guns, Chris Mullin and Mitch Richmond who shot quickly and often as they immediately stole the home court advantage by winning in Utah.

In game two, the Jazz converted the game from a horserace to a chess match, but Jerry Sloan should have known better than to play chess with Nelson. Malone scored 37 points as the Jazz led after three quarters, but was put into checkmate in the fourth quarter as each and every one of the Warriors helped disrupt him, holding him scoreless, and allowing the Jazz only seven field goals in the final period.

The Warriors knew that game three would be tougher than the previous two, but they also knew that if they lost, each succeeding game would more challenging than the one before. So, in front of the home fans, the Warriors took the bull by its horns and mercilessly attacked the Jazz while they were still reeling from two losses at home.

Can't play it safe

The Warriors did what Nelson said they would have to do, attack the opposition and not play it safe. For Golden State to win, Nelson knew that the team would have to take risks against quality opposition. Nelson is the master of risking putting an extraordinarily small lineup on the floor, with the possibility that the lineup could be dominated and dig a hole for the team, and allowing them the freedom to play their game without fear of being reprimanded from the sideline.

Although they will have a tougher time of it against the Phoenix Suns, one of the hottest teams in the league, the Warriors showed the country the value of big hearts and good coaching.

They also sent a message that if Ralph Sampson can be rejuvenated and the Warriors draft a productive player, they will be a serious force to be dealt with in the coming years, and not only in the first round of the playoffs.

Express runs wild at BVC finals

Runners on track for NorCal

By Rick Waters
Staff writer

The Express women overshadowed the men in last week's Bay Valley Conference Trials in Sacramento, as both teams had a successful meet.

The women, all four of them, placed second in the BVC while the men brought home a third place team finish.

"The team did all it could do to win," track coach Steve Greer said. "The other schools had a full compliment of field athletes that we could not compete against."

The women boast six conference champions.

Michele McNair led the way with a victory in the triple jump, soaring 36-feet-4-inches, followed by a win in the 100-meter high hurdles, with a time of 15.5 seconds, and finally taking first in the long jump with a leap of 13-feet-5.2-inches.

McNair also teamed with Yonetta Olden, Pam Terrell and Kenia Lockhard to win the 4x100-meter relay.

Olden took the 200 with a personal best 25.92 as well as placing second in the 400, which ended her streak of first place finishes in league competition.

Terrell breezed by the competition with a victory in the 100 clocking a time of 12.72. She also finished second behind Olden in the 200 with a time of 22.6. Lockhard took third in the 800 meters.

"The effort by the women is a testimony to their competitive spirit and their never say die attitude," said Greer. Although they did not make as much noise as the women, the men managed to take third in the conference trials.

Sean Cumby and Brent Merritt took center stage in the 400, as they posted their best times of the season. Cumby won in a time of 47.5 and Merritt finished a fraction of a second behind his teammate, also being timed at 47.5.

Both times would have won the California-Stanford meet, held on the same day. The winning time at that meet was 47.57.

Cumby and Merritt later combined with Dave Williams and Byron John to win the 4x400 meter relay.

In the 1500, Shane Healy first lapped the entire field, then cruised to victory in 4:00.9 seconds. Healy returned to win the 5000 in 16:21.9.

Rodney Tucker took second in the 100 in 10.85 and also helped Cumby, Meritt and Williams take second in the the 4x100 meter relay. Doug Conners won the 100-meter high hurdles with a seasons best 14.4.

The Express will compete in the NorCal meet today and next Friday with state meet bids on the line.

Corey Penaluna/The Advocate

Running on air

Sean Cumby and Brent Merritt finished first and second in the 400 meter race at the Bay Valley Conference meet finals. Cumby edged Merritt by less than a tenth of a second. Both runners have advanced to the NorCal meet which starts today at West Valley College in Stockton.

Comets clobber Mendocino in vain

No post-season play for sluggers

By Neil Keck
Staff writer

Now playing for pride, the Comet baseball team showed some of that Tuesday in its final home game of the season, clobbering Mendocino 10-2 to up their conference record to 13-7.

CCC travels to Yuba College for a doubleheader Saturday to wrap up the 1989 season.

They also have a game remaining against conference leader Cosumnes River as head coach Larry Quirico's protest of a game two weeks ago was upheld by Bay Valley Conference officials.

Quirico played the second game of a doubleheader against Cosumnes under protest because Mark Bonini was not allowed to continue playing as a designated hitter after being taken out as a relief pitcher in the fifth inning. The Comets ended up losing the game in extra innings. A date for the game had not been announced as of press time.

Against Mendocino, CCC was helped by effective pitching from Renee Johnson and five Mendocino errors in its victory Tuesday.

Johnson, despite issuing nine walks, hurled seven innings of one-run, four-hit ball while striking out four. He said he could have pitched better, but was satisfied nonetheless.

"My change-up was outstanding today," Johnson said. "It got me out of some jams, and I struck out batters with that pitch. I had a lot of walks, but I'm glad I went seven innings."

The Comets, meanwhile, jumped out to a 4-0 lead and never looked back. A four-run sixth inning iced it for CCC.

In the sixth, after two were out, Roger Tsurumoto grounded a single and advanced to third when Brian Basso lashed a double. Bonini then drilled a single to knock in both runners. Reggie Robinson continued the onslaught by blasting an inside-the-park homer to center for his sixth round-tripper of the year, and second inside-the-parker.

Basso also had a run-scoring single, Tsurumoto went 3-for-4 with two RBI, and Bobby Barton smacked an RBI double to contribute to the Comets' run production.

CCC looked like it would rather be in a boxing ring than on a baseball diamond during a 7-4 loss to Solano College here last Saturday.

Solano fought back from a 4-0 deficit, scoring a run in the sixth before getting to pitcher Jim Greenlee for five runs in the seventh, capped off by Ray Dobard's monstrous grand slam to left.

"I was proud of the way we played," Quirico said. "Jim pitched a good game, but unfortunately we didn't score enough runs for him."

Greenlee scattered six hits over seven-plus innings, allowing seven earned runs while striking out five.

Falcon pitcher Paul Perkins, after a shaky start, silenced the Comet bats, firing a seven-hit complete game while striking out ten.

Comet infielder Curtis Crews was slapped with a one-game suspension after he attempted to hit the Solano catcher seconds after he swung and missed an inside pitch to end the eighth inning. Both benched emptied, but no punches were thrown.

"I felt the umpires started more than they controlled," said Quirico, referring to the ump's constant warnings to both dugouts to quiet down the verbal barrages both teams were exchanging.

Hot-hitting Reggie Robinson went 3-for-4 with three RBI, including another inside-the-park homer as the Comets manhandled Napa Valley 13-3 last week.

Bonini cracked an RBI double for one of his two RBI, and Mike Lawn went 2-for-3 with one RBI for CCC.

Skip Plover held Napa scoreless until the ninth, when the Chiefs scored three runs off him. Plover didn't issue any walks during his complete-game stint to record his fourth BVC victory.

Four-year schools recruit eight cagers

By Michael Cosgrove
Staff writer

The men's and women's basketball teams having completed championship seasons will send a host of players on to four-year universities.

Brent Merritt, an All-Bay Valley Conference performer, who led the 28-6 Comets in scoring and is currently running for the Express track team, has signed a letter of intent to attend the University of Washington on a full scholarship.

"I think he's going to represent this institution well," said basketball coach Odis Allison. "You couldn't paint a better picture for opportunity than he's got."

> ***I won't be totally satisfied until they receive their bachelor's degree.***
> **—Paul DeBolt**
> **women's basketball coach**

Comets' sixth man and All-BVC guard Demetrius Mitchell possibly will attend the University of South Carolina, while power forward David Barksdale is leaning toward neighboring South Carolina State University.

Big man Maurice Dickens has been contacted by Akron University, the University of Cincinnati, and Fullerton State University, but has not yet made a decision on what school he will attend next year.

All-BVC small forward Scotty Thurman is considering attending Cal Poly Pomona where he will continue his basketball career.

All-BVC sharpshooter Charlotte Wiley, the fourth leading scorer in California, has signed a letter of intent to attend Fullerton State. She will receive a scholarship to play softball for one of the top women's college softball programs, and also plans on playing basketball for the Lady Titans.

All-NorCal guard Shelby Cox has committed to attend UC Davis where she was the Aggies number one junior college basketball recruit. Cox is slated to play small forward for Davis according to CCC head coach Paul DeBolt.

Mary Jeffries, who led the state in rebounds last year for the Lady Comets, is headed to Hayward State University where she will continue to pull down boards for the Lady Pioneers.

Point guard Lisa Nakamura will find a familiar face no matter which school she decides to attend next year. The state's leader in assists, Nakamura, will either join Cox at Davis or Jeffries at Hayward.

"I'm really proud that they're transferring," said DeBolt. "But I told them that's one step and I won't be totally satisfied until they receive their bachelor's degrees."

Netters set sights on league tourney

By Michael Hughes
Sports editor

After a disappointing season the tennis team is hoping to gain some respect in the Bay Valley Conference Tournament that continues today and Saturday at Yuba College. The event began Thursday.

Each league team will send six players to the tournament and each player will play singles and doubles. The tournament is single elimination, with the quarterfinalists advancing to the Northern California Regional Tournament at West Valley College May 11 to 13.

Twelve of the 64 players will be seeded. Coach Louis Toschi said that the bulk of the seeded players will be the number one player from their school, but a few of the number two and three players from the stronger schools will also be seeded.

Although CCC finished sixth in the BVC, Toschi feels his players have a good chance to make some noise in Marysville. Billy Barton, Mike Mee, Ed Alfaro, James Knox, Mark Channell and Leonard Malherbe will represent CCC at Yuba and the three doubles teams are Barton and Mee, Alfaro and Knox and Channell and Malherbe.

"Billy (Barton) has a good chance," Toschi said, "Even our three, four, five and six players could win a couple of matches in the league tournament."

While the team as a whole has not looked impressive the last couple weeks of the season, number one seed Barton has been a bright spot, being named the team's most recent player of the week. Barton has won six of his last seven matches, and the one he lost was against Marin's number one, who Toschi feels will be the top seed in the tournament. Three of Barton's wins during his late streak have come against opponents who had defeated him earlier in the year.

The team finished with a record of 4-12, 5-17 overall, but Toschi feels the team had a good year nevertheless.

"We had good team spirit, we just didn't have a lot of tennis background," Toschi said. "There is no losers on this team, because everybody played as hard as they could every match."

Billy Barton
Hopes to win league tourney

Figure 9–3. A sports editor must select a wide variety of sports features. (From *The Ranger*, San Antonio College)

Dodger Dollies entertain baseball crowd
Sports
Texas stompers romp
in gooey wrestling pits
XAS ARMADILL

Useless Wilson case, strike take the fun out of sports

carl
walworth

Any day now, all little league baseball managers and members of the Major Indoor Soccer League are going to go on strike and a third-teamer on the Illinois football team is going to sue the Big Ten for $72 million and another year of eligibility.

Well, of course, that's a big hoax, but what would happen if that were the case.? Not many people would care. Most wouldn't even give it a second thought.

After all, who cares? It's a long time before the indoor soccer season starts, and it hasn't become a favorite sport of many Americans.

Little league baseball is kids stuff, and only affects the parents and players involved. And if someone who never played a minute for the Illini decided to sue, the problem would never get the attention the Dave Wilson case has received.

Why has the Wilson case and the baseball strike remained the two top stories sports stories in Illinois?

Not because they are entertaining, interesting or fun, but because they deal with a starting quarterback whose case eventually led to the University being heavily sanc-

tioned by the Big Ten and, with America's pasttime. It's just not summer without baseball, and without it, there has to be something to fill the pages with.

Neither is really sport. Both belong in the crime/courts roundup with a couple of paragraphs each.

But the implications and effects of each make them worthy of the headlines. Headlines which are unnecessary.

Nobody really benefits from all of this except the lawyers. Who ever heard of Robert Auler or Byron Gregory before Wilson's suit. Marvin Miller and Ray Grebey weren't big names nationally before the compensation issue arose.

The baseball players aren't going to starve. The owners aren't hurting either.

They don't have to pay salaries, maintenance men or big light bills and they still have their insurance.

The Big Ten has not become any stronger since the sanctions. In fact, many people have lost a little respect for the prestigious league. And the torturous legal battle hasn't been the thrill of Dave Wilson's life.

And since everybody else suffers, one would think reasonable people could strike a compromise and get back to business as usual.

But reason doesn't appear to enter the picture. Egos, greed and stubbornness are the big factors.

Rather than settle an issue which seems to come up every year, the baseball players and owners have consistently put things off to the last minute and then started calling each other names. Again, the lawyers are the primary beneficiary since they get many months, rather than a few days, at the bargaining table. This is their chance for the national spotlight.

The owners aren't going to be able to turn the tables on free agency, so why don't they

give in a little bit? The players have to give some too, because if they break the bank, they will be a big loser.

The Big Ten is in a save-face situation with the questioning of the appropriateness of the sanctions. The University is not the only school involved whose integrity has been attacked. Many people's sentiment questions the integrity and responsibility of the faculty representatives—the core of the conference.

And Wilson certainly isn't reaping rewards, except for a little publicity. But the quarterback would likely rather be remembered for his 621-yards passing against Ohio State instead of being the guy who sued the Big Ten.

Now he has to decide whether he wants to continue his lawsuit, which is looking dimmer as time goes on, or enter the National Football League's supplemental draft July 1. His fight has come a long way, but he'll be taking a big chance if he continues his eligibility case after July 1.

The sad part of both situations is that things don't have to be this way.

It's time to put the sport back into sports.

Figure 9–4. A sports section serves an opinion function through a regular column. (From *The Daily Illini,* **Illini Publishing Company, Champaign, IL)**

A good sports section always has a column written by the editor or sports staff members. The sports section is the only place in the newspaper where certain events are reported. Just as with events in the news columns, the paper is responsible to the reader for placing these sports events into a context, for helping the reader understand what is going on in the world of sports.

The sports column can take a stand for or against something, explain an action by the state legislature or school administration, or analyze a recent trend (a rash of knee injuries on the old track). In this way the sports column acts as an opinion column (Fig. 9–4). Other opinions on sports issues may be voiced in a pro/con format. A column can also talk about a personality or an event more personally than a feature story can. Whatever the make-up of the column, it must be a regular part of a sports section.

The sports section can print its own letters to the editor. Though small papers rarely receive enough letters to warrant a regular spot in the sports section, most major papers print letters to the sports editor in this section.

The sports section also should include game summaries (box scores), statistics, and schedules. Sports fans love statistics! Game summaries may appear with the story (Fig. 9–5) or in a section all to themselves, in which case a line at the end of every story should refer the reader to the summary section.

Statistics, such as a list of league leaders in various sports or a list of school-record holders, can be used as fillers. Set them in type at the beginning of every season and you'll have an easy solution to the recurrent problem of how to fill a hole in the page. Publishing sports schedules regularly, either sport by sport or game by game, will help sports fans plan their attendance at games.

Weekly or less frequently published newspapers should concentrate their sports coverage on *preview*, not *review*. Leave the game coverage to the local daily paper. Let's say that a weekly newspaper published on Friday covers a football team that plays on Saturday. Were the paper to write the game story for last Saturday's game—which many papers do—the news would be very old indeed. Most followers of the team would know the results and details of the six-day-old game. The important game is not last week's, but tomorrow's. Lead off stories on sports that are still in season with the preview of the upcoming game and conclude with a wrap-up of the previous week's game, preferably with lots of quotes and analysis (Fig. 9–6). Read *Sports Illustrated* to see how events are covered a week after they happened. You'll be reading some of the best sports reporting in the country.

sports — the campus 5/2/80 5

Teed off?

Photo by Jerry Pfefferkorn

Ted Walters chips his way out of a sand trap on the seventh hole during a match against Fresno City College last Tuesday. The Giants as a team did not qualify for Valley Conference tournament play but two golfers, Terry Treece and Greg Miller, individually qualified for NorCal.

Golfers over par, win over Mustangs

For the first time in several years, the COS golf won't be participating as a team in the Valley Conference tournament next week.

The Giants, 7-6-1 suffered their first sub par season in over 10 years and closed out regulare season play Thursday with a stunning upset over conference leader San Joaquin Delta College, 363-383, to send the VC race into a tie between the Mustangs and Fresno City College.

Only two golfers, freshmen Terry Treece and Greg Miller qualified for the Northern California match which starts Monday at the Rancho Miranda course in Sacramento.

Even though the Giants did not have the kind of season a COS team is used too, according to coach Roy Taylor, every conference team rose to the occasion to play the Giants.

"Every team shot its best round of the year against us," he said. "Tuesday, Fresno shot a 374, its best mark to date and Modesto for the first time shot a round under 400, against us."

But the Giants didn't let the conference end without having their presence felt. Going down the stretch Thursday, Delta needed a victory to clinch the VC title outright but a victory for the Giants would send the conference race into a log jam between Delta and the Fresno Rams.

"Our guys were really looking forward to playing Delta," Taylor said. "They knew they could play the role of spoilers and they wanted to have something to do with the staging the conference champion."

And that's exactly what the Giants did, trouncing Delta by 20 shots on the Giants home course. It was the best match points a COS team has shot in over two years, carding the 363 for a two over par.

"It was a nice way to end the season," Taylor said in a telephone enterview. "The team played an excellent round of golf today (Thursday) and I'm very proud of them."

Ted Walters, the only sophomore playing for the Giants, ended the season a key note. He came away with the medalist honors carding an unbelievable three under par 69 with three birdies to wrap up his career with COS.

However, Miller was hot on his tail finishing the 72 hole course with a 70, recording four birdies along the way.

Paul Baxley, the second of four freshmen playing against Delta finished the afternoon with an even par 72.

The next two golfers to finish the 18 hole course were Treece and Rod Banks with 76's. For Banks it was his first match play and according to Taylor he played a very good round of golf.

"Going with the four freshmen worked out very well for us," Taylor said. "It has been the freshmen all season long that has been our strength. This season was kind of a rebuilding one, after their performances today (Thursday) will be back in the running next year."

Giants' doubleheader: last chance

Tomorrow the Giants host Modesto Junior College for an afternoon of baseball in a doubleheader.

There's nothing special about that — nothing special except that it's a pair of games the Giants would desperately like to win.

There's no title at state, but the Giants would like to win it as much as if it was a championship game.

The 1980 season has been a disappointment, according to coach Bert Holt, who has seen his Giants fall to a 8-11 Valley Conference record, 2-7 in the second half. They are 15-15 overall.

Holt believes a win might salvage the season in the players' eyes.

"The season has definitely been a disappointment," Holt said. "It's been disappointing to me and the players. The kids didn't play as well as they're capable of playing, and I didn't do the job of coaching I would have liked. Looking back on the season, I would have definitely done some things differently.

"We may have overestimated the background, knowledge and experience of the players."

Holt described Modesto as the kind of club that "battles."

"There's nothing special about Modesto," he said. "They're basically a defensive ball club, but they peck away at you — that's how they beat us before (7-3).

"They're like us offensively. They don't have much power, so we might have the edge there."

Modesto is 3-6 in the second half of VC play, and 9-20 overall.

There is, however, one bright spot for the Giants: next season.

Holt is hoping that this year's experience will help out next year. He'll have returning starters everywhere except at first base. He's also looking to a few incoming freshmen to round out the team.

In the meantime, however, there's always the summer and winter leagues to compete in between now and next spring's conference season.

Sports shorts

Women nine tie for title

The women's softball team gained a three-way tie for the Valley Conference title Wednesday afternoon as they swept a twin bill from American River College. They won the first game, 4-3, behind the pitching of Deb Camacho, and then trounced the Beavers, 11-1, with Sherri Gillan picking up the win. San Joaquin Delta College, which was leading the VC race by one game, needed to sweep Modesto Junior College to win the title out right. But the Panthers had a different idea as they lost the opener but took the night cap, sending the conference into the three-way tie. Cosumnes River gained the other spot with its double-header victories over Reedley College. The play-off game has been set for 1 p.m. tomorrow at Sacramento City College. All three teams ended the VC race with 11-4 records.

Intramural Expo winners

Tom Conda battled it out with Peter Logan and Terry Doss in the Frisbee competition to win the overall title. For his efforts, Conda received a world class Frisbee with Logan and Doss winning a free meal ticket. Logan also was the individual winner in the run/throw competition with Doss capturing the distance/accuracy event. Conda won the accuracy event which consisted of throwing the Frisbee through a huge hoop. In backgammon, Verni Vilhauer defeated Gahram Govderzian to win the first place award, a new backgammon set. Bruce Brown won the first place trophy in the mini slot car racing, edging out Roy Rinderle for the winners circle honors. Nobody was able to defeat Larry Kilen in the chess tournament as he took on over 10 students—all at the same time. His foes had a 90 minute time limit to defeat him. In wrestling, Joe Knoblauch won the 160-pound-and-under title defeating Brown, as little but mighty Dennis Townsend defeated Joshua Washington for the 160-pound-and-up title. Each winner received a trophy.

Tankers send six, two divers to state meet

The COS women's swimming team sent its strength to the State Swimming Meet which got underway Thursday in East Los Angeles.

The women's team took only five members of its third place Valley Conference team and will compete in four relays with two individuals competing in the 50 and 100 backstrokes.

The men's team only has one swimmer, John Blair, who qualified for the state meet. He will compete in the 200 and 400 Intermediates (IM).

COS also will be represented in the diving area with Bill Ryan and Melanie Jennings qualifying for the event. Ryan captured a second place finish in the one-meter and a third place in the three-meter boards in last weekend's Northern California diving competition. Jennings took 10th as the top 12 placers qualified for the state meet.

The 200 freestyle team consisting of Carol Fast, Allison Case, Karen Allen and Pam Scholl have clocked 1:46.3 this season, but Bricker said the team is three tenths off last year's sixth place finish of the COS relay.

"The women are capable of bringing their times down," Bricker said. "If they can do that they should end in the top 10."

And to Bricker, that is one thing she hopes every team will do—finish in the top 10.

Besides the 200 freestyle relay team, the Giants' 400 freestyle, 200 and 400 IM relays qualified for the meet.

Teri Holt, Fast, Case and Allen will each swim on the IM teams while Scholl replaces Holt for the freestyle relays.

Fast and Allen also will swim in the 50 and 100 backstroke events. According to Bricker, Fast should be seeded third or fourth in the 50 while fifth in the 100.

"Last year, Carol was seeded pretty well," Bricker said. "But she had one bad turn and it was over for her.

"In this competition one little slip up, whether off the ladder or on a turn you can almost count yourself out."

Case should be seeded in the top 15, according to Bricker, who receives the times of all the junior college swimmers in California in a swimming booklet weekly.

Fast also qualified for the 200 and 400 freestyle events but because those events would be swam back-to-back, Bricker thought it would be better for her to concentrate on the relays and the backstroke events.

The Giants finished Valley Conference play last week with a 6-3 mark and a 8-3 overall.

Tennis teams aim for title

The teams' seasons are over.

Now it's the players' turn.

Both tennis teams are currently involved in their respective Valley Conference tournaments — the men in Fresno and the women at Modesto.

Rounds started yesterday for both teams, run through today and conclude tomorrow.

Everyone making it to the third round qualified for next week's NorCal tournament as well.

The women, after going through conference action undefeated (14-0), were expecting (before leaving for Modesto yesterday morning) to do well, while the men were less confident.

"In the past, we've usually qualified (for NorCal) two singles and a doubles team," women's coach Barbara Strong said. "But this year we're expecting to qualify twice as many."

Four players, the doubles teams of Patti Guevara-Lisa Jacobo and Patti Hobbs-Jackie Simon, qualified for NorCal without so much as lifting a racket.

Both teams received first-round byes, and because to go to NorCal doubles competition it's only necessary to make it to the second round, all four women automatically qualified.

The doubles teams of Guevara-Jacobo and Modesto Junior College's Nami Kouzu-Lynn Waddell shared the top seeded positions.

Strong said before start of tourney play that Debbie Hamblin and Patti Boghosian, the remaining COS doubles team, should have had no trouble with their first-round draw against San Joaquin Delta's Lynn Brockman and Trish Bledsoe, and was therefore also expected to make the second round.

Women's first and second round results

Singles—Guevara bye. Jacobo bye. Boghosian bye. J. Simon def. Bledsoe, SJD, 6-1, 6-1. Hobbs def. Lyon, ARC, 6-0, 6-0. Hamblin def. Chappelle, FCC, 2-6, 6-4, 6-2.

Second round

Guevara def. Sagara, SCC, 6-0, 6-1. Jacobo def. Beagle, ARC, 6-2, 6-1. Boghosian def. Wong, SCC, 6-2, 6-0. Cadlimes, FCC, def. J. Simone, 7-6, 2-6, 6-2. Hobbs def. Miller, ARC, 4-6, 6-3, 6-2. Dean, ARC, def. Hamblin, 6-2, 6-3.

Third round

Guevara def. Louie, SCC, 6-3, 6-2. Jacobo def. Rock, CRC, 2-6, 6-2, 6-2. Kouzo, MJC, def. Boghosian, 6-0, 6-0. Metz, ARC, def. Hobbs, 7-6, 6-0.

Doubles competition

Guevara-Jacobo bye. Hobbs-Simon bye. Hamblin-Boghosian def. Bledsoe-Brockman, SJD, 6-1, 6-1.

Second round

Guevara-Jacobo def. Rock-Schoemer, CRC, 6-1, 5-7, 6-0. Hobbs-Simon def. Sagara-Louie, SCC, 6-1, 6-4. Hamblin-Boghosian def. Metz-Dean, ARC, 6-0, 6-2.

Mike Penn (seeded No. 4) and Robert Lombardi (placed), the No. 1 and No. 2 singles players on the men's squad, also received first-round byes. Penn and Lombardi also received a bye as the No. 3 doubles team.

Drew Smith received a good draw, according to coach Al Anderson, in the form of opponent Paul Nesley of Cosumnes River College.

The rest of the team played Reedley's Dan Mitchell (Mike Jackson); Delta's Scott Lockheed (Jack Nelson); and Sacramento City's Miquel Hernandez (Dan Wright).

The roughest time for the Giants is most likely to come in the third round when, if all goes as expected, Boghosian will meet the top-rated singles player, Kouzo, from Modesto.

Boghosian, who was undefeated in nine straight-set matches at the No. 5 position, and undefeated in doubles competition (with three different partners), is up for the occasion, however.

"I can't wait," she said. "It'll be nice playing someone who's pretty good."

Strong also thinks an upset may be in the works.

"It's possible that we could have three or four players play Kouzu if Patti (Boghosian) loses," Strong said. "If Boghosian loses, Jacobo should meet her in the fourth round, and if she loses, Guevara or Hobbs could meet her in the semi-finals."

"I'm glad that it's Boghosian who's playing her first," she said. "Patti is our best players to mix up her shots, and she has a positive attitude; but if she loses, there'll be more of us to go against her."

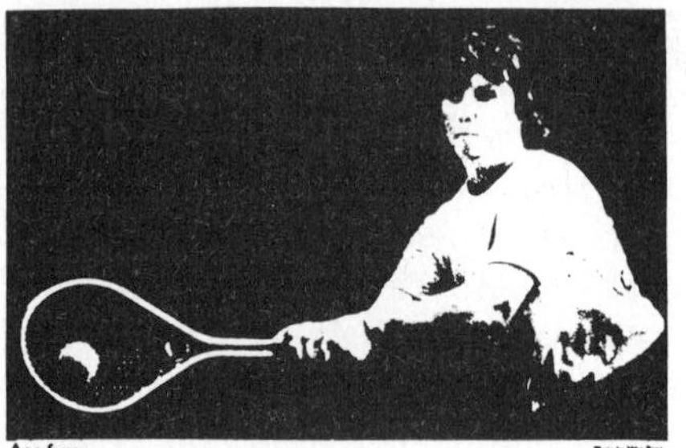

Ace form

Photo by Mike Penn

PattiHobbsshows the style that took her to a perfect 14-0 this season. This outstanding record qualified her for NorCal, along with three other teammates, in the doubles division.

Figure 9–5. The tennis story on this page has a scoring summary inserted as a "pullout" in the middle column, thus displaying the scores while breaking up a big gray block of type. (From *The Campus,* College of the Sequoias)

By Wendy Vasquez
Sports editor

Coming off a big 27-0 win over DeAnza in their season opener last Saturday, the Giant football team will be looking to do more of the same tomorrow night when they travel to Ventura for their second game of the 1980 season.

The game is scheduled to start at 7:30.

Ventura will be out to avenge last year's 20-9 loss to the Giants and hopefully initiate a more productive offense. They were beaten decisively last week by Saddleback, 42-7.

In last year's game, Ventura was held to just 205 yards in total offense, while the Giants gained 206 yards in rushing alone.

Under first year head coach Greg Mohns, the Pirates will be operating a wishbone offense, a new system for their team. According to Giant mentor Al Branco, they have the ingredients for making it work.

"Their running backs are tough and their quarterback is not afraid to run," Branco said.

Branco went on to add that Ventura has a personnel of about 90 players and are a very physical team.

"We'll have to hold up physically, they're a big team."

Although the wishbone is a traditionally difficult offense to defend against, Branco is not overly concerned.

"It's early, they're still learning the style," he said.

If last week's game was any indication of future contests, the Giants should have little trouble defending against opposing teams' offense.

Behind the leadership of veteran linebacker Brian Benko, the Giant defense kept DeAnza deep in the hole most of the game.

Figure 9–6. This weekly newspaper story leads off with a brief look at the upcoming game, then covers the previous week's game with lots of quotes, not just a play-by-play. (From *The Campus,* College of the Sequoias)

Writing

All the rules about good reporting and writing apply as well to sports news, sports features, and sports opinion stories. Reporters must cover the event with all the objectivity and professionalism of reporters who cover their beats on the news side.

Sports reporters have to recognize and deal with one particular writing pitfall that news reporters do not: sports clichés. Many coaches are guilty of speaking solely with time-worn words and phrases. Many sports reporters, having heard these same phrases from their sports heroes all their lives, are also guilty of this special sports sin. In the last 50 years many—but not all—of the colorful clichés have disappeared. In baseball coverage, all home runs were then "circuit clouts" or "four-masters," foul balls were "cackle clouts," left-handed pitchers were "southpaws" or "port-siders," and ground balls were "daisy-cutters."

Today new words and phrases become clichés almost overnight because of immediate media overuse: "We play them one game at a time." "I believe his future is ahead of him." "It felt good to win." "The teams locked in combat on the gridiron."

A good writer avoids sports clichés. Good writing is clear, concise, and descriptive. It re-creates the event for readers or sits them down with the sports figure being interviewed. Review the "20 Rules for Good Writing" listed in Chapter 6, follow them all, and you'll be one of the best sports reporters around— especially if your opposing hoopsters don't throw bricks often or miss crucial caroms off the glass.

Sports reporters need to develop sources and poke around behind the scenes just as news-side reporters do. A good reporter looks behind the obvious and tells the reader the *why* and *how* behind the *what*. Detachment from the sports event, the team, and the school is necessary for solid reporting to take place. A sports reporter cannot be a fan or cheerleader.

The most obvious item to be reported when writing about a sports event is the final score. You do not necessarily have to place it in the lead graf, however, especially if you work for a weekly paper and are concentrating on previewing next week's game. The final score should be included early in the story, but the lead can focus on any part of the event (see the lead in Fig. 9–9). For instance, the story can begin with an outstanding individual play or series of plays that led to the winning score. Or the game's importance in the league race can be featured. Don't just list the final score and the high-scoring individuals as a list of statistics. Quote the competitors, not just the coaches. Your readers like to know about the *people* who play, not just how many points a numbered jersey scored.

Even though sports news stories should focus on people and the how-and-why background needed to answer all the reader's questions, statistics play an important part in a sports story. Stats can lead to interesting and revealing questions in a postgame interview. Be sure to include statistical information in the news-gathering process. Many newspapers have developed special stat sheets for each sport to help the reporter record important information as the game progresses. Although many teams and schools have sports publicists to compile scoring summaries and statistics after a game, the stats may not be available in time for the reporter's deadline. Rely on your own work.

Sample sheets for football and basketball are shown in Figures 9–7 and 9–8. Notice how the columns make it easy for a reporter to follow the statistics of the game as it develops, yet leave room for observations. The time of all scores should be noted in a football game, but not in a fast-moving basketball game. When covering basketball, write down the time when the lead changes.

Sports news stories for daily newspapers should be structured in a basic inverted-pyramid format, with the most important facts first. If you are writing a

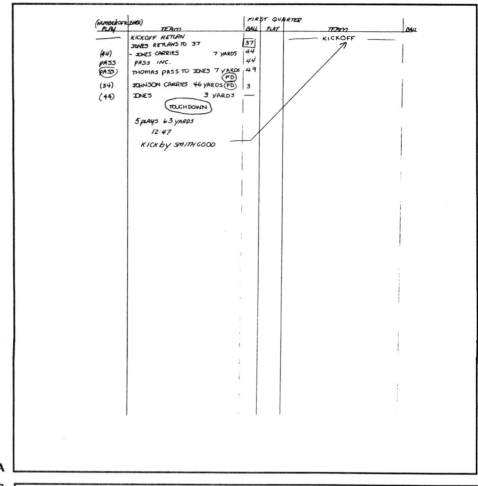

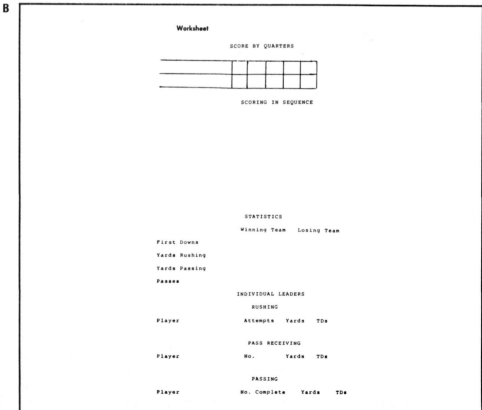

Figure 9–7. (A) A sample reporter's score sheet for keeping track of the play-by-play at a football game. The first column is for the player, the second for an abbreviated description of the play ("FD" for first down), the third for the yard line the play started on. Each team has half the page. (B) The form on which *The Knoxville News-Sentinel* likes to receive results from correspondents.

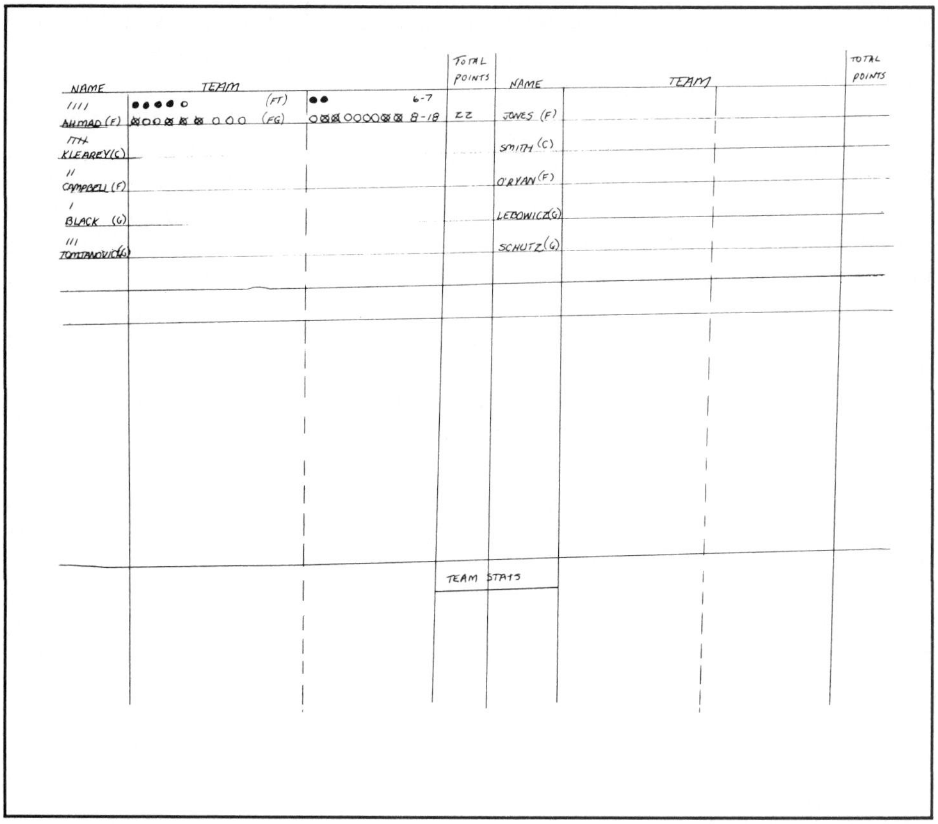

A

B

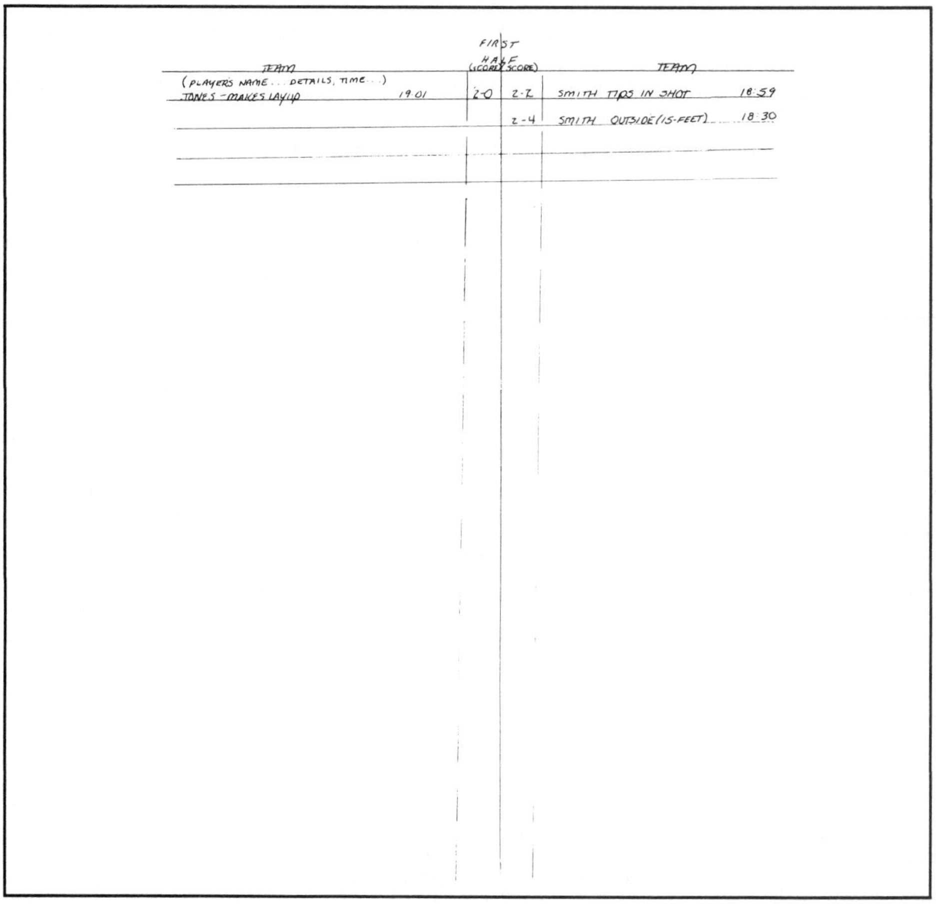

Figure 9–8. Basketball is a difficult sport to cover because so much happens quickly. (A) This system lists the player's name and personal fouls in the first column, indicates field goals and free throws (shots attempted and shots made) in the second column (with a dotted line separating the halves of the game), then totals points in the third column. A reporter may also be able to keep track of rebounds. (B) This form keeps a running total of the score in the column separating the two teams. It allows for a description of each shot rather than just its outcome.

story that will be published the following day, lead off with the key event or the turning point of the game. Mention the final score in the lead as well as "when" and "where," just as in a news story.

From that point on, the most important happenings that affected the outcome of the game should be covered in descending order of importance, leaving the least important details for the "bottom" of the story. Games should rarely be covered in chronological order. Professional football reporters often spend their halftimes writing the bottom of their story, because the outcome of the game is rarely decided in the first half. The bottom is the part of the story that starts out, "In the first half," and is usually a simple account of the highlights of that half. This early writing saves time after the game, when the daily reporter is on deadline.

Weekly reporters have the luxury of time, and they can put the story together more leisurely. They can spend more time getting quotes from the coaches and important players. Phone calls the next day or follow-up interviews on Monday morning can add other facets to the story that the daily reporter must miss. Sports reporters for weekly school papers should take advantage of all this time to dig deeper and use a feature story approach (Fig. 9–9).

Features play as important a part in the sports section as they do in the rest of the paper. Features should be a major portion of sports coverage for a weekly paper. Sports features, like news features, may use the *Wall Street Journal* formula (see Chapter 7). A feature story on a long-distance runner might begin:

> Sitting in the sporting goods store trying on training shoes, Benson Jones doesn't look like a world-class athlete. He's 5–8, he weighs 135 pounds after a spaghetti dinner and he's going prematurely bald.
>
> "These fit fine," Jones tells the shoe salesman. "I'll take three pair."
>
> Jones isn't gift shopping, he really *needs* three pair of shoes. He goes through shoes like the rest of us go through those knit slippers we got for Christmas. Jones is a marathon racer, one of the best in the world.
>
> His 2:09:48 at the Valley Marathon last month ranks him in the top 25 marathon racers in the country. As with most marathon racers, it's the long hours spent training and wearing out shoes that give him the ability to run—not jog—for 26.2 miles.

Figure 9–9. Many sports stories should take an analytical or feature approach. Find out why the game turned out as it did. Be descriptive. Be complete. (From *The Daily Pennsylvanian*, University of Pennsylvania)

The story starts out with a specific incident, a detail about Jones that gives the reader a feel for what he does. The detail (buying three pair of shoes) furnishes

By BOB SAPORITO

This one was very strange. It resembled a baseball game, four bases, a mound, nine fielders, but it was more on the line of a Marx brothers skit. And there were more weird turns than a game of Twister. The most unusual being the final score: Pennsylvania, 11, Haverford, 11.

Pay tribute for this oddity to darkness. The game was ended after only eight innings. Why then did it take over three hours to play eight innings? First, there were more walks than usual for a 2-1 game, but this one saw 28 free passes. It looked like a welfare merry-go-round.

"Our pitchers just didn't throw strikes," said Coach Bob Seddon. "We were putting too many men on for free (15 walks), and we won't win that way. We can't afford to give it away by walking in runs." Four of the Fords' runs were gratis.

Second, there were close to 350 pitches thrown in the game, enough to put a pitching machine out of commission. One reason was obvious lack of control, another was an inordinately small strike zone. "The umpire was forcing the ball to be perfect for a strike," said Seddon, "that's just not right. But he did miss pitches for both teams."

The game started out innocently enough. Lefty Joe Howley breezed through the top of the first. The Quakers (4-6) picked up three runs in their half thanks to a two-run single by Paul Kupcha, but Steve Criscuolo was caught in a rundown heading for third and all normalcy gunned down as well.

In the top of the second, Seddon asked where a ball four pitch was. He was yanked from the game by home plate umpire Tony Iacone like greased lightning. He was gone before he was three steps from the dugout.

"I asked one simple question, and I was gone," said Seddon. "This is a college game, and things like that take away from it." Iacone contends that the coach should know his place. "He

shouldn't question balls and strikes."

Then in the top of the third, Howley lost the plate. He walked five of seven batters, and freshman Joe Adams took over. His second pitch was lined to center by Dave Martin, rolling under the normally dependable glove of Steve Flacco, letting in three runs and giving the Fords a 6-4 lead.

In Penn's fifth, an RBI double by Kupcha and a run-scoring single by Pete Shutte, who reached base all five times up with two runs scored, pulled the Quakers even. But the top of the sixth brought more disaster for the nine. With two outs, bases loaded, and three runs already in, Eric Blank hit a smash to the backhand side of second baseman Criscuolo that deflected off his glove clear into left field for two more runs.

The Quakers battled back with four in the seventh as they batted around. Hits by Shutte, Jerry Smith, and John Vasturia knocked in the tying runs while knocking Haverford ace righthander Rick Pressler out of the

box in favor of lefty Paul Forshay, who did his fireman impression.

"We like to bring in Forshay because he comes from the other side and is much slower than Pressler," said Ford coach Greg Kannerstein. "The two styles compliment each other very well, and Penn is weaker against the lefties."

Interim coach Bill Wagner sent in junior Andy Sailor in the top of the eighth. He salvaged a lead off walk with a nifty pickoff move and eased out of the inning. This set the stage for the classic bases loaded, two out confrontation. Forshay put himself in a ravine by filling the diamond with Quakers on walks. Then with two outs he ran the count to 2-0 on Smith before getting a called third strike on the lefthanded power hitter to end the inning, and according to Iacone, the game.

Sports reporter, not sports writer

Ron Fimrite, a senior writer for Sports Illustrated *since 1971, made it to the top without a journalism degree. He was graduated from the University of California (Berkeley) with a degree in liberal arts. After a two-year stint in the Army, he worked for the* Berkeley Gazette *for four years, where, as he put it, "I did just about everything there was to do on the paper." He left the* Gazette *in 1959 to work for the* San Francisco Chronicle, *where he covered news and sports and wrote a sports column for five years before leaving for SI.*

Q: Why is it "news reporter," but "sports *writer*"?

A: I don't think there should be any distinction. You should be a reporter. I don't believe in the separation that has gone on between the news and sports departments. The sports department should be more aware of what's going on in the rest of the paper. They [the sports department] tend to be totally separate and maybe even sneered at by the people on the news side. By the same token the sports writers exclude themselves from the newsside people. Sports writers and reporters aspire to the same skills. I don't like it when someone calls me a sports writer. I tell them I'm not a sports writer, I'm a magazine writer.

Q: Why do you think it has been this way?

A: I think because in the old days the people in the news department didn't have much respect for sports writers. They felt they were not really reporters and that they weren't part of the paper; they were just jocks or publicists for the teams more than reporters. I think that's changing now, or should be changing. Sports reporters are becoming somewhat more knowledgeable. Certainly they are better educated than they were and they are not simply fans anymore. Regrettably, some still are, but they are beginning to take their craft seriously enough to realize that they are covering news.

Q: What makes a sports story and a newspaper sports section a good one?

A: The writing first—bright writing, not gimmicky. Good writing means good reporting. If a story is not well written, then the coverage becomes less important. There's nothing better than a well-written story. Not in the old-fashioned, flowery sort of way that was fashionable for so long. A well-written story is clear, succinct, and not overwritten. I think the biggest problem in most sports pages is that there is an awful lot of overwriting because reporters just don't do the kind of editing job that they do in other parts of the paper.

That's not to say that a story should be dull or dry; it should certainly be humorous because, after all, you're covering something that's a game. It's entertainment. Good fundamental writing skills are much more important than knowledge of sports. It doesn't matter how much you know if you can't make it clear—it's knowledge wasted.

Q: What should a sports reporter keep in mind when writing a feature story?

A: He should look for the unusual, the out-of-the-ordinary. Obviously, in a single interview you can't get to know a person real well, but some aspect of personality will come through. Readers will usually know what a sports personality has done; you should show what he's like.

In a game there is usually something that makes it different from any other game, some turning point or some moment that expresses the situation. That's basically the same in all kinds of reporting.

I had a city editor once who said, "Look for the cat on the windowsill." If you just covered a fire in an ordinary way, then yours and everybody's story would be exactly the same. But if you see a cat on a windowsill that needs to be rescued—that's what you should look for.

Q: What is your opinion of a New Journalism approach, in which the facts may be embellished or fictionalized a bit to help the story?

A: I disapprove of that kind of New Journalism, which is carrying it to its unfortunate extreme. I am violently opposed to making things up. If you have to make things up, you're really not being a very good reporter.

Q: When you cover a story, how do you go about it? How much time preparing and researching, how much writing and rewriting?

A: It depends on the kind of story. But I always try to at least familiarize myself with a topic. I try to do as much research as I possibly can, so I know the right things to ask and I know what to look for. I like to do a lot of research (although many people don't), mainly because I'm interested in that sort of thing. If I'm doing a historical piece, I may go to the library and spend a whole day reading.

When I write, I first go over my notes and then I take notes of my notes—of the significant notes. I take a lot of notes. During an interview you write down a lot of things and many of them are useless. From them I do a very rough sketch, not so much an outline, but a sketch of how I'm going to go through the story. Then I'll write a draft and heavily edit that draft. The second draft is usually the final version. In a longer story I might go as many as three drafts. I wouldn't do that working for a newspaper because you don't have the time, but that's how I write a magazine story. I have spent as long as 29 or 30 hours just writing a story and that much time also preparing for it.

Q: What's the best preparation for someone who wants to be a professional sports reporter?

A: I don't think you should go into journalism with a specific thing in mind. I think you'll miss a lot if you say, "I want to be a sports writer." Sports reporters could benefit from going into newswriting first and sports writing later because the training is a lot tougher in news. The situations change more. It's much better training for a writer to go into newswriting first.

Q: What are some tips of the trade for students training to be sports reporters?

A: Don't take yourself too seriously. Emphasize good, clean writing. Don't get sloppy or too flamboyant. That looks sophomoric. And have fun with it. But at the same time, work hard at developing a good, clean style.

insight into the nature of long-distance training. It's not just *any* incident; it tells the reader something.

After the story follows Jones on a training run, relays comments from fellow runners and his coach, and describes his special vegetarian diet and rigorous training method, it ends with another specific incident—a little story, if you will, to leave the reader with a last impression of Jones.

> It's three o'clock and Jones is preparing for his second run of the day. This one will be a "short" seven-miler. Before breakfast he ran 14.
>
> He takes a long swig at the drinking fountain next to the athletic field at MVC and looks down the road leading toward the river.
>
> "Really too hot," he says. "But I've got to get in at least 20 today. I managed only 15 yesterday. You want to come along?"
>
> The reporter declines, still sore from a four-mile "fun run" at a 5:45-per-mile pace with Jones the day before.
>
> "Okay, then, talk to you later." He looks at his watch. "I've got to run."
>
> And run and run and run.

The scene works in two ways. It gives the reader another personal look at Jones, and it sets the scene for the reporter's final point.

Today's sports reporters are working hard to shed the "sports writer" tag. Solid, hard-nosed reporting needs to take place in sports as well as in news. Team up this reporting with interesting and creative features, and the sports section will be a winner.

— Suggested Projects

1. Study last semester's sports pages and measure the approximate column inches that were devoted to intercollegiate and intramural sports, women's sports (compared with men's), and physical education classes. Also compare sports "news" coverage with sports features coverage. How does the section rank? Should sports coverage be apportioned more evenly?

2. Watch a televised sports event or a school sports event that you know will be covered the following day in your local paper. Write a story based on the event and the postgame interviews and compare it to the professional story. Evaluate differences in lead, facts, and analysis of the game itself, in use of quotes and overall structure.

3. Follow a local sports reporter around a college sports event. Watch what the reporter does during the event, who the reporter interviews, and how the reporter writes down information and statistics. Then compare your notes with the reporter's. Evaluate the reporter's story after it is printed. Invite the writer to attend a class question-and-answer session.

Exercises

1. Write an opinion-based sports column on a controversial issue: lengthy strikes, equality in the funding of men's and women's sports, violence or drug use in sports.

2. Write a daily-newspaper lead and a weekly-newspaper lead based on the following information on a football game. Then write a complete story using the lead of your choice.

Middle Valley College . . . 0 7 0 16—23
Johnsonville College . . . 8 0 0 14—22

JC-Elder, 3-yard run. PAT: Elder run.

MVC—Snapp, 17-yard pass from Cameron. PAT: Grant kick.

MVC—Christopher, 2-yard run. Kick failed.

JC—Elder, 68-yard run. PAT: Garcia kick.

JC—Orcutt, 18-yard interception return. PAT: Garcia kick.

MVC—Grant, 12-yard FG.

MVC—Schenz, 53-yard run (after lateral from Snapp). PAT: Grant.

Opening Central League game between two teams. Each had 3–0 preleague record. Cofavorites to take league title this year. Game held at Johnsonville's home field last night. JC's Alan Elder gained 155 years in game, including the two TDs and the two-point conversion. Best for MVC was quarterback Toby Cameron, who gained 72 yards. JC scored first after receiving opening kickoff. JC faked field goal and Elder, the holder, ran around left end for two points.

MVC scored just before halftime on flanker screen to Eddie Snapp. Neither team scored in third period. MVC opened fourth quarter with 83-yard drive capped by two-yard plunge over center by fullback Bob Christopher. JC scored on next drive when Elder scored around left end. Tony Garcia kicked the PAT. On MVC's first play from scrimmage after the ensuing kickoff, Cameron was intercepted by JC's Don Orcutt, the safety. Snapp, the intended receiver, had tripped and fallen on the play.

MVC drove down close to goal, but settled for field goal by Marty Grant with 1:43 remaining in the game. MVC successfully recovered an onside kick, but couldn't move the ball in three plays. Cameron was sacked twice, ending back on his own 17-yard line on fourth down. On next play, with 58 seconds remaining, he completed a pass to Snapp, who was being dragged down on his own 47-yard line when he spied halfback Jerry Schenz motioning for a lateral. Snapp passed to Schenz, who ran through five or six surprised JC players for touchdown. Grant's kick won the game.

Snapp: "It was like time was in slow motion. I looked up and there was Jerry wagging his arms like a madman. I figured there was nothing to lose at that point, so I flipped it in his direction. It was tough because my arms were pinned by the tacklers. And Coach (Coach Bob Jacobs) told us *never* to lateral when being tackled. All I could think of as I was falling to the ground was how mad Coach was going to be."

Schenz: "I couldn't believe it when I saw I was all alone and Eddie could lateral. I kept waving at him, but he didn't see me for what seemed to be the longest time. When I got the ball I just ran like hell. I'll never forget the look on Eddie's face when I was yelling at him to throw the ball; I knew he was thinking of Coach."

Jacobs: "Well, ol' Eddie might run some extra laps for breaking one of Jacob's cardinal rules. But, heck, I can't be too hard on the guy. I may have to add a new rule now to cover this situation in the future. It's great to get this game over with and to win. The guys played real hard tonight and it looks good for the rest of the season. We should only have trouble with Hidden Valley College. They've got a tremendous passing attack."

Next week MVC is home against Deer River College. The Deer River Bucks are 1–3 after losing last night to Hidden Valley 27–3 in their league opener. According to records, MVC should have no problems. "But you can never take anyone for granted in this league," Jacobs said. "We like to play 'em one game at a time. You've got to win the little ones to prove you're really a big one yourself. We'll work real hard this week, especially on our defensive line work, which should get a real workout against Deer River—they've got a real mastodon offensive line. My grandmother could gain 100 yards a game behind those guys."

Deer River's tailback, Aaron Rodgers, leads the league with 372 yards, an average of 93 yards a game. The problem is that the team has no defense and no passing offense to speak of.

10 | photo production

Pictures are the oldest method of communication, preceding writing by thousands of years. In an increasingly visual society, newspapers are using photographs more and more to lure the average reader away from the television set.

Newspapers today recognize the importance of good staff photojournalists. Photos are no longer frills—they communicate the news all by themselves.

This chapter assumes that the reader has already acquired a working knowledge of basic photography—f-stops, shutter speeds, depth of field, film development, printing techniques, and so on. Readers without this knowledge should consult a book on basic photography.

Photographer/Photojournalist

What is the desired end result of the photo? For the photographer, who is interested in quality first and foremost, the end result is the printed photograph itself. For the photojournalist, the end result is the published version of the photo in the paper. The photojournalist wants the photo to communicate something to readers and quality must sometimes be sacrificed in order to communicate an idea or an emotion. In actuality, photojournalists are reporters who work with cameras rather than with pens and paper.

Attributes of the Photojournalist

A good photojournalist must be (1) a journalist as well as a photographer, (2) a technician, and (3) an artist. A news photo has the same basic news values as a news story: timeliness, proximity, consequence, conflict, change, prominence, and human interest. The newsworthiness of a photo depends on the presence and intensity of these values.

Technical mastery of photography can only improve the photographer's ability to communicate the essence of a news, feature, or sports event. And last, all these technical details must be put into an aesthetically pleasing context.

In his excellent text *Photojournalism: Photography with a Purpose*, Robert L. Kerns lists four other elements that lead to success as a photojournalist:

1. *A desire to know.* Kerns says that curiosity is the most important of his four elements.
2. *A desire to communicate.* Enthusiasm and perseverance are critical to the photojournalist's success.
3. *An interest in others.* There is a story in every living thing, and standing aloof will not help a photographer figure out what makes a subject tick. The photojournalist should get *involved*.

116

4. *An ability to make decisions.* Which lens will provide the desired result? What method should be used to handle a tough person-to-person situation on assignment?

Photo Editor

Because writers and photographers have difficulty judging their own work objectively, editors need to help assess and improve quality in stories and photos. A photo editor should understand photojournalism well enough to make good decisions in photo selection for the newspapers.

Photo editors must also have good leadership qualities, an understanding of the nonphoto operation of newspapers, and darkroom management skills. Photo editors should be able to resolve conflicts between the section editors and the photo staff. An understanding of what section editors want in a photo, coupled with an understanding of what the photo staff is capable of producing, can help the newspaper get the best possible photos.

An important asset for a photo editor is the ability to devise and keep in operation an efficient photo and negative filing system. The photo editor must select a method that works for the staff and must make sure that each photographer follows the system.

Photo-Staff Organization

The ideal photo-staff organization includes an editor who supervises the staff, a chief photographer who helps the photo editor coordinate the work of the staff, and a darkroom technician who keeps the darkroom in working order so that photographers can concentrate on photography. Many small papers, however, don't have enough persons for all these editorial positions, so the chief photographer usually becomes the photo editor. The photo editor must be able to act as a manager, however, and not just as another photographer with management duties.

All communication between the newsroom and the darkroom goes through the photo editor. When a section editor makes a photo assignment, the photo editor looks it over, discusses any questions or problems with the section editor, adds any tips on the sheet itself, and then assigns the photo.

When the photo assignment has been completed, the photo editor screens the proof sheets and/or prints and suggests the best photos for publication. The most important job of the photo editor is this selection. Although many section editors have their own ideas about which photo they would like, the photo editor is the expert, not the section editor. The section editor should be in charge of photo selection only if the staff has no photo editor.

So the photo editor must be able to work with section editors as well as with the photo staff to get the best possible photos into the paper. Therefore, the photo editor should sit in on planning meetings with the other editors and should chair meetings of the photo staff to make sure operations run smoothly.

In addition to these management and liaison duties, the photo editor keeps track of all activities on campus and in the community. A master calendar of all events, posted in the newsroom or outside the darkroom, will keep photographers aware of photo possibilities outside their assignments. (You can get information for the master calendar from the public information office, the school calendar for special events, the student government or activities office calendar, calendars in the local paper, and so on. Coordinate this newsgathering activity with news and features editors.)

If the paper has no photo editor, a chief photographer has to perform all the duties of an editor as well as supervise other photographers and take photographs. When the paper has a photo editor, however, the chief photographer can concentrate on taking pictures and working closely with the other photographers.

Best advice is "shoot, shoot, shoot"

Stan Denny is an athlete turned sports photographer. After playing for the farm teams of the Los Angeles Dodgers and San Francisco Giants, Denny began working for the Louisville Courier-Journal *as a free-lance artist. He did some editorial and sports cartooning for the paper, then began reporting and "carrying a camera with me." He moved into the photo department full-time in 1968. Now he is a contract photographer, covering only certain assignments, usually sports events.*

Q: What attributes should a good photojournalist have?

A: Beyond a shadow of a doubt, the first thing to have is a deep and abiding interest in what you are doing. If you don't like taking pictures of people or events rather than a stationary object, then photojournalism isn't for you. A high level of interest is more important than equipment.

Q: What makes a photograph a good one?

A: That's a very difficult question to give a definitive answer to. In sports photography, for instance, we're constantly battling ourselves over which is the best picture—the one of the important play or the "great" sports picture that has nothing to do with the outcome of the game. Sometimes you don't have the luxury of choice, but when you do it's a very hard decision to make.

More specifically, a good photo is one that conveys a feeling of the story it illustrates. It makes no difference whether it's sports, feature, news, fashion, or whatever. The photo should set off in the reader's mind the statement, "I want to read that story, I want to know more about that photo."

Q: What part do photos play in a newspaper?

A: The more interesting newspapers have the best use of art. Personally, I think the worst newspaper I ever see is *The Wall Street Journal* because it hasn't any photographs except in ads. The front page just has that graph every day.

From a journalistic standpoint—not a *photo*journalistic stand-point—I think concern about use of art in the paper should be paramount. The average reader of a newspaper approaches the paper in two ways: (1) He wants to know the news, and (2) he wants to see what will interest him. And most readers are attracted to a story because of some piece of art.

Q: Do you select your own photos for publication and do your own cropping, or does a section editor select and crop?

A: Seventy-five or 80 percent of the assignments you get as a photojournalist are not earthshaking, so the photographer has complete control over what he wants to print. For instance, after a given event I may print half a dozen photos in different sizes and composition to show to the department head or editor for final selection. I'll probably follow the photos to the department and make my suggestions on the ones I prefer. Because I was there, I know which ones best tell the story. If I have more time I make a contact sheet and have the editor look the shots over to see what he needs. It's really a matter of time.

Q: When shooting an assignment, do you try to compose the photo in the camera, or do you wait and do that in the darkroom?

A: It would have to be both. On assignment you should try to get yourself into a position where that position, coupled with your equipment and the event itself, gives you the best perspective on what you are shooting. Even though you try to do this, there is still a great deal of composition in darkroom cropping. I know very few photographers who print full-frame and say, "That's just the way I wanted it." There's always composition done in the darkroom.

Q: What do you look for when you have to crop a photo to a certain size to fit the page layout?

A: Sadly enough to say, that's usually determined by someone else. One of the problems you face as a photojournalist is that someone lays out the page at three in the afternoon although the event doesn't occur until eight that night. This prelayout of the pages is a problem. You'll come in and the editor will say, "What have you got in a nice horizontal?" and you've been out shooting basketball!

If you had the time, say for a weekly paper, you could print a couple of compositions that would give you freedom in the layout four days from now. If you've got a strong vertical and a strong horizontal, make two prints. I'm not opposed to prelayout of pages, but don't rivet the layout so tightly that it can't accommodate a different shape.

Q: What specific tips do you have for sports photographers?

A: First, the answer is not equipment. Many student photographers see a professional photographer at a game with Nikon F3s and motor drives and 600 mm lenses, and they think that if they had that kind of equipment they could take good pictures too. This simply isn't true. You couldn't give me a million-dollar car and expect me to go to Indy and win the race. Don't get into new equipment until you are bored with and have completely exhausted the tools you already have.

To take a good sports picture, you have to have some knowledge of what you are shooting. I would be an average photographer of polo, for instance, because I have no idea what they do other than ride horses and hit a ball up and down a field. But if I were assigned a polo match in six weeks, I'd get a book out on it, I'd talk to a few people who play, and I'd go see the field.

I'd go out and look over *any* field, whether it's a baseball field or a football field. Find out where the sun's going to be at the time you're going to be shooting. If it's a night game, find out how much light you're going to have. Do some research on what you will be shooting.

Then have enough of a knowledge of the game so that you can predict where the action will be. Let's say you're shooting night football and you have 50 mm and 135 mm lenses. These are your tools, so to speak. Don't sit there and pine for what the guy from *Sports Illustrated* might have at some place with great light. You're at a dirty high school field with poor lighting. So don't try to shoot the pictures out in the middle of the field. Get way ahead of the ball or way behind. Don't do what everybody else does: Cluster eight yards ahead of the ball at the yard markers.

Finally, and I believe in this last tip like an 11th commandment, *ask a professional for help.* But the worst time to do that is when he is working. Don't walk up to him at a game and smile and say, "Hi, how ya like yer Nikon?" Talk to him before the game or at halftime. Ninety percent of the photographers I know would love to come to school and talk to a class or to a few interested students. The first way to alienate a photographer is to try to start a conversation with him while he's in a working situation. But give him your name and ask him to come to the school, and he'll be there when he can get the time and he'll probably have a slide show with him.

Q: What are the most important points to remember for a beginning photojournalist?

A: The first is: Shoot pictures. It's nice to look at books and read about it, but you have to shoot. It's like teaching people to swim. I can talk to them about it, I can show them movies, and I can give them books about techniques. But unless they get in that pool and get at it, they're going to drown. The same thing applies to people who want to be involved in photography. You must take photographs, and I'm talking on the excess side now.

When I first started I shot a lot more film than I do now. That was a trial-and-error situation for me. So don't be afraid to use film. I know this is a cliché, but the cheapest thing you've got is film. Your camera is worth hundreds of dollars, your time is worth something, and there you are worrying about saving the last six frames for your next assignment. Go

ahead and shoot it. I think that's paramount.

Then get someone you respect to help critique your work. Be tough-skinned. Know that you're starting out and that some of the pictures you really like are going to be shot down. Ask that person to tell you not just that he doesn't like it, but *why* he doesn't like it, why the photo doesn't work.

A lot of young photographers will also do one of two things. Sometimes they shoot a very safe picture that they've been taking for two or three years, and they feel very comfortable with it. It's their blanket. When someone tells them it's nothing exceptional, it really hurts them because two years ago someone told them, "Oh, that's good." Or a young photographer will stumble onto a shot that's good for him in terms of what he has done. It's lucky for him, yet it's still not a good photo.

A darkroom technician can help a busy photo staff by keeping an adequate supply of paper, chemicals, and equipment; keeping the darkroom clean and organized; and developing film and printing photos for photographers who are busy on assignments.

Staff photographers are like general assignment reporters on the news desk: they have no specific beats to cover. Some photographers, however, may be superior in a given subject, such as sports photography. Giving this person the majority of sports photo assignments is fine. The other photographers should not, however, be precluded from shooting sports events. Because professional newspaper photographers have to shoot every kind of assignment, student photographers should broaden their experience whenever opportunity allows.

Many schools have several publications, including a newspaper and a yearbook. Staffs can save money and improve the photography of both publications by cooperating on assignments. There is no reason to send a newspaper *and* a yearbook photographer to cover an on-campus concert. Staffs can often share photographers and economize on film and proof sheets. The staff can then concentrate on quality instead of being spread too thin by the dictates of quantity.

Photo Flow

"Photo flow" refers to the movement of every photo that appears in the paper from the assignment through the stages of negatives, proof sheet, print request, and final print. A good photo flow system should run something like the following: First, the news editor determines the need for photo coverage, fills out a photo assignment sheet (Fig. 10–1)—to indicate the time of the shooting, persons to be seen, special effects desired, and so on—and signs the form. The news editor then gives the assignment to the photo editor, who scrutinizes it, enters the photographer's name and the deadline on both the assignment sheet and the

Figure 10–1. Photo-assignment forms should be complete. The photographer needs to know what the editor has in mind, but he or she should be allowed to work out specific shots without editorial demands.

PHOTOGRAPHIC ASSIGNMENT

Cameraman: *Jones*

When: *Mon (10/14)* Time: *2 p.m.*

Location: *Haskins Hall*

Subjects: *Science Fair Winners*

Person to Contact: *Dr. Susanne Dowling (x 2372)*

Instructions: *individ. shots w/ winners & project. Be creative!*

Prints Needed:
When: *mon (10/21)*

What Poses: *also get mugs*

Number of Prints: *1 ea. (2 per person)*

master sheet, and delivers the assignment sheet to the assigned photographer. The photographer reviews the assignment, requests any necessary clarification from the news editor who made the assignment, and proceeds to shoot the assignment. After shooting the assignment, the photographer returns the completed assignment sheet to the photo editor and develops the film in the darkroom. Early the next morning, the photographer turns in a *proof sheet* (negative sized prints of an entire roll of film) to the photo editor, who marks the best frames and sends the proof sheet to the news editor. The news editor, with the photo editor's assistance, then makes the final decision on which photo is to be used, sending the proof sheet and request through the photo editor (who suggests cropping) to the darkroom. After printing the photo, the darkroom technician sends it to the news room and returns the proof sheet and negatives to the photo editor's file. This sample photo flow system should be amended to the individual needs of each newspaper.

When the photo editor determines how the photo should be cropped— either by marking the proof or the *full-frame* (not cropped in printing) 8 × 10 prints—he or she should work closely with the section editors. The "best" cropping may not meet the needs of the section editor's page layout or news value decisions.

Photo Filing

Photo-filing systems seem to be a problem with many student-newspaper staffs. There are many different ways to set up an effective system, but even the simplest won't work if staff members don't perform the needed steps. The key to any filing system is fulfilling responsibilities at every step in the process. As long as there are no weak links in this chain of responsibility, a photo-filing system can be very simple.

Figure 10–2. The front of the proof envelope lists the contents of the envelope so that it doesn't have to be opened unless a print is to be made.

FILE NO. 83-123	COLOR _____	B&W ✓

EVENT OR SUBJECT **WOMEN'S TENNIS vs. M.S.U.**

DATE PHOTOS WERE SHOT **OCTOBER 11, 1982**

PHOTOGRAPHER'S NAME **MIKE MESSING**

SEMESTER **FALL**   YEAR **1982-83**

FOR TRAIL BLAZER USE:	FOR NEWS SERVICES USE:	FOR PUBLICATIONS USE:
Contact received _____	Contact received _____	Contact received _____
Prints requested _____	Prints requested _____	Prints requested _____
Prints completed _____	Prints completed _____	Prints completed _____
Contact returned _____	Contact returned _____	Contact returned _____

ALL CONTACT SHEETS MUST BE RETURNED TO THE RACONTEUR OFFICE WITHIN 72 HOURS OR SOONER UPON REQUEST.

Paul Wright, a former yearbook adviser at Morehead State University in Morehead, Kentucky, had a system that worked well for his staff and for the student newspaper that shared photographers with the yearbook.

After making a proof sheet, the photographer places the negatives in an envelope and firmly tapes the envelope to the back of the proof. The proof (with negatives attached) is slipped into a preprinted 8½ × 11 envelope (Fig. 10–2). The large envelope is marked with the photographer's name, the date the photos were shot, the subject, and a file number that consists of the year and a three-digit number—91–123, for instance. The year, of course, easily identifies when the photos were shot. The three-digit number represents a certain subject area. For example, numbers 001–150 may be sports, 151–250 campus activities, 250–300 faculty and administration photos, and so on. When a set of negatives needs to be filed, the photo editor writes the next available number in the subject area on the envelope.

But the job is not done. Before filing the envelope, the photographer types all identifying information on a preprinted info sheet and inserts that in the envelope with the proof (Fig. 10–3). This information includes not only name, major, hometown, and club or fraternity/sorority affiliation of persons pictured in each frame, but also a brief description of the situation or activity in the frame. Only then is the envelope ready to be filed.

Then, to index photos for easy reference, the editor types the subject of the photos on an index-card system along with the file number. If there is already a card in the file with the same subject heading, the new file number is added to that card. If there are photos of several different activities on a proof sheet—for instance, the homecoming proof sheet includes shots of the football game, the crowning of the queen and/or king, the parade, and so on—the editor could make a card for each separate event. One proof sheet may end up with several cards in the file.

At the end of every year, the old files are moved from active to inactive storage, and blank envelopes are prepared for the following year. Prints are filed by section and discarded after a month or so.

Because the newspaper, the yearbook, and the public-information office at Morehead all look at and select photos from the same proof sheet, Wright devised a way to keep track of who was using which photo. Each group uses a different-colored grease pencil to mark desired frames on the proof. If a photographer shoots an assignment specifically for the yearbook, the yearbook editor draws an X through frames not to be used by the newspaper or public-information office. This way it is easy to see which photos have been used and by whom.

Ideally, Wright would like to print two proof sheets for each assignment to minimize handling of the sheet with the negatives attached, but costs prevent such a practice. Still, Wright says, his staff didn't lose an attached negative in five years.

IDENTIFICATION INFORMATION	
FRAME NO.	NAME(S), GROUP AFFLIATION, LOCATION, ETC.
1,2,44	BECKY McCLELLAND JR. KNOXVILLE
3–19	SUE ROBBINS SR. N.Y.
29–43	GEORGIA WILSON SOPH. MIAMI

Figure 10–3. Photographers should gather the necessary information for each frame and write it on the proof sheet, or on a sheet attached to it, at the time of the photo session, not later.

Elements of a Good Photo

A good photograph needs to have both technical and artistic merit. Figure 10–4 lists several technical details to look for in a good photograph.

Artistically, the most important part of a photo is its composition. "Composition" refers to the harmony of the proportions of the photo. Good composition can be achieved by setting up with proportion in mind or by cropping the photo after it has been printed. The former is done by the photographer. The latter is done by the photo editor. Whether it is the photographer or the editor who is trying to create good composition in a photo, four major principles should be

Figure 10–4. What to look for in selecting photos.

remembered: (1) the rule of thirds; (2) balance; (3) leading lines, or lines of force; and (4) contrast.

The *rule of thirds* states that the center of interest of the photo should not be in the center of the picture, which gives a feeling of rest and inactivity to the subject. Unless that is the effect you want, divide your picture into thirds, both horizontally and vertically. Then place your center of interest at or near one of the intersections of those lines (Fig. 10–5).

Balance refers to the visual balance of the picture. According to the rule of thirds, your center of interest is off to one side of the picture. Try to balance this strong focus with another, weaker focal point on the other side by having an element lead into the larger part of the picture (Fig. 10–6) or by having a secondary subject on the opposite rule-of-thirds line (Fig. 10–7).

Leading lines, or lines of force, help balance a picture. Every photo has lines: An arm, a road, a row of bleachers, or a shadow force the eye to move in its direction. These lines should move the eye *toward* the center of interest, not away from it or off the newspaper page (Fig. 10–8). But don't have *all* the lines in the photo lined up in the same direction, unless the purpose of the photo calls for it.

Compositional contrast has little to do with the tonal quality of the printed picture (although contrast there is important, too). Here *contrast* means to make sure your center of interest stands out from its background. If you are shooting something dark, make sure that the background is light and vice versa. You can also create contrast between the foreground and background of your picture. Landscape photographers almost always try to frame a shot with a tree or some flowers in the foreground.

Figure 10–5. The center of interest in a photo should be placed at or near one of the *rule-of-thirds* lines. The boot in this photo points to the calf's eye, the other center of interest. (Photo by Mike Penn)

Figure 10–6. The action in a photo—like this ball-carrier—should lead *into* the larger portion of the photo, and *into* the page as well. (Photo by Mike Penn)

Figure 10–7. Balance can also be achieved by having one emphasis on one thirds line and another element on the other. (Photo by Michael Messing)

Figure 10–8. Lines in a photo should lead the eye toward the center of interest, not away from it or off the newspaper page. Also see Figure 10–6. (Photo by Ron Osborne)

You should also make sure that no one in the photo is looking directly at the camera, avoid posed shots, select a photo that emphasizes the general subject of the story rather than a small part of it, and avoid "stock" shots, or photographic clichés, such as the ubiquitous clinch-and-grin trophy-acceptance photo (Fig. 10–9).

Figure 10–9. Stock shots such as this one of University of Tennessee basketball players Dale Ellis (*left*) and Michael Brooks should be avoided. (Photo by Michael Messing)

Figure 10–10. These two shots show alternatives to the stock shot in Figure 10–9. Pose winners in an informal way or, better yet, catch them in a candid pose. (Photos by Michael Messing)

Whenever a photographer is required to shoot—and the photo editor select and use—a photo of the local charity president accepting a school fund-drive check, or of the new cheerleaders, or of the state chess champion with her trophy, boundless imagination is necessary to avoid the cliché. Look for ways to get the subjects in a different pose from the usual handshake or the St. Valentine's Day Massacre group shot in which subjects line up against a wall. Just remember that the people, not the plaque or trophy, are the most important part of the photo. Sit them down and let them talk. Photograph them in an informal, casual pose (Fig. 10–10).

Photo Production

After a photo has been turned in, the editor must *crop* and *size* the photo. The act—and art—of cropping is similar to the editing of a reporter's story. The idea is to cut all unnecessary details. Rough cropping can be done on the proof sheet, and more precise cropping on an 8 × 10 full-frame print. In the latter case, the editor should crop the photo slightly larger than desired to allow for error. A velox that is too small cannot be pasted up; one that is too large can still be trimmed and used.

When cropping a photo, an editor should (1) crop so that there is one and only one center of interest; (2) crop tighter than might be thought reasonable (very few photos can be cropped *too* tightly—the error is usually made in the other direction); (3) *not* crop bodies at elbows, knees, wrists, and other joints.

It is a rare shot indeed that cannot be cropped at all. As a safety precaution, a photographer always tends to get more material on the negative than is needed in the print. What is there can be cropped, but what is missing cannot be added.

Cropping out parts of bodies is fine. Some of the best *mug shots* focus on part of the face, leaving out the top of the head, the ears, and sometimes the chin. An outstretched arm included in the photo would bring with it much unwanted empty space. So crop it out, but don't crop at the elbow—the cut there is too obvious and it distracts the reader. On the other hand, many readers don't even notice nonjoint crops.

Some editors like to use L-shaped pieces of paper or cardboard to help visualize various cropping choices (Fig. 10–11). Though very useful for visualizing, these pieces of paper should not be used for measuring. Use a ruler when sizing the photo. Accuracy here is very important.

Cropping never means actually cutting the photo with scissors or a paper cutter, practices that could damage the emulsion and create a ragged edge on the published photo. Instead, crop marks are drawn in the margin or occasionally on

Figure 10–11. L-shaped photo croppers can help visualize the final, cropped version of the photo. (Photo by Michael Messing)

Figure 10–12. Crop marks are drawn on the margins of the photo (*left*) with a grease pencil. The photo also can be cropped on the proof sheet. (Photos by Michael Messing)

the photo itself with a grease pencil (Fig. 10–12). These marks show the printer what area of the photo the editor wants to use.

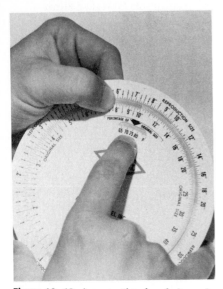

Figure 10–13. A proportional scale is used to tell the printer photo enlargement or reduction. Here the "original size" inner wheel refers to the size of the cropped photo (10"). Line up the 10" with the size you want the photo to be in the paper (the "reproduction size") on the outer wheel—7½". The percentage window shows that the photo should be marked for a 75 percent reduction.

Ideally, a photo should be cropped to the width and height that make it a good photo. Newpapers, however, use columns of set width, and photos must fit into these widths. A photo must be sized or *scaled* to fit the required column width either with a *proportional scale* (Fig. 10–13) or by mathematical formula.

When cropping a photo, an editor should keep in mind the planned proportion of the photo on the page dummy. In other words, if the page dummy calls for a vertical shot, the editor should mark on the photo a roughly vertical crop in a similar proportion.

The width of the cropped photo should be measured for enlarging or reducing to fit the preselected column width from the dummy. The width measurement—always given first—needs to be measured and sized first because it must fall on certain column-width measurements. Height can fluctuate; width cannot, unless you are doing a special display not using the standard columns.

Line up on a proportional scale the actual width of the cropped photo (the inside wheel) with the desired width (the outside wheel). The percentage of the enlargement or reduction is next to the arrow in the window of the inside wheel. A number over 100 means the photo must be enlarged for printing; a number under 100 means it must be reduced. Generally, the original photos should always be 8" × 10", then cropped and reduced for printing. The quality of the reduced photo is better than the enlarged one.

Let's look at an example. You have a photo that you have cropped to 9½" × 6". (Good job. These dimensions are close to the golden mean proportion of 1 to .62, the most pleasing proportion to the eye.) If you would rather work in picas—which is sometimes easier—the dimensions are 56 × 36 (picas are discussed in Chapter 12). You need to make the photo fit into three columns, which in your paper is 6⅞" (41 picas). Look closely at Figure 10–13. The inside (or "original") wheel's 9¼" mark is lined up with the outer wheel's 6⅞". In the percentage window you see that the photo needs to be reduced 75 percent.

To find out how high the reproduced photo will be, check the 6" mark on the inside, original wheel. The corresponding height on the outside reproduction wheel is 4½". The photo in the paper will be 6⅞" × 4½".

The mathematical formula uses cross multiplication of a ratio. You will always know three of the four numbers—photo width (PW) and height (PH) of the original photo and the reproduction width (RW) of the photo in the paper. You just need to know how high (RH) the photo will be. All these calculations can be made in inches or picas.

$$\frac{PW}{PH} = \frac{RW}{RH}$$

$$\frac{9\frac{1}{4}}{6} = \frac{6\frac{7}{8}}{X}$$

$$9\tfrac{1}{4}X = (6)\ (6\tfrac{7}{8})$$
$$X = \frac{41\frac{1}{4}}{9\frac{1}{4}} = 4\tfrac{1}{2}$$

Some printers want to know the desired height and width of the photo so they can calculate the percentage of reduction themselves. Others want to know the percentage. Regardless of which figures you give your printer, write the information on a slip of paper—never on the photo itself—and tape it to the back of the photo.

The printer then turns the photo into a *halftone*. Because newspapers use black ink on white paper, the many shades of gray in a photo must be made

Figure 10–14. A halftone enlarged to show the dot pattern.

through an optical illusion. The grays are reproduced by using thousands of tiny black dots per square inch. Dark grays use very large dots and small white space; light grays use very small dots separated by large areas of white (Fig. 10–14).

This process is also called *screening* because a sheet called a screen (it looks like a very fine window screen) is placed over the photo when converting it into a halftone. Most newspapers today use screens of 85 dots to the inch. The more dots per inch, the finer the detail that can be reproduced, and the higher the quality of the reproduction of the photo in the newspaper. Modern offset printing presses are capable of using fine photographic screens.

Photo Pages

Photo pages are being used more frequently by newspapers. As modern presses improve their photo reproduction capabilities, editors find ways to use more photographs. Many times complete pages are devoted to photos or photos with very little copy.

Photo pages fall into three categories: the photo group, the story, and the essay. The photo group is usually centered around an event, such as homecoming or a campus job fair (Fig. 10–15). All the photos on the page are independent of

Figure 10–15. A photo group.
(From *The Ranger*, San Antonio College)

Figure 10–16. This photo spread is from an award-winning special section on gangs in Southern California. (Courtesy of the *Daily Forty-Niner*)

Figure 10–17. A photo essay. (From *The Ranger*, San Antonio College)

one another and each shows a different aspect of the event. The photo group uses the most copy of the three types of photo pages. A photo story is usually about people, and the sequence of photos constitutes a narrative (Fig. 10–16). The photo story is used when a series of interrelated photos tell the story better than a long written story could. Most of the copy is written in long cutlines that explain each photo. A photo essay usually centers on an issue in the news, such as violence in sports or drugs on campus (Fig. 10–17). The photos may tell a story (as in a photo story) or the photos may be independent (as in a photo group). The photo essay, like a written essay, makes a personal statement about the issue.

Pointers on picture pages

1. One photo should dominate the page. A few photos make a better, more appealing page than do many photos.
2. One photo should be cropped severely horizontally or vertically. At any rate, the photos should be a variety of shapes. Don't overuse the "golden proportion."
3. Use ample white space. White space makes the photos stand out. The space between all elements should be equal, but the outside white space (between the photos and the edge of the page) *should* vary.
4. Vary the design of picture pages. Don't make today's look like the one you used last week.
5. Captions (or cutlines) need not be as wide as the photo.
6. Keep the captions as brief as possible. Don't repeat information. Let the photos tell the story.

Figure 10–18. Stop-action or blurring can be used to achieve different effects. Panning—stopping the focus element in a photo, but blurring the background—can also be used. (Photos by Mike Penn)

Photos are important and effective ways to communicate news (Figs. 10–18 through 10–22). Good photojournalists who are also good photographers need to be recruited and then given creative freedom. Section editors and the photo editor must work together in assigning, selecting, and cropping photos for use in the paper. Good photographs are of no use to readers if they are not used properly.

Figure 10–19. Good feature photos don't always have to have faces in them. (Photo by Ron Osborne)

Figure 10–20. Good sports photos usually focus in tightly on the action. (You can't get high-quality photos by blowing up small sections of negatives in the darkroom.) This close-up shot puts the reader right in the pool with the players. (Photo by Mike Penn)

Figure 10–21. The mug shot on the left shows effective use of very tight cropping. The photo on the right needs cropping. The person is looking out of the photo, not into it, and empty space fills much of the photo. (From *The Daily Pennsylvanian*, University of Pennsylvania)

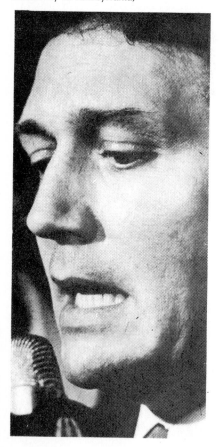

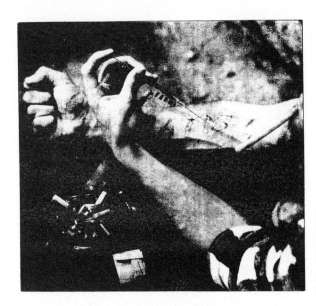

Figure 10–22. Sometimes the best way to illustrate a story is with a photo illustration. This one, from *Spectator* at the Eau Claire campus of the University of Wisconsin, is properly tagged as a photo-illustration in the credit line. (Courtesy of *Spectator*)

Suggested Projects

1. Look through issues of last year's paper for photos that show an effective use of center of interest, balance, leading lines, contrast, blurring, panning, and stop-action. Post them for the staff to see. Also look for photos that could have been cropped better. Draw crop marks on these photos and post them.

2. Invite a local photojournalist to visit your darkroom facilities. Ask for comments on your photo flow system. Get tips on photo coverage, photo pages, and more effective ways to use the technical tricks of the photojournalist's trade.

3. Evaluate your photo flow and negative-filing system during a staff meeting.

Vocabulary

crop
full frame
halftone
leading lines
mug
proof sheet
proportional scale
rule of thirds
screen
size

11 editing

After the copy has been written and the photographs taken, editors review the work to make sure that it is marked properly for the printer, that it represents good journalism, and that no legal problems will follow publication. A good editor can improve a reporter's story by judiciously cutting out extraneous words, correcting misspellings, and double-checking the story for accuracy. A good editor can also improve a photograph by cropping it and writing an appropriate caption or cutline.

Most writing and editing at modern newspapers is done on video display terminals (VDTs) or personal computers (PCs). Some larger universities have electronic newsrooms that rival even the most up-to-date professional papers. But because the vast majority of school newspapers still write and edit on paper, and because the fundamental editing skills and techniques needed by professional journalists are the same whether a pencil or an electronic cursor is used, this chapter does not discuss VDT editing techniques.

Editing, the careful second look at copy or photographs, can and should be done by the reporter or photographer who did the original work before turning it over to the copy desk or photo editor. A third look is *proofreading*—reading for minor corrections after a story has already been typeset.

Someone other than the reporter should read a story before it goes into the newspaper because reporters are not perfect typists. Reporters often work under deadline pressure and may overlook an error that a careful editor will catch and correct, and they need someone with an objective viewpoint to help them make their work even better.

Many beginning journalists and nonjournalists see reporting as the glory job on a newspaper. Perhaps it is, because the reporter usually gets the byline and the awards for an excellent story, even if an editor rewrote it. The better wordsmiths on a newspaper staff usually become editors, however, because good word skills are more important at the editor's desk than at a reporter's typewriter. Many papers will put up with a sloppy writer (for a while, anyway) if he or she is a good *reporter*. A good editor can make a story more readable, but only a good reporter can dig up the facts that go into the story. The ideal combination is a good reporter who is a good writer as well.

After reporters finish stories, they should revise them using the proper copy-editing marks (see Fig. 6–18) to correct typographical errors and to add to, delete, or change what they have written. As long as the copy does not contain a great many corrections, the story can be handed in. The editing should be printed legibly so that the typesetter is not slowed in setting the copy (Fig. 11–1). Most important, the reporter should try to *improve* the story through editing, not just add paragraph marks and "30."

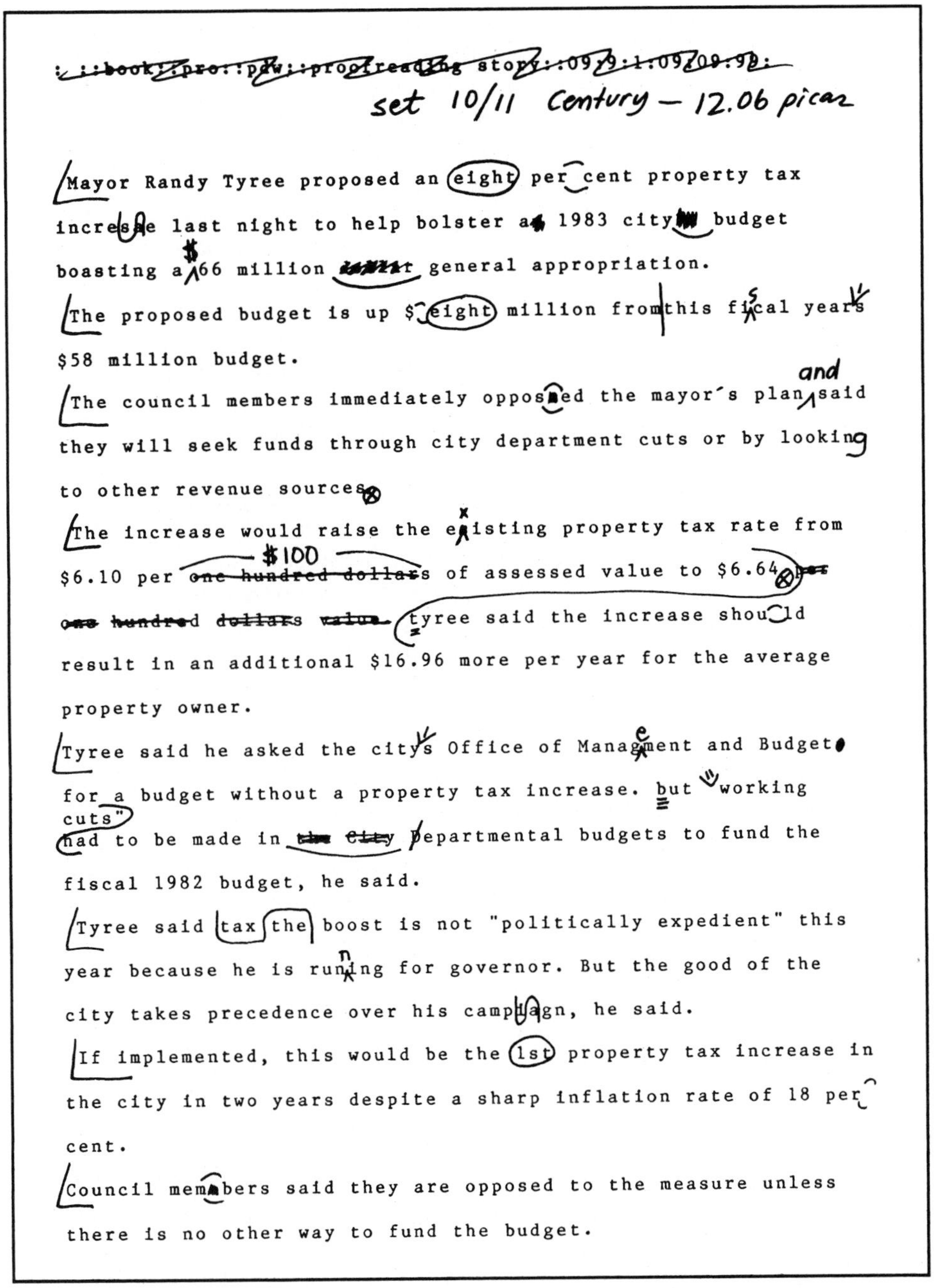

set 10/11 Century — 12.06 picas

Mayor Randy Tyree proposed an (eight) per cent property tax increase last night to help bolster a 1983 city budget boasting a 66 million general appropriation.

The proposed budget is up $ (eight) million from this fiscal year's $58 million budget.

The council members immediately opposed the mayor's plan *and* said they will seek funds through city department cuts or by looking to other revenue sources.

The increase would raise the existing property tax rate from $6.10 per *$100* one hundred dollars of assessed value to $6.64 per one hundred dollars value. Tyree said the increase should result in an additional $16.96 more per year for the average property owner.

Tyree said he asked the city's Office of Management and Budget for a budget without a property tax increase, but working cuts" had to be made in the city departmental budgets to fund the fiscal 1982 budget, he said.

Tyree said the tax boost is not "politically expedient" this year because he is running for governor. But the good of the city takes precedence over his campaign, he said.

If implemented, this would be the (1st) property tax increase in the city in two years despite a sharp inflation rate of 18 per cent.

Council members said they are opposed to the measure unless there is no other way to fund the budget.

Figure 11–1. Stories need not be typed perfectly. As long as the person keyboarding your copy can easily read the copy, corrections can—and should—be made with the proper copy-editing marks.

Copy Desk

At the copy desk copy is edited, pages are laid out, headlines are written, and editors' hair is often ripped out because of sloppy work by reporters. The copy desk is one of the last places where work can be improved or errors caught.

On professional papers the copy editor is sometimes called the *slot*, because traditionally the copy desk has been horseshoe shaped with the editor inside the U, or the "slot," of the desk.

Sitting outside the U are the *rim* persons. The copy editor selects stories for a page, lays the page out, and then turns the story and attached headline request figures over to someone on the rim. That person edits the story, writes a head for it, and returns it to the copy editor for final approval. The copy editor then marks the page layout with the appropriate slug for the story and headline and sends the copy to be typeset. (In modern electronic newsrooms, where editors can call up stories on a VDT no matter where they sit, the familiar U-shaped desk and the terms "slot" and "rim" are becoming bits of nostalgia, although the terms are still used.)

On larger school papers, the setup is often the same as on professional papers. The larger the volume of material to be edited, the more likely a newsroom will have a separate copy editor and copy desk. On smaller papers copy desks are a rarity—copy may go through one person to be edited, or the section editors themselves take care of all the editing for stories in their section.

Editors need to perform six basic tasks as they look over work by reporters: (1) mark the copy for proper typesetting; (2) check for mechanical writing errors (that is, punctuation or spelling errors, typographical errors, and so on); (3) check for accuracy of fact; (4) check for logic, clarity, usage; (5) estimate the length; and (6) write a headline for the story.

Because an editor needs to know beforehand how wide the story is to be set, the page should be designed (on a *page dummy*, or miniature map of the final product) before the editing process begins. By checking the page layout, the editor can mark the proper column width of the story, the point size and style of the type, the size and style of the headline requested, and any other special type effects the page designer has called for. All this information is marked in the space at the top of the first page. This information also is necessary for the electronic copy desk.

Next, the editor should correct all the mechanical errors. This first time through the editor should add or delete paragraph marks; change spelling, punctuation, and style errors; add "more" at the bottom of every continuing page and "30" or "#" at the end of the story (if the reporter has forgotten them); and correct minor grammatical errors, such as pronoun or subject/verb agreement. The "electronic" editor does not have to worry about these details. With wire stories, however, extraneous code words, the date and city of origin, and so on must be deleted.

These errors should be rectified the first time through because to the careful editor, they stand out blatantly. Not correcting them until later would interfere with the next step—reading the story for logic and idea flow. The last part of this mechanical check should be a very careful look at all facts: spellings of names, dates, places, and so on. Libel suits often stem from carelessness, so *everything* ought to be checked, even if reporters insist they are correct.

Editors need to be skeptics. It's not good enough for the reporter to be sure; the editor should be sure as well. A good editor knows a little about a lot of things, the better ones a little about nearly everything. They may not know if a figure is correct or if the spelling of a strange chemical is right, but they know to doubt their accuracy, and they know where to check the information.

Next comes the most difficult reading of the story: the check for logic and idea flow. Note how the editing process has moved from specific to general. First the very specific items, such as graf marks and "more," get the editor's attention. Then come the common misspellings and style errors, and next a check for accuracy of names and other facts in the story. Now the editor takes a general, overall look at the organization and flow of the entire story. Some editors may prefer to go from general to specific, but getting the picky little errors out of the way first works better for most people. Multiple readings are always necessary, because if you stop every other line to correct some small typo, you aren't going to be able to follow the reporter's story.

If a story is well written, the lead will grab the reader's attention and convey the important point of the story, either through a summary or through some kind of characterization. From there the story flows logically from idea to idea so that any reader can quickly comprehend what the reporter is communicating. But any writer can tell you that this type of writing does not come easily. So the editor often must help. The editor, who comes to the story fresh, can objectively judge the story's merits and repair its shortcomings.

First, look at the lead. Does it grab the reader? If it is a summary lead, does it accurately summarize the major point(s) of the story? Is it too long, too short? If the lead is weak, fix it by editing or write a better one.

Then mentally pick out the major points of the story and outline them. Are the major points listed first, with minor points following? Are the points in a logical sequence? Are points supported? Do the transitions move the reader easily from point to point, graf to graf? If it is a news story in inverted-pyramid format, can the story be cut after nearly any graf and still make sense? When the story ends, does the reader have an understanding of what was just read? Are all the questions a reader may ask answered in the story?

If the answers to all these questions are affirmative, then the editor can thank the reporter for doing a good job. If any of the answers are negative, then it is up to the editor to make the necessary corrections, additions, or deletions. Of course, for major work the story should be sent back to the reporter.

Copy Counting

Before setting a story in type, an editor should estimate approximate length. If the story is too long or short, the editor should deal with the story before it has been set in type. Stories should always be a little longer than the page dummy calls for. If the dummy calls for a 12″ story, set approximately 15″ in case last-minute adjustments to the design require more copy. On the other hand, too much unused copy set in type is a waste of money. If a story is too short, the editor can make sure that filler material is on hand.

The easiest copy-counting method requires character counting of both the news copy and the typeset story. First, determine how many characters (including punctuation and spaces) are in the average inch of typeset material in your paper. Let's say the answer is 240. If you set the margins on your typewriter or PC at 10 and 70 and keep the lines as close as possible to 60 characters, four lines on your typewritten page will equal one inch of copy in the paper. Thus, an assignment for a 12D story will require at least 48 *full* typed lines. Short end-of-paragraph lines should be counted as half lines. Many PC word processing programs or spelling check programs have character-count or word-count capability. These can assist in estimating the length of the story on the page.

It is also a good idea to write a graf or two more than required because an editor will probably tighten the writing. Extra grafs can always be cut; a short story cannot easily be lengthened. Some staffs have copy paper printed with the required margins indicated (Fig. 11–2). Because elite and pica typewriters fit a different amount of characters within a certain length line (elite type has 12 characters to the inch, pica 10), reporters need to know what kind of typewriter they are using. Regardless of the length of the line, however, it is the number of characters on the line that is important. Ask your printer to set up samples of different-size columns and type using the same page of copy. This way, different lengths of the same copy can be displayed graphically.

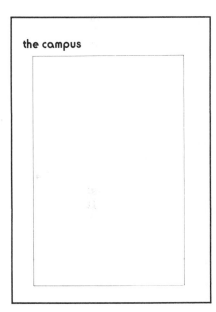

Figure 11–2. The margins on this copy paper, set at 60 characters on a pica typewriter, make copy counting easy: Four lines of typing equal one inch of type in the newspaper.

Examples of Editing

Many beginning reporters misunderstand the role of the editor and resent the editing done by the copy desk. These neophytes believe that every word that spills from their teeming minds onto their typewriter keys is sacred and that editing changes are akin to editorial heresy. This is simply not the case. *Every* reporter gets edited; *every* story can be improved. Sometimes the reporter may not agree with

Grammar: Calisthenics of writing

Most beginning journalists cringe at the very mention of the word "grammar." Nonetheless, using good grammar is part of being a good journalist. Mastering every aspect of the English language is a lengthy and difficult task, but nearly anyone who applies himself or herself can learn the rudiments of grammar. There are many good texts for this (listed in the bibliography for this chapter), but a quick look at several weak areas should get you started in improving the mechanics of your writing. Just like calisthenics, which are a tedious but necessary part of learning ballet, grammar study is a tedious but necessary part of learning to be a writer.

Spelling seems to be a major weak point of students today. Many believe that, as in horseshoes, closeness counts. But a good writer is precise and will not stand for anything but the correct spelling. Professional editors are complaining more and more about the poor spelling skills of journalism-school graduates. Now is the time to polish your spelling skills so that when you hit the job market, your correct spelling will stand out.

Spelling is little more than applying certain rules (such as the proverbial "*i* before *e* except after *c*") and a lot of memorization. If you didn't have a rigorous spelling education when you were young and more interested in acquiring new words, you may have difficulty. But remember that learning to spell is just a matter of memorizing the words you have trouble with. Make a list of your problem words and refer to it constantly. When you have mastered a word, cross it off. Learn to use the dictionary and *use* it; most terrible spellers have dusty dictionaries.

Most punctuation problems stem from misuse of the comma and problems with the semicolon and colon. Use punctuation marks sparingly. When in doubt, leave them out. Beginning writers tend to use commas too frequently, inserting the mark as a cue for the reader to inhale. A comma is not placed in the sentence by sound or by breathing patterns; it is placed there by rules of grammar.

Commas separate items in a series: *Our flag is red, white and blue.* The comma before the coordinate conjunction (and, but, or) may or may not be used, depending on the style of the publication for which you are writing. Most newspaper stylebooks—following the general dictum of "When in doubt, leave it out"—do not use a comma before the conjunction in a series. Commas do appear before coordinate conjunctions in this book because books do not follow newspaper-style rules.

Commas and conjunctions also come together in compound sentences. A compound sentence is really two sentences, or independent clauses, of common meaning joined together by a conjunction *and* a comma. A conjunction alone or a comma alone is just not strong enough to hold two sentences together. An example of a compound sentence is "We have missed the bus, and now we will be late for school." The two clauses, which could stand by themselves as separate sentences, are related in meaning, so they may be joined. Notice the presence of both a comma and the conjunction *and.* Don't join unrelated ideas in a compound sentence: "We have missed the bus, and the exam is tomorrow."

Commas are also used after introductory phrases or clauses. The general rule is that if the introductory phrase or clause is short—about five words or fewer—no comma is necessary. "By morning the rain had ended" needs no comma after *morning* because the introductory phrase consists of only two words. "Because the rain had turned the field into a puddle of muck, the game was canceled" does need a comma after the introductory phrase because the phrase is longer than five words.

Commas are used with nonrestrictive adjective clauses. Restrictive clauses, which may look similar to nonrestrictive clauses (and which in fact may often be *exactly* the same), do not take commas. The difference between the two clauses depends on *meaning*, not on any kind of grammatical rule.

A restrictive adjective clause restricts, or limits, the *meaning* of the noun it modifies (its antecedent) to a smaller group within a larger body.

For instance, in the sentence "The drivers who had selected rain tires were having no problems with the downpour," the clause *who had selected rain tires* restricts the meaning of the noun *drivers* to the small group in the field who were using rain tires instead of dry-weather tires. *Only* those drivers with the rain tires were having no problems.

Because the clause is so important to the meaning of the word *drivers,* no commas are used. But what if *all* the drivers had selected rain tires before the race and the writer merely wanted to tell the reader that fact? Then the clause would be nonrestrictive and commas would be called for: "The drivers, who had selected rain tires, were having no problems with the downpour." Here the information is additional, parenthetical information; it does not restrict the meaning of *drivers* to only a small group.

Confused? No one said this was easy. The process, however, is simple, if not easy. First, you have to identify the clause. *Who, which,* and *that* introduce the vast majority of restrictive/nonrestrictive clauses, so just look for those words. Then, after you have identified the beginning and end of the clause, pull it out of the sentence. Does the removal change the intended meaning? If so, it's restrictive. *Do not separate it* from the main clause with commas. If its removal does not change the meaning, put commas on *both* sides. There is *never* a comma on just one side of a nonrestrictive clause.

If you use commas only in these situations and in the place listed below in the discussion of semicolons, you will make few comma errors. If, when copy-reading a story, you find a comma that doesn't fit any of these rules, get rid of it!

Semicolons are misused so much that beginners are often told not to use them at all. If your sentences are so long that you need a semicolon, make them two sentences. The semicolon must be used, however, in a series of items that use commas internally. Otherwise, the reader wouldn't be able to tell the difference between a minor break *within* the item and a major break *between* items. A good example of this is a list of names and organization titles:

> The following were elected officers of the MVC Chess Club last week: Fred Fenwick, president; Trudy Truesdale, vice-president; Eddie Wilson, treasurer; and Sally Brown, secretary.

Note how the comma is needed to separate the name and the title. If there were also commas after each title, it might confuse the reader as to which title went with which name. So the commas provide the minor breaks in a complex list and the semicolons the major breaks. Note also that there is always a semicolon before the conjunction in a series using semicolons.

Both the semicolon and the colon may be used to join complete sentences (independent clauses), but beginners would do well to avoid using them that way; the uses of the colon especially are sometimes based on subtleties. It's better to make compound sentences with only a comma and a conjunction.

Colons *should* be used to introduce a quote or a list. (See the sentence preceding the semicolon example.) Think of the colon as the Ed McMahon ("He-e-r-r-e's Johnny!") of punctuation marks: He's always introducing what follows. If you can't replace a colon in your work with the words "And here it is," you've probably used it incorrectly.

The last common problem area for beginners is agreement. Subjects and verbs, and pronouns and their antecedents, must agree in number. In other words, singular subjects must have singular verbs, and plurals must go with plurals. The same goes for pronouns. Although there are many types of agreement violations, two seem to be especially common. Consult a grammar book for work on the rest.

Beginners often make agreement errors when there is a prepositional phrase or other intervening words between the subject and the verb. You should identify the subject and the verb, no matter how far apart they may be in the sentence, and make sure that they agree. For example, in the sentence "The two little girls, along with the man who claims to be their father, were seen at the lake yesterday," the tendency is to say "father *was* seen"; but *father* is not the subject, *girls* is. Remember that grammar is not an auditory skill: It doesn't matter what it sounds like. "Father were seen" may sound awkward, but it is grammatically correct in this case. Be sure you know the subject(s) and verb(s) in your sentences, and make sure they agree in number, no matter how far apart they may be.

The other agreement violation has to do with the agreement of antecedents with indefinite pronouns. Indefinite pronouns are words such as *somebody, anybody, nobody, no one, each, every, all, either,* and *neither*: words that refer to no particular person. The common error here is that a plural pronoun is often used after an indefinite pronoun when a singular pronoun is called for. For example, in the sentence "Everyone on the team tried her best," the usual tendency is to substitute *their* for *her*, the justification being that *team* is plural because there are many team members. But the subject is every*one*, team members as singular individuals. The same goes for "Did somebody lose her [not *their*] book?" and "Neither of the boys is [not *are*] coming." Again, the trick is no trick at all. Merely know your grammar well enough to identify the proper antecedents of your pronouns, and make sure they agree.

The one monkey wrench in the indefinite-pronoun works can be illustrated by the word "all." *All* can be either singular or plural, and it is up to you to decide how to use it. If what you are talking about can be separated into component parts, then use *all* as plural ("*All* the dollar bills *are* gone"). If *all* refers to a concept that cannot be broken up, use the word as singular ("*All* the money *is* gone").

This list doesn't begin to touch upon all the facets of grammar, punctuation, and usage. Reporters and especially editors need to hone their grammar skills to a fine degree. It does take study and practice. But careful writers care enough about their readers and about their words to make the conscientious study of grammar and spelling second nature.

the changes and should consult the editor. But in most cases the editor has improved the story.

Dealing with the creative work of another person is always a tricky business. Good editors will make only those changes that are necessary. They make changes not in the reporter's writing style, just in mechanics. The editor's main responsibility is to the readers, not to the reporter's ego.

Here are some examples of fuzzy thinking that slipped by the editor's pencil. How would you edit these?

1. Down the hall from the Student Personnel Center is an office that few people hear about—the Enablers Office which benefits the many handicapped students on campus.

   The Enablers Program helps the many handicapped students on campus. It gives these students the opportunity to go to college and benefit from the areas that they need.

Not only are these programs offered, but also easy access to all facilities is provided. Elevators, ramps and automatic doors are only a few of these facilities. Plans are always being developed to eliminate the remaining architectural barriers.

2. While other colleges, such as the University of Long Beach, San Jose State, Pasadena College, and Fresno State, will also be participating in the competition, the bands will be rated individually—not in comparison to the other college bands.

3. Monies from these activities are drawn from gate receipts at football and basketball games and a large district subsidy. Next year's $99,044 budget includes $33,000 in anticipated gate receipts and $58,000 in guaranteed district subsidy.

Example 1 consists of the first three paragraphs of a story on the Enablers Office at Middle Valley College. The first graf shows that the student does not know the difference between a restrictive and a nonrestrictive adjective clause. The clause "which benefits the many handicapped students on campus" is an adjective clause that modifies "Enablers Office." But the writer—and the editor—have incorrectly punctuated the clause as restrictive; it should be nonrestrictive and a comma should be added after "Office." A restrictive clause *restricts*, or limits, the meaning of the noun it modifies. As punctuated (without a comma), the clause restricts "Enablers Office" to only that one office that benefits the many handicapped students on campus, implying that some Enablers Offices on campus do not benefit handicapped students. This is absurd because there is only one campus Enablers Office. Inserting a comma, thus making the clause *nonrestrictive*, is correct because the clause *adds* information to the noun; it does not restrict the meaning of the noun.

The second graf of example 1 begins with an obvious redundancy. The writer had just defined the function of the Enablers Office in the opening graf. Also, we have Enablers *Program* (capital *P*), which is a change from the reference in the lead graf. Why the change? And what is meant by "benefit from the areas that they need"? Do the students need *areas?* It is an example of fuzzy thinking, and both the reporter and editor missed it.

The third graf is another example of poor grammar and weak editing. What are "These programs" that the writer is referring to in the first sentence? The writer seems to think he has mentioned them already, and the reader is only going to get confused. The third sentence refutes the statement in the first sentence that the Enablers Office provides "easy access to all facilities." In other words, if plans for removing the remaining architectural barriers are always being developed (third sentence), there must be some barriers to remove, which the first sentence says is not true. It also sounds as if the Enablers Office is always coming up with plans it cannot follow through on. Example 1 is an example of a story that needed a heavy rewrite by a careful editor.

Example 2 shows a common misuse of the word "while," which means "at the same time as." Is that what the writer intended the word to mean in that sentence? The sentence is also much too long and unwieldy. Lastly, the University of Long Beach doesn't exist; California State University, Long Beach, is the correct name of the school.

Example 3 reads pretty well at first glance. But good editors are nuts about checking numbers. The income figures given here don't add up: $8,044 of income is not mentioned, and its absence is not explained. It is not fair to the reader to print this kind of inattention to detail.

Good editing can improve the work of even the best reporter on the staff. Editors are necessary to organize the putting together of the newspaper in the newsroom after the reporters have brought in the news and features. But editors are also necessary to make reporters' stories more readable. Editors and reporters can and should work together toward the same goal: the best possible story.

PROOFREADER'S MARKS

⊗	Period	✐	Delete	
∧	Comma	*tr*	Transpose -- letters, words, or lines	
:	Colon	⌗	Insert space	
;	Semicolon	‿	Close up	
⌄	Apostrophe	✓	Less space	
⌄ ⌄	Quotations	⫽	Equalize space	
=	Hyphen	*wf*	Wrong font	
⊢⊣	Dash	◻	Indent one em. Double for two ems	
Cap	Capitalize	⊓	Move up	
lc	Lower case	⊔	Move down	
¶	Paragraph	⊏	Move to left	
No¶	No paragraph	⊐	Move to right	
spell	Spell out	*stet*	Let stand something that has been marked out	
∧	Caret			

Figure 11–3. Proofreading marks are similar to copy-editing marks, but because different changes are needed when copy has already been set in type, additional marks are used. These would be used only on the page proof in the electronic newsroom.

Proofreading

The last chance to catch errors before they become part of history in print is during proofreading and reading page proofs. Proofreaders look over the story after it has been set in type but before it has been trimmed, waxed, and pasted up on the page. In the electronic newsroom, the editing and the proofreading are, in essence, done at the same time. What the editor does with a story comes out in type. Thus, extra care must be taken to ensure accuracy. Proofreaders should not look for (nor, theoretically, should they find) parts of the story that need editing. Instead, the proofreader looks for typographical errors and double-checks common facts. Good proofreaders may sometimes find errors of logic or idea flow that both the editor and reporter missed. The proofreader should query the editor to see if a change is warranted.

Proofreaders use many of the same marks that editors do (Fig. 11–3), but there are some variations because proofreaders are dealing with type, whereas editors deal with typewritten words. Proofreaders use a special blue pen (sometimes called *photo-blue*) that is invisible to the camera that takes a picture of the page for the printing plate. Because the camera will not "see" the nonreproducible blue ink, the proofreader can mark a correction directly on the proof and mark the symbol indicating the needed correction in the margin (Fig. 11–4). Unlike copy editing, where marks are made between lines of the story, proofreading corrections are always made in the margin; there is too little room between the lines of type to make the corrections clearly.

Figure 11–4. Proofreading changes are always indicated in the margin of the page proof. A photo-blue pen is used so that the correction marks will not appear in the printed paper.

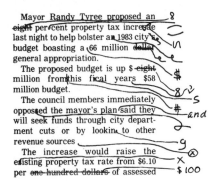

Page proofs (the completed paste-up of the page) are the last checkpoint in the process before the paper is put to bed. This is the last chance that bleary-eyed staff members have to catch and correct errors. If the proofreading process has been effective, page-proof time can be spent looking for big errors only—heads over the wrong stories, cutlines under the wrong photos, entire columns of type transposed in a multicolumn story. Sometimes these big, obvious errors are the hardest to see—until the paper is on the newsstand.

Photo Editing

The section editor or the photo editor initiates the photo process by making an assignment for a photo. A good editor who knows why the photographer was sent out in the first place can help the photographer by making suggestions on the assignment sheet. The editor should not necessarily suggest camera position, shutter speed, and f-stop but rather make sure the photographer understands what angle the story will take. If a photographer doesn't understand what the editor is looking for, he or she may turn in an excellent photo, but it won't fit the editor's needs. The responsibility for a good assignment lies with the editor.

By working closely with the photo editor, the section editor can be sure that the purpose of the photo is made clear to the photographer. The primary purpose of newspaper photos is to *communicate*. An inexperienced section editor may want to select a photo based on news values alone, regardless of quality. An inexperienced photojournalist may want to use the best shot, regardless of news value. A photo editor who can step in, evaluate both sides of the situation, and select the best photo for the job is a plus for a staff. Without a photo editor, this problem must be worked out by the section editor and photographer.

If the staff has no photo editor, then the section editor should crop the photos. The photographer should provide full-frame shots to the editor or follow the editor's suggested cropping on the proof sheet.

Describing the Photo

Few photos can stand by themselves. Even scenic photos can communicate better with a *cutline* telling the reader where the photo was taken and under what circumstances. The best news photos can always be enhanced by adding explanation in a cutline and/or *caption*. The cutline is the main text of the description of the photo. The caption, used in various typographical ways, is a one- to four-word tagline for the photo. Although newspapers have differing rules concerning the use of cutlines, several basic rules should be followed.

Writing a cutline requires as much skill and attention to detail as writing a news story does. Because a cutline should be brief, the words must be packed with meaning. A cutline should describe the photo, not the event itself, but it should not state the obvious. If, for instance, the photo shows water spouting out of a broken fire hydrant, the cutline should not say that. It should explain *why*. Also, be specific. Don't say that the lineman in the photo is heavy; say that he is 6'4" and weighs 285 pounds.

Cutlines should never make obvious statements: "Shown above is" or "Pictured here with her prize." When identifying persons in a photo, use as simple a method as possible, as dictated by the formation of persons in the photo. Use "from left," instead of "from left to right." Use the front-row, back-row method or the clockwise method for larger groups. If only two persons are in the photo, identify one as being on the left, then just name the other person. The reader will know whom you are referring to.

If there are persons in the background of a photo, never say that they are "looking on." Crop them out of the photo if they are just "looking on." Instead, identify the person somehow: "Behind Jones is 1954 Homecoming Queen Rebecca Peterson," or "Clyde Hamilton, background, is immediate past president."

If the picture is humorous or lighthearted, then the cutline should be as well. But don't get carried away. A cutline is not the place to editorialize or be sarcastic. Captions are the best place to use humor—perhaps a pun or a play on words. Then the cutline can explain the photo as well as the pun, if necessary.

Cutlines should be written so that every line in the paper is nearly a full line. A very short line at the end of a cutline adds unwanted white space to a page. Some papers have special printed forms that assist in character counting. Cutlines with a series of photos side by side should all be the same approximate depth, regardless of the photo width. Cutlines for multicolumn photos should be set in several columns. If the typeset columns are uneven, the "short" leg of type should be the last one.

Cutlines are written for two kinds of photos—those that stand alone (sometimes called *feature photos*) and those that accompany a story. Cutlines for *stand-alone* or *wild photos* may be long and should convey the basic who, what, where, when, how, and why of the story behind the photo. Cutlines for photos with an accompanying story do not need to be as long. The story provides the detail.

The layout style of a paper sometimes calls for a separate headline with the photo. Called either a *catchline* or an *overline*, this is similar in function to a caption (Fig. 11–5). Catchlines and overlines are usually used in place of captions on stand-alone photos.

Photo Credits

Writers get by-lines for their work; photographers get *photo-credit* lines. As with by-lines, photo-credit lines should be given for excellent work, not for every photo that appears in the paper. Many papers have a standard photo credit—such as "Clarion photo" or "Photo by the Daily News"—for standard shots.

Cutting up

Barby Cobb

Carole Brewer, left, freshman in education, receives directions on fetal pig dissection from her instructor, Vicki Major, graduate student in zoology. Dissecting the pigs is a laboratory requirement for Biology 1220 classes.

Figure 11–5. Sometimes a small head can be used above the photo—as an overline—instead of as a caption beneath the photo. (From *The Daily Beacon*, University of Tennessee)

Stride for stride chase

Photo by Brian K. Johnson

UW-Eau Claire forward Steve Manning (right) and a UW-Stout player were in pursuit
of the ball in this soccer action Sunday at Simpson Field. UWEC won, 6-1.

Water music

While students enjoy the cool water in IMPE pool Monday
afternoon lifeguard Steve Mason, senior in engineering,
spends some free time practicing his oboe in the hot sultry
weather. (photo by Steve Buyansky)

Snow job

Old Man Winter played a late April Fools' joke and dumped, ahem, the last snowfall of the season Friday night. Ralph Rickgarn, director of Centennial
Hall, walked across the snow-covered Mall Saturday afternoon to Walter Library.

**Figure 11–6. Photo credit lines can be used in many ways. The upper left photo uses a credit line at the lower right corner of the photo,
the upper right uses one at the end of the cutline, and the bottom uses one vertically at the lower right corner. (From *Spectator,* University
of Wisconsin, Eau Claire; *The Daily Illini,* Illini Publishing Company, Champaign, IL; *Minnesota Daily,* University of Minnesota)**

Newspapers use photo credits in many different ways (Fig. 11–6). Try to be fair with the size and play of the photo credit compared to the writer's by-line. On some papers the writer gets a large, prominently displayed by-line, and the photographer gets a small credit line run up the side of a photo or at the end of the cutline. Even worse, the writer of a photo essay gets a by-line in 18-point type and the photographer is still stuck with little 6-point lines. Give photographers credit for their work, and give them as much credit as the writers get.

Editing is important because it is the last step in preparing original work for publication in the paper. The tasks of copy-editing, proofreading, photo selection and cropping, and cutline writing—along with page layout—bring together in an attractive and coherent package all the news, entertainment, and opinion for that news day or week. Creative writers and photographers are not enough to make a good newspaper; skilled editors are also needed to coordinate and improve work.

— *Suggested Projects* —

1. Go over back issues of your paper and look for stories that needed more editing. Why weren't they edited well in the first place? If they came in on deadline and there was still not enough time for a solid editing job, could the deadline be moved up an hour to allow more time on the copy desk? Now that you have the time, how would you change those stories?

2. Invite a local editor to discuss editing techniques. Perhaps he or she can bring a sample story that needs editing. What editorial skills does the editor believe are important?

3. Develop a system (or review the one you have) for reporters and photographers to give feedback to editors on how they believe their work was handled. Make sure the internal communication lines are open.

4. Invite a local photographer or photo editor to visit your newsroom and discuss photo-selection processes with the editors and the photo staff.

Vocabulary

caption
catchline
cutline
feature photo
overline
page dummy
page proof
photo credit
photo-blue
proofread
rim
slot
stand-alone photo
wild photo

Exercises

1. Edit the following story. Use the proper copy-editing symbols.

MCV proffesor Sara Grayson who was aquitted last month of conspiracy to sell stolen movie and copywrite infringements, against movie studios, has filed a six hundred thousand dollar lawsuit in Federal Court against a New York man and his wife who testified against him in thecase

Grayson flied the suit against Bruce Troute and his wife Brooke, both of Albany, N.Y. claiming they sold her several hundred films under false and fraudulent pretenses.

Grayson claims to have suffered substantial expsnses in herself defending and irreparable damage to her reputation. as a result of the criminal prosecution.

> Troute is currently serving an 18-month sentence in a federal penitentiary in Massachusetts as a plea bargain he struck with the United State's Attorneys office for his testimony against Grayson.

2. Edit the following story.* Watch for libel problems. Cut unnecessary information. This story needs heavier editing than the story in exercise 1. Publication day for this story is Wednesday, April 27. The incident occurred on Friday, April 22. The correct names are Leonard G. Zelmin, Glen Harder, and Joann Hanson.

ASB veep busted
Middle Valley College Clarion
Susan Daniels

A major xxx Middle Valley College student body officer was arrested on a serious criminal charge.

Associated Student Body (ASB) Vice President Leonard J. Zelmin, was alledgely arrested last night for possession of Cocaine.

According to police records, Mr. Zemlin, who is twenty-eight, was taken into possession by city police lieutenant Glenn Harder, two miles from campus after he was seen weaving severely in his car on College Rd.

Harder searched the suspects car and found 5 ounces of Cocaine in the trunk. This inflormationis from the official pulice record. report.

Zelmin was taken to city jaill, booked,, incardcerated overnight, and, finally, released on $1500 bail this morning. He will be preliminarily arraigned this Wednesday afternoon Apr. 27th, in Jefferson County Superior court.

Elected ASB Vice President in the February elections, Zelmin has also formerly served in the offices of ASB treasurer and Sophomore Class Council President. A Physics major, Zelmin is on th Admissions Office list to graduate in June. He is a veteran of the Army war in Vietnam and was honored withboth the Medal of Honor and the Burple Heart.

more

---

*From a copy-editing exercise by M. M. Jacobson.

ASB veep busted
Middle Valley College Clarion
Susan Daniels

add 1

A 4th semester student, carries a 3.7 grade point average and has had his name three times on the dean's scholarship list.

Zelmin, is an honor graduate of Thomas Paine High School in 1990, where he was elected to the post of ASB president twice.

Givinghis xxxxx version of what happened in a campus interview, Zelmin revealed "the pigs have been on my case for years just because they know I hate faschist authority and have spoken out publically against it."

"I was framed. That cop planted the Cocaine in my car, and I'm innocent.

Zelmin says that he will enter a plead of innocent to the charge Wednesday afternoon at his hearing.

ASB president Joann Hanson had no comment on Zelmin's arrest, except to say that it, "Would have no effect on his status on the campus of this college.."

30

12 typography and printing

News is worthless unless it can be printed in mass quantities and distributed to the public. Good journalists—reporters as well as editors—should have a working knowledge of typography and the printing process of their newspaper. A knowledge of what happens to stories and photographs after they leave the editor's desk not only helps staffers avoid asking for something that cannot be done by the printer, but this also helps them use all the available typographical tricks of the trade to make the paper easier to read and more attractive.

Before learning typeface styles and different printing methods, journalists should learn the basic vocabulary of printing. Since the fifteenth century, when Johann Gutenberg invented movable type (individual, reusable letters instead of page-size carved wooden blocks), an informal vocabulary of printing has developed. But not until the French printer Pierre Fournier formalized the point system of typesetting in the eighteenth century did all printers speak the same language.

Fournier selected the *point*—the approximate size of a period, or $1/72$ of an inch—as the basic measuring unit for type (Fig. 12–1). Today the height of a letter is measured in points (Fig. 12–2). A newspaper may use type sizes of five and one-half or six points for classified ads, legal notices, stock market reports, and sports summaries and box scores. Nine- or 10-point type is standard for other editorial material. Headlines range from the small 14-point heads of news briefs to 60-point, 72-point, and larger headlines of the stories on page 1. Newsstand editions

Figure 12–1. This photo shows the relationship between an inch, a pica, and a point. Picas are shown on the bottom. The black box around the six indicates that six picas equal one inch. Since there are 12 points to a pica, 72 points equal an inch.

Figure 12–2. The height of a letter is usually measured in points.

This is 9-point Univers 55

This is 14-point Univers 55

This is 24-point Univers 55

This is 36-point Univers 55

This is 72-point

This copy is set 12 picas, 3 points wide, a common measure in 6-column broadsheet newspapers today.

This copy is set 14 picas wide, a common measure used on 4-column tabloid newspapers. All line measures are made in picas and points.

Figure 12–3. Column width or column measure varies, depending on the size of publication and the design plan. On a given page, varying the standard width on one story is a good way to help that story stand out.

of metropolitan dailies use big-story headlines as large as 144 points (approximately two inches high) to catch the reader's eye.

The width of columns is specified by the *pica* (see Fig. 12–2). Twelve points make up a pica, and six picas make an inch. Newspaper-column widths range from approximately 10 picas in *tabloids* (papers the size of *Rolling Stone* or *The Sporting News*) to 12 to 14 picas in six-column full-size papers (Fig. 12–3). Readability studies have shown that the optimum width for 9- or 10-point *body type* (the type size in standard newspaper stories) is 13½ or 14 picas. The width in picas should be about 150 percent of the point size of the type. Some full-size papers have switched to the six-column format to achieve this optimum width. Because of a move to narrower paper to save money, the standard width of most newspaper columns today is about 12 picas, 3 points.

Because creative page design calls for some variety in column widths, editors should understand this print-shop terminology. The editor will have to do pica and point calculations for redesigned column widths. A story set in a standard column width of 12 picas, 3 points, for instance, will become narrower (and thus longer) if reset at 11 picas to be set off inside a box.

Two other commonly used type measurements are the *em* and the *en*. The em is equal to the width of the capital letter M. Because the M in most typefaces is square, the width of an em is usually equal to the height of the letter. For example, an em in 12-point type is 12 points, in 36-point type it's 36 points, and so on. Paragraph indentations in typesetting are usually one em space (Fig. 12–4). The en is one-half the em measurement in a given typeface. Therefore, an en in 12-point type would be 6 points, and an en in 36-point type would be 18 points. These two measurements—along with a third measurement, called a thin space (one sixth of an em)—are not used nearly as often by page designers as the pica and point, but the designer should understand them nevertheless. These measurements are used most often in setting up tabular material or in special effects such as *initial letters* (larger-than-normal letters that begin a paragraph) and *copy wraps* (columns of type made to fit around an unusual shape).

Figure 12–4. Paragraph indentations are usually one em space. An en space is one half an em, and a thin space is one sixth of an em.

1 em

This example shows a one em indentation preceding the first line.

One em.

One en.

One thin space.

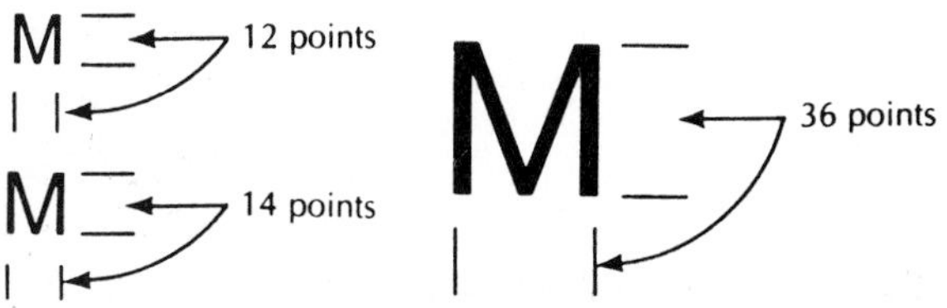

M 12 points

M 14 points

M 36 points

One last term concerning type measurement is leading (pronounced "ledding"). *Leading* refers to the amount of space—including white space—that surrounds a line of type (Fig. 12–5). (On many modern phototypesetters as well as in word processing and PC pagination software, leading is called *linespacing*.) Technically, a line of type is always designed with a few points of white space above and below the line; thus 12-point type is not precisely 12 points high. But in a column of 12-point type set solid (or with 12 points of linespacing), the measure between the bottom of one line of type and the bottom of the next line of type will be 12 points. It is simpler to think of leading as the amount of space *between* lines of

Figure 12–5. Leading is one specification a typesetter must know before setting a story or headline.

Leading refers to the measurement of the white space that surrounds a line of type.

26 points

24-point type, 26-point leading

Writing and editing the news are only the first half of the newspaper process. The news is worthless unless it can be printed in mass quantities and distributed to the public.

10-point type, 10-point leading

Writing and editing the news are only the first half of the newspaper process. The news is worthless unless it can be printed in mass quantities and distributed to the public.

10-point type, 11-point leading

Writing and editing the news are only the first half of the newspaper process. The news is worthless unless it can be printed in mass quantities and distributed to the public.

10-point type, 12-point leading

Writing and editing the news are only the first half of the newspaper process. The news is worthless unless it can be printed in mass quantities and distributed to the public.

10-point type, 15-point leading

type. The width of the line and the boldness of the type are factors that determine how much leading is to be used.

A story set without extra leading is said to be *set solid*. Most newspapers today set their stories with one extra point of leading. For example, 10-point stories are set with 11-point leading (often written 10/11). The extra white space between the lines, even though a mere 1/72 inch, makes the type easier to read.

A typesetter needs to know four specifications about a story before it is set in type: (1) type style, (2) point size, (3) pica width for the column, and (4) linespacing. Without these markings at the beginning of a story, the typesetter cannot begin. Some news departments set up standard measures for all four specifications. Only copy that is to be set differently is marked. The typesetter assumes that unmarked copy is to be set according to agreed-upon standard measurements.

Typography

In addition to typeface measurements, there are several categories of typefaces the journalist should know. All typefaces fall into one of these categories, called races. The main three races of type of use to the newspaper journalist are *roman, sans serif*, and *square serif*, sometimes called slab serif (Fig. 12–6).

Roman type is probably the most common of these races. Roman type has letters made up of thick-and-thin strokes and serifs, which are little extra finishing strokes at the tips of letters (Fig. 12–7). Modern romans exaggerate the thick-and-thin strokes and their serifs are thinner than those of older romans. Old-style romans minimize the difference in the strokes and the serifs are small and are

ABCDEFGHIJKLMNO
PQRSTUVWXYZ
abcdefghijklmnopqrstu
vwxyz
1234567890$?!&

ABCDEFGHIJKLMNOPQRSTUVWXYZ
abcdefghijklmnopqrstuvwxyz
1234567890$?!&

ABCDEFGHIJKLMN
OPQRSTUVWXYZ
abcdefghijklmnopqrs
tuvwxyz
1234567890$?!&

Figure 12–6. Bodoni (top) is an example of roman type, Helvetica of sans serif, and Clarendon of square serif.

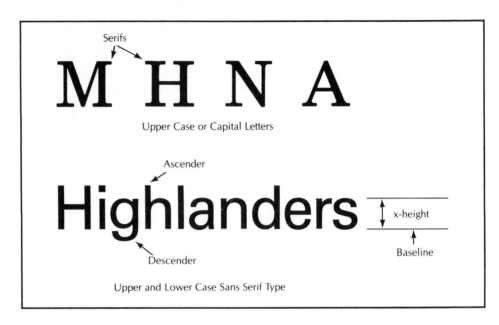

Upper Case or Capital Letters

Upper and Lower Case Sans Serif Type

Figure 12–7. Knowing and understanding typographical terms is important for journalists.

bracketed (the serifs are rounded into the stroke of the letter). Roman type—and usually old roman type—is easy to read and is therefore used in most books, magazines, newspapers—and even on typewriters.

In sans serif the letter is the same thickness throughout and there are no serifs. (The word "sans" is French for *without*.) Sans serif is popular as a headline typeface because of its clean, crisp look. Many papers use roman body type for readability and sans serif headlines for a modern look.

Square, or slab, serif is the in-between face: It has rectangular serifs, but the strokes of the letters are all the same thickness (as with sans serif). Square serif typefaces, popular 50 years ago, are not used nearly as much today, except in small doses of body copy or in large and loud headlines.

Within these races of type are smaller groups called families. A type family is a group that has one design feature in common, and although many types may share a family name (Souvenir, Century, Futura), each typeface is slightly different in weight or width. The "weight" of a letter is its relative boldness or the width of the strokes of the letter. The Souvenir family, for instance, is available in light, medium, demi-bold, and bold. Figure 12–8 shows that the shape of the letter is

Figure 12–8. The Souvenir family of type is available in various letter weights.

Souvenir light
Souvenir light italic
Souvenir medium
Souvenir medium italic
Souvenir demi-bold
Souvenir demi-bold italic
Souvenir bold
Souvenir bold italic

HELVETICA REGULAR

ABCDEFGHIJKLMNOPQRSTUVWXYZ
abcdefghijklmnopqrstuvwxyz
1234567890$&¢.,;:-'?!

HELVETICA REGULAR CONDENSED

ABCDEFGHIJKLMNOPQRSTUVWXYZ
abcdefghijklmnopqrstuvwxyz
1234567890$&¢.,;:-'?!

HELVETICA REGULAR EXTENDED

ABCDEFGHIJKLMNOPQRSTUVWXYZ
abcdefghijklmnopqrstuvwxyz
1234567890$&¢.,;:-'?!   ßÆÇŒıæçœ

**Figure 12–9. Type families can also vary in
the width of the letter as a whole, not just the width of the stroke.**

exactly the same (the Souvenir family characteristic), but the width of the letter
gets thicker as you read down the list.

Type families can also vary in the width of the entire letter, not just in the
width of the strokes making up that letter. The Helvetica family, for example, is
available in regular, condensed, and extended widths (Fig. 12–9).

Italic typefaces are so numerous they could almost form a race of their own.
Italics, originally designed as a separate typeface by an Italian (thus the name), are
now little more than variations within a type family. Italic typefaces should not be
confused with *script* or *cursive* type. Italics lean to the right, as do cursive and
script, but italic letters are not connected (like script), nor do they have visually
linking strokes (like cursive) (Fig. 12–10). Italic typefaces are not simply romans
leaning to the right. Trus italics are drawn differently (note the shape of the italic
"*a*" and the roman "a" in this paragraph. Because italics are more difficult to read
than roman type, their main use in newspapers is in headlines or cutlines.

When type families and styles are to be selected for a newspaper, the
designer considers several important items. First, the body type should be pleasing to the eye and easy to read. When considering the design of your newspaper,

ABCDEFGHIJKLMNO
PQRSTUVWXYZ

abcdefghijklmnopqrstu
vwxyz

1234567890$?!&

ABCDEFGHIJK
LMNOPQRSTU

abcdefghijklmnopqrs
tuvwxyz

1234567890$?!&

ABCDEFGHIJKLMNOPQRSTUVWXYZ

abcdefghijklmnopqrstuvwxyz   1234567890$&.,;:='?!

Figure 12–10. Italics, cursive, and script are similar, but they are not the same. Script letters (*bottom*) actually connect, cursive letters (*upper right*) have visually linking strokes, and italic letters are designed to lean to the right.

Figure 12–11. The x-height of a typeface makes a difference in readability.

This is Century Textbook, a readability typeface. Because of its large x-height, and its small ascenders and descenders, it is very easy to read.

This is Holland Seminar, set in the same type size and leading as the Century Textbook. Because it has a small x-height, it looks smaller than the Century and it is harder to read.

work on the body type first. Other typographic choices should follow. Typeface designers have designed several very good typefaces with large *x-heights* (the height face of the lowercase *x*). A large x-height makes the type seem bigger and easier to read than a standard-height face of same size type (Fig. 12–11), even though the letters don't take up any more space horizontally. A readable face, combined with an extra point of leading, makes modern newspapers pleasant to look at and easy to read.

Another consideration for the designer is the *headline schedule,* a list of headline types and sizes used in the paper. The headline type style should be compatible with—should look good with—the body type, even if the head schedule is sans serif and the body type roman. With modern photocomposition machines and modern typefaces, many newspapers use only one family—such as Franklin Gothic, Times Roman, or Bodoni—in the headline schedule but vary the width and weight. Within one family there are often eight different faces available for headlines. Many schools and most well-designed professional newspapers have typefaces and sizes standardized for various parts of the paper (Fig. 12–12) in a type and design stylebook.

Most type for newspapers today is set by the phototypesetting method, a photographic method using negatives and paper. Light is shone through a "negative" alphabet on a photocomposer filmstrip. Lenses enlarge or reduce the image to form different type sizes. The light coming through the alphabet exposes photographic (light-sensitive) paper, which is then taken out of the phototypesetting unit and run through developing and fixing solutions to create the final *galley* of type (a long column of type to be cut and pasted onto the page). Coupled with a computer, the photocomposer can set a thousand lines or more per minute.

Figure 12–12. (*Opposite*) Besides its own headline count sheet, the staff of *The Ranger* (San Antonio College) also has a typography style. Different kinds of copy and headlines have set type styles.

TYPOGRAPHY STYLE FOR THE RANGER

Element		Type Face	Size	Leading	Measure
Body Copy		Bodoni	P09	F010	13 picas
News Briefs (boxed)		Bodoni	P010	F011	25 picas
Editorials		Bodoni	P010	F011	20 1/2 picas
Jump Lines		Bodoni Bold	P09		(See Sam, Page 3) (Con'd from pg. 1)
Staff box		Bodoni	P010	F011	25 picas
Bylines	Name:	Helios Bold	P010		
	Position:	Helios Lt. Italic	P08		
Cutlines		Helios Bold	P010	F011	25 picas (2 or 4 col.) 19 picas (3 col.)
Photo Credits		Helios Lt. Italic	P08		Photos by . . .
Photo Essay, Story Credits		Univers #56	14 pt.		Photos by . . .
Namelines, Singletons		Helios Bold	P012		
Catchlines		Univers #65	18 pt.		Count
Briefs heds		Univers #65	24 pt.		22 count
Editorial heds		Univers #55	36 pt.		Count
Letters to editor heds		Univers #56	14 pt.		Count
Folio		Helios Light and Bold	12 pt. caps		

Main line on kicker head indented three picas.
News Summary, Marquee, Sports Shorts indented 1 1/2 picas from box edge.
2-point rule encasing photographs, boxed. 1-point rule beneath kickers, wild art.
10-percent screen on flag, mast, special page headings, box headings.
10-percent screen inside boxes when type is overprinted.
Leave 1/4" for folio at top of page.

Univers Type Faces: #55 - light
#56 - light Italic
#65 - medium
#66 - medium Italic
#67 - medium condensed
#76 - bold Italic

Column Widths:
1 column   13 picas
2 column   27 picas
3 column   41 picas
4 column   55 picas
5 column   69 picas
6 column   83 picas

Figure 12–13. Huge rolls of paper are fed into the web press at one end, and they weave an intricate "web," moving from one end of the press to the other. After printing, the web paper is folded and cut. (Photo by Michael Messing)

Printing

After stories have been set in type, the paper needs to be printed before the reader can enjoy it. The first printing presses used for repetitive impressions of a wood-block printing plate were grape presses, normally used for making wine. The press operator had to carefully place a sheet of paper on the inked wooden block, then spin the round handle until the press plate came into contact with the back of the paper. Too much pressure and the block might break; too little and the impression would be weak. Each sheet had to be handled carefully so that the ink would not smudge.

This tedious process of sheet-by-sheet printing—although improved somewhat over several centuries—was basically how newspaper printing was done until the invention of the rotary press about 1890. The rotary press allowed the printing plate to be curved and attached to a rotating cylinder. Continuous feeding of sheets of paper meant that thousands of pages could be printed in a short time.

Next, the *web press* (Fig. 12–13), a system in which huge rolls of paper were fed into a press and cut into individual issues at the end of the printing process, sped up the process. Today most newspapers are printed on modern web presses using rolls of newsprint that are two pages wide, six miles long, and weigh 1,800 pounds.

Letterpress and Offset

Two major methods of printing are *letterpress* and *offset*. The letterpress method is the modern version of the old grape press. Curved lead plates with raised and reversed letters are *pressed* against the paper as it rolls by (Fig. 12–14). This method, although still used by some professional and student newspapers, is being replaced by the faster and higher-quality offset process. Letterpress printing plates usually are made of heat-formed lead and weigh approximately 40 pounds. This weight—combined with the fact that plates wear out after a long press run, much like the centuries-old wooden plates—makes letterpress plates less desirable than offset printing plates. Many newspapers have modified their

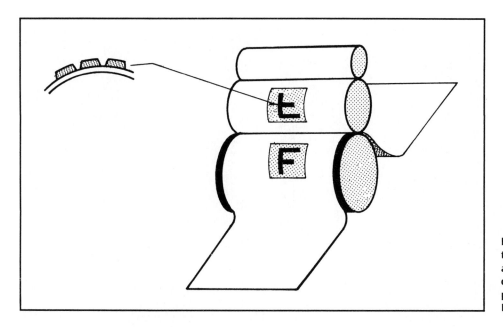

Figure 12–14. In the letterpress process, the raised surfaces on the printing press are inked (*top roller*) and then pressed directly onto the paper. The image on the printing plate is reversed. (Drawing by Dana Warren)

presses to accept lighter, aluminum letterpress plates that use a thin, light-sensitive coating of plastic. But all letterpress presses still have the disadvantages of plates wearing out and poorer reproduction quality than offset.

In offset printing the plate never touches the paper itself. Thus the plate is "offset" from the paper (Fig. 12–15, 12–16). The plate is a thin sheet of light-sensitive aluminum. After it has been exposed to light through the negative, the plate is treated with a solution so that ink sticks only to that part of the plate that light has hit (where the letters and photos are). The rest of the plate is washed clean of ink during the press run. The impression is transferred to a blanket roller, which then presses against the paper as it rolls through the press.

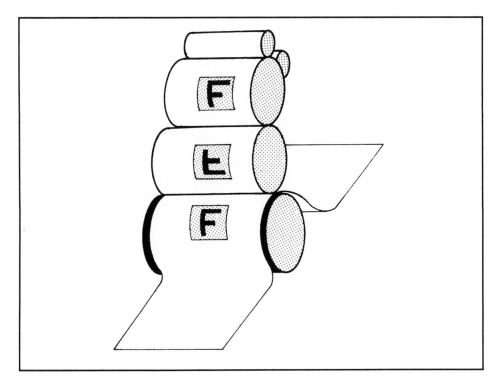

Figure 12–15. In the offset process, the image is transferred from the plate to a blanket roller and then to the paper. Thus, the plate is "offset" from the paper. The image on an offset plate looks like the final version; that is, it is not reversed as with letterpress. (Drawing by Dana Warren)

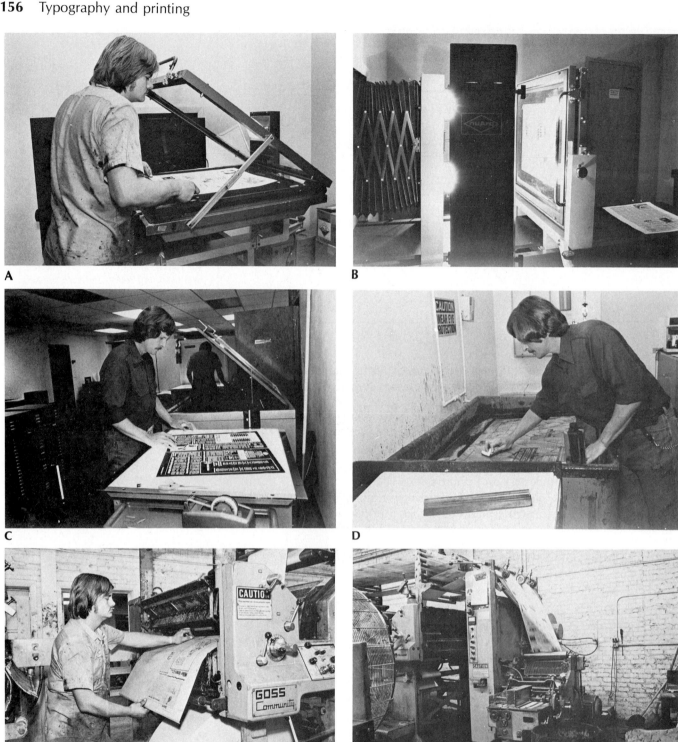

A

B

C

D

E

Figure 12–16. The offset press. The completed paste-up is under glass (A) so that a large negative can be made of it by the copy camera (B). The negative is then checked on a light table (C), and stray clear spots (which would show up as "dirt" on the printed paper) are blocked in, or "opaqued." After the printing plate has been made, it is washed with a solution (D) that makes the image visible and also treats only that part of the plate that is to hold the ink for printing. The plate is then attached to the press (E). (Note that only one page is to be printed from the plate.) Then as papers reach the end of the press, the roll of newspapers is folded, and individual issues are cut, folded again, and sent out on a conveyor belt. (Photos by Michael Messing)

Offset printing, a form of lithography, is better than letterpress in three major ways: First, it makes a much clearer and sharper reproduction and prints high-quality color photos. Second, offset is faster because the press doesn't have to deal with the 40-pound lead plates of letterpress. And third, offset is cleaner and easier to work with because of its light printing plates. Coupled with photo-typesetting, which sped the typesetting process from seven lines of type per minute 20 years ago to thousands of lines per minute today, offset printing has changed the look of modern newspapers.

Flexography is a printing method that is now being improved to the point that it is a viable alternative to offset. Using a water-soluble ink on a letterpress web press, high-quality photo reproduction—at least as good as offset—has been achieved. Flexography uses a resilient printing plate, unlike letterpress, which uses a hard lead plate.

Computers and Printing

Computers have forever changed the way newspapers are produced. Up until even the late 1960s, Johann Gutenberg could probably have worked in the back shop of a newspaper and not had too much trouble keeping up. But today, computers have replaced most of the back shop workers. The number of people involved in the production of newspapers has dropped dramatically during the last 20 years.

Many major newspapers are moving toward *pagination* systems, or computers that will allow pasting up of various elements totally within the computer. Even photographs can be handled this way. Then, at the push of a button, a complete page can be produced, with all elements in their proper position. The page negative can then be made from a page that had not been touched by human hands. The next goal is to get a complete page from the editor's terminal directly on the printing press, reducing even further the steps and personnel needed to produce a newspaper.

Even personal computers are now powerful enough to paginate complete tabloid or even broadsheet pages without paste-up. The main limitation is that photo reproduction is still too memory intensive for most PCs, and personal printers cannot handle page sizes bigger than a legal sheet of paper.

Although the software works around this by producing the page in sections or "tiles," the next big step for small professional newspapers and for college papers will be the large paper personal printer.

Because of the time lag in producing a book, there is no telling what is available to you as you are reading this—maybe even those tabloid sized personal printer sheets. But regardless, computers will continue to become more sophisticated and even cheaper. Progressive publishers will always find ways to harness the power of the computer to the efficient and fast transformation of information into news.

Suggested Projects

1. Study your paper's present body type and headline schedule to see if the typefaces are compatible. Do you use too many different typefaces for headlines? What other typefaces are available from your printing facility? Can you change the type style of your paper to improve its appearance?

2. Visit your local newspaper and tour its composition room and press room. Do the personnel there have any ideas that might help you improve your typeface selection? Your paste-up techniques? Your photo quality?

Vocabulary

body type
copy wrap
cursive
em space
en space
flexography

full-size
headline schedule
initial letter
italic
leading
letterpress
linespacing
offset
pagination
pica
point
roman
sans serif
script
set solid
square serif
tabloid
web press
x-height

3. Meet with the foreman of your printing facility and devise a list of ways to improve your work flow.

4. Gather type specimen books from local newspapers and print shops. Look for typefaces that might enhance your headline schedule or standing typography.

page design $\boxed{13}$

Good design can act as a lubricant for content. In other words, a well-designed presentation makes getting information easier—and perhaps even pleasurable—for the reader. Let's be clear here: People read newspapers for their content, not for what headline typeface they use, how big they play their photographs, or what colors they display. But good, functional newspaper design is crucial if you expect to gain or even retain readers. Too many other visually exciting choices exist in the media world today for newspapers to remain dull and gray, as, frankly, they once were.

Design is also important because it helps form that first impression in a reader's mind. Just as you can tell a lot about a person in the first few seconds of an encounter, readers learn a lot about your paper based on the way it looks.

- Is it old-fashioned and standard, or is it contemporary, breezy, or even flashy?
- Is it neatly dressed, or is it sloppily put together?

Good design can make all the difference here.

Design is the attractor, even though it must not be so obvious after the initial attraction that it gets in the way of reading. Good design really functions at two levels: (1) It is a plan that allows the reader to access required information as quickly and easily as possible, and (2) it attracts the attention of the reader (Fig. 13–1).

Attention and Gestalt

The eyes process much visual information that the brain never deals with on an active level. When we aim our eyes in a direction, we *see* a lot more than we can *look at*. The focus area is only about 3 degrees of the approximately 180 degrees we can see.

For instance, as you see these pages, you can only "look" at a certain portion at a time. As you read these words, you can see the other words on the page, but you can't read them because your attention area is limited. It is rather like trying to read a barn-sized sign in the black of night with a small-beam flashlight: You have to run the beam over the sign bit by bit to understand the entire message.

Attention is sometimes an active process: You choose where your eyes want to point when you read. But it is also often a passive process: Your eyes are drawn—outside your will, if not actually against it—to certain areas of a visual field. This is visual attraction. Attention is *more* than attraction because it involves meaning. When you try to extract meaning from something, you must pay attention to it.

159

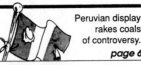

Figure 13–1. This community college front page was an award winner in a student Society of Newspaper Design competition. Notice the treatment of the above-the-flag teasers, the second-deck headlines, and the boxes at the bottom of the page. This work shows that quality presentation of the news is possible, even at the two-year-college level with its frequent staff turnover. (Courtesy of *The Advocate*)

For instance, when the average reader looks at a newspaper page, he or she is drawn first to the photographs, then to spot-color elements, and then to headlines. Research projects by The Poynter Institute for Media Studies in 1985 and in 1990 showed this. Generally speaking, this eye movement is true of all readers: The eyes are attracted to certain kinds of visual elements. Continuing research in eye movement done by The Gallup Organization should continue to better inform those who present information.

The first-seen elements on a page tend to be larger or bolder or irregularly shaped or in color. Although these are important, content can draw the eye as well. Try putting a large, bold, irregular splotch of color next to an equally large, black-and-white photo of a naked person and you'll see what I mean. After stopping at these points, the eyes become much more under the active control of the reader, and returns can be made to the most interesting points, either in terms of the visual stimulation or of the content.

Attention also tends to be given to the familiar and to patterns. The attention span is limited, so the most easily "excitable" portions of the memory area of the brain seek matches from the visual stimuli the eye is sending along.

The most easily excitable portions of the memory tend to be those most frequently excited in the past. The power of this tendency to match with familiar patterns is so strong that it is almost impossible to see a new pattern as "new" if it looks like something familiar.

For instance, look at the following shape. It is a unique shape, but because it *looks like* an O and an E, that's how we see it. The brain wants desperately to make sense out of the universe, to force the unknown into previously known patterns, or into the "known," in whatever way it can.

Or look at the following:

to get her

Some readers probably saw "to get her" and others saw "together": The spacing was set purposefully so that the meaning (as defined by the space) was ambiguous. Depending on what you wanted to see or what you expected to see, the brain decided to "see." The way you display your type and other design elements can work in the same way. You can either make communication easy and clear or you can make it ambiguous.

There are two major theories on how the brain deals with visual information from the eyes. The first says that the brain compares the new stimuli with previously stored patterns or *templates*. If the brain finds a match with a familiar pattern, even if it has to stretch a bit to make the match, the new stimuli are identified.

The second theory says that the brain analyzes new stimuli as combinations of elemental features. For instance, letters of the alphabet are combinations of horizontal, vertical, diagonal, and/or curved lines.

Given the right combination of features, no matter how oddly they may be combined, the brain can identify a letter. The template-matching theory would require many templates to identify letters because of all the possible forms for any given letter. The features-analysis theory says that as long as the elements are aligned in the correct basic structure, the letter can be identified.

Figure 13–2. The eye/brain tends to group information quickly in an attempt to make sense of what the eyes see. Here, the brain organizes the top grouping by shape, but at the bottom, tone (or color) is the organizing factor. Tone is more quickly and easily processed, so it dominates shapes in organizing visual information. You can use this to help guide the reader through your pages.

Regardless of which theory is correct, you can see that perception relies on certain structures made up of lines and shapes. Publication design is little more than paying attention to these basic shapes and using them in such a way as to not confuse the reader. Although "creativity" certainly plays a part, it is not strictly necessary in order to become a competent page designer.

Another helpful set of principles for the inexperienced designer is the gestalt principles of perceptual organization, named after gestalt psychologists.

In essence, the main gestalt principle says that the whole is greater than the sum of its parts, that the pattern is more important than the individual element. In fact, there is some evidence that we see the pattern much more quickly and more accurately than we see the individual units.

Here again, we have the brain sifting through visual information looking for the familiar and for patterns.

The gestalt principles, according to John R. Anderson,[1] are:

Similarity.   Objects that look alike tend to be grouped together (Fig. 13–2). This involves shape, color, size, position (and attitude or angle), and texture. A relationship is implied when elements are similar, as with the uniforms of an athletic team, or the same color and shape corporate logo. Therefore, on a publication page, similar shapes and colors, and so on, imply that the content is related. Unfortunately, this principle is frequently ignored, adding unnecessary confusion.

Proximity.   Similar elements closely grouped will be seen as a unit and not as individuals. Tightly spaced elements have an almost magnetic attraction to each other. If a pattern is evident, the grouping of elements may be loose.

Good Continuation.   Segments of shapes or lines are put together in their easiest and most pleasing configuration. Or, the brain wants to connect lines or shapes that appear to be aligned.

Good Form and Closure.   If an incomplete shape would become a familiar shape by mentally completing it, that is what the brain does. Again, this is an effort by the brain to make the unfamiliar familiar. Even completely novel shapes are divided into units.

What does this have to do with laying out decent-looking pages?

If you can understand and then control the eye movement, from the initial entry point, through the other stopping-off points, to the departure point for a page, then you can make the information-gathering process easy. This is what good functional design is all about.

You can move your readers' eyes around the page in a calm and coherent manner, making the information-gathering process easy and pleasurable. Or you can ignore what we have learned about how people both see and look and create random design, leaving poor readers to wander aimlessly on the page (Fig. 13–3).

Readers like their information quick and easy. It's not enough to give them information: The getting of that information must be easy and pleasurable. One communications theorist (William Stephenson) has gone so far as to say that media use is an act of "play" by readers.

[1] John R. Anderson, *Cognitive Psychology and Its Implications,* 2nd ed. (New York: W. H. Freeman and Co., 1985).

Daily Bruin

Vol. CXXX, No. 128
Circulation: 22,000

Monday
May 21, 1990

Young offers aid for $1 million L&S deficit

Regents may not provide money to troubled college

By Eugene Ahn and Christine Hagstrom
Staff Writers

A $1.2 million deficit spurred by faculty overhiring in UCLA's College of Letters & Science has prompted Chancellor Charles Young to provide the college with financial relief that the UC Board of Regents will not give if the shortfall resulted from an administrative foul-up, officials said Friday.

UC President David Gardner, in an interview at the regents' meeting in San Francisco, vowed the regents would intervene with emergency funds only if the college's financial problems were caused by "unexpected events" that were no one's fault.

The chancellor's long-term and short-term plans to help the college cope with financial strains, including a snap move to use $400,000 in campus-wide funds to hire additional course instructors,

- Economics/business major passes first stage of unprecedented retroactive approval **See Page 10**
- UC President David Gardner calls situation with Chicano Studies major hard to imagine **See Page 11**
- College spokesman says provost didn't mean exactly what he said last month when addressing faculty recruitment **See Page 11**

was explained by Vice Chancellor Michael Granfield and in a five-page "state of the college" letter written by Provost Raymond Orbach, who sent copies Friday to 90 administrators, department chairpersons and program directors.

Although Orbach's letter did not specify dollar amounts, Granfield said an overhiring of professors last year — in which the college recruited more faculty than it had funds to pay for — was "primarily responsible" for the school's current deficit of $1 million to $1.2 million.

Gardner said the college's deficit would likely remain UCLA's problem. "If the chancellor came to me and said, 'Hey, I have this terrible problem blah-blah-blah-blah,' and the problems are a result of decisions he or his colleagues made, I am going to say, 'Thank you, glad to hear it, now solve it.' I am not going to reach in and tell

him how to deal with it — that is his problem. That is what he is paid for."

The overhiring, a result of recruitment misprojections and an unexpectedly high number of "top-notch" candidates who accepted job offers, has resulted in a financial shortfall many department administrators expect will lead to sweeping cuts in the number of temporary faculty and the undergraduate courses they teach.

Granfield placed partial blame on the college's rigid planning timelines. "This happened because they do things way in advance. By

See **DEFICIT**, page 10

Inside

Kosher food to be sold at UCLA

The student union will begin distributing kosher deli sandwiches and salads today.
See page **5**

Viewpoint

Water, water everywhere?

Susan Rinderle takes the plunge into some solutions for California's water shortage, and looks at one of the biggest water-wasters: UCLA.
See page **16**

Arts & Entertainment

Unprecedented presentation

A symposium on Latino films and filmmakers spotlights articulate new voices and talents.
See page **18**

Sports

You're out, but we're in

The UCLA softball team advanced to the college world series by eliminating Northern Iowa this weekend in a two-game sweep.
See page **36**

SUZANNE STATES/Daily Bruin
The Rev. Jesse Jackson waits to speak at the UCLA School of Law commencement on Sunday.

Jackson speaks at UCLA law school

Graduates give standing ovation to former Democratic candidate

By Kathy Lo
Staff Writer

The Rev. Jesse Jackson called for "quality leadership" when he spoke to the 329 graduates of the UCLA School of Law on Sunday at Dickson Plaza.

"Without vision the people perish. Students, you have the power to transform America," said Jackson, who received a standing ovation from the 39th graduating class.

Jackson also urged the audience to recognize world diversity. "Most people in the world are yellow, are brown, black, non-Christian, poor, female, young and

don't speak English.

"It is the demand of that world that obligates you to a multi-cultural, diverse education, reflective in faculty and students and administrators or the demands of our time will reduce you to obsolescence," said Jackson, who was wearing a black commencement robe and a green sash to signify strength, pride and dedication to diversity.

Although the audience applauded Jackson, one woman intermittently heckled Jackson. "I'm Jewish. He is anti-Jew and I don't appreciate him speaking here as if he was some kind of egalitarian, and I don't like him being here," said Agnes Frenka,

whose son graduated that day.

But during the commencement ceremony, Jackson voiced concern for the oppression of Jews, as well as other minority groups.

"Students must not transmit the diseases of ancient fears and barriers, but rather hope and dream your way into a new day and a better way. The resurrection of racism, or personal and institutional sexism, anti-Semitism, anti-Arabism, anti-Hispanicism, Asian bashing and homophobia represent spiritual surrender and ethical collapse," he said.

UCLA's 1990 Professor of the Year Julian Eule said that he shared Jackson's message. "Our races are different, our religions are different and our perspectives are different. But if you just listen, it would not surprise me if the messages sound a little more alike."

IFC set to investigate fraternity

Beta Theta Pi said to have violated policy

By Tina Anima
Senior Staff Writer

UCLA's Beta Theta Pi fraternity is being investigated for possible violations of university policies on theme parties and alcohol, university officials said Friday.

The fraternity's "Sunrise" party early Friday morning prompted MEChA to file a complaint with the university later that day, alleging that the fraternity violated a university policy forbidding groups from sponsoring parties that promote ethnic stereotypes.

The Interfraternity Council will appoint students to investigate the charges and report to the Office of Fraternity and Sorority Relations on Wednesday, the office's director Chris Fishburn said.

Beta Theta Pi sponsored the bash at its Gayley and Strathmore house where partygoers gathered at dawn for a celebration with beer and music, leaving at about 11 a.m.

MEChA denounced the "Sunrise" party in a draft complaint to university officials Friday, saying that it related to "past racist and sexist incidents." The Chicano-Latino student group will give a final version of the letter to her today, Fishburn said.

Five years ago — before the theme party policy existed — Beta's "Tequila Sunrise" party sparked a string of protests by MEChA members and community members who said the event violated a year-long university mandate against ethnic theme parties. During demonstrations some members of the Greek system heckled the protesters and hurled tortillas at them.

University officials decided the party promoted negative stereotypes of Mexicans. Partygoers wore Mexican garb, listened to a mariachi band and displayed a banner of a tequila worm with a sign that read "Eat Me" next to it.

"That was a blatant theme party," said Assistant Vice

See **SUNRISE**, page 14

Figure 13–3. This *Daily Bruin* **(UCLA) page exhibits good design, with modular layout, second decks and pullouts for the scanners, good typographical contrast, and teasers to give a high story count on the front page. The** *Daily Bruin* **was an award winner in the University of Missouri Show Me Design competition.**

Design Tools of the Trade

After understanding the above general principles on *how* we look and see, editors next need to understand the more specific available tools. It is through the use of these visual tools that the principles can be put into practical use on your pages.

Basically, anything on your pages is made up of line, shape, tone, and (visual) texture. With these, you can manipulate reader response to your presentation.

Line

Lines can be classified into horizontal, vertical, diagonal, and curved. Each has a connotative, or second-level, meaning that can add to or detract from your message.

Horizontal lines are restful and at peace with their surroundings. Horizontal lines, then, should not be used as part of a design on highly active content, such as football games, county fairs, and so on.

This concept carries over into the width of columns of type on your page. Wide columns of type (though it depends on the size of your page, let's say 24 picas or more) say "quiet" and "bookish." The wide lines of type emphasize the horizontal.

If you want to add action and excitement to a spread, you would use narrower columns of type. Don't go so narrow, however, that readability of the type is hampered (Fig. 13–4).

Vertical lines are dignified and strong, like the columns in classical architecture. The very columns of type in your publication represent vertical lines. They add order and stability to the content. They also show potential for movement. Horizontal lines emphasize the passive, the non-moving.

Column rules represent simple vertical lines that help balance the horizontals of the headlines and flags. Vertical lines create up and down movement. On a tall page, such as a broadsheet newspaper page, or even a "tall" tabloid, vertical lines in a layout can help the reader see the layout as one unit.

Diagonal lines show the most movement and action. Diagonal lines can very easily lead the eye through a layout. You would use diagonal content elements in "avant-garde" spreads as well because they break the rules of the format grid that the rest of your publication follows. The very breaking of a rule adds power to the diagonal.

Curved lines are sensuous and classy. Curved lines also show motion, but they are more controlled than is a diagonal: Diagonal lines are rocket launchings; curved lines are figure skaters doing a spiral on ice.

In design, lines are both real and imaginary. Real lines are made up of the alignment of the tops of several columns of type, or the columns of type themselves, which end up being long, thick (though gray) lines.

Imaginary lines are also part of the content of many photographs and illustrations. These lines can continue through and across the rest of your design and create motion, and so on.

Because any of these real or imaginary lines can cause the eye to move, a good designer will use them to get the eye to travel to other important parts of the design, such as the story or the body copy in an ad.

A

B

Figure 13–4. Wide columns, which say "slow read," are well suited to an opinion page, but narrower columns work better for lists and other quick reads. The five-column grid on the six-column, broadsheet *Battalion* provides a good foundation for the page (A); the narrow, ragged five-column format stands out on the normally four-column format elsewhere in the *Daily Lobo*, a tab (B). (A, Courtesy of *The Battalion*; B, Courtesy of the *New Mexico Daily Lobo*)

Shape

Because type is set in columns of type, graphic design ends up being mostly horizontal and vertical lines. Thus, the most frequent shapes on a page are rectangles and squares. But triangles and circles also are useful shapes to consider in design.

The basic page size of your publication is the most obvious rectangle. Your columns of type and photographs on a page also are rectangles. Because of the plethora of rectangles in any publication design, the occasional use of a triangle or a circle can add emphasis to that element.

Circles are especially good as parts of nameplates or column logos, the constants in any publication. Circles are good for logos because the eye movement stays within the shape. And again, because most everything else on a page will be a rectangle, using circles with your constants can add a special flavor.

Triangles are either solid—with the point up—or they show potential to tip over—point down. Either way, triangles have good eye movement around the three points. Squares, on the other hand, show little movement around the four corners. Thus, the triangle is a good shape to keep in mind for a layout, especially an ad layout. The use of three focal points in a design creates visual interest in the design by forcing the eyes in a restless move around the three points.

This is where an understanding of perception and gestalt comes in. The eye naturally looks for patterns, as we have learned, and having three points enhances the pressure to search your design. A four-point design is much too stable to stimulate good eye movement.

Tone

It is tone and shape that give our eyes something to see. Tone is the relative darkness or lightness of an object. In a sense, tone is the black-and-white equivalent of color in design.

Color helps us to differentiate objects and, in a black-and-white design, it is the tone that does this: pure black, through various shades of gray, to pure white, or at least as white as the paper stock allows us to get!

Tone in a design is usually achieved with *halftone* screens. Screens consist of dots of various sizes and proximity to one another. Light-gray tones are made up of small dots relatively far apart. With dark-gray screens, the dots have gotten so large that the screen appears to be a black background with white dots. The eye mixes the combination of black and white—as you might mix black and white paint—to create the impression of gray.

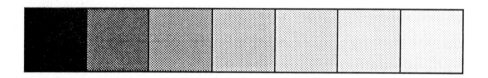

The tone of a screen is called for by using the percentage of an area that is filled with dots. For instance, a light-gray screen would be a 10 percent or 20 percent screen because only that portion would be covered by the dots.

Sometimes screens are used over type, and sometimes simply as background to an entire design. When using screens with type, be very careful not to make the screen so dark that the type becomes hard to read. Use either bigger or bolder type under a screen.

An aspect of tone that is not often considered by designers is the tone of the type itself on the page. Especially from a distance, the line after line of body type adds tone to a design. The type you choose, the size, the line width, and the leading all affect how dark or light your columns of type appear (Fig. 13–5).

The more leading you add to a block of type, for instance, the lighter it appears. The principle is the same as that of a halftone screen: The more white paper that shows between the little dots of black, the lighter the element will appear. Control the tone of your type by making typographical decisions on a sample page, not just on the drawing board. A column logo that may look great by itself may be lost on a page with heavy type.

Texture

Anything you see gives you an impression of what it would feel like were you to touch it. This is true in graphic design. Usually a graphic designer adds texture to a design through the use of specialty screens. Besides the pure grays of halftone screens, designers can use screens that simulate a variety of textures, such as mezzotint or steel etching. Certain typefaces also can appear "soft" or "hard," masculine or feminine.

Lorem ipsum dolor sit amet, consectetuer adipiscing elit, sed diam nonummy nibh euismod tincidunt ut laoreet dolore magna aliquam erat volutpat. Ut wisi enim ad minim veniam, quis nostrud exerci tation ullamcorper suscipit lobortis nisl ut aliquip ex ea commodo consequat.

Duis autem vel eum iriure dolor in hendrerit in vulputate velit esse molestie consequat, vel illum dolore eu feugiat nulla facilisis at vero eros et accumsan et iusto odio dignissim qui blandit praesent luptatum zzril delenit augue duis dolore te feugait nulla facilisi. Lorem ipsum dolor sit amet, consectetuer adipiscing elit, sed diam nonummy nibh euismod tincidunt ut laoreet dolore magna aliquam erat volutpat.

Ut wisi enim ad minim veniam, quis nostrud exerci tation ullamcor-

Lorem ipsum dolor sit amet, consectetuer adipiscing elit, sed diam nonummy nibh euismod tincidunt ut laoreet dolore magna aliquam erat volutpat. Ut wisi enim ad minim veniam, quis nostrud exerci tation ullamcorper suscipit lobortis nisl ut aliquip ex ea commodo consequat.

Duis autem vel eum iriure dolor in hendrerit in vulputate velit esse molestie consequat, vel illum dolore eu feugiat nulla facilisis at vero eros et accumsan et iusto odio dignissim qui blandit praesent luptatum zzril delenit augue duis dolore te feugait nulla facilisi. Lorem ipsum dolor sit amet, consectetuer adipiscing elit, sed diam nonummy nibh euismod tincidunt ut laoreet dolore magna

Lorem ipsum dolor sit amet, consectetuer adipiscing elit, sed diam nonummy nibh euismod tincidunt ut laoreet dolore magna aliquam erat volutpat. Ut wisi enim ad minim veniam, quis nostrud exerci tation ullamcorper suscipit lobortis nisl ut aliquip ex ea commodo consequat. Duis autem vel eum iriure dolor in hendrerit in vulputate velit esse molestie consequat, vel illum dolore eu feugiat nulla facilisis at vero eros et accumsan et iusto odio dignissim qui blandit praesent luptatum zzril nulla facilisi. Lorem ipsum dolor sit amet, consectetuer adipiscing elit, sed diam nonummy nibh euismod tincidunt ut laoreet dolore magna aliquam erat volutpat. Ut wisi enim ad minim veniam, quis nostrud exerci tation ullamcorper suscipit lobortis nisl ut aliquip ex ea commodo consequat. Duis autem vel eum iriure dolor in hendrerit in vulputate velit esse

Figure 13–5. Body type ends up being long columns of a gray tone on your page. Depending on your typeface and leading, that tone can range from a light to a medium gray. Here, only the leading differs, but you can see that the density of the negatively linespaced right-hand column is darker than the other two columns. Make headline and logo typeface selections only after you have settled on a body type, so you can pick the proper optical weight.

Design Principles in Newspapers

Once these elements are considered and controlled, the editor is faced with placing elements in an attractive and coherent package on a piece of paper. Luckily, other principles regarding how individual elements should be related are also available. According to Roy Paul Nelson, these are *balance, proportion, contrast* or *emphasis, sequence, unity,* and *simplicity.*

Balance

Elements on your page have a visual or optical "weight." The more a reader is attracted to an element, the more "weight" it is considered to have. A good design has elements with visual weights in balance. In general, large objects are visually "heavier" than small objects, color elements heavier than black and white (B&W), irregular shapes heavier than common shapes (circle, square, etc.), and so on. In fact, if white space on a page is sufficiently large, it can have quite a "heavy" visual weight. The page designer's job is to use these attributes to create a balanced design.

The simplest way to achieve balance in a design is to center everything: symmetrical or formal balance. However, centering is used to a fault in many smaller newspaper ads. It is the easiest but often not the best way to achieve balance.

Symmetrical balance is boring, just as the square is probably the least interesting shape because of its ho-hum regularity of four even sides. Symmetrical balance is great for formal occasions, but it does not surprise and/or please the reader as much as asymmetrical design.

For instance, two photos don't have to be the same size and played in mirror-image column positions to achieve balance. Play a large photo near the center line and play a smaller photo at the edge of the spread; that is, farther from the visual fulcrum point (Fig. 13–6). This puts the two photos in visual balance.

In general, designs should balance side to side—or across pages in a magazine—top-to-bottom, and even diagonally, especially on a broadsheet newspaper page.

Understanding balance and using it properly come with practice. After a while you will just "feel" what is right and what isn't, without having to think so hard to do it. Patience and practice are called for.

The school's jazz ensemble rocks amphitheater.
page 4

The college celebrates Cinco de Mayo today.
page 5

Students strut their stuff in lip-synch contest.
page 6

The Advocate

Friday, May 5, 1989   Contra Costa College, San Pablo, Calif.   Vol. 59, No. 26

On line

Co-editors Anna Armstrong (right) and Laura Carcango, with the help of adviser Brown Miller, are reviving the college's literary magazine Current. The publication's goals are to showcase student works and to protest the lack of literature offerings at the college.

Revival of magazine forum for protest

Students object to lack of literary courses

By Julie Schliesser
Scene editor

After a five year absence, Current, Contra Costa College's little known literary magazine, is back, but with more in mind than just the showcasing of student literary works.

"Reviving Current is a form of protest," Anna Armstrong, one of the magazine's editors said. She and co-editor Laura Carcango, both English majors, are frustrated by the lack of literature offerings here and said that it is the responsibility of the college to provide it.

"They have abandoned their role as educators," Armstrong said of her belief that it is the administration and faculty's responsibility to provide courses in literature to all students, regardless of their skill level.

"I don't know what that means," said President D. Candy Rose. "They sound unnecessarily bitter."

The bitterness may come in what Armstrong said she perceives as an underlying attitude at the college that "people (students) don't have the skills to understand, appreciate and use literature in their lives. I think they're wrong."

"I believe it's something that needs to be guarded against, (that is) becoming an exclusively remedial, vocational college," College Dean Robert Martincich said. He said that the college can't be considered comprehensive for very long if it doesn't offer literature.

"The department has been dragging its heels with this one," Baji Majeste-Daniels, English department chairperson, said.

"We need to create new, exciting literature courses that are designed to attract students," she said. "It won't be a problem to be solved overnight."

English 210A, an overview of English literature taught by instructor Sheila Wander, will be offered in the fall along with two creative writing sections taught by William Lawson. Martincich and Rose both said that an honors literature course that was cancelled this semester because of the instructor's death is still in the works and may be offered by the spring semester of 1990.

Armstrong said of the aims of their protest, "I want to take it as far as until the administration's policies are changed, doing anything that has to be done."

"We're not all business majors," Carcango said. She and Armstrong said they feel as if English majors are getting "gypped" while science, business and vocational majors are provided with a variety of classes pertaining to their majors.

After being told by the UC Berkeley Admissions Office to go to Diablo Valley College if she wanted to take literature classes, Armstrong became angry.

"I think I fit in well in this atmosphere. I don't think I'd be happy at DVC. I don't think I should be pushed out of my community."

"I expect no more from such students except patience," Martincich

See Magazine/8

Bay Area womb to hi-tech boom

(Editor's note: With this issue The Advocate continues its series entitled, "Bay Area Focus." This week we examine the advanced technological capabilities that characterize the region. CCC has responded by developing a number of programs designed to train students for these new and growing industries. These articles appear on page 3.

In coming weeks we will examine transportation problems and health issues. The "Bay Area Focus" logo will accompany these articles when they appear.)

By Kevin Cunningham
Senior associate editor

The garage has been the oil stained womb of many a Bay Area high-tech company. The computer maker Hewlett-Packard got its start in one, as did Apple Computer.

Now a new kind of high technology is coming into its own — biotechnology. The biotech industry is not only giving the Bay Area another reason to call itself the high-tech

capital of the world, but is also exploiting a new part of the home.

"It (Berkeley Antibody) was originally in a kitchen in the married student housing in Albany," Dr. Tom Anderson, president of Berkeley Antibody, said of his company's lowly beginnings while he was at UC Berkeley. The company, called BABCo for short, was started in 1981 with about $8,000 in equipment, including a typewriter, Anderson said.

This year it made "several million dollars," Anderson said. He said BABCo is now located in the Hilltop area of Richmond and works with more than 140 other companies and institutions.

BABCo is only one of a number of companies making profits from new biological techniques developed here, much the same as the computer industry did after a Stanford University researcher developed the transistor. Part of the reason the high-tech and biotech industry located in the Bay Area is the large number of universities and research labs here.

"Three of the top universities in

the country are here in the Bay Area," said Sally Didomenico, spokesperson for the Bay Area Economic Forum. "They're just the top of the heap in the whole country."

While UC Berkeley, Stanford and the UC San Francisco Medical Center dominate the local scene, two national laboratories and the state universities in San Jose, San Francisco and Hayward contribute to the area's pool of well-drained workers.

Andy Evangelin, a spokesperson for UCSF Med Center, said the school

has produced many of the area's top companies.

"Three of the country's leading biotech companies, Genentech, Chiron and California Biotech, are in the Bay Area," Evangelin said. "They were all started by UCSF researchers."

Didomenico also said the large amount of venture capital in the area helped small businesses. Venture capitalists provide money to entrepreneurs with good ideas for a share of the profits.

"This is the venture capital capitol of the world," she said.

Anderson said he did not know about venture capital when he was starting BABCo, but he wishes he had.

"If you have three new ideas on back of a paper towel, you could get $1 million from those guys," Anderson said.

Bay Area institutions are continuing to advance the cutting edge of high technology.

"UC San Francisco is at the forefront of modern biomedical research

See Womb/3

Major Bay Area biotech research firms

District, state, seek diversity through hiring

(Editor's note: This is the second of a two-part series looking at the state's new efforts in affirmative action hiring.)

By Kevin Cunningham
Senior associate editor

Affirmative action is often portrayed as a welfare program by its opponents.

They fear that poorly qualified minorities will get hired and promoted while hard working, well qualified white males languish. But as California community colleges make stronger efforts toward hiring minorities, those involved in affirma-

tive action agree that one of the qualifications of an instructor is the ability to communicate to a diverse student body.

Michael Anker, chair of CCC's Affirmative Action Committee, said, "Part of what makes an instructor qualified is the ability to relate to students — to be sensitive to their particular needs, to know about the cultural background and be able to serve as a role model for them."

College President D. Candy Rose agreed, saying more diversity in the faculty and administration is needed. She said she wants Hispanics and Asians to fill the three open assistant dean positions, because CCC now

has neither on its administrative staff.

"I'm one of those who believe there is such a thing as a role model," Rose said. "Since our student body is diverse, so should our faculty and staff."

District actions

With this in mind, community colleges are setting out to improve staff diversity in response to the passage of Assembly Bill 1725 last fall. AB 1725 reworked much of the community college system, including the establishment of a general plan for diversification.

It also set a goal that by the year 2005, the diversity of community

college employees should be the same as the diversity of California's general population.

Dr. Rose said CCC already exceeds local diversity goals, which compares CCC to the county's population make up. Likewise, district Personnel Director Richard Livingston said the district was the fourth best affirmative action achiever in the state. "We have not done poorly, but we're not satisfied," Livingston said.

The district-wide Affirmative Action Committee and the newly appointed district director of affirmative action, who chairs the committee, have been created to improve

affirmative action.

The director is Louis Watts who helped set up the affirmative action program at the California Department of Education. He began his new job last month.

"We've got a real good person," Livingston said. "(We) recommended Watts to the (governing) board because he set up the affirmative action office at the State Department of Education. He has the kind of experience we were looking for."

Watts said he is looking forward to his new job, which is building an affirmative action program from the

See Diversity/5

Louis Watts
Affirmative action organizer

NEWSLINE

Club meets

The International Club is having a meeting on May 9 in L-3 at noon. The topic of discussion will be the club picnic. Everyone is invited to attend.

Performance opens

The multi-cultural theater project, "As WE Like It," is opening in the Performing Arts Center tonight at 8 p.m. In addition to tonight's performance, the production will be presented on May 6 and 7, and next Friday through Sun-

day, May 12, 13 and 14. Friday and Saturday performances will be at 8 p.m. and Sunday performances will be at 2 p.m. Ticket prices are $3. For ticket information, call 236-3323.

Plant sale to be held

The Disabled Students Union is sponsoring a plant sale on Wednesday and Thursday, from 10 a.m. to 1 p.m. The plants, which will include dozens of indoor and outdoor varieties, will be sold in the campus amphitheater.

Orientations set

Students interested in attending UC Berkeley, CSU Hayward or Mills College for the upcoming semester/quarter through the Concurrent

Enrollment Program must attend one of the following orientation meetings, to be held in LA-103: May 10, from noon to 1 p.m., or May 11, from 12:30 to 1:30 p.m. Attendance at only one of the two orientations is mandatory for enrollment in the program.

Information sheets will be posted and distributed throughout the campus. For further information, contact the Counseling Office in H-42, or call ext. 251 or 347.

Test off campus

The next SAT test will be administered by the Testing Center on May 6 at an off-campus location. The CHSPE will be given on May 20 in the library. The Testing Center is a walk-in center, but interested students need to report to

director Phyllis Goldman at least one day before the test date. For more information, contact Goldman in A-3 or at ext. 250 or 314.

Conference slated

The Foods of Grandeur Club will have its next dinner on May 19 at 7 p.m. The gourmet dinner will be held in the Culinary Arts Dining Room, AA-239. Advance reservations are required and should be received no later than May 16. The cost per person is $27.50.

The menu will include seafood ravioli in cream sauce, vichyssoise, pink grapefruit sorbet, filet of beef with two sauces, tossed salad with champagne vinaigrette and cappuccino. For further information, contact Penny or Gary at ext. 311 between 9 a.m. and 1 p.m.

INSIDE

Science division irons out the final details for its new biotechnical program. **3**

The Comet baseball team clobbers Mendocino College, winning 10-2. **7**

Local One, the classified workers union, protests the ban on smoking in buildings. **8**

Figure 13–6. This page exhibits good balance. First, the heavy nameplate at the top is balanced by the reverse logos at the bottom. The art on the page is balanced left to right in a nice, three-point layout, which creates more eye movement than one with two or four. (Courtesy of *The Advocate*)

Proportion

Visual communicators and artists have known for centuries that certain relationships between elements—certain distances, shapes, and so on—are more visually pleasing than others.

The "golden proportion," approximately 0.62 to 1 or about 3 to 5, provides a relationship between the sides of a rectangle that is more interesting than the obvious 1-to-1 ratio of a square. We can see the relationship between the sides of a square immediately. It is routine, even boring.

With a "golden rectangle," however, the relationship between the sides is not so obvious. The eyes/brain have to spend a little more time checking out each side to look for the pattern, the gestalt. Thus, it is more visually interesting.

Another accepted formula is the "root-2 rectangle," a little closer to a square. The root-2 rectangle is formed by taking the diagonal of a square as the radius of an arc. Where the arc crosses the baseline is the proper width for the long side of the rectangle. A golden rectangle can be made in similar fashion. After dividing a square in half and drawing the diagonal of a half, an arc is swung down to the baseline again to locate the proper distance for the rectangle.

These shapes can be used in graphic design for the shapes of pages themselves, the shapes of photos and drawings within those pages, the depth of type blocks, and so on. This is not to say that you need to try to fit everything into these shapes. But you should remember that symmetry and total precision and similarity are not visually interesting.

Contrast or Emphasis

A good design has a starting point or focal point. Mario Garcia calls this the *center of visual impact* (CVI). The CVI is where the reader enters the page, an action that the designer must control (Fig. 13–7). Without a CVI, a page is a mass confusion of elements competing for attention. Readers may simply go elsewhere.

The CVI is given *emphasis* by making it *contrast* with the other elements on the page. The attributes listed under "Balance" above work here as well: The CVI gains emphasis by its placement (high), its size (large), its tone (bold or in color), its shape (unusual), or even white space (surround the element with a much larger amount). Elements that break a margin or any other visual "rule" on your page gain emphasis as well.

Typographical contrast also is an important point to remember. Your message is delivered in type, but in various kinds of type: headlines or titles, blurbs or subheads, body type, captions, large quotes pulled from a story, or in maps and graphics.

These different parts of your message should not look the same. Captions, for instance, should *look* very different from body type. Readers should be able to identify immediately what they are reading.

This is done by contrasting all caps with uppercase and lowercase letters, roman with italic, bold with light, serif type with sans serif, large with smaller, and so on. This not only helps communicate the information more quickly but it makes your page look more interesting and attractive.

Figure 13–7. This page exhibits a strong CVI photo at the upper left. Most readers will enter this page there before moving on to the other photo, the graphics, and the headlines, and then settling to read a story. (Courtesy of *Central Michigan LIFE*)

Sequence

After the reader has been attracted to your CVI, you want to walk that reader through your page(s) in a pleasurable and interesting fashion. This means that the sequence of stops after the CVI must be clear.

Generally, readers start any page or spread in the upper left corner, sort of a default CVI. By thoughtfully using proper emphasis, however, you can induce readers to start nearly anywhere on a page, even the lower right-hand corner, the traditional departure point for the page. Be aware, however, that asking readers to fight gravity by starting at the bottom of a page, or by asking them to return to the top after a trip down page is usually asking too much. Readers simply don't like to defy reading gravity.

Proper sequence is achieved in a number of ways. The most obvious way would be to start at the top and number or letter photos or elements in the sequence you wish. But that would quickly get boring or tiresome.

Another way is to use the "imaginary" line created by the content of a photo or illustration or by the edges of artwork or columns of type. By aligning elements, the designer creates movement by forcing the eye to follow the imaginary line.

This action is a result of the gestalt principles, which explain that the brain likes to look for patterns in a visual field.

Another design manipulation is to use the concepts introduced under contrast and emphasis. If a reader will look at a large item first, then that reader will move to a smaller element next.

For instance, if you play a large photo, a medium-sized photo, and then a small photo on a page, that is exactly the order readers will follow as they look over the page. Sequence is created with large-to-small, color-to-B&W, irregular-to-normal shape, and so on.

Consider CVI and a diminishing sequence of visual impact and you get a coherent design. Ignore them and you get random design, a potpourri of placement principles. The idea is to use design to increase reader traffic on your page. Attract readers, intrigue them to pay attention, and then let your sparkling content take over.

Designer Robert G. Scott says to "keep the eye moving within the format until attention is exhausted. There must be no leaks where the eye is allowed to escape from the pattern by accident."

Unity

Design is a function of content. Therefore it must support the content by giving serious matters serious display and less serious content "fun" display. In the same way, the typeface, design style, color, and layout must fit together in a unified package to truly help communicate the content.

If you have an illustration with bold, thick lines, the type you use should also use bold, thick lines, such as a bold Helvetica. If your artwork is made up of delicate lines, a heavy Helvetica would look out of place. The same goes for border tapes. Bold type and bold tape go together, bold type and thin tape may not, unless the unusual contrast is what you want.

In a simpler sense, unity also refers to keeping some things constant throughout your publication. All standing headlines or column logos should be in the same typeface. The design should be similar, if not exactly the same.

Some people argue that contrast and unity are opposing principles. How can you have both?

The overarching principle is unity, but it is the unity of *constants* in your publication, not boring unity of layout. The unity comes in the framework, in the design plan. Contrast and emphasis enter in how you lay out individual pages.

Again, a good way to look at this idea is in architecture and construction. Unity is the foundation, the framework of the house. Contrast is the outer skin, the architectural design that allows the same basic structure to take on a unique look.

The design plan is set up and solidified well before any individual publication begins, or at least it should be. The layout of individual pages, following the principles of the overall design plan, comes later. First freeze the pond, then let the skaters dance.

Simplicity

The best designs, the best layouts, are simple ones. Even complex page designs that at first blush appear complicated turn out to be mere embellishments of a simple plan.

Tastes in any kind of design change in cyclical patterns: Ties get wider and narrower; skirts get longer and shorter. Tastes in graphic design also change and go in cycles. But simple, functional design is one of those universal principles that will work anywhere, anytime.

Keep your designs simple. A simple design helps communicate the information at hand: just what you are trying to do. A flashy design calls attention to itself, not to the content. People pick up publications to get the content, not to admire a wonderful design. If that wonderful design attracts readers to the content and then makes that visit easy and rewarding, then great! The design worked.

The old KISS formula is worth remembering, but let's defuse it a bit. Instead if "Keep It Simple, Stupid!" write this above your work station:

KEEPING IT SIMPLE = SUCCESS

Simplicity in design means:

- few elements instead of many
- more white space, instead of crowding in many elements
- grouping similar elements for easy reading
- few typographical changes.

A good test to use on any design element is: Remove it. If the design falls apart and becomes confusing, then you've gone too far in your editing. Yes, design can and must be edited too. If nothing happens when you remove it, then leave it out and congratulations! You have just made your design simpler. And better.

The Column Grid

All newspapers are designed on a basic grid of columns of type. Within the margins of the page, all elements are somehow attached to this grid structure (Fig. 13–8). This is much like architecture or house construction: First build a solid foundation, then on that design whatever kind of house you wish. The foundation, however, is always first.

So for whatever size newspaper you have, first set up the basic column grid. Once this is done, the design principles mentioned earlier can all be used freely. Broadsheet newspapers usually use six columns, tabloids four or five, and 8½ by 11-inch publications three. From this basic structure, deviations can be made, but most of your pages should start out on the same grid.

A grid is a rather precise structure within the page: The columns and gutters between them are precisely drawn down to a point, or 1/72 of an inch. The type from your laser printer or typesetter dances out line by line with utmost precision.

Figure 13–8. The column grid underlies all newspaper pages, no matter how many columns you are using. This six-column grid is standard for broadsheet papers. Many papers are taking a trick from magazine design and building pages on double the "half-column" grid, or one based on your normal half-column size. This way, dropping in half-column photos or pullouts or gaining more flexibility in photo and feature layouts becomes easier and more standardized.

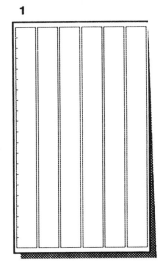

Unless you are paginating within a computer, you then must take separate pieces of type, art, or photos and paste them down onto another sheet of paper or a paste-up board. To be sloppy and imprecise makes no sense, yet many newspaper staffs pay little attention to the spacing of the elements on the page.

Regardless of whether you paste up or paginate, a basic principle applies. Remembering always that the basic structure is important and comes first, set up strict guidelines for the spacing of elements on a page. The basic principle is:

related elements should be more tightly spaced than unrelated elements

This is the "visual magnetism" rule that springs from the gestalt principles, as discussed earlier in this chapter. Spacing related elements more closely than the unrelated elements around them forces the eye/brain to group the elements together. This is exactly what you want to happen. Paying attention to this principle will help guide your readers through your content.

For instance, if your gutters are one pica, you may want to use 1.5 picas around all elements in a box. This somewhat larger "frame" around the elements (larger, that is, than the gutters between legs of type or between type and art) sets off the box from the rest of the elements in the content and forces together the related elements within the box (Fig. 13–9).

If you use one pica between a headline and the story that goes with it, you should use 1.5 picas *above* that headline, between it and the story above. This helps set off the headline/story combination from the rest of the page. In fact, a good newspaper staff has set spacing guidelines for every combination of elements on the page, all following the general rule of more space between unrelated items than between related items. Following these guidelines religiously will improve the looks of your page, even before you improve basic layouts. Be precise!

After the basics are set up, you are ready to deviate. Line measures help separate stories on a page. You may, for instance, wish to emphasize a story. One way to do that would be to run the type a little wider than normal, taking the space

Figure 13–9. Whenever you place type—or any other element—in a box, be sure to leave a little more white space framing the element(s) than you use as a gutter between legs of type, which is your basic spacing unit. The extra white space on the outside "forces" the eye to see the related elements as a grouped whole.

Lolloh hoy ohlo lhoyh hlolly ohyloyh hlyhol

Lorem ipsum dolor sit amet, consectetuer adipiscing elit, sed diam nonummy nibh euismod tincidunt ut laoreet dolore magna aliquam erat volutpat. Ut wisi enim ad minim veniam, quis nostrud exerci tation ullamcorper suscipit lobortis nisl ut aliquip ex ea commodo consequat.

Duis autem vel eum iriure dolor in hendrerit in vulputate velit esse molestie consequat, vel illum dolore eu feugiat nulla facilisis at vero eros et accumsan et iusto odio dignissim qui blandit praesent luptatum zzril delenit augue duis dolore te feugait nulla facilisi. Lorem ipsum dolor sit amet, consectetuer adipiscing elit, sed diam nonummy nibh euismod tincidunt ut laoreet dolore magna aliquam erat volutpat.

Ut wisi enim ad minim veniam, quis nostrud exerci tation ullamcorper suscipit lobortis nisl ut aliquip ex ea commodo consequat.

Duis autem vel eum iriure dolor in hendrerit in vulputate velit esse molestie consequat, vel illum dolore eu feugiat nulla facilisis at vero eros et accumsan et iusto odio dignissim qui blandit praesent luptatum zzril delenit augue duis dolore te feugait nulla facilisi. Nam liber tempor cum soluta nobis eleifend optiobnn coutngue nihillis imperdiet doming id quod mazim placerat facer possim assum.

Lorem ipsum dolor sit amet, consectetuer adipiscing elit, sed diam nonummy nibh euismod tincidunt ut laoreet dolore magna aliquam erat volutpat.

Lorem ipsum dolor sit amet, consectetuer adipiscing elit, sed diam nonummy nibh euismod tincidunt ut laoreet dolore magna aliquam erat volutpat. Ut wisi enim ad minim veniam, quis nostrud exerci tation ullamcorper suscipit lobortis nisl ut aliquip ex ea commodo consequat.

Duis autem vel eum iriure dolor in hendrerit in vulputate velit esse molestie consequat, vel illum dolore eu feugiat nulla facilisis at vero eros et accumsan et iusto odio dignissim qui blandit praesent luptatum zzril delenit augue duis dolore te feugait nulla facilisi. Lorem ipsum dolor sit amet, consectetuer adipiscing elit, sed diam nonummy nibh euismod tincidunt ut laoreet dolore magna aliquam erat volutpat.

Ut wisi enim ad minim veniam, quis nostrud exerci tation ullamcorper suscipit lobortis nisl ut aliquip ex ea

commodo consequat.

Duis autem vel eum iriure dolor in hendrerit in vulputate velit esse molestie consequat, vel illum dolore eu feugiat nulla facilisis at vero eros et accumsan et iusto odio dignissim qui blandit praesent luptatum zzril delenit augue duis dolore te feugait nulla facilisi. Nam liber tempor cum soluta nobis eleifend optiobnn coutngud nihillis imperdiet doming id quod mazim placerat facer possim assum.

Lorem ipsum dolor sit amet, consectetuer adipiscing elit, sed diam nonummy nibh euismod tincidunt ut laoreet dolore magna aliquam erat volutpat.

Ut wisi enim ad minim veniam, quis nostrud exerci tation ullamcorper suscipit lobortis nisl ut aliquip ex ea commodo consequat. Duis autem vel eum iriure dolor in

Figure 13–10. Even when you use an odd measure—such as two legs of type in three columns—be sure to keep the gutter the same measure. The gutter is one of those structural grid elements that should not normally change.

of, let's say, four columns, and running just three legs of type in that space (Fig. 13–10). One way to refer to this is to refer to the type as "legs" and keep the columns for the structure of the page. The example then would be three legs of type in four columns, or just three-in-four.

The exact line measure for this should be already set out in your spacing guidelines. There is no time to reinvent the wheel each issue by having to calculate each and every odd measure. The guidelines should have all the odd measures

"A Checklist for Functionally Integrated Design" by Roger F. Fidler, from the out-of-print *newspaper design notebook,* vol. 2, no. 1. Reprinted by permission.

A checklist for
Functionally Integrated Design

Functionally integrated layouts are not created with magic wands or rigid rules. They require organized and creative thinking developed through experience. And even with experience, not everyone has the visual sensitivity and judgment to become a good layout editor.

The following checklist is by no means all-inclusive. It is merely a tool for assessing layouts and should not be regarded as a newspaper design dogma.

If you can answer *Yes* to all questions designated with an open ballot box and *No* to all those designated with a solid box, the page layout is probably well-designed.

ORGANIZATION
☐ Are readers guided smoothly and naturally through the page?
☐ Do all elements have a reason for being?
☐ Are all intended relationships between elements readily apparent?
☐ Are packages clearly defined?
■ Does the design call attention to itself instead of the content?
■ Does the page appear cluttered?
■ Do any type or art elements appear to be floating on the page?
■ Do any elements appear lost?
■ Are any editorial elements easily confused with advertising?

READABILITY
■ Do any elements interrupt reading or cause confusion?
■ Are any legs of type perceptually truncated by art or sell lines (i.e quotes, liftouts, etc.)?
■ Is the line width of any text too narrow or too wide for easy reading?
■ If text is set to follow the shape of adjacent art, is the story difficult to read?
■ Do any headlines or sell lines compete with headlines or sell lines in adjacent columns?
☐ Are the starting points for all stories easily determined?

ACCURACY and CLARITY
☐ Does the layout accurately communicate the relative importance of the stories contained on the page?
☐ Do the art elements accurately convey the tone and message of the stories?
☐ Are logos consistent and differentiated from headlines?
☐ Are the devices used in a layout appropriate for the content of the page?

PROPORTIONING and SIZING
☐ Are all elements sized relative to their importance?
☐ Are the shapes and sizes of elements appropriate for the content of the elements?
☐ Do the shapes of elements add contrast and interest?
☐ Does the page have a dominant element or package of elements?
■ Does the shape of an element appear contrived or forced?
■ Do any logos or headlines seem out of proportion with the size of the story or column?
■ Are several elements similar in proportion and size?

EFFICIENCY and CONSISTENCY
☐ Do all areas of white space appear as if they were planned? (When it appears as if something fell off the page, the white space is not functional.)
☐ Is spacing between elements controlled and consistent?
☐ Are areas of white space balanced on the page?
☐ Is all type, especially agate material, set at the most efficient measure for the information contained?
☐ Is the size of column gutters constant?
■ Does the number of elements and/or devices used in a package seem excessive?

already figured, even those within a box. So if you want to run that three-in-four inside a box—which would mean that the legs of type would have to be even narrower because of the framing white space—you can just look up the necessary measure in the guidelines.

Remember that wider horizontal lines tend to say "quiet" and "slow, book-ish read." Narrower lines—and columns—say "quick read" and "excitement." Opinion pages, for instance, often use a wider measure, a different grid that indicates a more thoughtful approach to information. On the other hand, calendars and some feature fronts—the sort of "what's happenin'?" pages—need to portray action, so narrower legs of type are preferred.

For instance, if you have a standard, six-column grid, you may want to go to five columns for the opinion page and other "slow reads" and seven columns for briefs, calendars, listings, and other quick-n-dirty reads. This is one way that your design can support your content and add to the ease of reading—and perhaps even comprehension—of your readers.

Typography in Design

Because type plays such a large part on a newspaper page, designers must treat type as a design element. A designer spends a lot of time thinking about typeface selection for body type and for headlines before making a decision. Sometimes a new typeface will even be designed to fit a specific need. Typefaces can evoke different moods. Bold sans serif faces are active, splashy, aggressive. Old romans are distinguished and quietly beautiful. A designer selects the typeface that fits the mood of the paper.

Several other factors concerning typography on a page need to be considered: the readability of all-capital-letter headlines, the readability of italics, and the number of typefaces to use. Not long ago, newspapers used many all-cap headlines. Today a few papers still use them on occasion. Studies have shown, however, that all-cap heads are hard to read, largely because there is no difference in height between capital letters—a major factor in recognizing lowercase letters. Also, capital letters take up more horizontal space than lowercase letters. On a newspaper page, where space is at a premium, avoid using all-cap headlines unless the story is a big one.

Italic typefaces are also not as easy to read as their roman cousins. Some papers use italics for cutlines and for an occasional headline to counterpoint the many romans on the page. If usage is kept to a minimum, italics are fine. But cutlines may be better set off typographically by using sans serif type, one or two points larger than the body type.

Following the trend toward simplicity, many newspapers have reduced the number of headline styles and/or weight to one or two. Differences in emphasis are achieved by changing the size, the number of columns, and the number of lines in headlines. Many papers use a bold typeface for the majority of headlines and a medium-weight head for emphasis. When using a second deck or readout head, vary the weight from bold to medium (or light). Italics are fine here, too.

One last note on mixing serif and sans serif typefaces on a page: Although many designers may tell you that mixing the two in headlines is taboo, careful choice of typefaces will lead to an attractive head schedule, and mixing the two as body type and headline is all right and perhaps preferable (Fig. 13–11). Because readers are used to reading serif type in books, magazines, and newspapers, a

Figure 13–11. Mixing two faces of type in your headline used to be taboo. Now, if you pick the proper typefaces, you can achieve an attractive mix that both grabs the readers' attention and looks good.

Dude: 'The sun, the surf, the bods'
Former Bruin spikers kick sand in little kids' faces

sans serif body type is unusual and harder to read. The common trend in today's newspaper design is to use a modern serif typeface with a large x-height for body type and roman or sans serif type for headlines.

Justified versus Unjustified

A designer needs to consider whether to use justified or unjustified type (Fig. 13–12). If the lines of type are automatically spaced by the computer so that all lines are exactly the same width, they are *justified*. Unjustified type, also known as *ragged right*, can be set highly ragged or just slightly so. The latter is preferred for readability.

Tuesday night's Student Government Association meeting was again the scene of heated debate as a bill that would reinstate salaries for the president and vice president of the organization was voted down.

The stipends had been repealed by the student body in a referendum during last month's SGA election balloting by a vote of 1,672 to 1,030.

Debbie Sears, commuter senator and one of the bill's supporters, said the reason the stipends were still an issue to be voted on by the senate was because most students don't know what the officers do.

"The president and vice president spend all that time working for SGA and for the students," she said. "Surely they should receive some incentive to work besides the personal satisfaction of it."

Senator David Sharp said reinstating the salaries for the officers would be a "slap in the face" to the students who voted.

"Who can expect students to participate in the future in an election if you turn around and reverse their decisions?" asked Sharp.

Tuesday night's Student Government Association meeting was again the scene of heated debate as a bill that would reinstate salaries for the president and vice president of the organization was voted down.

The stipends had been repealed by the student body in a referendum during last month's SGA election balloting by a vote of 1,672 to 1,030.

Debbie Sears, commuter senator and one of the bill's supporters, said the reason the stipends were still an issue to be voted on by the senate was because most students don't know what the officers do.

"The president and vice president spend all that time working for SGA and for the students," she said. "Surely they should receive some incentive to work besides the personal satisfaction of it."

Senator David Sharp said reinstating the salaries for the officers would be a "slap in the face" to the students who voted.

"Who can expect students to participate in the future in an election if you turn around and reverse their decisions?" asked Sharp.

Tuesday night's Student Government Association meeting was again the scene of heated debate as a bill that would reinstate salaries for the president and vice president of the organization was voted down.

The stipends had been repealed by the student body in a referendum during last month's SGA election balloting by a vote of 1,672 to 1,030.

Debbie Sears, commuter senator and one of the bill's supporters, said the reason the stipends were still an issue to be voted on by the senate was because most students don't know what the officers do.

"The president and vice president spend all that time working for SGA and for the students," she said. "Surely they should receive some incentive to work besides the personal satisfaction of it."

Senator David Sharp said reinstating the salaries for the officers would be a "slap in the face" to the students who voted.

"Who can expect students to participate in the future in an election if you turn around and reverse their decisions?" asked Sharp.

Figure 13–12. Type columns may be set justified (*left*), unjustified or slightly ragged (*center*), or highly ragged. Notice that the unjustified column is no longer than the justified story. The highly ragged story uses four more lines of type.

Unjustified, or ragged type, can add a different "look" to your pages, but use it carefully. The message it delivers does not say "hard news." Reserve unjustified type for soft news, columns, or letters to the editor (Fig. 13–13). Some papers use *rules*, or thin vertical lines, in the *gutter* between columns of unjustified type. Other designers dislike unjustified type, believing that the extra white space created by the shorter lines is too large and visually distracting. Generally, reduce the gutter size when using unjustified columns of type.

Unjustified lines are easier to read than are justified lines, which have to be spaced or squeezed, or words have to be hyphenated to make every line precisely the same width. But with unjustified columns, the typesetter does not have to letter-space, squeeze, or hyphenate. The word-spacing is always the same and thus easier to read. Unjustified columns are best used to give emphasis to special soft news stories.

Layout

To lay out a page means to combine the design elements in a pleasing pattern through *organization* and *emphasis*. "In the well-designed newspaper, contents are organized to help the reader and are presented in simple, clear, readable form," Wallace Allen says. "First of all, the newspaper must *look inviting* to the reader. Then it must *help him read*."

Newspapers can use largely vertical or largely horizontal layouts. Newspapers started out as highly vertical. In fact, they were so vertical that story No. 1 started in the upper left corner and ran one column all the way down until it was

BUZZY

Buzzy is an unusual name for a man, but then Buzzy Wicker is an unusual man. "When you meet him he's a little off-the-wall," says his former roommate, Cade White, senior photojournalism major from Temple. "When you get to know him, he's still off-the-wall."

Cade met Buzzy, a graduate mass communications major from Memphis, Tenn., at a basketball game a few years ago. Cade was photographer for the *Prickly Pear;* Buzzy worked with the video yearbook.

"Buzz just walked up and introduced himself," Cade recalls. "I thought he was really forward, but once I got to know him — that's just his nature. He doesn't have any inhibitions. He's just a good 'ole boy from Tennessee."

Buzzy admits to being unusual. "I'm different for sure," he says. "I don't worry a lot about what people think of me."

In fact, Buzzy doesn't worry much period — another quality that makes him unusual. "I don't let things upset me," Buzzy says. "I'm not a worrier. They say that things you worry about don't come to pass anyway. It's kind of a needless stress."

Cade says, "He takes life as it comes — just one day at a time. The things that he worries about are very limited. He worries about school."

Buzzy, who served as executive director of the 1987-88 video yearbook, is just a few hours short of a master's degree. Unfortunately, an overseas trip he needed to complete his thesis was canceled this summer, leaving him with a problem he still has not worked out.

Still, Buzzy isn't worried. "I think he worries in the sense that he contemplates stuff," says Kevin Marshall, a close friend and fellow graduate student. "He's thoughtful more than he worries. He's pretty logical."

Buzzy says the most stressful period of his life came in the years between graduating with a bachelor's degree in 1982 and his return to ACU for graduate work in 1987.

After graduating with a degree in radio/TV, Buzzy immediately went to Abilene's KTXS as newscast director. After a year, he went to CNN in Atlanta, Ga., as a technical director.

"The first week I was there the Marines got blown up in Lebanon, and we invaded Grenada," he said. "It was a little too much hard news for me. Seven hours of hardcore news everyday — it kind of made your outlook on life a little grim."

When CNN made budget cuts, Buzzy, being low on the totem pole, found himself without a job. He spent the next few years in a variety of jobs, including newspaper work, advertising and youth ministry. Unemployment sometimes lowered his spirits.

"That was by far the most difficult period of my life," he said. "I can really sympathize with people who are unemployed."

Luckily, Buzzy had a good church and family to help him through the difficult times, and after landing a job with a public television station in Memphis, he decided to return to school for a master's degree.

He said he had often contemplated graduate work, and he wanted to be around good equipment in a situation where he would have free reign to use his creativity.

"Sure enough, the video yearbook came along and that was a nice outlet for my creative urges," he said.

Buzzy helped with the video yearbook his first year back, and last year, he was executive producer. He said he enjoys putting the yearbook together, and that many of the events he attends for filming are just plain fun.

Although Buzzy loves using a camera, he also loves music, and sometimes he finds himself in front of the camera. During Welcome Week he took center stage to do his popular Willie Nelson imitation.

He plucked his guitar and growled out the tunes of "Blue Eyes Crying In The Rain."

His appearance in the Welcome Week Talent Show wasn't his first performance before an audience. He said he has done his Willie Nelson act in a variety of places, including with a band at Casa Herrera.

Buzzy says his love for music goes back to his childhood.

"I was really young when the Beatles were coming up," he said. "I had a Beatles wig, and I used to entertain people by doing the twist."

Cade, who also plays the guitar, said he and Buzzy would sit around and pick and sing when they were roommates. "Buzzy likes all kinds of music, but his main musical interests lie in his homeland of Tennessee. He loves Blue Grass; he likes Country and Western," Cade says.

Buzzy loves the guitar, but he learned to play only in the last few years. He did not get his first guitar until after he graduated with his bachelor's.

He said when he was working at KTXS, his roommate, who also worked there, owned a guitar. "One day I went to Lake Brownwood to go skiing, and he got the keys to my motorcycle and had a wreck and got killed," Buzzy says in a low voice. "I inherited his guitar."

The incident was difficult for Buzzy, and the guitar has remained very special.

"He hardly ever puts his guitar in the case," Marshall says. "It sits on a stand in the front room." Buzzy taught himself to play it, and he still uses it.

Although music is very important to Buzzy, he doesn't know where it will lead him. He has written a few songs and says he might try to get them published, but his long-term goals focus on his mass communications skills.

"I'd like to go to work in corporate communications," he says. "I think I could do that pretty well. I wouldn't mind one day teaching. I think God's got something in store for me, and it will come around eventually."

As for his unusual name, Buzzy, whose real name is Charles Wicker, says it was a gift from his family. "They didn't want to call me Chuck or Charlie," he said. "So one day Mom said, 'We'll just call him Buzzy. It stuck like glue.' "

Buzzy said he has tried several times to lose the name, which isn't good in professional circles, but he can't. He says if he ever does rid himself of the name, he will know he finally has matured.

"I'll know I'm really grown up then," he said. "People will call me Charles." — *by Candy Holcombe*

Buzzy often can be found in the ACU Video Productions Studio on the first floor of the Don H. Morris Center, where he spends a majority of his time editing tapes — *Roy Cade White/Optimist*

or in Moody Coliseum videotaping basketball or volleyball games for the video yearbook — *Roy Cade White/Optimist*

and at his home, 1401 North 21st St., playing with his dog, Zulu, or strumming on his guitar. *Roy Cade White/Optimist*

Figure 13–13. This page uses ragged right type as one way to show that the content is not hard news. Ragged right type calls for smaller gutters than normal, by the way, because most lines in the column are much shorter than full length. (Courtesy of the *Optimist*)

completed, then story No. 2 started, and so on, each wrapping top-to-bottom, column-to-column until the page was filled. The decade of the 1970s was probably the age of the purely horizontal layout. Many newspapers reacted against the old-fashioned verticality of most of the eight-column newspapers of that time and ran everything in short, wide boxes across the page. But the all-wide spreads sometimes looked static and boring, even though everything was neatly organized and displayed.

176

The best and most interesting presentation, of course, combines the vertical and horizontal. Long stories are better displayed horizontally because the lack of depth hides the often intimidating length of the story. Long verticals seem to appear longer to the reader. But photos and shorter stories can be displayed vertically. Playing the horizontals off verticals such as these (Fig. 13–14) makes for a more visually exciting page.

Outside

Clear

Sunny with highs in the upper 70s to low 80s. Santa Ana conditions most of the day. Seventy-five percent chance of being overcome by a wall of sliding mud.

THE GRAPHIC

CAMPUS WEEKLY

Inside

Poloists on fire. Page 5.

Vol. 18, No. 6 SEAVER COLLEGE, PEPPERDINE UNIVERSITY--MALIBU, CA November 9, 1989

NOTEWORTHY

Amnesty International

Everyone is welcome to contribute their thoughts to the Human Rights Board located outside the campus bookstore.

The next Amnesty meeting will be Tuesday Nov. 14 in MSC 105 at 8 p.m. The meeting will highlight news about South Africa. Call Marie at x3792 for more information.

Health & Counseling

The center will be sponsoring an educational/support group for Adult Children of Alcoholics on Nov. 13, 20 and 27 from 4 to 5 p.m. in PLC 100. Carolyn Nicks, M.A., will be leading the group.

Hockey Club

Tonight is the last home game of the semester. The team will be playing UCLA at 9 p.m. in the Conejo Valley Ice Arena.

Intramurals

Aqua Aerobics classes will be meeting every Monday evening from 6 to 7 p.m.

Anyone interested in cardiovascular and muscular work, a Contracted Fitness program is being offered Monday through Friday, 6-7 a.m.

SGA

The Student Government Association is sponsoring the First All-Campus Steak and Shrimp Banquet. It will be held Thursday, Nov. 16 from 4:30 p.m. to 6:30 p.m. at Alumni Park.

The banquet is free to meal card holders. It will also be free to the first 800 students, faculty, staff and administrators who RSVP to the SGA office, x4360.

Student Accounts

There is now a drop box in the mail room specifically for payments to Student Accounts.

This will help to alleviate the lines encountered at the Cashier window.

Volunteer Center

Volunteers are needed to help work at the Food Drive, Saturday Nov. 11, 10:30 a.m. - 1:30 p.m. or 1:30 p.m. to 4:30 p.m.

The drive will provide food for people in need this holiday season.

Donations will also be taken Nov. 11 at Vons on PCH and Sunset.

The "Friend to Friend" program needs a limited number of students who want to spend a few hours a month at Villa Esperanza. Call x4143 for more information, or contact Tad Benson, x3757 to sign up.

Pacific Palisades landslide closes PCH

Tumble down

Graphic photos / Scott Eslinger

Cal- Trans workers monitor the unstable hillside using an airhorn to warn others if a further slide should occur. Tree and cement slab (inset) were removed Wednesday. Pacific Coast Highway reopened to traffic Wednesday evening about 6:30.

By ANDREW McCARTHY
Graphic Managing Editor

A massive concrete slab and a large tree hung precariously over Pacific Coast Highway Wednesday, the result of a landslide just north of Chatautaqua Boulevard in Pacific Palisades.

The highway remained closed until 6:30 p.m. Wednesday when two of the four lanes were opened. Cal-Trans workers spent most of Wednesday removing the tree and concrete which were considered a danger to motorists.

The slide, which blocked all lanes of the highway, occurred at approximately 11 a.m. Tuesday. Gustavo Ortega, a Cal-Trans worker, just happened to be near the site when the hillside broke away.

"It (the land slide) didn't make a lot of noise...I just saw the dust," he said. Ortega immediately reported the slide via the radio in his truck. Cal-Trans responded to the slide around 11:15 a.m.

Two people were injured, and three cars wrecked in the slide. The Mercedes of Barbara Phillips, 47, was flipped over by the slide. The GMC Jimmy driven by Ed Withers, also 47, of Thousand Oaks was buried in the dirt. Phillips sustained two broken ribs and Withers only cuts and bruises.

The slide covered the highway with approximately six feet of earth. Using skiploaders and a number of dump trucks, workers had the majority of the earth and debris cleaned up by 3 p.m. Tuesday.

The highway, however, remained closed throughout the night because of concern that the earth under the concrete slab or the tree might give way and cause further earth movement.

By Wednesday, Cal-Trans officials had decided to make a "Declaration of Emergency," a Cal-Trans spokeseman said.

It was necessary to declare the emergency "in order to secure the hill," said

SEE LANDSLIDE / PAGE 2

Controversy increases as Km sales escalate

By TAMI MARKO
Executive News Editor

Km, manufactured in Canada by Matol Botanical International, is a liquid potassium, mineral supplement which currently earns $12.8 million in monthly sales. The product has been met with enthusiasm and skepticism on Pepperdine's campus.

The Km controversy centers around the lack of scientific evidence proving Km's health benefits verses the rave testimonial reviews of those who have used the product.

Dr. Karl Jurak, who invented the product more than 60 years ago, believes the unique combination of 14 herbs and plants aids the body in eliminating toxins that inhibit its potential to function at an optimum level.

The lack of scientific proof should "make people cautious about the product," said Susan Speer, a visiting professor at Pepperdine.

"I find it hilarious that ... a nutrition teacher, with a few years of academic study," said Brett Baggett, a user and distributor of Km, "would assume she knows more about biochemistry, agrobiology, and how nutrients are used in the blood stream than a world-famous biochemist/agrobiologist (Jurak) who has...two Ph.D.s with 25 medical patents to his name, who furthermore, received a doctorate with honors at age 19, after presenting this molecular formula (now called Km) as his thesis project."

"The body works to eliminate excess potassium (K)," Speer said, "Taking more potassium cannot raise the potassium level in the body unless there is a deficiency."

Many people do, however, feel they benefit from the product.

"I started taking (Km) and felt better in certain regards," said Doug Horn, former Pepperdine Lacrosse coach and supervisor for Matol Botanical.

"I don't have the aches and pains I had for 10 years prior to taking it," he said. Horn plans to pursue a full-time career in Km distribution.

Another point skeptics of Km raise is all of the product's ingredients "are essential nutrients found in many other foods," Speer said.

The Student Dietetic Association sponsored a booth last month at Seaver College's Oktoberfest where members distributed flyers explaining that the nutrients in Km can be obtained from eating regular food.

Because the nutrients in Km are found in many natural food sources, "there's really no sense in spending $30 on Km," said Kim Criss, president of the SDA chapter at Pepperdine.

Advocates of Km agree that the product's ingredients can be obtained through a healthy, well balanced diet.

Those that support and use Km, however, believe that the product's molecular combination of nutrients increases the body's potential to absorb the nutrients.

With that logic in mind, a dosage of Km may be more beneficial than one banana.

Other Km skeptics also raise the possibility that the product's success lies in the mind of the user, known in psychology circles as the placebo effect.

"Because there is no scientific evidence, no one can say whether it works or it doesn't work," Speer said.

Whether the effect is psychological, many Pepperdine students have faith that the product has definite health benefits.

"I really think the stuff works. I started using it last year during Lacrosse," said junior Lenny Asaro, member of the Pepperdine Lacrosse team.

"Since then it has given me more of a physical edge...more energy, helped me think clearer on the field, and my running, without a doubt, has improved," Asaro said.

Dan Voss, a junior business major who used Km for three months said, "At first I didn't need as much sleep, but it could have been psychological."

SEE NUTRIENT / PAGE 2

PRSSA chosen for campaign

25 chapters compete for NutraSweet

By TRACY MARCYNZSYN
Graphic Staff Writer

Pepperdine's chapter of the Public Relations Student Society of America was one out of 25 chapters nationwide chosen to implement a campaign for the NutraSweet company's competition, "The College Beat with NutraSweet."

PRSSA, a national pre-professional club for students, began their eight-week campaign Oct. 18. The campaign ends Dec. 18.

The Pepperdine program, "Is NutraSweet In What You Eat?" is designed to increase the public's awareness about NutraSweet brand sweetener.

"Pepperdine and Cal State Long Beach are the only West Coast schools in the competition," said Shelly Walker, the president of Pepperdine's PRSSA chapter.

According to a PRSSA newsletter, each campaign includes a budget, time line, slogans, media techniques and planned events on the Pepperdine campus and in the Malibu community. Each chapter will receive $800 from the NutraSweet company to cover campaign expenses.

The winning chapter will receive $2,000 and five representatives will be flown to Deerfield, Illinois to present their chapter's campaign to the NutraSweet company.

Pepperdine's campaign consists of seven different events designed to inform Pepperdine students and the Malibu community about the benefits of NutraSweet Brand Sweetener.

The program officially began at Pepperdine's celebration of "Oktoberfest" where PRSSA had set up a booth and a contest in which students guessed the number of NutraSweet gumballs in a jar. Gretchen Gubbrud guessed the correct amount and won the $25 gift certificate for Hughes Market.

Other events included "Trick or Treat with NutraSweet," on Oct. 31 at the Malibu Community Center. NutraSweet was introduced to parents who may have been worried about the amounts of sugar their children were consuming, especially on Halloween.

Future events will include a drawing in which one can win $50 worth of groceries at Hughes Market. Sampling tables will be set up in the store so customers can sample products sweetened with NutraSweet. Customers can enter the drawing by filling out a questionnaire about their knowledge of NutraSweet or by circling a product on their receipt that contains NutraSweet.

Car Wash aids relief cause

By JIM LAURITZEN
Graphic Staff Writer

As the dust from the San Francisco earthquake settled and the damages were assessed, many students felt there was not much they could do to help the situation.

One group of students, led by freshman Leyla Sohaey, was able to make a difference.

A car wash was organized on Saturday, Oct. 21, from 9 a.m. to 5 p.m., and all the proceeds went to the Red Cross.

This event raised approximately $2,000 dollars.

It made a great impact on the people of Malibu, many of whom contributed to the success of the event.

"The community really came together to help," Sohaey said. "Hughes donated some supplies, Malibu Inn donated 20 hamburgers, Printing Square donated 500 flyers, and Chevron donated their parking lot," he added.

Many people who did not have time for a car wash just drove through and gave donations.

Junior Karen Brune, who was involved in the project, said, "What impressed me the most is how everyone pulled together in a common concern. It was incredible how easily it went together."

Sophomore Rachel Naylor, another volunteer, said, "It made me feel a lot more connected to the community...we could share our time with someone we didn't know."

When asked how she became motivated to plan such an event, Sohaey said that the day after the earthquake, she had tried to help out by joining the Red Cross, but they were only accepting trained professionals.

Although she did not know anyone in San Francisco or the surrounding area, she organized the event "out of frustration."

Sohaey gave a great deal of credit to Beverly Ann Sohaey, who "made calls, bought supplies, got up at 5 a.m. on the day of the car wash, and gave a large donation to the whole project."

On the day before the car wash, a group of volunteers went into a beauty shop in the Hughes shopping center to post a flyer.

According to Sohaey, the people in the store started donating money when they heard about what the flyer was adver-

SEE CAR WASH / PAGE 2

Figure 13–14. This page is a modular layout with predominantly horizontal modules. What helps the page to work, however, is the vertical "Noteworthy" column in the upper left. The vertical keeps the page from being static. (Courtesy of *The Graphic*)

Modular layouts have been found to be more pleasing, probably because the reader can easily see the package's edges and thus know the limits of the commitment to read. All stories—or story/photo combinations—in modular layout fit into neat rectangles (Fig. 13–15). Modular layouts do away with the jagged shape that stories take in other layout styles. A benefit of modular design is that news elements are presented in neat organizational packages, fulfilling that major layout principle.

Figure 13–15. This page presents all its information in easy-to-see modules. Even legs of type in a story are preferred by readers over uneven columns. (Courtesy of *The Advocate*)

12 Friday, April 21, 1989 The Advocate NEWS

MORE NEWS

District says yes to three deans

In that wacky game of peek-a-boo assistant deans, the one that was gone has now reappeared.

Three assistant deans will be hired this summer, negating an earlier report that CCC would only be able to hire two assistant deans, college President D. Candy Rose said.

Dr. Rose said miscommunication between herself and the district concerning the new assistant dean of community education led her to believe that the newly reorganized managerial structure would have to be altered.

She said the district had already agreed to the community education position when they approved an additional two dean positions, totaling three assistant deans. Rose said she took the approval of the two new positions to indicate that the total number would be two.

Two of the three deans will support instructional programs, while the other assistant dean will focus on community education programs like the non-credit program and instructional outreach. In the five-year district hiring plan, there will be no new managerial positions for CCC, Rose said.

— Kevin Cunningham

Photography deadline coming

The art department is sponsoring the college's annual its Annual Photography Contest/Exhibition. Photographers may submit a total of five prints which must be turned in to the art department office by 4 p.m on Tuesday. The exhibition opens May 1 and ends May 19.

There will be an opening reception at Rhodes Gallery on May 2 from 5 to 7 p.m. For more information call the art department at ext. 261 or 262.

Annual scholarship dinner held

CCC's 30th Annual Scholarship Recognition Dinner will be held on Friday, May 5 at 6 p.m. Tickets are now on sale for $18 each. To purchase tickets contact Dianne McClain or Bruce Carlton in L-6, Ginny Watkins in LA-24 or Boyce McKelvey in AA-203. The deadline to buy tickets is May 2. For more information call Carlton at ext. 449 or 450.

DSU sponsors plant sale

The Disabled Students Union will be sponsoring a plant sale on May 10 and 11. There will be dozens of indoor and outdoor varieties of plants to choose from. This is a chance to support the DSU and buy plants at low cost. The sale will be held from 10 a.m to 1 p.m. in the amphitheatre.

Late applications accepted

The dental assisting program is now accepting late applications for the summer session. CCC's graduates have earned an high pass rate on the Registered Dental Assisting State Board Exam for the past seven years. Applications are available in AA-206. For more information call ext. 265.

Student poet rhymes again

By Ray Britt
Staff writer

Tim Fielding/The Advocate

Poet and student Claire J. Baker has published her eighth book, this one a book of poems, dedicated to Women's Center director Ruby Farris.

Seventh-semester student Claire J. Baker has been writing poetry since her teen years. According to Baker, since those early years she has written seven books, thousands of poems and won hundreds awards. Her latest book is entitled, "Women Centering."

"My mother never discouraged me or put me down for writing poetry, so I continued to write," Baker said.

Her latest book of poems is a compilation of numerous pieces she has written throughout the years. Baker re-edited the older pieces and assembled them with newer poems, dividing the poems into four sections. She said the process took a total of 60 hours. The result is an independently published book on the plight of women, in both a negative and positive light.

"I hope the book gives women a sense of kinship. Women can confront their fears," Baker said. "Man can learn about our struggles with understanding."

The book is dedicated to Baker's friend, Ruby Farris. Farris, the Women's Center coordinator here, said Baker's poetry reveals a lot about her.

"I've come to learn a lot about her through her poetry," Farris said. "Her writing says a lot about who she is. She probably doesn't realize how revealing she is."

The seed for the book grew from an independent contract which Baker signed when she entered the Woman's Center. Students in the center are required to sign up for projects, and Baker decided her project would be to write a book of poetry.

Baker says the center gives her a place of identity.

"I am very happy with my association with the center. It makes me feel like someone special," Baker said. In gratitude to the center and its director, the central poem of the book is, "Strong Woman," and is dedicated to Farris.

"I think Ruby is a strong woman and that inspired the poem," Baker said. "She has made the center a place of reception and peace for me."

Farris said she was humbled by the gesture. "I never looked at myself as being a strong person. The dedication was very touching."

Baker has resisted the opportunity to be published by major firms because she likes the freedom of her independence. She doesn't like the competitiveness of big firms. She says that she is content with the way her career is going. She added that she doesn't feel poetry is commercially feasible.

Last year, she published the book, "Re-Entry," which she composed on a Macintosh computer. She said she really enjoyed that project which was about her experiences attending college. She said the experience of working on a computer was exciting.

...Withdrawal

Continued from page 1

will drop them when the instructor's policy is not to drop students.

"If it's obvious to me that students aren't coming to class I'll drop them," said Buescher, whose classes contain roughly 50 to 60 students. "But it puts me in a difficult position to make decisions for students, and I don't like to make students' decisions for them."

Some students claim that because they are getting these mixed messages they are finding failing grades on their report cards in courses they registered for, but never attended.

Anthony Woods said he signed up for an English course, but after attending class for a few weeks he stopped going with the understanding that the instructor would drop him.

"She told me she was going to drop me because I wasn't coming to class, and when my grades came in the mail I got an 'F'," said an angry Woods.

"I never even went to this history class and the teacher kept me on the roll," said student Raephel Jackson. "He gave me a 'D' and I never went to the class."

Not all students are confused by the college's withdrawal policy and some have benefitted from instructors who drop students for non-attendance.

"Every teacher I've ever had has announced at the beginning of class that it's the student's responsibility to drop classes," student Sharon Faerber said.

But Georgia Haley knew she was responsible for dropping a class that she never attended and was glad to see a "W" on her grade report even though she didn't file a drop card.

"The teacher was really nice about it and dropped me," Haley said. "I know I was supposed to drop the class but I just flaked on it."

Biological sciences instructor Dr. Debbie Draves said that teachers don't always drop students for non-attendance because occasionally students return and have a legitimate excuse for their absence.

"I always announce at the beginning of the semester that it is the student's responsibility to drop the class," said Draves, who is also a member of the Student Services Committee. "But I will drop students who never show up to class."

Students can appeal a grade received in a class they never attended according to Maryanne Werner-McCullough, chairperson of the Appeals Committee.

"The Appeals Committee can't change a student's grade, but if a student claims that he never went to class we will send the information on to the instructor," said Werner-McCullough. "We ask to have the grade changed from an 'F' to a 'W', but only the instructor can change the grade.

"We get that a lot in the Appeals Committee," Werner-McCullough said referring to students who assume that instructors will file drop cards for students who don't attend class. She also pointed out that the appeal process can take several months, sometimes causing problems if a student wants to transfer.

...Plan

Continued from page 1

Rose said, "We simply have to increase our use of space."

One of the reasons the college hasn't received funds recently in this area is due to low enrollment, Rose said. Additional students would increase the college's use of space. "We have to expand our offerings."

"What we need to do is examine how we're using the space right now and come up with a way of using it more efficiently and effectively," said Director of Business Services Pete Goodson, a member of the college Space Committee.

"We probably do not need new building space," Brown said, "but the space that we do have probably should be remodeled."

The Space Committee was formed at the beginning of this semester specifically to review space-usage on the campus.

"We're trying to develop a philosophy and policy on the utilization of space," Goodson said.

The request for state funds was first sent to the state Chancellor's Office in February, Brown said. From there, it will be sent to the state Board of Governors for approval in May or June, and will then be sent to the Department of Finance. In January 1990, it will go through the legislative process to be signed by the governor in June, when the final decision will be made.

Brown said that if CCC receives the funds, it can be expected that they will be spent to take care of the handicapped barrier removal in the fiscal year 1991-92.

"So we'll just have to wait and see," Rose said. "There are no guarantees."

...Harley

Continued from page 1

or eight blocks, Simpson said, he realized he couldn't logistically or legally continue to chase the guy, so he headed for the San Pablo Police Department.

At the SPPD, he filled in the police officers on duty, "four of whom were my former students, including the sergeant," and they picked up the pursuit.

"(Officer) Dave Lewellyn got on the guy. The guy abandoned the bike and got away about six blocks northeast of campus. They recovered the bike there."

Semons, who was routed out of bed by Simpson and driven back to reclaim his bike, was ecstatic. "It was recovered in perfect condition. There was just some cosmetic damage, about $200 worth." He said a quick trip to a repair shop would have the machine up and purring again soon.

Simpson, reluctant to take credit for saving the day, said the San Pablo police did the work.

"It was just pure dumb luck that I saw it," he said. "The cops deserve the credit. They recovered the bike in excellent condition.

"(The bike) was El Cheapo Junko when Ralph bought it," said Simpson, who is in the process of "personalizing" a BMW motorcycle for himself. "He put about $1,000 on it to make it HIS."

"Motorcycles are very personal," Semons said, obviously glad to get his own personal statement back in his garage. "We express ourselves through our bikes."

Semons has already planned his next adventure — his wife is expecting a baby on Labor Day.

Simpson said he hopes his services won't be required for that event.

...Cocoon

Continued from page 1

ommend the kind of educational program that is right," Allums said.

However, one black student, a business major who asked that her name be withheld, said counseling does coddle black students.

"They treat you like a baby because you're black. The counselors protect blacks because they feel they don't have the knowledge that other students have," the student said. She said a counselor did quite a bit for a cousin of hers, "getting her classes and talking to her instructors — everything."

English major Regina Rodgers said counselors often do not advise black students to go into challenging classes.

"If your goal is to transfer, then they will tell you what classes to take, but nothing that will help you to develop the ability to think. It's a continuation of high school," she said.

Hector Razo, an engineering major, had a different experience. When he first came here, he was told to take harder classes in philosophy, speech, biology and engineering. He said he rarely sees students being directed into easier classes.

"The only time I see that is when people take the placement test. They tell them not to jump into higher classes," he said. He said some students are placed lower than they should be, because they did poorly the day they took the test.

The student services approach

Director of Special Programs and Services Sodonia Wilson, who directs EOPS, said that student services does not conflict with the instruction of students.

"Student services has a responsibility to meet the needs of the students. (We support) good academic standards and certainly support the standards of the campus," Dr. Wilson said. She said the goals of instructors and student services personal were similar.

> *I wish the teaching faculty were aware of the other needs of students besides academic needs.*
>
> —Charles Allums

"Without student services, you would probably find very few students here," she said. EOPS provides tutors, peer counselors, and book grants, among other things, to students with economic or educational need.

"I don't see that as being overly protective," Wilson said.

Art student Alicia Gilliam agreed that student services increases the number of minority students here.

"(EOPS) is a good thing because there are students who need it. Without student services you wouldn't have many minority students in academics," Gilliam said.

Greer said not many people know what counselors do. Greer, who is the women's track coach, likened counseling and instruction with coaching.

"You help them (students) reach whatever potential that they have, whether it's on the playing field or in the classroom," he said.

Counselor Wayne Daniels said student services may have a "cocoon" effect on students, but it applies to all and does not have a negative effect on learning. He said student services is the "nurturing heart" of the campus and instruction is the "logical, impersonal head" of the campus.

"It's motivating students and inspiring students, giving the student a sense of mission for himself or herself. Those things that nurture the heart and soul of the campus create a cocoon, and rightly so. The cocoon effect is a benefit to all students," Daniels said.

The needs of black students

Allums said Martincich may be perceiving the "togetherness" that is part of black culture.

"(Martincich) may be right in the sense that black people tend to be more spiritual and tend to form more caring relationships. He may not understand that," Allums said.

"He just wants you enrolled in class and doesn't care about all the other things that are part of a modern college." Allums listed health, financial and family concerns as non-academic things which affect learning.

"I wish the teaching faculty were aware of the other needs of students besides the academic needs," Allums said. He cited the case of a student who needed a grade of C or better in Mathematics 120 to transfer, and the instructor gave her a D. Allums said she worked full time, had a child and generally earned good grades.

"I don't see the difference between a C and a D grade when the student understands the concepts of Math 120," Allums said.

As an example of "cocooning," Martincich referred to Allums' suggestion that minority students should get 15 points added to their placement test scores. Allums said the extra points would make up for the cultural bias in a test that favors whites.

Allums said that giving minorities extra points was not protecting students, but challenging them by allowing them into college-level courses. He said part of the problem blacks have with education is that they have been routinely tracked into remedial courses, giving them a negative image of themselves.

"(The education process says) 'You're not going to make it. You're not college material.' It happens in hundreds of subtle ways," Allums said. "Don't lean backwards to develop this remedial thing. We've got to challenge students."

Psychology student Denise Anderson said that she can see this process working in her 8-year-old daughter. Anderson is white, but her daughter is part black.

"Somehow she's getting a negative cultural image of herself in school," Anderson said. Anderson said black classmates of hers in English also have negative images of themselves when it comes to academics.

> *Without student services, you wouldn't have many minority students in academics.*
>
> —Alicia Gilliam

Greer said not underestimating students is important.

"If we have high expectations of them then they will have high expectations of themselves as students," he said.

Abuse of the system

College President D. Candy Rose said she did not know of any abuse of the student services, but if any is occurring, it will be solved in part by new statewide standards, including matriculation requirements and Title V course standardization requirements.

Dr. Rose said there is an historical tension between counselors and instructors in California community colleges, which was why she placed counseling under instruction in a recent reorganization in CCC's management structure.

Martincich said that, at the committee meeting, he described a split between the student services and the instructional services managers along racial lines. Most instructional managers are white, while almost all student services managers are black. Martincich said he raised the issue of "cocooning" because he thought the new structure would give the student services group more autonomy and so more ability to protect students.

Two of the committee members present at the meeting where Martincich spoke said he used the term "white college" when referring to instruction and "black college" when referring to student services. Martincich denies this.

Greer said the comments bothered him. He said that problems should be clearly identified, possible solutions should be provided and, then, the problems should be discussed. Otherwise, disharmony can result, Greer said.

Allums said the choice of the word "cocoon" was not appropriate.

"Bob (Martincich) should watch his metaphors. I think that was a very distasteful way of referring to what we do to students. There's a joke going around about the 'coons' in student services," Allums said.

"Since the 60s, the white world has become more aware and sensitive," Allums said. "We seem to be coming together as people rather than races.

"We all have an opinion as to how we should go about this work of providing a well rounded college education. We should try to find ways to cooperate and work together instead of seeking ways to divide," he said.

A side head needs to have more leading

Lorem ipsum dolor sit amet, consectetuer adipiscing elit, sed diam nonummy nibh euismod tincidunt ut laoreet dolore magna aliquam erat volutpat. Ut wisi enim ad minim veniam, quis nostrud exerci tation ullamcorper suscipit lobortis nisl ut aliquip ex ea commodo consequat.

Duis autem vel eum iriure dolor in hendrerit in vulputate velit esse molestie consequat, vel illum dolore eu feugiat nulla facilisis at vero eros et accumsan et iusto odio dignissim qui blandit praesent luptatum zzril delenit augue duis dolore te feugait nulla facilisi. Lorem ipsum dolor sit amet, consectetuer adipiscing elit, sed diam nonummy nibh euismod tincidunt ut laoreet dolore magna aliquam erat volutpat.

Ut wisi enim ad minim veniam, quis nostrud exerci tation ullamcorper suscipit lobortis nisl ut aliquip ex ea commodo consequat. Duis autem vel eum iriure dolor in hendrerit in vulputate velit esse molestie consequat, vel illum dolore eu feugiat nulla facilisi. Nam liber tempor cum soluta nobis eleifend optiobam coutngue nihillis imperdiet doming id quod mazim placerat facer possim assum.

Ut wisi enim ad minim veniam, quis nostrud exerci tation ullamcorper suscipit lobortis nisl ut aliquip ex ea commodo consequat. Duis autem vel eum iriure dolor in hendrerit in vulputate velit esse molestie consequat, vel illum dolore eu feugiat nulla facilisi.

Lorem ipsum dolor sit amet, consectetuer adipiscing elit, sed diam nonummy nibh euismod tincidunt ut laoreet dolore magna aliquam erat volutpat. Duis autem vel eum iriure dolor in hendrerit in vulputate velit esse molestie consequat, vel illum dolore eu feugiat nulla facilisi.

Lorem ipsum dolor sit amet, consectetuer adipiscing elit, sed diam nonummy nibh euismod tincidunt ut laoreet dolore magna aliquam erat volutpat. Ut wisi enim ad minim veniam, quis nostrud exerci tation ullamcorper suscipit lobortis nisl ut aliquip ex ea commodo consequat. Duis autem vel eum iriure dolor in hendrerit in vulputate velit esse molestie consequat, vel illum dolore eu feugiat nulla facilisi.

qui blandit praesent luptatum zzril delenit augue duis dolore te feugait nullaissimo facilisi.

Lorem ipsum dolor sit amet, consectetuer adipiscing elit, sed diam nonummy nibh euismod tincidunt ut laoreet dolore magna aliquam erat volutpat. Ut wisi enim ad minim veniam, quis nostrud exerci tation ullamcorper suscipit lobortis nisl ut aliquip ex ea commodo consequat. Duis autem vel eum iriure dolor in hendrerit in vulputate velit esse molestie consequat, vel illum dolore eu feugiat nulla facilisis at vero eros et accumsan et iusto odio dignissim qui blandit praesent luptatum zzril delenit augue duis dolore te feugait nulla facilisi.

Lorem ipsum dolor sit amet, consectetuer adipiscing elit, sed diam nonummy nibh euismod tincidunt ut

Figure 13–16. Running a headline along the side of a story—usually at the top of a page or within a box—is one acceptable variation of the usual headline-over-story. Side heads look better with a little extra leading.

Some modular pages become dull and static when designers create series of nearly equal rectangles. The designer can set a story in a different measure, perhaps using unjustified type or column rules. This method of emphasis is preferred to the shopworn solution of simply using larger or bolder headlines. Emphasis by isolation can be achieved by using more white space in and around the main element. A flush-left headline at the side of the copy (Fig. 13–16) will leave white space at the outside edge.

Special Design Elements

Good design can help the looks and organization of the paper in many less significant places: regular features such as the nameplate, section logos, folios, column heads, graphs, and charts. Special effects such as initial letters and quoteouts break up large gray blocks of type. Other special effects—boxes, over-printing, and screens—simply add emphasis to a design element.

The *nameplate* is the name of the paper on page 1 and in the masthead on the editorial page. A distinctive type style should be used in a well-designed total nameplate package. The name of the paper is its "corporate identifier." Put lots of thought into designing the nameplate. Section *logos,* or *flags,* are names of the various sections of a paper. The typeface of these should be the same as, or complementary to, the nameplate typeface. The design for all flags should show similarity.

According to Roger Fidler there are four basic requirements for logos: (1) Their typeface should be different from, but compatible with, the typeface of headlines. (2) The logo should be boxed or separated from the rest of the page by rules. (3) Typeface and other design devices used in the logo should be distinctive. (4) Logos should be simple. They should attract readers, not distract them. Column logos and story identifiers are useful tools to help the readers find the content they are interested in.

Folios are small lines of type that indicate the page number and the publication date of the issue. Dates are necessary on inside pages to verify to advertisers that their ads were published on the date requested. Just because folios are necessary doesn't mean they have to be unimaginative.

Some papers tie the folio to a rule at the top of the page (Fig. 13–17). Others use large, bold page numbers. Whatever your paper uses, be sure that it follows the design rules for logos and that all folios are consistent. The usual placement of folios is at the upper outside corner of the page. Traditionally, the page number is on the outside of the page and the date is on the inside.

Page 4, New Mexico Daily Lobo, Thursday, April 26, 1990

FORUM

OCTOBER 20, 1989 • THE LOYOLA MAROON • 3

January 10, 1990   □   **Central Michigan LIFE**   ■   **3C**

Figure 13–17. Folio lines usually run at the top of each inside page. These are only a few possible ways to use them. On the front and on section fronts, folios usually are worked into the flag.

Figure 13–18. Columnist photos are a good way to add a personal touch to opinion or humor columns. The photos themselves can be run normally, cropped tightly along the side, or cropped tightly along the top and bottom.

Columnists often have logos, either with a photo or without. This is a good opportunity to put a face with the comment. You can play the photo any number of ways, and it certainly does not have to be run large (Fig. 13–18). The logo can be run on top of the column, with the headline an integral part of it, or it may be run as a *drop-in logo*, or one that is inserted into one of the legs of body type.

Bar charts, fever-line charts, and pie charts are useful because they can better display visual data. Written narratives are frequently preferred for a simple retelling of a story. Charts and graphs, however, are often better to show comparisons of numbers. If the story involves questions, such as How far? How many? How much? How often?, and so on, an information graphic may be better (Fig. 13–19). *Time* and *Newsweek* magazines are excellent in their use of graphs.

Initial letters are large letters at the beginning of a paragraph. This common device in magazines has unfortunately not been used much in newspapers. Initial letters are an effective way to break up long columns of gray type. Some papers use them only in the first paragraph of a story, and others spot them throughout the story.

Another device used to break up long columns is the *quoteout*—a quote from the story set in larger type and inserted in the middle of a story (Fig. 13–20). Larger than normal quotation marks can set off the quote. Quoteouts should be set in 14- to 18-point type and on a narrower measure than the body type to add white space and air out the gray look. In a multicolumn story, quoteouts can run across two or more columns of type. Quoteouts need not be placed near where the quote appears in the story.

Overprinting is a technique in which a second image is printed on top of one already on paper. The most common uses of overprinting are to make *screens* and *spot color*. A screen uses a halftone-dot pattern to create a light-gray area. It is usually used in conjunction with a boxed story (Fig. 13–21), although the screen

Figure 13–19. Information graphics are sometimes the best way to tell the story. Bar charts, pie charts, fever-line chasrts, and maps can add much display type, and a quoteout is a good way to add a graphic element when you don't have art. In a short story, it is best placed as near the lead photograph as possible to act as an additional draw to begin reading. (Courtesy of The Advocate)

Plan for AC Transit timed transfer center at CCC

VA

Current bus stop

SA

AREA ENLARGED BELOW

76

200

70

70

74

78

72

Waiting area

69

71

Buses that will serve this site	
69 El Sobrante/ Richmond	76 El Cerrito Plaza BART
70 Hilltop Mall	78 Richmond BART
71 El Cerrito Del Norte BART	West County Justice Center
72 Oakland/ Hilltop Mall	200 Crockett
74 Kaiser Center	

Tim Fielding/The Advocate

Bus transit center proposed for college

Plan creates bus round where Lot 2 now stands

By Claire Anselmo
Associate editor

"All roads lead to CCC."

By next fall, this statement that has been a public relations slogan for the college for years, will ring true for all students catching the AC Transit bus to the campus, when an interim timed transfer center will be in operation here.

District Chancellor Jack Carhart has approved $80,000 in funding from the district to initiate construction this summer. The new bus transfer center is designed to tie seven bus lines together and to reduce the wait time for

a transfer to five minutes.

The interim project, will cost a total of $150,000. It is set for finalization this September. AC Transit transportation planner for West Contra Costa County Peter Tannen said the plans are not 100 percent definite, though, because the AC Transit is still settling negotiations with CCC and the city of San Pablo.

By the fall semester 1990, the interim plan will be completed and the AC Transit will then begin work on a permanent transfer center to include a building that will house a public restroom and possibly a concession stand. The final, permanent transfer center will be completed by 1994 and will be situated in parking Lot 2 behind the Student Activities Building.

The final plan will cost an estimated $1.5 million, which AC Transit has requested federal funding.

Tannen said the largest expenditure will go toward connecting the pavement of the circled driveway to parking Lot 2. Tannen said the paving and construction will be done in a permanent manner so it will not have to be redone during the construction of the final transfer center.

"We're trying to make the bus lines more efficient," Tannen said. "We're trying to make it easier to ride the bus. It'll be easier for

'It's potential for reducing traffic congestion is good.'

—Dr. Rose

See **Bus transit**/6

College faces huge hiring task

By Mary Bodvarsson
Editor-in-chief

Facing some 45 interviews in the next few weeks, college President D. Candy Rose said that one of her primary tasks before the fall 1989 semester begins is to complete the hiring of three assistant deans, a director of business services, a campus police lieutenant and nine faculty members.

"It's a very time-consuming process, but extremely important," Dr. Rose said of the hiring effort. "This is a million dollar-plus investment. It's definitely worth the time to get excellence."

The assistant deans should be in place before the fall 1989 session begins, she said. The three positions are two assistant deans of instructional support services, one for occupational programming and one for instructional technology, and an as-

> "
> *This is a million dollar-plus investment. It's definitely worth the time to get excellence.*
> —Dr. D. Candy Rose
> college president

sistant dean of community education.

The job announcement for the three positions has gone to the district for final preparation and should go out to the public "this week or next," Rose said. She expects to begin

the interviewing process by the end of June.

"We'll be asking for volunteers from the faculty to participate in the hiring," Rose said. "We are looking forward to having a full complement of administrators on board. It's been a long time and we need the help."

While some people have questioned the success of finding qualified applicants during the summer months, Rose said she doesn't anticipate a problem.

"Administrative hirings go on all year, unlike faculty hires. Also, administrative jobs aren't tied to the semester like teaching jobs. There are a number of administrative jobs open all the time. I foresee no problems."

College Dean Robert Martincich said that while the hiring process may be beginning late in the hiring season ("if there is a hiring season"),

the college will not "settle for less than qualified personnel."

"The temptation is to settle for the first person who shows up with a smile on his face and is willing to help," Martincich said. "We've also had the experience of not making the right choice and going through the whole process again.

"The cost (of not having the assistant deans in place) is in the accumulation of things not done. We'll really be in trouble if we go another year (without the assistant deans)," Martincich said, however, that the college should have little trouble in attracting quality candidates.

"We are very competitive as a place to work," he said, "with good pay, a good location, good campus. We don't have to be Disney World to get people to come to work here.

"It is the policy of the district to

See **Hirings**/12

16A   Wednesday, April 25, 1990   Daily Forty-Niner

Figure 13–20. Pulling a quote from a story and placing it in display type near the beginning of the story is always a good idea. It acts as a graphic element on the page, perhaps attracting readers to the story who otherwise may have missed it.

Figure 13–21. Placing a gray screen—or a color screen—over type can work well as long as the screen is not too coarse or dark. Don't let anything get in the way of easy reading. (Courtesy of the *Daily Forty-Niner*)

SPORTS

49er Notes

Tree planting

Coach George Allen is taking time out from coaching the football team today to do his part for Earth Day.

Allen will be replacing a dead tree with a new one at noon near the VEC building on Lower Campus.

Hitting streak at 25

Third baseman Todd Guggiana kept his hitting streak alive last weekend against UC Irvine. Guggiana has hit safely in 25 straight games and needs hits in the next four games to break the school record.

The current record is held by Rob Townley, who hit in 28 straight games in 1979. Guggiana was also named Big West co-player of the week for last week.

Record breaker

Townley also holds the school record for batting average (.422) and hits in a season (100).

But first baseman Don Barbara is on track to break both of those records. With 11 games left in the season, Barbara is batting .478 and has 85 hits.

Finally No. 1

The men's volleyball team was finally voted No. 1 in the AVCA-Tachahara coaches poll Tuesday.

You would think Coach Ray Ratelle would be happy, but he seemingly could not care less.

"It doesn't make a bit a difference to me," Ratelle said. "The only thing that matters is this Thursday night."

Volunteers needed

All those interested in working on the 1990 Homecoming week are invited to attend an orientation meeting Thursday at 3 p.m. in the University Student Union Formal Lounge.

The committee plans and organizes the activities during Homecoming Week and other home 49er athletic events.

For information call Cindy Regnier at 985-4662.

Compiled from staff reports.

Ginny Dixon/Daily Forty-Niner

CSULB No.4 tennis player Scott Potthast practices his volley during a workout. He has an overall record of 15-13.

Potthast breaks the mold

Canadian 49er opts for tennis

By Heather Smalley
Daily Forty-Niner

Occasionally, Scott Potthast gets tired of answering the same questions.

"What's a nice Canadian boy like you doing in Southern California?"

Playing tennis.

"Shouldn't you be playing hockey or skating?"

You mean, like ice skating?

Potthast, the No. 4 player on the Cal State Long Beach men's tennis team, was born in Saratoga, then migrated to Vancouver, Canada, when he was 6 years old.

He does not play hockey.

"I loved to shoot around in the gym," he said. "Floor hockey, I mean. In high school.

"Look, everybody stereotypes Canadians," Potthast said. "They automatically think we harpoon whales and live in igloos."

Potthast's igloo, disguised as a townhouse, nestles in Burnaby, a small suburb of Vancouver. There, he pursued his

Men's tennis

dream of tennis fame for 12 years.

He began playing at age 4, following in the footsteps of his father, Bob, who captained the U.S. Junior Davis Cup team in the mid-1950s, turned professional and was a Top 5 doubles player with USC coach Dick Leach.

"They were a hell of a team, at least from what I heard," Potthast said.

Potthast's parents met while on the pro circuit. "My mom was No. 2 in Canada in the 18s, and they met on the Pacific Northwest circuit. He was 11 years older than she — she was 20. Mom had my brother, Chris, at 21, me at 24."

And at 4, Bob Potthast presented his son with a little sawed-off wooden racket, which Scott took to immediately.

"People used to tell me I could bang the ball constantly off this net that would rebound — I'd never miss," Potthast said. "So I thought I was good and I might try the game. But it went to my head."

Bob Potthast died of cancer shortly after seeing his son take up the sport he loved, and the three remaining family members went back to Mrs. Potthast's hometown, Vancouver, where Scott and Chris began following a legacy.

Not the least of which was physical — besides tennis, the 6-foot-3-inch, 210-pound Bob Potthast played linebacker for the 1957 University of Iowa football team that won the Rose Bowl.

"My brother got the height and I got the build," Potthast said, referring to Chris, 23, who plays tennis for San Jose State. "He's the tall skinny bonerack; I'm the short fat one."

At 6 feet, 170 pounds, the 49er is anything but dumpy.

The brothers played tennis, although not together. "I don't think we got along that well," Potthast said. "We used to brawl."

But about the same time Chris left for California and college, their mother remarried, to Larry Isaac, a television sports producer. "It must be six years now," Potthast said.

All of a sudden his eyes widened, the brows nearly disappearing into his hairline. "I forgot their anniversary," he choked. "It was April 19."

Things have been peachy throughout the Potthast-Isaac clan ever since, he said.

But while his brother was schooling and his mother was marrying, Potthast was playing in Vancouver, staging scenes on court.

See POTTHAST—Page 15A

CSULB's season rests on CS Fullerton series

By Brady Rhoades
Daily Forty-Niner

With the NCAA Regionals looming large in the near future, this weekend's series pitting the floundering Cal State Long Beach baseball team against Big West Conference leader Cal State Fullerton grows ever more significant.

Only nine conference games remain. The 49ers, 29-18-1 overall and 6-6 in the Big West, remain in fourth place after blowing a 8-0 lead against UC Irvine Sunday and eventually succumbing, 12-11, to the Anteaters in 11 exhausting innings.

The loss prevented the 49ers from a clean sweep. Behind explosive hitting from Don Barbara and Todd Guggiana, the top two hitters in the Big West, CSULB took games Friday and Saturday, 9-2 and 9-4.

Guggiana, who holds a 25-game hitting streak, went 4 for 4 with two RBI and three runs scored in Game 1 and continued his hitting assault in Game 2 with a solo home run and double, to finish with three RBI.

Baseball

Rob Townley set the school record for longest hitting streak in 1970 when he hit safely in 28 consecutive games.

Barbara, batting .478, had three hits, including a ninth-inning home run, in Game 1 and batted over .600 for the series.

But 49er fortunes turned to folly in Game 3. Leading 8-0 after two innings, CSULB coach Dave Snow pulled starter Eric Gruben with one out and two men on base in favor of reliever Greg Hays.

Hays, leading the team with a 2.75 ERA, did not have his best stuff and, along with Jimmy Griego, gave up 11 hits in 4½ innings as the Anteaters rallied for five runs in the bottom of the ninth and two more in the eleventh.

"It was the same story," Snow said. "Greg has been our guy, and today he

See SERIES—Page 15A

Weekend series is a family affair

By Steve Carpenter
Special to the Daily Forty-Niner

For the mother of Cal State Long Beach softball pitcher Karrie Schott, the 4-3 CSULB loss in the second game of Saturday's doubleheader at UC Santa Barbara was an ambivalent affair.

She saw her daughter's seven-game, 50-inning scoreless string come to an end, despite Karrie's allowing just two hits through six innings. An error and two costly walks amounted to a disastrous four-run sixth that transformed a 2-0 49er lead to a 4-2 deficit in the blink of an eye.

Just as the University of Hawaii did last month, a league doormat tripped up second-place CSULB in the last game of a four-game season series. The Gauchos

Softball

appeared well on the way down to 4-18 and the 49ers seemed on the verge of 21-7, until catcher Leslie Sheperd's two-out grand slam off Mary Letourneau, in relief of Schott, ambushed CSULB's hopes of a 4-0 road trip.

But a four-day tour that stopped in San Jose before hitting Santa Barbara was still a success. The 49ers, 20-8, avenged an April 9 split by dispatching San Jose State 6-1 and 3-1, Letourneau and Ruby Flores picking up the wins. Center fielder Sandra Ross had two RBI singles in Game 1 and shortstop Kim Kostyk lashed a three-run triple. CSULB

See FAMILY—Page 14A

A

Lorem ipsum dolor sit amet sed non seduntio nunc quid alor

Lorem ipsum dolor sit amet, consectetuer adipiscing elit, sed diam nonummy nibh euismod tincidunt ut laoreet dolore magna aliquam erat volupat. Ut wisi enim ad minim veniam, quis nostrud exerci tation ullamcorper suscipit lobortis nisl ut aliquip ex ea commodo consequat. Duis autem vel eum iriure dolor in hendrerit in vulputate velit esse molestie consequat, vel illum dolore eu feugiat nulla facilisis at vero eros et accumsan et iusto odio dignissim qui blandit praesent luptatum zzril delenit augue duis dolore te feugait nulla facilisi. Lorem ipsum dolor sit amet, consectetuer adipiscing elit, sed diam nonummy nibh euismod tincidunt ut laoreet dolore magna aliquam erat volupat.

Ut wisi enim ad minim veniam, quis nostrud exercitation ullamcorper suscipit lobortis nisl ut aliquip ex ea commodo consequat. Duis autem vel eum iriure dolor in hendrerit in

vulputate velit esse molestie consequat, vel illum dolore eu feugiat nulla facilisis at vero eros et accumsan et iusto odio dignissim qui blandit praesent luptatum zzril delenit augue duis dolore te feugait nulla facilisi. Nam liber tempor cum soluta nobis eleifend option congue nihilis imperdiet doming id quod mazim placerat facer possim assum.

Lorem ipsum dolor sit amet, consectetuer adipiscing elit, sed diam nonummy nibh euismod tincidunt ut laoreet dolore magna aliquam erat volupat.

Ut wisi enim ad minim veniam, quis nostrud exercitation ullamcorper suscipit lobortis nisl ut aliquip ex ea commodo consequat. Duis autem vel eum iriure dolor in hendrerit in vulputate velit esse molestie consequat, vel illum dolore eu feugiat nulla facilisis at vero eros et accumsan et iusto odio dignissim qui blandit praesent zzril delenit augue

duis dolore te feugait nulla facilisi. Lorem ipsum dolor sit amet, consectetuer adipiscing elit, sed diam nonummy nibh euismod tincidunt ut laoreet dolore magna aliquam erat volupat.

Ut wisi enim ad minim veniam, quis nostrud exercitation ullamcorper suscipit lobortis nisl ut aliquip ex ea commodo consequat.

Duis autem vel eum iriure dolor in hendrerit in vulputate velit esse molestie consequat, vel illum dolore eu feugiat nulla facilisis at vero eros et accumsan et iusto odio dignissim qui blandit praesent luptatum zzril delenit augue duis dolore te feugait nulla facilisi. Lorem ipsum dolor sit amet, consectetuer adipiscing elit, sed diam nonummy nibh euismod tincidunt ut laoreet dolore magna aliquam erat volupat. Duis autem vel eum iriure dolor in hendrerit in vulputate velit esse molestie consequat, vel illum dolore

aliquip ex ea commodo consequat. Duis autem vel eum iriure dolor in hendrerit in vulputate velit esse molestie consequat, vel illum dolore eu feugiat nulla facilisis at vero eros et accumsan et iusto odio dignissim qui blandit praesent luptatum zzril delenit augue duis dolore te feugait nulla facilisi.

Lorem ipsum dolor sit amet, consectetuer adipiscing elit, sed diam nonummy nibh euismod tincidunt ut laoreet dolore magna aliquam erat volupat. Ut wisi enim ad minim veniam, quis nostrud exercitation ullamcorper suscipit lobortis nisl ut aliquip ex ea commodo consequat. Duis autem vel eum iriure dolor in hendrerit in vulputate velit esse molestie consequat, vel illum dolore eu feugiat nulla facilisis at vero eros et accumsan et iusto odio dignissim qui blandit praesent luptatum zzril delenit augue duis dolore te feugait

This is a caption. This is a caption. This is a caption. This is a caption. This is a caption. This is a caption.

More lorem ipsum et alia, quid dolore

Lorem ipsum dolor sit amet, consectetuer adipiscing elit, sed diam nonummy nibh euismod tincidunt ut laoreet dolore magna aliquam erat volupat. Ut wisi enim ad minim veniam, quis nostrud exerci tation ullamcorper suscipit lobortis nisl ut aliquip ex ea commodo consequat.

Duis autem vel eum iriure dolor in hendrerit in vulputate velit esse molestie consequat, vel illum dolore eu feugiat nulla facilisis at vero eros et accumsan et iusto odio dignissim qui blandit praesent luptatum zzril delenit augue duis dolore te feugait nulla facilisi. Lorem ipsum dolor sit amet, consectetuer adipiscing elit, sed diam nonummy nibh euismod tincidunt ut laoreet dolore magna aliquam erat volupat.

Ut wisi enim ad minim veniam, quis nostrud exercitation ullamcorper suscipit lobortis nisl ut aliquip ex ea commodo consequat. Duis autem vel eum iriure dolor in

hendrerit in vulputate velit esse molestie consequat, vel illum dolore eu feugiat nulla facilisis at vero eros et accumsan et iusto odio dignissim qui blandit praesent luptatum zzril delenit augue duis dolore te feugait nulla facilisi. Nam liber tempor cum soluta nobis eleifend option congue nihilis imperdiet doming id quod mazim placerat facer possim assum.

Lorem ipsum dolor sit amet, consectetuer adipiscing elit, sed diam nonummy nibh euismod tincidunt ut laoreet dolore magna aliquam erat volupat.

Ut wisi enim ad minim veniam, quis nostrud exercitation ullamcorper suscipit lobortis nisl ut aliquip ex ea commodo consequat. Duis autem vel eum iriure dolor in hendrerit in vulputate velit esse molestie consequat, vel illum dolore eu feugiat nulla facilisis at vero eros et accumsan et iusto odio dignissim qui blandit

B

Lorem ipsum dolor sit amet sed non seduntio nunc quid alor

Lorem ipsum dolor sit amet, consectetuer adipiscing elit, sed diam nonummy nibh euismod tincidunt ut laoreet dolore magna aliquam erat volupat. Ut wisi enim ad minim veniam, quis nostrud exerci tation ullamcorper suscipit lobortis nisl ut aliquip ex ea commodo consequat.

Duis autem vel eum iriure dolor in hendrerit in vulputate velit esse molestie consequat, vel illum dolore eu feugiat nulla facilisis at vero eros et accumsan et iusto odio dignissim qui blandit praesent luptatum zzril delenit augue duis dolore te feugait nulla facilisi. Lorem ipsum dolor sit amet, consectetuer adipiscing elit, sed diam nonummy nibh euismod tincidunt ut laoreet dolore magna aliquam erat volupat.

Ut wisi enim ad minim veniam, quis nostrud exercitation ullamcorper suscipit lobortis nisl ut aliquip ex ea commodo consequat. Duis autem vel eum iriure dolor in hendrerit in

vulputate velit esse molestie consequat, vel illum dolore eu feugiat nulla facilisis at vero eros et accumsan et iusto odio dignissim qui blandit praesent luptatum zzril delenit augue duis dolore te feugait nulla facilisi. Nam liber tempor cum soluta nobis eleifend option congue nihilis imperdiet doming id quod mazim placerat facer possim assum.

Lorem ipsum dolor sit amet, consectetuer adipiscing elit, sed diam nonummy nibh euismod tincidunt ut laoreet dolore magna aliquam erat volupat.

Ut wisi enim ad minim veniam, quis nostrud exercitation ullamcorper suscipit lobortis nisl ut aliquip ex ea commodo consequat. Duis autem vel eum iriure dolor in hendrerit in vulputate velit esse molestie consequat, vel illum dolore eu feugiat nulla facilisis at vero eros et accumsan et iusto odio dignissim qui blandit praesent luptatum zzril delenit augue

duis dolore te feugait nulla facilisi. Lorem ipsum dolor sit amet, consectetuer adipiscing elit, sed diam nonummy nibh euismod tincidunt ut laoreet dolore magna aliquam erat volupat.

Ut wisi enim ad minim veniam, quis nostrud exercitation ullamcorper suscipit lobortis nisl ut aliquip ex ea commodo consequat. Duis autem vel eum iriure dolor in hendrerit in vulputate velit esse molestie consequat, vel illum dolore eu feugiat nulla facilisis at vero eros et accumsan et iusto odio dignissim qui blandit praesent luptatum zzril delenit augue

aliquip ex ea commodo consequat. Duis autem vel eum iriure dolor in hendrerit in vulputate velit esse molestie consequat, vel illum dolore eu feugiat nulla facilisis at vero eros et accumsan et iusto odio dignissim qui blandit praesent luptatum zzril delenit augue duis dolore te feugait nulla facilisi.

Lorem ipsum dolor sit amet, consectetuer adipiscing elit, sed diam nonummy nibh euismod tincidunt ut laoreet dolore magna aliquam erat volupat. Ut wisi enim ad minim veniam, quis nostrud exercitation ullamcorper suscipit lobortis nisl ut aliquip ex ea commodo consequat. Duis autem vel eum iriure dolor in hendrerit in vulputate velit esse molestie consequat, vel illum dolore eu feugiat nulla facilisis at vero eros et accumsan et iusto odio dignissim qui blandit praesent luptatum zzril delenit augue duis dolore te feugait

This is a caption. This is a caption. This is a caption. This is a caption. This is a caption. This is a caption.

More lorem ipsum et alia, quid dolore consectetuer elit aliquam

Lorem ipsum dolor sit amet, consectetuer adipiscing elit, sed diam nonummy nibh euismod tincidunt ut laoreet dolore magna aliquam erat volupat. Ut wisi enim ad minim veniam, quis nostrud exerci tation ullamcorper suscipit lobortis nisl ut aliquip ex ea commodo consequat.

Duis autem vel eum iriure dolor in hendrerit in vulputate velit esse molestie consequat, vel illum dolore eu feugiat nulla facilisis at vero eros et accumsan et iusto odio dignissim qui blandit praesent luptatum zzril delenit augue duis dolore te feugait nulla facilisi. Lorem ipsum dolor sit amet, consectetuer adipiscing elit, sed diam nonummy nibh euismod tincidunt ut laoreet dolore magna aliquam erat volupat.

Ut wisi enim ad minim veniam, quis nostrud exercitation ullamcorper suscipit lobortis nisl ut aliquip ex ea commodo consequat. Duis autem vel eum iriure dolor in

hendrerit in vulputate velit esse molestie consequat, vel illum dolore eu feugiat nulla facilisis at vero eros et accumsan et iusto odio dignissim qui blandit praesent luptatum zzril delenit augue duis dolore te feugait nulla facilisi. Nam liber tempor cum soluta nobis eleifend option congue nihilis imperdiet doming id quod mazim placerat facer possim assum.

Lorem ipsum dolor sit amet, consectetuer adipiscing elit, sed diam nonummy nibh euismod tincidunt ut laoreet dolore magna aliquam erat volupat.

Ut wisi enim ad minim veniam, quis nostrud exercitation ullamcorper suscipit lobortis nisl ut aliquip ex ea commodo consequat. Duis autem vel eum iriure dolor in vulputate velit esse molestie consequat, vel illum dolore eu feugiat nulla facilisis at vero eros et accumsan et iusto odio dignissim qui blandit

praesent luptatum zzril delenit augue duis dolore te feugait nulla facilisi.

Lorem ipsum dolor sit amet, consectetuer adipiscing elit, sed diam nonummy nibh euismod tincidunt ut laoreet dolore magna aliquam erat volupat.

Ut wisi enim ad minim veniam, quis nostrud exercitation ullamcorper suscipit lobortis nisl ut aliquip ex ea commodo consequat. Duis autem vel eum iriure dolor in hendrerit in vulputate velit esse molestie consequat, vel illum dolore eu feugiat nulla facilisis at vero eros et accumsan et iusto odio dignissim qui blandit praesent luptatum zzril delenit augue duis dolore te feugait nulla facilisi.

Lorem ipsum dolor sit amet, consectetuer adipiscing elit, sed diam nonummy nibh euismod tincidunt ut laoreet dolore magna aliquam erat volupat. Ut wisi enim ad minim veniam, quis nostrud exerci tation

Figure 13–22. Be careful with photo placement. Example A shows ambiguity: Does the photo go with the story to the right or below? Example B shows one of several ways to counteract this problem in an intelligent layout: Never lay out an unrelated story beneath a photo that is the same width.

can set the story off without the box. Screens can add visual variety when there is little or no art available for a page. Spot color is the use of one color in addition to black. It can either be run as a solid 100 percent color block or screened to achieve lighter tints. With only one extra color, a creative designer can get three tones by using 100 percent, 50 percent, and 10 percent screens, which would give, for instance, a full-tone blue, a medium shade of blue, and a very light shade of blue. The color lends a special emphasis to an element. It is expensive, however, and should be used sparingly. But if an advertiser has ordered color for an ad, you can also use that color on the same and certain other pages for no additional charge.

All these special effects work only when used frugally. Boxes, screens, and spot color should be used only for a story that needs extra emphasis. If you use them every week, they are no longer unique when you really need special play.

Use of Photos

Readers look at photographs before they read anything. The designer should therefore direct the reader's attention from the photo to the first word of the story by making sure that one of the photo's leading lines points to the beginning of the story.

Most designers agree that photographs should be anchored on another element or to the edge of the page. A photo floating in the middle of a page looks out of place. Three ways to play a photo with a story are horizontally, vertically above the copy, and vertically below the copy.

The vertical play of photo over story seems natural: Readers tend to look at photos first and then below them for information. Playing a photo horizontally with a story is fine, on either the right or left of the type. Remember to have the action in the photograph move you toward the story, however, and not off the page or into an adjoining story. Also, don't run a two-column photo tied horizontally to a story and then another two-column story below it (Fig. 13–22). The reader may be confused initially as to which story the photo goes with.

A special effect that occasionally works well with photos is the *COB* (*Cut Out Background*) silhouette (Fig. 13–23). COBs can be either partial or full. Partial COBs are called *walkoffs*. But remember that 99.9 percent of the time, the rectangle is better for a photograph than any other shape. Because COBing takes away from the basic design element of the rectangle, use it only for extra emphasis. Don't destroy a perfectly good photo just because you like the COB effect. But if the photo would be improved by cutting out useless background or if the 3-D effect of a partial COB would add another dimension to the photo, do it. Type set with a ragged edge that approximates the shape of the photo can enhance the effect of the COB (Fig. 13–24).

Cutlines, captions, and photo credits can be used many different ways with photographs. Cutlines nearly always appear beneath a photo. In a series of photos, cutlines can be bunched together beneath or to the side of the series. On photo-essay pages, cutlines should appear beneath each photo (in which case they should be very brief).

Although many designers use different terminology, here "cutline" refers to the body of type that explains a photograph. "Caption" refers to a small headline above the cutline. This is sometimes called a "catchline" or "overline." Sometimes captions appear as the first few words of the cutline, either as a separate sentence or as the first few words of the cutline. In this case, the caption is often capitalized or set in bold-face type.

Dance production opens tomorrow. *page 4*

Figure 13–23. In feature situations, or in teasers such as this one, creating a silhouette photo can be an effective way to draw the readers' eyes. Silhouettes can be difficult to do well, and please don't overdo it.

Figure 13–24. Copy wraps—having the type run around art placed within the type columns—are much easier to do in PC-based pagination systems than they were on many phototypesetters. As with most "gimmicks," they should be used with caution and sparingly. But in the right situation, they can help a dull layout stand out.

Lollo hoy loh oh yhol glyh

Lorem ipsum dolor sit amet, consectetuer adipiscing elit, sed diam nonummy nibh euismod tincidunt ut laoreet dolore magna aliquam erat volutpat. Ut wisi enim ad minim veniam, quis nostrud exerci tation ullamcorper suscipit lobortis nisl ut aliquip ex ea commodo consequat.

Duis autem vel eum iriure dolor in hendrerit in vulputate velit esse molestie consequat, vel illum dolore eu feugiat nulla facilisis at vero eros et accumsan et iusto odio dignissim qui blandit praesent luptatum zzril delenit augue duis dolore te feugait nulla facilisi. Lorem ipsum dolor sit amet, consectetuer adipiscing elit, sed diam nonummy nibh euismod tincidunt ut laoreet dolore magna aliquam erat volutpat.

Ut wisi enim ad minim veniam, quis nostrud exerci tation ullamcorper suscipit lobortis nisl ut aliq- uip ex ea commodo consequat.

Duis autem vel eum iriure dolor in hendrerit in vulputate velit esse molestie consequat, vel illum dolore eu feugiat nulla facilisis at vero eros et accumsan et iusto odio dignissim qui blandit praesent luptatum zzril delenit augue duis dolore te feugait nulla facilisi. Nam liber tempor cum soluta nobis eleifend optiobnn coutngue nihillis imperdiet doming id quod mazim placerat facer possim assum.

Lorem ipsum dolor sit amet, consectetuer adipiscing elit, sed diam

Photo Pages

Two important design questions have to be answered about photo pages, whether they are a photo group, story, or essay: First, should the photos be grouped together in the center of the spread, or should they be spread out on the page? And if the photos are bunched in the center, should white space be allowed on the outside of the group, or should the total package of words and photos fill the margins of the newspaper page?

Although designers differ on the first question, the majority believe that *internal* white space, the space between all photos, should be equal and small. The photos should be tightly clustered on the page. External white space can and probably should vary (Fig. 13–25). Too much internal white space makes the

Figure 13–25. With photo essays, be sure to keep the space between photos tight and consistent. The outside white space can and should differ. (Courtesy of the *Optimist*)

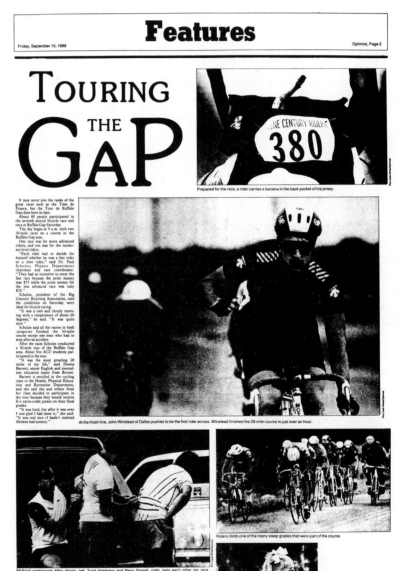

photos look like they have "exploded" to the far corners of the page. But some good photo essays have broken this rule. The final decision should depend on the content of the photos.

The second question is more difficult to answer. Some designers believe that magazines and yearbooks may have large blocks of external white space on a photo page, but that a newspaper page ought to be filled to all four page margins because too much white space on the outside of a photo essay will look like wasted space to the reader. White space should *never* be just unfilled space—it should have a design function. But a little white space on the outside will direct attention to the design of the photos and words themselves.

Advertising

Ads are always placed on the newspaper page first, and the page designer has to work with the space that is left. For an effectively designed page, articles and ads should look pleasing together. Editors and designers need to think about ad placement, not just lay ads out haphazardly.

Ads are usually laid out in a stair-step pattern from the upper right of the page to the lower left (Fig. 13–26). Other papers stack ads in a pyramid up the middle of two-page spreads, and still others reverse this pattern. Because these methods leave awkwardly shaped news holes for the designer to deal with, modular design for ads has become more popular.

If ads leave a rectangular shape for the designer, he or she can achieve more pleasing page designs. Another good reason for positioning ads in rectangular shapes is that ads then are usually kept below the fold. When ads creep above the fold, they sometimes interfere with the graphic display selected for the news hole. Even if the pyramid, stair-step method is used, the smart designer will try to "modularize" a page anyway, using each step as a breaking-off point for a design element (Fig. 13–27).

In magazine-sized papers and even tabloid newspapers, the modular concept can be used vertically by placing the ads in the outside columns of the pages. Full-size newspaper pages may be too large for vertical ad modules.

A page designer should never move an ad without the ad manager's permission, even if it stands in the way of an improved design. Ad placement is the decision of the advertising department. Some ads can be moved; some can't. Check before you do it on your own.

The design of the ads themselves deserves a few words, even though good books have been written on the topic. The basic design principles, mentioned earlier in this chapter, apply to ads as well. Remember these few things:

- Have a strong Center of Visual Impact (CVI), whether it is art or simply type.
- Leave a bit of extra white space at the top of each ad to separate it visually from the editorial content or other ads.
- Write the headline so it acts as a caption to the art.
- Have the CVI lead the reader to the body copy.
- Give each ad a "look" unique to the client. Use that look in each ad.

Now, let's look at and critique a number of college newspaper pages:

Figure 13–26. Ads are generally laid out in a stair-step pattern from upper right to lower left. (From *Roundup,* Pierce College)

Figure 13–27. If you have to deal with stair-step ads, try to create modules on your pages by evening off the page at every "step." Research has shown that a modular ad hole is superior to a pyramid-shaped one.

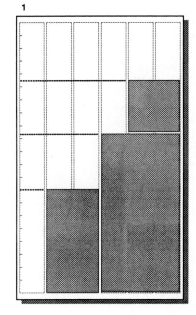

Figure 13–28. Try to create a unique "look" for each advertiser. That way the look, as well as the information in the ad, will always clearly represent only that advertiser. Here, a special border is used.

Figure 13–29. The UCLA *Daily Bruin* is an award winner for design, graphics, and typography. This front has an eye-catching photo, three stories, and a column of teasers on the left. The use of bold sans serif headlines with the lighter, roman second decks is particularly effective. (All following pages courtesy of the *Daily Bruin*)

Figure 13–30. This *Daily Bruin* sports front is actually the back cover of the 60-page tab. Note the teasers along the bottom that refer the reader to inside pages near the back. The classifieds are placed between the news and feature up front and the sports section in the back.

Figure 13–31. The *Daily Bruin* has an effective news brief presentation with reverse-bar organizers and bold, two-line heads. The reverse-bar logos would look better if they were all CAPS.

Figure 13–32. With the use of white space to give special emphasis to the illustration, readers understand right away that this presentation is not just the standard news page.

188 Page design

16 **Friday, June 1, 1990** Daily Bruin **Viewpoint**

Viewpoint

Viewpoint

Asians are excluded by admissions policy

By Jo Yang

Regent Vice Chairman Roy Brophy's statement in the UC Board of Regents' meeting ("Regents debate UC admissions," *Bruin*, May 18) that hundreds of 4.0s are turned away" because of "reverse discrimination" is untrue. In fact, hundreds of Asian students with 4.0 GPAs were rejected by the University of California not because their slots were reserved for underrepresented minority students in the affirmative action program, but discrimination by the UC admissions officers.

These regents and administrators oppose affirmative action programs because they hold an elitist concept of education — that education is a privilege for a few social and economic elite only, not a right for all people.

The fact is that administrators and most regents don't care about hundreds of Asians with 4.0 GPAs who were denied admission because white students were admitted in their place. These officials are only concerned about the declining white admits. One such administrator is UCLA's Director of Admissions Rae Lee Siporin who wrote an official memo a few years ago stating that UCLA needed to stop the decline of white student admissions. Administrators apparently felt that there were too many Asian Pacific Islander students and not enough white students.

Many misguided people (including Asian students) relate the existence of anti-Asian quotas in colleges to affirmative action programs. In fact is that discrimination against Asian Pacific students is the result of racism by college administrators, not due to the existence of affirmative action. According to a report, Asian American's admit rate (number admitted versus number that applied) is among the lowest of all ethnic groups, including whites. Asians' admit rate is 13 percent while the whites' is 17.5 percent.

In a 1989 *Public Interest* report, Harvard's Asian Pacific admits averaged 1467 on the SAT score while the white admits only averaged 1355, or 112 points lower. It seems that when an Asian applicant has the same GPA and SAT indexes as a white applicant, Harvard admits the white applicant. This explains why the Asian's SAT average was higher than that for whites. Simply, Asian students had to surpass white students academically to be admitted.

It may seem that Asians have "friends" in high places (such as the UC Regent Roy Brophy) who care about them. However, these administrators and regents are enemies of affirmative action program. They want to divide opinions of students of color and push their admissions policy to benefit the white students.

The university even tried to convince Asian Pacific students that they would benefit by the serious weakening of affirmative action programs. Its representative, Tom Lifka, assistant vice chancellor on student academic services, said that computer simulations of the new UCLA admissions plan show that Asian and Pacific Islander students would actually gain from it — by gaining 100 additional slots.

The truth is that in the new UCLA admissions policy, almost 60 percent of the admits are accepted solely on the basis of their academic performance — GPA, SAT score, number of honors classes taken, etc. So the Asian students who on average have higher GPA and SAT indexes don't compete with the underrepresented minority students for admissions, but with the white students.

Some of these administrators and regents also want to present the Asian American "success" as evidence that the American system is "so fair to all that Afro-American and other minorities jolly well better look to themselves, not to the government or 'reverse discrimination' for solutions to their problems," according to UCLA professor Don T. Nakanishi.

Twenty years ago, many people of color and community people demanded open admissions, where education is a right and that anyone who wanted to attend college would be able to do so. Universities were unwilling to yield to these nationwide demands but provided a compromise. The compromise was affirmative action.

In today's prevailing conservative political climate, students of color cannot afford to lose affirmative action programs. Losing them would mean turning back the clock to the pre-civil rights era when education was bestowed only to the whites. So affirmative action is symbolic of people of color's history and struggles in America.

Students of color, especially Asian students, must show compassion and solidarity with other oppressed minorities because like them, Asians continue to remain oppressed and excluded.

Yang is a junior majoring in economics.

Counterpoint

The importance of Islam to Malcolm X

By Hassan el Nouty

Andrew K. Milton is to be commended for his article commemorating the late Malcolm X's birthday ("Remembering Malcolm X and his valuable legacy," *Bruin*, May 21). One may regret, however, that Milton chose to give us a truncated image of that great historic figure.

First there is the question of Malcolm X's "embrace-of violence-employed-in-self-defense." The article's attempt to water down that position runs, I am afraid, into a contradiction. Referring to the famous photo showing the black leader "holding a shotgun over the ominous threat 'By any means,'" Milton writes: "This is the combination of an out-of-context statement about the right of self-defense and a photograph of the measures he took for protection following the firebombing of his home."

Under whatever circumstances the statement was made, it cannot be described as an "ominous threat." Violence-employed-in-self-defense, whether in a personal perspective or a collective one, cannot be seen as a "threat" except by the aggressors/oppressors against whom it is directed. Are we to espouse their viewpoint and share their fear that their victim might resist "violently"?

The issue of "means" cannot be dissociated from that of "ends." It can be argued that whenever the end is just (and what is more just then the liberation of the oppressed?), "any means" used to achieve it becomes *ipso facto* just. At least that was Malcolm X's feeling. He lived in a world — which is still our world — where the oppressors, in order to perpetuate their oppression, do not recoil from using "any means" at their disposal: bloody physical violence and ideological violence that is no less abhorrent (the daily brainwashing of the people by the media).

In the name of what logical or moral principle, it can be argued again, should the oppressed be restricted from using "any means" they can dispose of to strike back?

Malcolm X was a model of courage. We owe it to his memory not to "edulcorate" what he stood for. Some may find it difficult to accept. But the fact is that he stood for revolutionary violence in response to oppression and repression (which makes him so different from Martin Luther King who believed in working "within" the system in order to "reform" it).

In a sense, Malcolm X belongs to the era during which Mao Tse Tung's teachings had a resounding impact. Precisely Mao advocated people's armed struggle, which can be translated into "violence-employed-for-collective-self-defense," as the only road towards total liberation.

Before Mao, Islam had made of armed struggle against "zolm" (injustice) a religious duty for every Muslim. That is what "Jihad" (Holy War) is about. Today, with the Moslem masses reeling under the domination of East and West imperialisms imposed on them directly (in the Russian Empire and in occupied Palestine), or indirectly (by local puppet regimes in the American Empire), "Jihad" means more than ever "people's armed struggle" against "injustice."

No wonder that Malcolm X's path led him to Islam. He repudiated his "Christian" names which bore the mark of the "white" masters and adopted the Islamic name of El Hajj Malik al-Shabaz. By doing so he was simply rediscovering his roots. Many of the Africans brought to the New World came from Muslim Africa. In Africa, Islam has been a formidable opponent of European colonial penetration. Think of Abdel Kader in Algeria, Samory in West Africa, and the Mahdi in the Sudan. Therefore, fighting under the banner of Islam was for Al Hajj Malik part of his African heritage.

An altered version of Islam, which can be explained as a reaction to the centuries of degradation by the white man, had been introduced in the United States in the early thirties by Elijah Muhammed. He perceived Islam as a religion for the blacks exclusively (no Arabian or Asian or European Muslims were permitted in his places of worship). But Al Hajj Malik turned to authentic Islam, which is a non-racial, non-tribal and non-ethnic universal religion.

If Al Hajj Malik gave top priority to the cause of his black brothers, the most disinherited segment of the American society, it was for tactical reasons as he explained it himself: "This in no way implies discrimination or racialism, but rather shows that we are intelligent enough to plant the good seed of Islam where it will go best . . . Later we can "doctor up" or fertilize the less fertile areas, but only after our crop is already well planted in the hearts and minds of these black Americans who already show great signs of receptiveness."

In Milton's article there is not the slightest hint of the essential Islamic dimension in Al Hajj Malik's life and combat. That curious omission must be corrected for the sake of truth, and because the presence of Islam will have to be increasingly reckoned with in America. By conservative estimates, there are already six million Moslems in the United States. That number is growing. It is expected that during the next two decades, Islam will become this country's second largest religion after Christianity.

El Nouty is a professor of French.

Daily Bruin
112 Kerckhoff Hall
308 Westwood Plaza
Los Angeles, CA 90024
(213) 825-9898

Editorial Board

Editor-in-Chief: Valarie De La Garza
Managing Editor: Kenneth Kecskes
Senior Copy Editor: Matthew Fordahl
Viewpoint Editor: Lisa Hamilton
A & E Editors: June Pinheiro, Rob Winfield
Sports Editor: David Gibson
Design Editors: Nancee LeNormand, Albert Poon

Unsigned editorials represent a majority opinion of the Daily Bruin Editorial Board. All other columns, letters and artwork represent the opinions of their authors. They do not reflect the views of the Editorial Board, the staff or the ASUCLA Communications Board. The Bruin complies with the Communication Board's policy prohibiting the publication of articles that perpetuate derogatory cultural or ethnic stereotypes. Written material submitted must be typed or written legibly.

All submitted material must bear the author's name, address, telephone number, registration number or affiliation with UCLA. Names will not be withheld except in extreme cases. The Bruin will publish anonymous letters on a case-by-case basis if the letter is deemed to be of a sensitive nature, but the above information is required for purposes of verification. If a letter is printed anonymously, all biographical information will be kept confidential.

When multiple authors submit material, some names may be kept on file rather than published with the material. The Bruin reserves the right to edit submitted material and to determine its placement in the paper. All submissions become the property of The Bruin. The Communications Board has a media grievance procedure for resolving complaints against any of its publications. For a copy of the complete procedure, contact the Publications office at 112 Kerckhoff Hall.

Figure 13–33. This Viewpoint page follows the general concept of wider columns for the slower reads, but this page ends up as being too gray, even with the bold heads and reverse logos.

Figure 13–34. The *Daily Bruin* designers use the double truck—or center spread—of the paper well by ignoring the fold. This two-page spread is really designed and seen by readers as a whole. The designer was careful not to allow the fold to go over a face in the photograph.

Page Dummies

A page is not designed on a full-size sheet unless it is a magazine page. Instead, the page designer uses a page dummy (Fig. 13–35), the "map" followed by paste-up personnel. A good page dummy is proportional to the final page. For instance, Figure 13–35 is printed on paper 8½" × 14" to closely approximate the final shape of a full-size newspaper page. Don't use standard 8½" × 11" paper unless you adjust the dummy size because the proportions will not match the final proportions on the paste-up.

Regardless of the dummy used, several rules for indicating different elements on the page should be followed. The first and most important rule is that the dummy should be neat and legible. A map that cannot be deciphered is useless. Other rules include using X's to indicate photos; arrows to indicate copy; a diagonal line from the upper left corner to indicate ads; and "fit," "cut," or "jump" to show the desired status of the story. Stories, headlines, cutlines, ads, sandwiches, and any other design elements should all be marked on the dummy. Leave nothing to the imagination of the paste-up person.

The keys to a good dummy are neatness and clarity of instructions. Clear and complete instructions ensure that the page will come together quickly and will be close to the designer's plan.

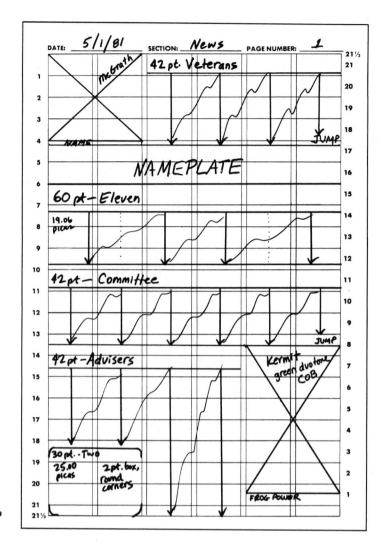

Figure 13–35. Note that photos and heads on this dummy are slugged for quick and easy identification. Stories that jump are so indicated.

Good page design works hand in hand with good content. Remember that design is meant to *organize* the content logically for the reader and to *emphasize* the important items. Keep the design simple and use special effects only for special occasions, and your design will make your paper popular with your readers.

— Suggested Projects —————————

Vocabulary

art
box
broadsheet
COB
cutoff rule
double truck
flag
formal balance
golden mean
gutter
informal balance
jump
justified
layout

1. Practice making page dummies by selecting pages from your paper and turning a completed page back into a dummy. Indicate all necessary items to the paste-up person.

2. Clip layout ideas you like from other publications, both student and professional. Post these or keep them in an idea file. Professional designers are constant borrowers. For that special layout, turn to your idea file for inspiration.

3. Ask art students or an art instructor to help you redesign your newspaper. Select a new typeface for the nameplate and for body type and headlines. A design class in your school might want to redesign the paper as a class project.

4. Invite a local journalist to discuss the realities of laying out pages, not just the theories as discussed in this and other books.

5. Get copies of design and type stylebooks from well-designed school and professional papers. How can you "borrow" and improve your paper?

logo
nameplate
optical weight
overprint
quoteout
ragged right
rules
screen
spot color
standing headline
tombstoning heads
walkoff

Exercises

1. The following two lists of story summaries are from the exercise in Chapter 2. (You may want to review your answers to that exercise before doing this one.) Use these lists as page budgets, and design a front page and an inside page. The inside page has one large ad covering the bottom half of the page.

You do not have to use the art with a story, nor do you have to use the entire story. Indicate the length of the story you use on the dummy. You may use the inside page for jumps from the front page. Indicate headline size and number of lines.

Note: For both A and B, you have a stand-alone, or feature, photo available. You may also use a small filler. Use an index box on the front page if you wish. Use the same nameplate design and size as on your own paper. Also, you may use any additional special design elements, such as quoteouts, initial letters, photo COBs, boxes, or screens. Just be sure that these are properly marked on the page dummy.

A.
  1. The county chess champion, who comes from your school, won a tournament last weekend in your city. 10 inches; 1 mug shot.
  2. The Sigma Nu fraternity wins the campus blood drive. 5 inches.
  3. The projected school budget for next year means that $500,000 in financial aid will have to be cut. 22 inches; 2 mug shots.
  4. A bike-theft ring on campus is broken when five bikes are found in the garage of a house near campus. 12 inches; photo of garage interior with bikes.
  5. A local parent group wants to outlaw drug paraphernalia sold in several record shops near campus. 18 inches; photo of parent meeting.
  6. A former art student opens a tattoo parlor near campus, saying tattoos are for everyone. 20 inches; photo of artist at work and several close-up shots of his tattoos.
  7. The state college board discusses raising tuition next year by 35 percent. 25 inches.

B.
  1. The student government declares war on free faculty parking privileges. The associated student government wants faculty to pay because students have to. 16 inches; map of campus parking areas.
  2. Tomorrow is Chinese New Year and you have a sizable group of students of Chinese heritage on campus who have a celebration planned. 20 inches; illustration of symbol for new year.
  3. A bomb hurled in an assassination attempt on the leader of a military junta in Chile fails to go off and no one is hurt. 10 inches; wirephoto.
  4. Administrators prohibit the distribution of an underground magazine published by a campus antinuclear group because the material would disrupt classes. The antinuke group cries censorship. 23 inches; reproduction of magazine cover, mug shot of antinuke group leader.
  5. A swimmer from your school sets the state record in the 400-yard freestyle at yesterday's meet in another part of the state. 7 inches.
  6. Campus utility bills have doubled in the past three years, and trustees are considering lowering thermostats this winter to 60° in all classrooms. 13 inches; graph or chart.

14 headlines

Figure 14–1. This 1929 edition of *The Knoxville News-Sentinel* shows the extensive use of small second-deck heads above major stories. (Copyright © 1929, *The Knoxville News-Sentinel*. Reprinted with permission)

Complete Wire Reports of UNITED PRESS, the Greatest World-Wide News Service

The Knoxville News-Sentinel   HOME

Vol. XLIII.—No. 310   KNOXVILLE, TENNESSEE, WEDNESDAY EVENING, OCTOBER 30, 1929.   PRICE FIVE CENTS

COUNCIL VOTES TO RAISE ITS OWN SALARIES

Amendment, Given Approval, Would Go Into Effect as of Oct. 1, Dempster Says.

FOR LEGISLATIVE ACTION

Blanc and Fretz Vote Against Provision; Other Changes Are Recommended.

Washington Is Stirred By Mystery Of Girl's Death

Government Officials Take Part In Trying to Solve Murder-Suicide Puzzle; Suspect's Alibi Hold.

By RODNEY DUTCHER

MISFORTUNE NEVER REDUCES ITS BUDGET

Lean Months Are Upon Knoxville's Unfortunate Ones; Only Community Chest Can Cope With Widespread Want and Suffering in City.

EXPERT PILOT SAVES PLANE AND HIS FOUR PASSENGERS

Brings Western Air Express Liner Down In Meadow Covered With Snow When He Runs Into Blinding Snow Storm.

Workhouse Is Lot Of Youth Taking Pistol To Mother

KELLY SLATED FOR LAW POST

Expected to Succeed Peters Within Short Time.

FULTONS HAVE BABY GIRL

MORE UMBRELLA WEATHER

WEEMS ARRIVES

Father of Two Children Has No Statement to Make.

A Plan to Rescue The Stock Market

STOCK EXCHANGE TO CLOSE DOWN

OLD GANG IS TRYING TO GET BACK IN POWER

City Manager Forces In Cincinnati Fighting to Keep Control.

EXPECTED TO WIN

Under Non-Political Government Vast Improvements Made in Ohio City.

TURNS BEAR

DOORS SHUT UNTIL NOON TOMORROW

Trading Mart Will Suspend Business Friday and Saturday; Employes Exhausted.

WILL REOPEN MONDAY

Then Will Close Again Tuesday Because of Election; Curb Expected to Act.

DELAY ACTING ON KNOX VALUATION

State Board Asks Atty.-Gen. Smith for an Opinion.

By BENTON J. STONG

WEEMS BOYS THRILLED BY THEIR FIRST MOVIE SHOW

Taken By Mrs. Hardinge, Their Mother, to See 'The Taming of the Shrew'; Talk About 'Goober' Testimony To Be Heard Monday.

GLASGOW TO STAY

Informs Church He Will Turn Down College Offer.

KNOX UTILITIES ASSESSMENT UP

Power-Light Increase $932,000; Gain Over State.

WON'T BROADCAST

You Must Have Ticket to Follow Auburn Game.

STOCK LOSER SHOOTS SELF

WHEN PEOPLE BECOME FRIENDS—

Jo Jo Says

RAIN

192

Headlines must summarize an often complex story in a handful of words that have to fulfill some rather strict wording and space requirements. That summary must not only be accurate and complete, it must also be clever enough to entice the reader to look at that particular story.

Functions

Headlines have two major functions. First, they summarize the basic news of the day for the reader who doesn't have the time to read every story in the paper. Because the head may be the only information many readers will receive about a story, most headlines are written from the lead of a news story (but not necessarily of a feature or other non-news stories). If the headline writer has summarized the story correctly, the headline information should be found in the first three paragraphs. Second, headlines visually "grade" the relative newsworthiness of each news story. It is a fair bet that the editor thinks the story beneath a four-column headline on page 1 is more important than the story beneath a one-column head on page 4. A hurried reader can scan the paper and confidently read only the important news of the day—the stories under the larger heads.

A good editor uses typographical traits such as weight (boldness) or type style to indicate the story's importance or tone. For example, feature or "People" pages of newspapers often will use lighter, less serious-looking typefaces than would be appropriate on page 1 above a murder story. Feature sections use italics more often than do news sections.

Headlines also introduce large areas of black and white to give the page more visual interest. Newspapers have been very gray throughout most of their history. Before large multicolumn headlines became common, headlines had deck after deck of 10- to 18-point type (Fig. 14–1). With the advent of yellow journalism around 1900, a newspaper had to demand more attention than the next paper to attract readers, so editors began using larger and larger type across multiple columns to gain public attention. Today, banner lines of 72-point and larger type across page 1 of metropolitan-paper newsstand editions are the rule and not the exception (Fig. 14–2).

Figure 14–2. Newsstand editions use 72-point and larger headlines to attract persons walking past. (Copyright © 1982, *Los Angeles Times.* Reprinted with permission)

Different Kinds of Headlines

If all heads were of uniform size and placement, the appearance of the paper would be static and dull. Effective use of different kinds of headlines makes a newspaper page look more interesting to the reader. Before we look closely at headline writing, we should define some terms.

A *line* refers to just that: a line of a headline. A head usually has one, two, or three lines (Fig. 14–3). Occasionally, a paper will use four or five lines over a one-column story. Most papers today avoid more than three lines over stories that cover three or more columns.

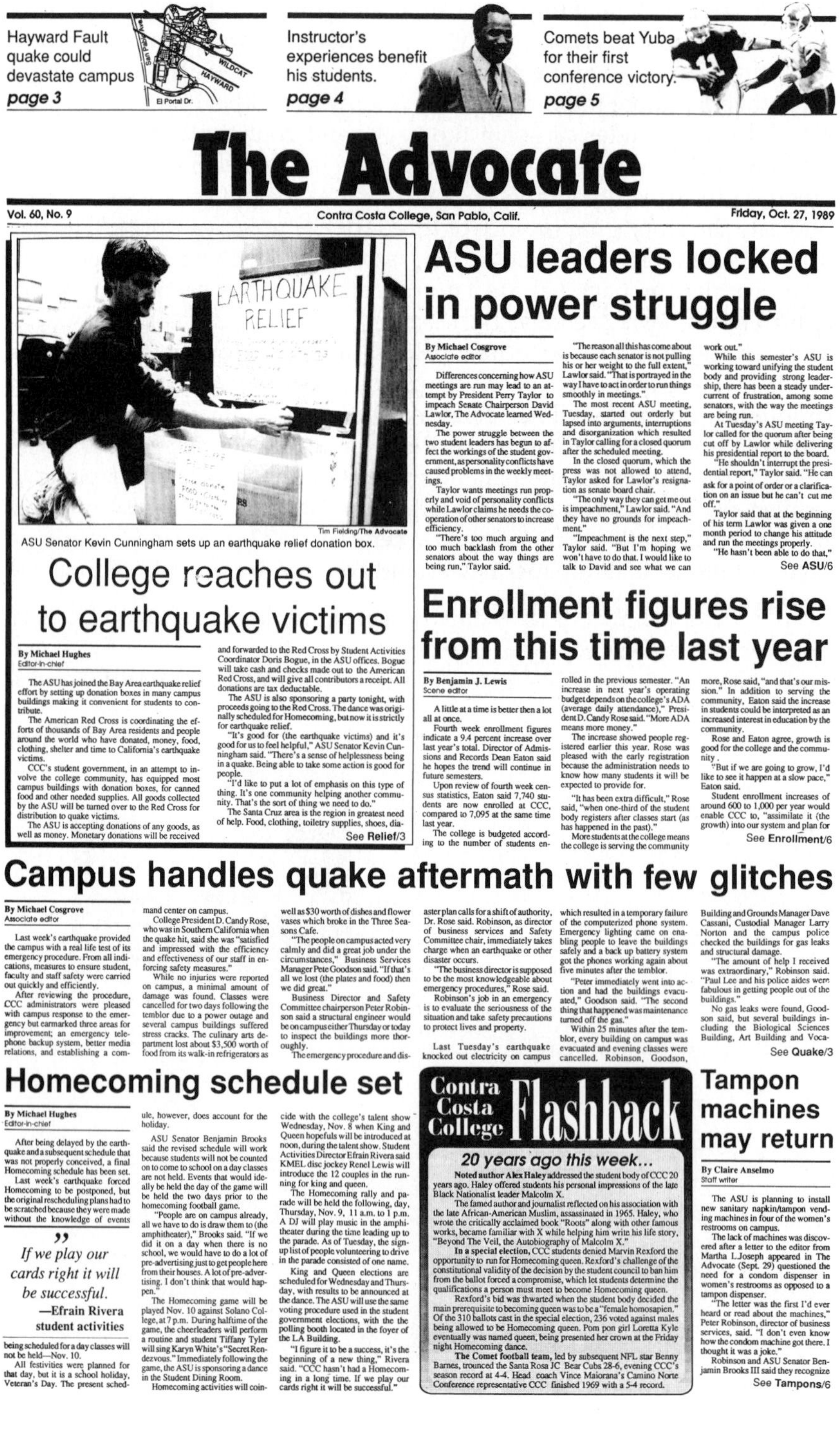

Hayward Fault quake could devastate campus *page 3*

Instructor's experiences benefit his students. *page 4*

Comets beat Yuba for their first conference victory. *page 5*

The Advocate

Vol. 60, No. 9 — Contra Costa College, San Pablo, Calif. — Friday, Oct. 27, 1989

Tim Fielding/The Advocate

ASU Senator Kevin Cunningham sets up an earthquake relief donation box.

College reaches out to earthquake victims

By Michael Hughes
Editor-in-chief

The ASU has joined the Bay Area earthquake relief effort by setting up donation boxes in many campus buildings making it convenient for students to contribute.

The American Red Cross is coordinating the efforts of thousands of Bay Area residents and people around the world who have donated, money, food, clothing, shelter and time to California's earthquake victims.

CCC's student government, in an attempt to involve the college community, has equipped most campus buildings with donation boxes, for canned food and other needed supplies. All goods collected by the ASU will be turned over to the Red Cross for distribution to quake victims.

The ASU is accepting donations of any goods, as well as money. Monetary donations will be received and forwarded to the Red Cross by Student Activities Coordinator Doris Bogue, in the ASU offices. Bogue will take cash and checks made out to the American Red Cross, and will give all contributors a receipt. All donations are tax deductable.

The ASU is also sponsoring a party tonight, with proceeds going to the Red Cross. The dance was originally scheduled for Homecoming, but now it is strictly for earthquake relief.

"It's good for (the earthquake victims) and it's good for us to feel helpful," ASU Senator Kevin Cunningham said. "There's a sense of helplessness being in a quake. Being able to take some action is good for people.

"I'd like to put a lot of emphasis on this type of thing. It's one community helping another community. That's the sort of thing we need to do."

The Santa Cruz area is the region in greatest need of help. Food, clothing, toiletry supplies, shoes, dia-

See **Relief**/3

ASU leaders locked in power struggle

By Michael Cosgrove
Associate editor

Differences concerning how ASU meetings are run may lead to an attempt by President Perry Taylor to impeach Senate Chairperson David Lawlor, The Advocate learned Wednesday.

The power struggle between the two student leaders has begun to affect the workings of the student government, as personality conflicts have caused problems in the weekly meetings.

Taylor wants meetings run properly and void of personality conflicts while Lawlor claims he needs the cooperation of other senators to increase efficiency.

"There's too much arguing and too much backlash from the other senators about the way things are being run," Taylor said.

"The reason all this has come about is because each senator is not pulling his or her weight to the full extent," Lawlor said. "That is portrayed in the way I have to act in order to run things smoothly in meetings."

The most recent ASU meeting, Tuesday, started out orderly but lapsed into arguments, interruptions and disorganization which resulted in Taylor calling for a closed quorum after the scheduled meeting.

In the closed quorum, which the press was not allowed to attend, Taylor asked for Lawlor's resignation as senate board chair.

"The only way they can get me out is impeachment," Lawlor said. "And they have no grounds for impeachment."

"Impeachment is the next step," Taylor said. "But I'm hoping we won't have to do that. I would like to talk to David and see what we can work out."

While this semester's ASU is working toward unifying the student body and providing strong leadership, there has been a steady undercurrent of frustration, among some senators, with the way the meetings are being run.

At Tuesday's ASU meeting Taylor called for the quorum after being cut off by Lawlor while delivering his presidential report to the board.

"He shouldn't interrupt the presidential report," Taylor said. "He can ask for a point of order or a clarification on an issue but he can't cut me off."

Taylor said that at the beginning of his term Lawlor was given a one month period to change his attitude and run the meetings properly.

"He hasn't been able to do that,"

See **ASU**/6

Enrollment figures rise from this time last year

By Benjamin J. Lewis
Scene editor

A little at a time is better then a lot all at once.

Fourth week enrollment figures indicate a 9.4 percent increase over last year's total. Director of Admissions and Records Dean Eaton said he hopes the trend will continue in future semesters.

Upon review of fourth week census statistics, Eaton said 7,740 students are now enrolled at CCC, compared to 7,095 at the same time last year.

The college is budgeted according to the number of students enrolled in the previous semester. "An increase in next year's operating budget depends on the college's ADA (average daily attendance)," President D. Candy Rose said. "More ADA means more money."

The increase showed people registered earlier this year. Rose was pleased with the early registration because the administration needs to know how many students it will be expected to provide for.

"It has been extra difficult," Rose said, "when one-third of the student body registers after classes start (as has happened in the past)."

More students at the college means the college is serving the community more, Rose said, "and that's our mission." In addition to serving the community, Eaton said the increase in students could be interpreted as an increased interest in education by the community.

Rose and Eaton agree, growth is good for the college and the community .

"But if we are going to grow, I'd like to see it happen at a slow pace," Eaton said.

Student enrollment increases of around 600 to 1,000 per year would enable CCC to, "assimilate it (the growth) into our system and plan for

See **Enrollment**/6

Campus handles quake aftermath with few glitches

By Michael Cosgrove
Associate editor

Last week's earthquake provided the campus with a real life test of its emergency procedure. From all indications, measures to ensure student, faculty and staff safety were carried out quickly and efficiently.

After reviewing the procedure, CCC administrators were pleased with campus response to the emergency but earmarked three areas for improvement; an emergency telephone backup system, better media relations, and establishing a command center on campus.

College President D. Candy Rose, who was in Southern California when the quake hit, said she was "satisfied and impressed with the efficiency and effectiveness of our staff in enforcing safety measures."

While no injuries were reported on campus, a minimal amount of damage was found. Classes were cancelled for two days following the temblor due to a power outage and several campus buildings suffered stress cracks. The culinary arts department lost about $3,500 worth of food from its walk-in refrigerators as well as $30 worth of dishes and flower vases which broke in the Three Seasons Cafe.

"The people on campus acted very calmly and did a great job under the circumstances," Business Services Manager Pete Goodson said. "If that's all we lost (the plates and food) then we did great."

Business Director and Safety Committee chairperson Peter Robinson said a structural engineer would be on campus either Thursday or today to inspect the buildings more thoroughly.

The emergency procedure and disaster plan calls for a shift of authority, Dr. Rose said. Robinson, as director of business services and Safety Committee chair, immediately takes charge when an earthquake or other disaster occurs.

"The business director is supposed to be the most knowledgeable about emergency procedures," Rose said.

Robinson's job in an emergency is to evaluate the seriousness of the situation and take safety precautions to protect lives and property.

Last Tuesday's earthquake knocked out electricity on campus which resulted in a temporary failure of the computerized phone system. Emergency lighting came on enabling people to leave the buildings safely and a back up battery system got the phones working again about five minutes after the temblor.

"Peter immediately went into action and had the buildings evacuated," Goodson said. "The second thing that happened was maintenance turned off the gas."

Within 25 minutes after the temblor, every building on campus was evacuated and evening classes were cancelled. Robinson, Goodson, Building and Grounds Manager Dave Cassani, Custodial Manager Larry Norton and the campus police checked the buildings for gas leaks and structural damage.

"The amount of help I received was extraordinary," Robinson said. "Paul Lee and his police aides were fabulous in getting people out of the buildings."

No gas leaks were found, Goodson said, but several buildings including the Biological Sciences Building, Art Building and Voca-

See **Quake**/3

Homecoming schedule set

By Michael Hughes
Editor-in-chief

After being delayed by the earthquake and a subsequent schedule that was not properly conceived, a final Homecoming schedule has been set.

Last week's earthquake forced Homecoming to be postponed, but the original rescheduling plans had to be scratched because they were made without the knowledge of events being scheduled for a day classes will not be held—Nov. 10.

If we play our cards right it will be successful.
—**Efrain Rivera**
student activities

All festivities were planned for that day, but it is a school holiday, Veteran's Day. The present schedule, however, does account for the holiday.

ASU Senator Benjamin Brooks said the revised schedule will work because students will not be counted on to come to school on a day classes are not held. Events that would ideally be held the day of the game will be held the two days prior to the homecoming football game.

"People are on campus already, all we have to do is draw them to (the amphitheater)," Brooks said. "If we did it on a day when there is no school, we would have to do a lot of pre-advertising just to get people here from their houses. A lot of pre-advertising. I don't think that would happen."

The Homecoming game will be played Nov. 10 against Solano College, at 7 p.m. During halftime of the game, the cheerleaders will perform a routine and student Tiffany Tyler will sing Karyn White's "Secret Rendezvous." Immediately following the game, the ASU is sponsoring a dance in the Student Dining Room.

Homecoming activities will coincide with the college's talent show Wednesday, Nov. 8 when King and Queen hopefuls will be introduced at noon, during the talent show. Student Activities Director Efrain Rivera said KMEL disc jockey Renel Lewis will introduce the 12 couples in the running for king and queen.

The Homecoming rally and parade will be held the following, day, Thursday, Nov. 9, 11 a.m. to 1 p.m. A DJ will play music in the amphitheater during the time leading up to the parade. As of Tuesday, the sign-up list of people volunteering to drive in the parade consisted of one name.

King and Queen elections are scheduled for Wednesday and Thursday, with results to be announced at the dance. The ASU will use the same voting procedure used in the student government elections, with the the polling booth located in the foyer of the LA Building.

"I figure it to be a success, it's the beginning of a new thing," Rivera said. "CCC hasn't had a Homecoming in a long time. If we play our cards right it will be successful."

Contra Costa College Flashback

20 years ago this week...

Noted author Alex Haley addressed the student body of CCC 20 years ago. Haley offered students his personal impressions of the late Black Nationalist leader Malcolm X.

The famed author and journalist reflected on his association with the late African-American Muslim, assassinated in 1965. Haley, who wrote the critically acclaimed book "Roots" along with other famous works, became familiar with X while helping him write his life story, "Beyond The Veil, the Autobiography of Malcolm X."

In a special election, CCC students denied Marvin Rexford the opportunity to run for Homecoming queen. Rexford's challenge of the constitutional validity of the decision by the student council to ban him from the ballot forced a compromise, which let students determine the qualifications a person must meet to become Homecoming queen.

Rexford's bid was thwarted when the student body decided the main prerequisite to becoming queen was to be a "female homosapien." Of the 310 ballots cast in the special election, 236 voted against males being allowed to be Homecoming queen. Pom pon girl Loretta Kyle eventually was named queen, being presented her crown at the Friday night Homecoming dance.

The Comet football team, led by subsequent NFL star Benny Barnes, trounced the Santa Rosa JC Bear Cubs 28-6, evening CCC's season record at 4-4. Head coach Vince Maiorana's Camino Norte Conference representative CCC finished 1969 with a 5-4 record.

Tampon machines may return

By Claire Anselmo
Staff writer

The ASU is planning to install new sanitary napkin/tampon vending machines in four of the women's restrooms on campus.

The lack of machines was discovered after a letter to the editor from Martha L.Joseph appeared in The Advocate (Sept. 29) questioned the need for a condom dispenser in women's restrooms as opposed to a tampon dispenser.

"The letter was the first I'd ever heard or read about the machines," Peter Robinson, director of business services, said. "I don't even know how the condom machine got there. I thought it was a joke."

Robinson and ASU Senator Benjamin Brooks III said they recognize

See **Tampons**/6

Figure 14–3. Headlines can come in all sorts of forms: bold, light, and with as many lines as you need, though rarely more than four. (Courtesy of *The Advocate*)

Banner and *streamer* usually refer to a headline that goes all the way across a page. A *skyline* head covers all columns at the very top of a page. It is often used for the most newsworthy story of the day for obvious reasons: to catch every reader's eye. Many papers, however, begin feature stories or long news analyses above the nameplate to give the story good play on page 1 and leave the straight-news section of the page untouched beneath the nameplate (Fig. 14–4).

A *combination* head covers two different but related stories, each of which has a smaller *drop* or *readout* headline as well (Fig. 14–5).

A *deck* refers to both the larger and the smaller parts of the headline. In Figure 14–2, the "Last Chance" head is the main part of the headline; the smaller head ("U.S. Urges") is the second deck. But both make up the total headline for the story. Some journalists use "deck" to refer to a "line" of a headline, but this method is clearer.

A *kicker* headline is a small headline above a main head. It is usually half the point size of the main head (Fig. 14–6). Some papers use a *reverse kicker* (or hammer head): The short, pithy head is in large type, and the longer head that covers all the columns is smaller (Fig. 14–7). A kicker is nearly always flush left, and the main head then always indents approximately two units. When a story is boxed, both heads can be centered. The kicker may be underlined. Some papers use an italic kicker if the main head is standard type, and vice versa (see Fig. 14–7).

Kickers add information that cannot be included in the main head. Because they also get more white space on the page, kickers should be no longer than approximately half the width of the main head. And because the main head is

Samelson describes imprisonment

The Ranger

Board appoints interim president

Expert sees savings through computer system

Faculty Senate sets two elections

Figure 14–4. Many newspapers will lower the nameplate on page 1 to run an important news analysis or feature story above it. The main news story is still below the nameplate. (From *The Ranger*, San Antonio College)

Figure 14–5. A combination headline with two readout heads. (From *The Campus*, College of the Sequoias)

Nursing permit changes: Will care be affected?

Fears exaggerated

By Carol Helding
Staff writer

The cry is "wolf."

Registered nurses are, by exaggerating present conditions and loudly voicing their unsubstantiated fears, falsely alerting the public to a health care "crisis."

The state Board of Registered Nursing (BRN) signalled the panic last March when it announced changes in the interim permit policy.

Previously, the BRN issued three-month work permits to nursing graduates who failed the licensing exam or who were awaiting exam results. Now such permits are valid for six months.

The BRN had also proposed a two-year work permit to be given in special cases.

But if there are more nurses, it should ultimately lead to lower nursing salaries, as the supply of nurses grows to meet the demand.

Not wanting their salaries lowered, nurses wanted something done.

If they could convince the public that medical care would be jeopardized by the board's action, then the nursing shortage, current salaries and high health care costs could be maintained.

Nurses are "howling" for two main reasons.

One, nurses have worked without problems under the old three-month permit. The BRN extended this period to six months because it believed that the current licensing exam discriminates against those who have problems with English, namely minorities and foreigners.

The BRN wanted time to study and revise the exam, while allowing those who may have failed because of the exam's discriminatory nature to work as nurses.

Two, the proposed two-year permit would not be given to exam flunkees. Instead, it would be reserved for foreign-trained nurses. It would allow them to work and become more proficient in English before taking the exam.

Naturally, nurses contend that the quality of health care will decline when permit holding nurses go to work.

Permit holders, however, might not even be hired. The BRN has left the decision to individual hospitals. One may choose the hire only licensed nurses, another to supplement its staff with permit holders. In other words, a work permit is not an employment guarantee.

Two advantages can be realized when hospitals hire permit holders.

First, permit holders can be paid less than licensed nurses, while they are capable of performing essentially the same duties. Hospitals —and patients—could save money.

Second, permit holders can perform the more mundane nursing tasks, freeing the limited number of licensed nurses for more vital functions. This will lower the number of licensed nurses needed on the shift and reduce costs.

Both advantages worry licensed nurses.

However, a patient's life won't be jeopardized. Obviously only licensed nurses will be assigned delicate tasks, such as monitoring a life support system, and permit holders will be well-supervised.

Even so, remember that permit holders have the same training as licensed nurses. Foreign-trained nurses were licensed and working with patients in their homeland. The BRN is not sending untrained idiots into the hospital.

The cry is "wolf" and California should recognize it as just that. The BRN's action could reduce the cost of healthcare—not the quality.

Competency questioned

By Chuck Rush
Staff writer

Nurse.

The word alone commands awesome respect, just slightly lower than the respect people associate with doctors. A nurse brings to mind many things: comforting angel of mercy, competent aid to doctors.....

Competent?

It should be a question you ask yourself when you see your doctor. In recent action, the state Board of Registered Nursing has moved to allow nurses unable to pass an already questionably lenient licensing exam to serve as nurses for up to two years.

What this means to the public is the chance that they may be placed under the care of an incompetent nurse. The nursing exam in question requires that the applicant be able to correctly answer 350 of 800 questions.

If a college student were to receive an "A" grade for an exam with a score of 35 out of 80 questions, most would reasonably doubt the validity of that grade.

In perspective, consider that these unlicensed nurses will have been unable to answer even the low requirement of 44 percent. How can one not question their competency?

The Board qualified its action by requiring these unlicensed nurses to be under the constant supervision of their licensed colleagues. This "solution," in itself, creates another problem.

If the licensed nurses are already in such high demand, how can they possibly devote their time to supervision? The logical conclusion is that unlicensed nurses will, at least some of the time, be working on their own, while their supervisors are performing their duties.

Another problem the supervising nurses will face is that they will have no way of knowing their charges' strengths and weaknesses. If they give an order, they will have no assurance that the unlicensed nurse can carry out the order or not.

Licensed nurses might become, in effect, babysitters and handholders with the danger of letting their own tasks slip. In this way, competent nurses become less effective and the whole system breaks down.

A doctor must be assured in his own mind that his nurse is tending to her chores so that he may devote his time and attention to his patients.

The Board's action has met with strong resistance within the nursing field. Nurses are, understandably, disturbed because the action affects their credibility very negatively. People looking at nurses will be unable to differentiate which nurses are licensed and which are not.

A strong lobby has risen up against the Board. Petitions being circulated by the Committee for Safe Nursing Care demand that the current Board be dismissed by the governor for their "incompetent, unprofessional conduct" and their "neglect of duty under the law." The committee hopes to obtain enough signatures from nurses and patients to have a significant impact.

Although new faces on the board would change future policy, it is the issue at hand that is most important. Allowing nurses who have not passed the state exam to practice does not solve the nursing shortage — it compounds it.

State law benefits those 65 or older

Senior citizens attend college at no cost

Figure 14–6. A kicker head can add white space to the page as well as give additional information about a story.

Food stamps

1 million people to be cut from program

Figure 14–7. A reverse kicker uses a large head above a smaller head—the opposite of a kicker.

ASB decides to restructure Student Senate

— ASB decision
• ASB decision
■ ASB decision

Figure 14–8. The top headline is the main headline. Jump headlines (*bottom*) use similar wording, don't need a verb, and often begin with a dingbat.

Figure 14–9. All-cap, up-style, and down-style headlines.

HAMILTON DECIDES THAT CITY SCHOOLS ARE UNDERSTAFFED

Hamilton Decides That City Schools Are Understaffed

Hamilton decides that city schools are understaffed

usually indented under a kicker, some white space is gained at the beginning of that line as well.

Jump heads appear above the continuing story as it jumps from page to page (Fig. 14–8). Large papers might begin a story on page 1 and continue it on pages 3, 28, and 29. The jump head, smaller than the original head, often begins with a typographical *dingbat*, such as dashes, *bullets* (circles or dots), or stars. It often repeats a key word or phrase from the main head to guide the reader quickly to it. On most smaller papers and most school newspapers, a story is jumped only once so more than one jump head per story is rare. Some papers use full headlines as jump heads. Others use the "key word" approach with one word jump heads. The key word is used in the turn line. Either method has its pluses and minuses.

A *subhead* appears within a story rather than above it, but it is a headline nevertheless because it summarizes or describes a part of the story (see Fig. 14–2, lead story). Subheads break up long, gray columns of type with brief statements in boldface type. Bold type surrounded by white space every three to five paragraphs makes the story less gray and more visually appealing. Subheads also function as signposts for readers who want to skim a story: Subheads can tell them where the story changes direction. Because so many of your newspaper's readers are really "scanners," using subheads over segments is a good way to capture their attention as they breeze through your pages.

Subheads may refer to anything in the several paragraphs that follow, but it is usually best when they refer to paragraphs immediately following to avoid confusing the reader. If the story is segmented well, the subheads act truly as mini-headlines over the parts of the story. Keep subheads terse: White space is desirable whether the subhead is centered or flush left.

The trend in the capitalization of headlines is toward the *"down" style*, in which heads are capitalized as they are in a sentence: Only the first word and proper nouns are capitalized. Heads with all capital letters are difficult to read, and most papers have phased them out. Many papers still capitalize the first letter of all words except short prepositions (*"up" style*). The "down" style makes heads easier to read and allows more letters to be fitted into a line (Fig. 14–9).

Headline Schedules

Most newspapers have booklets of headline typefaces and sizes they use. Called headline schedules, they usually include unit counts for each size and style of face (Fig. 14–10). The unit counts are very important to the editor but usually a thorn in the side of the headline writer.

Unit Counts

Because a headline has to fit into a certain size space on the page, the headline writer must know how much space the letters will take up. Obviously, larger letters take up more space than smaller ones, but less obviously, different typestyles take up different amounts of space with the same letters (Fig. 14–11). Within every typeface alphabet the letters W and M take up more space than n and x. The i and t take up even less space. Headline writers must be aware of the width of headline typefaces at their paper so they can count heads accurately.

Although the computerization of newspapers today gives writers an almost infallible headline counter with their video display terminals or PCs, most school newspaper staffs have to count their headlines to see if they will fit.

Counting heads is a good skill to know, and it helps learn typography.

A paper's headline schedule not only shows all the heads used by the paper, from the largest to the smallest, but also includes the headline count for each typeface and size (see Fig. 14–10).

HEADLINE SPECIFICATION SHEET

LOWERCASE LETTERS are one (1) count, except for the letters j, i, l and t, which are one-half (1/2) count, and m and w, which are one and a half (1 1/2) counts.

UPPERCASE LETTERS are one and one-half (1 1/2) counts, except for the letters J, I, L and T, which are one (1) count, and M and W, which are two (2) counts.

PUNCTUATION is one count.

NUMBERS are one (1) count except for the number 1, which is one-half (1/2) count.

SPACE between words is one-half (1/2) count.

For all hed depths add 1/4 inch if hed goes at top of page.

R = regular face   I = Italic face

72 POINT

R	I		1 col	2 col	3 col	4 col	5 col	6 col
75,	76 (Bold)		4	8 1/2	13	18 1/2	23	27 1/2
65,	66 (Med)		4	9	13	18 1/2	22 1/2	27
55,	56 (Light)		4 1/2	9	15	20 1/2	24 1/2	29 1/2

One line, 1 1/2 inches; two lines, 2 1/4 inches; three lines, 3 inches.

60 POINT

R	I		1 col	2 col	3 col	4 col	5 col	6 col
75,	76 (Bold)		5	10 1/2	16	22	27 1/2	32 1/2
65,	66 (Med)		5	10	16	21 1/2	27	31
55,	56 (Light)		5 1/2	11	18 1/2	24	30	35

One line, 1 1/2 inch; two lines, 2 inches; three lines, 2 3/4 inches.

24 POINT

R	I		1 col	2 col	3 col	4 col	5 col	6 col
75,	76 (Bold)		11	25	37 1/2	51	65	78
65,	66 (Med)		12	25 1/2	38	52	64	79
55,	56 (Light)		14	26 1/2	40 1/2	64	78 1/4	91

One line, 3/4 inch; two lines, 1 1/4 inch; three lines, 1 1/2 inch.

Cutlines	2 col -	25 picas
	3 col -	19 1/2 picas
	4 col -	26 1/2 picas

All cutlines set Helios Bold P010 on F011

All *taglines* set Univers #65 18 pt.

All *namelines* (1 col.) 12 pt. Helios boldface

All *briefs headlines* set Univers #65 24 pt. 2 col.

Figure 14–10. A good headline schedule includes all the information a headline writer will need.
(From *The Ranger,* San Antonio College)

Journalism is an exciting field

Journalism is an exciting field

Journalism is an exciting field

Journalism is an exciting field

W

M

i

t

n

Figure 14–11. Typefaces have varying widths and therefore take up differing amounts of space in headlines, even if the point size is the same. Individual letters, too, vary in width.

Figure 14–12. A Univers 55 headline schedule.

To standardize headline counting, editors long ago adopted a set unit space for each letter and figure used in newspapering:

Capitals

M, W:	2 counts
I:	1/2
All others:	1 1/2

Lowercase letters

m, w:	1 1/2 units
f, i, j, l, t:	1/2
All others:	1

Others

Space:	1 count
Numbers except 1:	1 1/2 (slightly less when more than 3 numbers
Number 1:	1
Punctuation marks:	1/2
Question mark, dash:	1 1/2
Symbols ($, %):	1

The unit space compensates for variances in the widths of letters in the alphabet. Caution is advised, however, on this count system: It is based on old hot-type headlines. With many of the modern phototypesetting (or cold-type) machines and with PC-based publishing software, the counts are not precisely the same. Because it is still reasonably accurate, this chapter will base its count on the count chart.

On the headline schedule shown in Figure 14–12, a 36-point Univers 55 headline has a unit count of 9 per column. For a head wider than one column, the

UNIVERS 55

Counts per Column:

14:	23 1/2
18:	19 1/2
24:	14
30:	10
36:	9
48:	7
60:	5 1/2

No. 1 14 Journalism: the collecting, writing, editing and publishing of news or news articl

No. 2 18 Journalism: the collecting, writing, editing and publishing of n

No. 3 24 Journalism: the collecting, writing, editing an

No. 4 30 Journalism: the collecting, writing,

No. 5 36 Journalism: the collecting, wi

No. 6 48 Journalism: the collec

No. 7 60 Journalism: the c

headline writer multiplies the counts for one column by the number of columns the headline will cover. The writer should also add half a count to compensate for the space between columns. Therefore, a three-column Univers 55 headline has a count of 28 units (3 × 8 per column, plus 1 for the two gutters).

If asked to write a 28-unit headline for a story about Senate passage of a new bill, a head writer might come up with:

Senate approves water bill

The head count is $24\frac{1}{2}$ units (S = $1\frac{1}{2}$, e = 1, n = 1, a = 1, t = $\frac{1}{2}$, e = 1, space = 1, and so on), which fits inside the maximum of 28. A few counts under, or approximately 15 percent, of the maximum is allowable, although short heads are acceptable in today's modern graphic design. In this case, $23\frac{1}{2}$ would have been an acceptable minimum. A headline cannot, however, be even a half count over the maximum. If a head is too long, it will carry into the gutter between columns or even into another story.

There are two good methods for counting heads on paper. The first is to write out the head on a scratch pad with plenty of space between the lines. Put a small line below the letter for every full count and a small line above the letter for every half count as you go across the line. When you have finished, go back and count all the full units and then add the half units.

Senate approves water bill

The second method is simply to count each letter's unit space, and write it above the letter, then total the spaces. You might get confused with all the addition in a long headline if you tried to do it mentally, but by writing down the numbers, you minimize the chances of error.

Headline Writing

These rules and limitations might be enough to scare all but the most dedicated away from head writing, but it is not as hard as it seems. Some do's and a lot of don'ts make the task simpler than it appears.

Have a firm idea of what the story is about before you begin to write a headline. Don't just glance over the first paragraph of a story; read the story carefully, several times if necessary, so that you can summarize it accurately in a few words.

Because headline writers have to be able to summarize long, complex stories in a few words, they need good vocabularies. If one word doesn't fit in a line, a longer or shorter synonym might. Keep a thesaurus around the newsroom. On the other hand, don't get carried away with synonyms. For example, don't substitute *wallop* or *trounce* for *beat* if the winning edge in a basketball game was only three points. And, as with good writing, don't use a complicated word when a simple one will do.

Headline writers need a good understanding of the English language and a determination not to accept the mundane, ordinary, verbless title for a headline (Fig. 14–13). Sometimes a mere shift in words or a reversal of the two lines will make the head fit.

Intramurals successful

Figure 14–13. Don't use a title—a verbless headline—for a newspaper story. In addition, this head could be used almost any time. It is a "generic" headline.

Most important, do not hurry a headline or accept any head that will fit. Headlines are among the most important writing in a newspaper; indeed, at most copy desks only senior desk persons write the headlines (or at least the heads above the major stories). Be prepared to work on a head for 15 to 20 minutes to make it just right. The five-minute-per-headline stage will come in due course.

It is all too easy for students to believe that headlines are not important or are too hard to write and therefore spend little time on them. But taking time to write good headlines—to "sell" the story to the readers—is well worth the effort, especially on feature stories. Coming up with creative word twists or puns for a feature story or humorous column can be among the more entertaining parts of producing the paper (Figs. 14–14 and 14–15). Remember that with features headline writers have some freedom to stretch a pun or to play with words, but they shouldn't go so far that the reader can't follow.

Do

- Know what the story is all about.
- Use present-tense verbs to indicate the past. Use "ing" forms for stories that are occurring when the reader gets the paper and infinitives for future occurrences. Past tense sometimes works, but present is used most often.
- Write headlines on a separate sheet, not on the story.
- Develop a large vocabulary.
- Be specific.
- Indent main heads under kickers one em space.
- Use numbers and abbreviations in headlines if necessary, but within reason.
- Use a verb in a headline—a strong, colorful one.
- Use single quotation marks for quoted material in headlines.
- Use a comma instead of the word *and*.

Don't

- Turn in a line that counts 6 when it should count 12. Don't exceed the maximum count.
- Use a period at the end of the headline.

Figure 14–14. This set of headlines won first place in a statewide competition in California.

Renee Ortiz-Wyckoff:
running for two this time

Faculty salaries
It takes class to move up

Feathers expected to fly when
Giants play West Hills Falcons

Artist aims below the belt
in shot at double standard

Mild-mannered Marchant
peels to new personality

Men's hoop
There's no business
like slow business

features
They share jeans as well as chromosomes

Figure 14–15. Feature stories, such as this one about twins, are a good place to use creative headline writing. (From *The Campus*, College of the Sequoias)

- Begin a headline with a verb.
- Use a name in a headline unless the person is well known.
- Split infinitives, prepositions and objects, nouns and modifiers from one line to the next.
- Use *to be* verb forms.
- Use more than one modifier per noun.
- Use *a, an,* or *the* unless the word is part of a title.
- Use pronouns.
- Accept mediocrity.

Headline Requests

A newspaper staff needs a method for telling the copy desk what kind of headline is needed for a story: A request for a "3-column, 2-line, 36-point Univers 55 main head with an 18-point kicker" is too long and bulky. Most newspapers develop systems to identify headlines quickly and easily.

Some papers assign numbers to all the different heads on their headline schedule. For instance, in Figure 14–13, 14-point Univers 55 might be No. 1, 18-point Univers 55 No. 2, and so on down the remainder of Univers 55 heads. An editor can request a three-column, and two-line No. 5 with a No. 2 kicker.

Other papers just list the necessary numbers in a set order and leave it to the desk person to write the head. The head request might look like this:

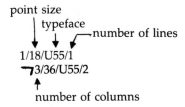

The request is for an indented main head and a kicker. The drawn-in line indicates the indentation of the main head to remind the desk person to shorten the count of the main head a few spaces. The kicker is 18-point Univers 55, one line. All kickers are one line, but putting the number in eliminates any possible confusion. The main head is three columns of 36-point Univers 55, two lines. The head writer should check the head schedule for unit counts per column.

Many school papers use the printed headline request form (Fig. 14–16). This form has blanks on which the editor indicates the headline style and size and lines on which the head writer writes the head. The form can also include information for the typesetter.

Figure 14–16. A headline request form from *The Campus*. This is used when body copy and heads are processed separately. (College of the Sequoias)

the campus
Headline Request Form

Date: _____   Page: _____

Typeface: _____ Size: _____ Pica Width: _____ Columns: _____

ALL CAPS: ☐

Set as is: ☐

_____

_____

_____

Writer's Initials _____

Pub. 2

The headline is usually written on a separate sheet of paper, whether it's a special printed form or a blank sheet of typing paper. It is better to process the heads and body copy separately.

Examples

Here is a typical headline-writing situation.

Milldale School has just selected a new principal to replace a person who will retire this year. The head requested has a count of 15 per line for a two-line head.

Principal selected	16 units
by Milldale School	16½ units

This head won't work because the lines are too long, and the verb is passive. Passive verbs should be used only in a pinch. So the head must be rewritten. All the important information is there, but it needs rewording.

A good trick to use if the head is slightly long or short is to reverse the lines, changing the verb forms as needed.

Milldale School	14 units
selects principal	14½ units

Now the headline fits the story as well as the required count, and the verb is active.

Another tip to remember is to use synonyms. If a headline is good but doesn't fit, maybe a simple word substitution will do. The headline writer must be cautious to make sure that the substituted word still means the same thing.

Take this head:

Raiders defeat Vikings, 31–14	27 units

If this head were too long, the writer could make several changes. *Defeat* could become *beat*, and if that weren't enough, *Vikings* could become *Vikes*. If the head were too short, the writer could use city names:

Los Angeles defeats Minnesota, 31–14	30½ units

Let's look at a sample story, and write it a down-style headline, an 18/U65/1 kicker with a 2/36/U65/2 main head.

> If estimates provided by the State Department of Finance are accurate, Middle Valley College may not receive an increase in state funding for next year, according to Dr. Fenton T. Harper, president.
>
> "We really don't know what we're going to get from the state next year," Harper said. "The Department of Finance says we aren't going to get any money next year because the so-called rainy-day funding is exhausted.
>
> "And we're due for a 10 to 11 percent increase because of inflation alone," he said.
>
> Harper explained that MVC has been relying on state money to provide 80 percent of the college's income. Without an increase, Harper said, many college programs may have to be cut back severely.

Begin with the main head, which has a count of 9 per column. Remember that main heads under kickers need to be indented about two counts, so the maximum here should be 9 + 9 + 1 (for the gutter) = 19 − 2 (for the kicker), or 17 units.

Just like a good lead, a good head usually focuses on the what-happened of the story.

No funding increase	18 units
predicted by state	16 units

This head says what happened, but the top line is one unit too long and the verb is passive. Let's try again.

MVC may not get   15½ units
increased funding   15½ units

Better. The verb is active and the count will fit without crowding. Now for the kicker.

A kicker should count about the same as the main head. A good rule of thumb is that if the kicker is approximately the same count as the main head, it will take up approximately half the space because it is half the point size. The rule on kicker lengths is flexible almost to a fault: It should be neither too long nor too short. It should be no longer than the center of the main head.

The kicker should give additional information or name a source but should rarely "read" into or out of the main head. It is usually better to have the kicker stand alone in meaning from the main head. Kickers do not need verbs.

'Rainy-day' fund exhausted   23½ units

This kicker can stand alone and tells the reader something else about the story. It also correctly uses single quotation marks, which are always used in headlines. But it is too long and it repeats a word that is in the main head (fund and funding). Let's try another one.

Dept. of Finance estimate   23½ units

Still too long.

State estimate   12½ units

Much better. "State" says the same thing as "Dept. of Finance," and it fits (Fig. 14–17). But maybe you can play with the "rainy-day" idea a little bit and come up with a headline that is informative and entertaining, a great combination (Fig. 14–18).

Now let's try to write a head for a sports story. It's a 3/48/U65/2. The count is 8 per column, or 25 including the gutters.

> With some hot shooting from the field that included four players scoring in double figures, the Middle Valley basketball team defeated the Johnsonville Pirates, 95–71, in a preseason game Tuesday night.
> Before a highly partisan crowd of 1,450 in the MVC "snakepit" gym, the Giants shot 58 percent from the floor. The Pirates shot only 36 percent.
> With the win, MVC improved its preseason record to 5–3 and dropped Johnsonville to 2–5.

Just as with a news story, a sports story headline should come from the lead:

Johnsonville basketball team   25½ units
loses to MVC, 95–71   19 units

The top line is too long, and the bottom line is too short. The lines in a head should rarely be more than two counts apart, three at the very most, or the head will look unbalanced. MVC should be mentioned first, not Johnsonville. The winning team should "beat" the other team, not "lose" to it; it might appear as if the losers lost on purpose—a doubtful occurrence.

MVC basketball team   19½ units
defeats Johnsonville, 95–71   25 units

State estimate
MVC may not get increased funding

Figure 14–17. This headline fits all the standard requirements, but it lacks color.

Figure 14–18. A little extra effort can turn a dull headline into one that can attract readers. The bottom example, with the second deck, is a good way to add more information without adding awkward whitespace.

Funding weather report:
'Rainy-day' surplus now all dried up

Now the winning team is listed first, but the top line is too short. And "MVC basketball team" takes up a lot of space without saying much. There is also no need to mention MVC in the head—the story is in the MVC paper. Why not work in a descriptive term from the story?

Hot-shooting Giant cagers	23½ units
defeat Johnsonville, 95–71	25 units

Now the head fits and it is livelier. It *tells* more of the story than just the score. Although a synonym for basketball players also was used (some editors cringe at certain sports nicknames, but they are needed too often in heads to be discarded completely), the headline is much better in this form.

Figure 14–19. Even professional papers can make mistakes. Because words often have double meanings and because the change of one letter can make a big difference, headlines need to be double-checked for accuracy as carefully as stories are checked. (Reprinted with permission of *Columbia Journalism Review*, copyright September–October 1981)

The Lower case

Medfly Finds No Cause For Worry
Daily Sun/Post (San Clemente, Calif.) 9/1/81

The Salt Lake City Track Club's All-Women's 10,000-meter race is scheduled Saturday at 8 a.m. at Sugarhouse Park. The entry fee is $4 with shirt or $1 without.
The Salt Lake Tribune 8/27/81

Giant roaches set fall practice
Highland Park (Ill.) News 7/30/81

Warden and Aide at Rikers Are Demoted After Escapes
The New York Times 8/15/81

Navy Finds Dead Pilots Flying With Hangovers
The Washington Post 9/18/81

The Star's demise makes Washington the largest one-city newspaper in the country
The Philadelphia Inquirer 8/8/81

Half of U.S. High Schools Require Some Study for Graduation
Los Angeles Times 8/10/81

Coed Climbing Out in Iran
Buffalo (N.Y.) Evening News 8/10/81

The noon gun at Major's Hill Park
The (Ottawa, Canada) Citizen 6/27/81

Fried chicken cooked in microwave wins trip
The (Portland) Oregonian 7/8/81

Local Charity Group Helps Disable Man
The Clayton (Georgia) News Daily 9/14/81

Guyer's widow rules out plans to replace him
The (Cleveland) Plain Dealer 4/28/81

Gisèle Berger, in the kitchen of La Bonne Table, with a display of the raw materials she uses for her innovative seafood specialties.
Food & Wine 8/81

CJR asks readers who contribute items to this department to send only original clippings suitable for reproduction; please include the name and date of publication, as well as your name and address.

At first glance, headline writing seems to be an almost impossible task. Students complain that the counts are too short to say anything and the rules restrict their creativity too much. But headline writing improves with practice; after a while speed and quality come together.

Writing heads is one of the most important and challenging tasks on a newspaper. Few areas in newspapering allow so much creativity. With a little practice and imagination, writing headlines can be fun.

— Suggested Projects

1. Ask for a copy of the headline schedule of your local paper. How many typefaces does it use? Does the schedule include headline counts as well as the faces themselves? Look for ways to improve your headline schedule.

2. Take stories from last year's paper and try to find heads that can be improved. Can you make the head fit better or better highlight the angle of the story?

3. Begin clip files of good and bad headlines from your own paper and from the professional press. Decide what makes them work well or fail. List and post your own do's and don'ts for writing effective headlines.

4. Invite a local copy editor to critique your headlines and give you tips on how to improve your work.

5. Have someone tape or mark out the headlines in a paper from another city. Then try to write heads to fit the stories. Compare to the heads that actually appeared. Which are better? Why?

Vocabulary

banner
bullet
combination head
deck
dingbat
down style
drop head
kicker
line
readout
reverse kicker
skyline
streamer
subhead
up style

15 production

The revolution in personal computer front-end systems and in PC-based typesetting and publishing systems has changed the way student newspapers are produced. Fewer and fewer send copy written on a typewriter to a typesetter—either on-campus or off—and then paste up galleys of type, headlines, and veloxes.

This has meant a tremendous savings for school-publication staffs, at least after the initial capital investment. Besides saving money, carrying ideas through from conception to production helps make better journalists. You will always be better off if you know enough to assist your work at any stage of the process. This chapter will discuss both traditional production and PC-based, in-house production.

By far the largest cost in producing a paper is labor. Student journalists usually provide the newsroom work for small salaries or for course credit. If the paper is turned over to an outside firm for typesetting, paste-up, and printing, the cost per issue can nearly double. If the staff, however, does the typesetting and paste up, or if it produces full pages on a PC, delivering *camera-ready* (completely pasted up) pages to the printer, a large part of the production cost of each issue can be saved. This savings means that a newspaper can publish more issues, buy improved equipment, or send more staff members to journalism conferences. The initial expense of purchasing paste-up supplies or PCs and software is soon regained by paying the local print shop less per issue.

Although some staffs may balk at what seems to be extra work, most students prefer to paste up their own pages because they can make the necessary last-minute changes in design themselves. By seeing a page through from beginning to end, many students also gain pride in their work and in the paper itself. When the paper is good, especially when it wins awards, the feeling of pride is great.

Traditional Paste-up

Traditional paste-up involves more of a separation between the newsroom and the production room. In the PC-based system, especially those with the Apple Macintosh® computer, the newsroom and production room are basically the same place: inside the computer.

Traditional paste-up usually is done in the composing room or back shop of a newspaper. At a professional paper, specially trained personnel follow the editor's page dummy (Fig. 15–1), preparing the page so that a page negative and printing plate can be made from it. Most composition rooms have the following basic materials: light tables or paste-up tables with T-squares, waxers, razor-blade knives, photo-blue pens, rolls of border tapes, a sharp paper cutter, storage areas, rollers or brayers, and cellophane tape.

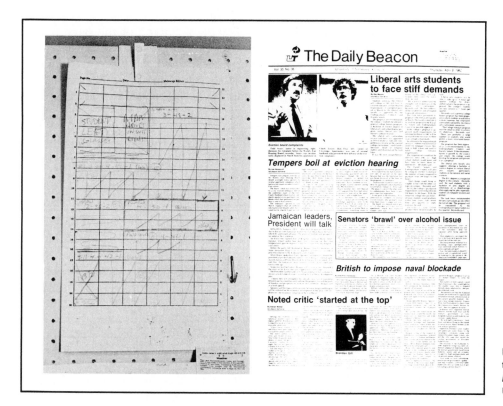

Figure 15–1. A page dummy is a map of the completed page. (Photo by Michael Messing; page from *The Daily Beacon*, University of Tennessee)

Even the smallest newspaper staff can have an adequate composing room in a workroom or classroom. Not much space is needed, but it should be separated from the newsroom so that materials don't get lost or mixed up. The paste-up area needs to be kept very clean and neat. Because the printed page is reproduced photographically—in essence, a photo of the paste-up is made into the printing plate—every smudge, thumbprint, speck of dirt, stray pen or pencil line, folded-over corner of a galley, or loose piece of copy shows up in the final product (Fig. 15–2).

The paste-up process is in one sense simple and in another difficult. The process of lining up all the copy, photos, and ads is a straightforward, obvious task. But it is one of those easier-said-than-done jobs that takes about twice as long as you thought it would.

A: There are five parking lots available for COS student use. Four of the lots are located on campus and there is on located between Mearle's and Visalia Sight und on Mooney Blvd. Parking rules and regulations can be referred to in the student handbook, the Sequoiana.

Figure 15–2. A completed paste-up is reproduced photographically. In this example a small piece of pasted-up material slipped before the negative was made.

Figure 15–3. Always place ads on the pages first. Then, as stories, headlines, and photos come to the paste-up area, place them on the flat according to the page dummy. (Photo by Michael Messing)

Pasting-up is, very basically, just following a "map" of the page that is provided by the editor on the page dummy. (See Figure 15–1.) The editor creates an ideal page with photos, headlines, and stories. The paste-up person should follow this design precisely whenever possible.

But the paste-up process is one of compromise. Stories always end up a little shorter or longer than designed, so the page often must be rearranged slightly. The editor or page designer should be the person who decides upon or okays any changes in the layout. If the student journalist pastes up the page, the changes can be done quickly and easily without any communication problems with the printer.

Paste-up is done on a full-size replica of the final newspaper page, often called a *flat*. Page borders and columns are printed in a light blue ink that will not appear on the page negatives. Inches and picas are also marked on the columns to assist in placing items on the page. The first items to be placed on a page should be those that *must* go on the page. On the front page, these items would be the nameplate, the index box, and any other regular features. Inside, "must" items include ads, section logos, folios, the masthead, and regular features. The rest of the material has to fit around these.

Under ideal circumstances, the paste-up person would have all the items for the page ready at the beginning of paste-up. It seldom works this way. Sometimes the photos are in first or all the headlines are ready, but the stories are not. Even though all the materials are not in, begin paste-up. Trim, wax, and place early materials on the page according to the page dummy (Fig. 15–3).

Trim carefully with a razor-blade knife or scissors. A slip can ruin several paragraphs and cause costly resetting. But you don't have to trim the galley of type right next to the letters. Leave some white space as a margin of error. Just be sure that galleys don't overlap in the gutter. Trim carefully between lines; don't accidentally trim off the ascender or descender of a letter.

Line up the legs of type in multicolumn stories so that the top line and bottom line of all legs are even and the lines align across all columns (Fig. 15–4). If one or two legs need to be *aired out* to align the columns, make the cuts in the center of the columns between grafs (never between lines in a graf). Add equal space between each graf in the leg of type. Avoid pasting up a column so that the top line is very short. This short line, called a *widow*, destroys the even line across the top of the story and adds white space where it is not needed.

Figure 15–4. The top and bottom of each column of type should line up with the others. If a column has fewer lines of type than other columns, add space equally between paragraphs within the column. (Photo by Mike Penn)

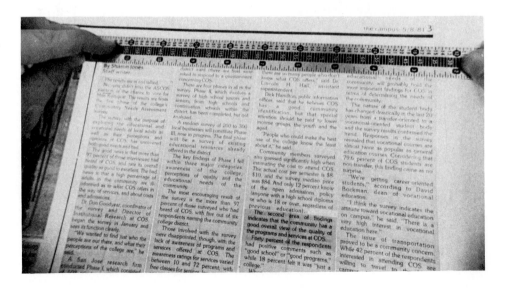

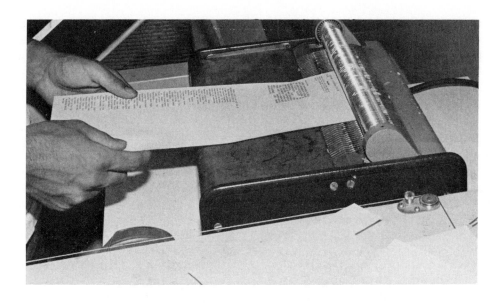

Figure 15–5. A waxer places sticky, melted wax on the back of the galleys. (Photo by Michael Messing)

The back of the galley is coated with a thin coat of hot wax (Fig. 15–5). When pressed down firmly onto the paste-up page, the galley will stick. Waxers range from expensive professional models to inexpensive, hand-held models. Special, waxable paper can be purchased if you use your own laser printer.

Photos and major headlines should be placed on the flat first. If all goes well, any adjustments later will be minor and made in story length, not in these major design elements. If you have to trim early stories to fit them in their intended place, *don't discard the overset material*—type that will not be used in the issue. Place it safely in a special tray and throw it away only when the issue has been sent to press and you're positive you won't need it for a last-minute change.

As the rest of the material for the page comes in, it can be trimmed, waxed, and pasted up to fit the design. If the page designer is not doing the paste-up, he or she should indicate on the page dummy whether a story must appear in its entirety, regardless of the other elements on the page; whether it can be cut to fit the space designed for it; or whether it can be jumped to another page. These marks—*fit*, *cut*, and *jump*—should be written on the dummy (see Fig. 15–1) to save the paste-up person a search for an editor to okay fitting, cutting, or jumping a story.

Positioning elements on a page is done with a light table or with a T-square or other straight edge. Actually, many experienced paste-up persons use a third method: a well-trained eye. This last method is not recommended for beginners.

Light tables have a piece of heavy plate glass over a piece of translucent white glass. Light shines through the glass and illuminates the flat. Because the lines on the flat show through the galleys of type, the galleys can be pasted over the lines on the page, assuring straightness. The vertical column lines are the borders of each line of type or cutoff lines for photos.

T-squares can be just as effective as light tables. Check vertical straightness and alignment with column lines first, regardless of method, and double-check horizontal lines of type. Seemingly slight differences show up as major flaws when the page is printed. Don't just eyeball the page: Check and double-check the straightness of every element.

After the page is completely pasted up and double-checked for straightness, someone other than the page editor or paste-up person should proof the page, looking mostly for big, blaring (and therefore usually invisible at this point) errors, such as headlines over the wrong stories or switched cutlines. After the page has been okayed and initialed, the paste-up person places a blank flat on top of the type and rolls over the page with a hard plastic roller or brayer to firmly attach the type and photos. The completed flats should still be handled carefully on the way to the printer. The printer can usually supply boxes for transporting camera-ready flats to the shop.

Other Techniques

If the page designer has done an effective job, some special design elements besides columns of type will be used on each page. These elements—photos, boxes, overprinting, and dropouts—require different paste-up techniques. Corrections also require special handling.

Photos can be handled two ways: (1) The print shop can make a screened version of the photo to paste on the page. This substitute photo is called a *velox* or *PMT* (for *p*hoto-*m*echanical *t*ransfer). Or (2) red or black "windows" can be placed on the flat in the exact size and position desired for a photo. When the page negative is made, the windows become clear. Later, print shop personnel will *strip in*, or tape into place, negatives made from the original photos.

The velox alternative makes it easy to check the accuracy of the photo cropping and the cutline because you can see exactly what will appear in the paper. The window process just gives the paste-up crew a blank rectangle to look at. The printer has to be trusted to get the correct photos in the windows and to get the cropping correct. But the window method produces a higher-quality photo in the paper. If you have a printer you trust, use the window process, especially if you use offset printing. The photos in the paper will look great. The final choice between methods, however, is probably the printer's.

Boxes are made by using rolls of border tape of varying width. Rolls with several hundred preprinted round corners are also available. Border tape is easy to use. To keep it straight as you lay it down, stretch it *slightly* when pressing it down on the page (Fig. 15–6). Stretching it too tightly, however, will make the flat wrinkle. To use tape with preprinted round corners, tape down the four corners first, then run the straight lines from corner to corner (Fig. 15–7). Straight corners should be mitred (cut at a 45-degree angle) for the best fit (Fig. 15–8). Overlapping tapes may cause distortion. Boxing within a PC software is so easy and accurate that being able to throw out those rolls of tape alone may well be worth the cost.

The process of overprinting—a second printing over an area on the page that has already been printed—is used most often in newspapers to screen copy blocks, print a headline on top of a photo, and print color. The paste-up process for these is similar.

One way to make a screen is to have the print shop do it in the printing process. Cut a window in the exact shape desired, paste it down on a piece of clear plastic acetate overlay, line it up properly over the copy block, and tape down one side of the acetate to the edge of the flat (Fig. 15–9). To ensure precise placement, use *registration marks* on both the acetate and the paste-up sheet. A registration mark is usually a cross inside a circle. If the printer lines up the registration mark on the overlay exactly above one on the paste-up sheet, the screen will end up in the desired place. Copy-block screens are usually very light gray, described to the printer as "10 or 15 percent" (of black).

A second way to use screens in the paper is to paste down your own on the flat or on an overlay. Shading screens from companies like Zip-a-Tone or Formatt come in many different tones and shapes—such as circles, spirals, and lines—as well as the normal range of dot patterns. These are attached to the sheet with their own adhesive substance. Then they can be cut to the desired shape with a razor-blade knife, positioned on the page, and rolled down securely.

To print part or all of a headline over a light portion of a photograph, place

Figure 15–6. Border tape should be stretched slightly as it is placed on the page. (Photo by Michael Messing)

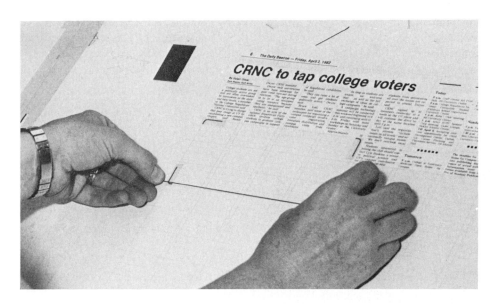

Figure 15–7. Round-cornered boxes are laid out by first pasting down preprinted corners and then stretching straight tape from corner to corner. (Photo by Michael Messing)

Figure 15–8. Square-cornered boxes should be made with mitre cuts (45° angles) through the corners to prevent problems during plate-making. (Photo by Michael Messing)

Figure 15–9. An overlay of Ruby-Lith indicates that the final exam schedule is to be a gray box. Note the two registration marks on the right margin of the screen. (Photo by Mike Penn)

the headline on a piece of clear acetate and attach it on one side (so it can be lifted for last-minute work) of the flat (Fig. 15–10). Then, just as with the screen, indicate proper position by registration marks. If you have the ability to do so, you could print the headline itself on a piece of clear acetate the same size as the velox. The printer might not have to do a second step this way.

A designer may want a copy block printed over a screened (or lighter) version of a photograph or a drawing. Again, use acetate and registration marks for positioning. Attach screening instructions to the acetate. Usually, any screen darker than 10 percent will make the type too hard to read and will ruin the effect.

Printing a color photograph using a *four-color process* is very expensive. In a four-color process, four overlays—one each for black, magenta (red), cyan (blue), and yellow—are lined up, four printing plates are made, and that area of the page gets four layers of ink. The registration here must be extremely precise or the photo turns out fuzzy. Offset presses are capable of better registration than are letterpress presses.

Spot color is cheaper and easy to use because it entails just one extra printing, as with a screened copy block. The process again involves clear acetate and proper registration. The cost can be minimized if you use a color the printer already has

Figure 15–10. Headlines can be overprinted on photos by placing the headline on a piece of clear acetate. If you paste the head directly on the photo, the white space around the letters will show, too. (Photo by Mike Penn)

Figure 15–11. The headline here has been "dropped out" of the black portion of the photograph during the negative-making process at the print shop. Dropouts work well, as in this photo, when the headline falls in a very dark portion of the photo. (Copyright 1981, *Lexington Herald-Leader.* **Used with permission)**

on the press (just ask). You can also enhance a black-and-white photo by adding a spot color to it (a sunset photo using orange is one example). The result is called a *duotone.* Duotones can be effective if done selectively. Check with your printer before you try one.

A *dropout* (or reverse) is the opposite of an overprint. Instead of appearing black on the photo, the headline will appear white (Fig. 15–11) because the halftone dots have been "dropped out" of the photo during the negative-making process. Dropouts are done in the print shop darkroom. Some printers want dropout materials a day earlier than the normal deadline because of the extra work they entail.

Corrections

On VDTs and PCs, corrections are usually made electronically before the story has been set in type. Nonetheless, some corrections still need to be pasted up. Those papers without VDTs will need to do corrections on the final paste-up.

Corrections should always be at least one line (Fig. 15–12). Three or four lines are better yet. The larger the patch, the less chance it will fall off or slip out of place before the page negative is made. Just place the waxed correction directly on top of the old lines. Occasionally a print shop will use cellophane tape—the "invisible" kind, not the glossy kind—to help hold down corrections. But many printers do not like this practice because the tape distorts the light during the page negative process, making the type beneath the tape appear lighter and thinner than type not covered.

Corrections are often set line by line in one block of type that needs to be cut apart and placed in the proper position. By following the order of the corrections and the proofreader's marks in the margin, the paste-up person can place correc-

Figure 15–12. Corrections should always be at least one line—three or four are better—of type, never just a word or letter. Modern typesetting systems should eliminate most correction paste-up. (Photo by Mike Penn)

tions where they belong. Carefully cut out the line or lines to be corrected with a razor-blade knife (scissors are too clumsy). A good technique is to attach one edge of the waxed correction on the blade of the knife and position the opposite edge on the galley. Then, after lightly placing down the knife-blade side, move the point of the blade up or down until the correction is lined up properly.

Tape may have to be used for emergency corrections. If the rare one-letter correction has to be made by swiping a letter from last issue's flat, put the letter on a piece of cellophane tape, and then line the tape up in the proper position. You'll never get wax to hold one letter. Better yet, don't get stuck in this situation.

Computer Production

Many newspaper staffs have moved to personal computers, and especially the Macintosh computer, as production tools. With these, type can be set; charts, graphs, and maps can be created; and entire pages can be put together totally within the computer memory. Then a complete (or nearly complete) page can be run out on a laser printer. The laser printer does not have the reproduction quality of the phototypesetting machines, but for general newspaper use, the 300-dots-per-inch printing is perfectly acceptable.

With the originator of the typeset copy—the reporter or editor—now able to, in essence, set type, proofread type, and even perform electronic paste-up, the work-flow process is dramatically different from that in the regular newsroom. It is critical not to bog down the "creative personnel" with production headaches. You can't ask editors to perform all the functions they did before and now pick up the paste-up (through electronic page composition programs) as well.

Going to a PC-based production system does not necessarily take less time, and, in fact, in the beginning it will probably take more time. The learning curve for these programs is simply not as steep as the companies and some of the magazines would like to have you believe. Also, you have to very jealously protect your editors' time and not let them become overwhelmed. Helping production—not doing all the production—is a better approach.

In general, the job of final production of the newspaper should be handled as before. Stories should be written, edited, and stored in the computer in a certain place when they are ready for production. Editors who try to do a little editing, a little headline writing, a little paginating, and a little proofreading all at the same time will hit a high frustration level quickly. If you are asking editors or other desk persons to do the pagination, you must free them from other tasks at that point, and you must have deadlines set so that most of the work is in and edited.

As an example, here is how I would suggest setting up a copy-flow/production system for a small Macintosh newsroom. This would hold whether you have a network or not.

The reporters write their stories and turn them in to a folder on the editor's computer called "To Be Edited" or something similar. Claris Corp. has a public domain software program called *Public Folder* (available to users of Claris products). It allows files to be shared from computer to computer without having to purchase expensive network software. After the editor reads the story and makes corrections and cuts, it should be saved under a new name in a different folder. From this folder, depending on your copy flow, the story can get a second read and/or a headline, or it can be ready for production at that point. This way, the original stories are still in one folder, and the edited work is passed on from folder to folder throughout the production process. To find stories that are "ready," you merely have to look in the proper folder, not look down the list to find the latest "Saved" times and dates for the edited versions.

It would probably be easier to organize the stories topically (for example, News, Features, Sports, Briefs, Calendar, and so on) or by pages, prior to calling them into the pagination program. Because you access one folder at a time from these programs, just entering one folder for each story you need for a particular page will speed up the process immensely.

Don't use this production time as creative time. Using the headline count system, write headlines ahead of time whenever you can. The heads can be adjusted easily to fit by almost anyone on the staff, but you really can't ask just any staffer to write heads while doing the pagination. Also, it takes longer this way.

In addition, be sure to have a page dummy for each page. Too many staffs have suffered by trying to put the page together in real time while looking at the computer screen. This is not the time to be thinking about placement; this is the time to be placing and adjusting where necessary. The page layout people are now free from getting bogged down at this important, last-minute stage of the process. Using dummies also allows more staffers to participate in production. Following a dummy is not a creative task, but this simple "paste-up" gives them an opportunity to learn the program, see how dummying works, and even learn a bit about effective layouts.

For certain pages, ignore the pagination programs altogether. Some of the inside pages have so little editorial content that it would probably be a better use of personnel to simply run out galleys of type and separate headlines and hand paste-up, just like in the "old days." The editors can then concentrate on the important pages—the front, section fronts, the editorial page—leaving the less important ones to other staff members. This also avoids the bottleneck of forcing all pages to go through certain desks or computers to be put together. One bad page slows everything, and the whole paper might be delayed more than necessary.

The last step, as always, is proofing. Look at the paste-ups in hard-copy form one last time before allowing them to go to the printer. Someone who was not intimately involved with the pages during production should do the proofing, if possible. It is always good to bring fresh eyes to this important last task of production.

The production process, whether by hand or electronically, is characterized by organization, careful handling of materials, neatness, and attention to detail. If the newsroom has done its job by producing effective page layouts and by getting in all stories and photos on time, then production time can be spent working carefully on the pages rather than waiting for last-minute work. Production is a critical part of the publishing process because if a paper *looks* sloppy, if headlines are crooked and photos are misidentified by switched cutlines, then no matter how good the content of the paper, readers will not have confidence in the staff. Don't send out your paper sloppily put together.

— Suggested Projects

Vocabulary

air out
camera-ready
cut
dropped out
duotone
fit
flat
four-color process
jump
overset
page editor
PMT
registration marks
strip in
velox
widow

1. Compare the labor costs of pasting up your own paper (or creating it all yourself with PCs) with the charge a print shop would make for the same thing. How much money do you save every issue if you buy a few items for your newsroom and do the work yourself? If you do your own paste-up, keep these figures handy when administrators start looking at your budget.

2. Either visit the back shop of a local newspaper or invite a paste-up person to visit your facility and share a few tips. Most professionals can paste up a full-size newspaper page in 20 minutes, a task that may take students several hours. How do they do it? Could you purchase any tools or materials that would make your job quicker, easier, and better?

3. Compare your paste-up area with the composition room at a local newspaper or other printing facility. Can you make more efficient use of space and storage areas? Can the staff use spare storage rooms or small classrooms as a permanent paste-up facility, not to be disturbed by other classes using the room? Do a general efficiency study of your entire production process, from deadlines to editing, proofing, paste-up, and printing.

advertising 16

Many journalists forget that newspapers are profit-making businesses. Owners of newspapers expect to see a profit from their investment in building space, equipment, and salaries. Journalists also sometimes forget that their salaries are paid by those same ads that take up news-hole space. Without advertising neither the owners nor the journalists are in business.

The first paid advertising in an American newspaper was from a man who advertised for two lost anvils in the *Boston News-Letter* on April 25, 1704. But advertising didn't play an important part in American newspapers until the penny press era of the 1830s. Merchants became more and more interested in catching the attention—and the money—of the new urban middle-class reader.

Today, advertising in newspapers is divided between display ads—both local and national—and classified ads. *Display ads* (Fig. 16–1) are those that appear throughout the newspaper interspersed with editorial material. Businesses trying to sell specific items use display ads. These ads are boxed off from editorial material and include large type, the name of the business, and often a drawing or photo.

The difference between a local display ad and a national one has to do more with the source of ad payment than the look of the ad. For example, General Motors may decide to advertise Chevrolet Caprices in a newspaper. The ad only advertises the worth of a Caprice, not necessarily the dealer where you can buy

Figure 16–1. Display advertising appears throughout the paper. (From *The Daily Illini,* Illini Publishing Company, Champaign, IL)

217

one. A local ad may also try to sell a reader a Caprice, but it will advertise Downtown Chevrolet, on Fourth Street.

Sometimes a national ad may also include a tie-in with one or many local outlets. In a *co-op ad* the national firm and local outlets cooperate in buying space in the paper. Co-op ads, a good way for local merchants to save money, will be discussed in greater detail later in the chapter.

Classified ads (Fig. 16–2) are usually set in small type and grouped together in their own section. This section may also carry display ads. For instance, under "Autos" where private individuals are trying to sell their cars to other individuals,

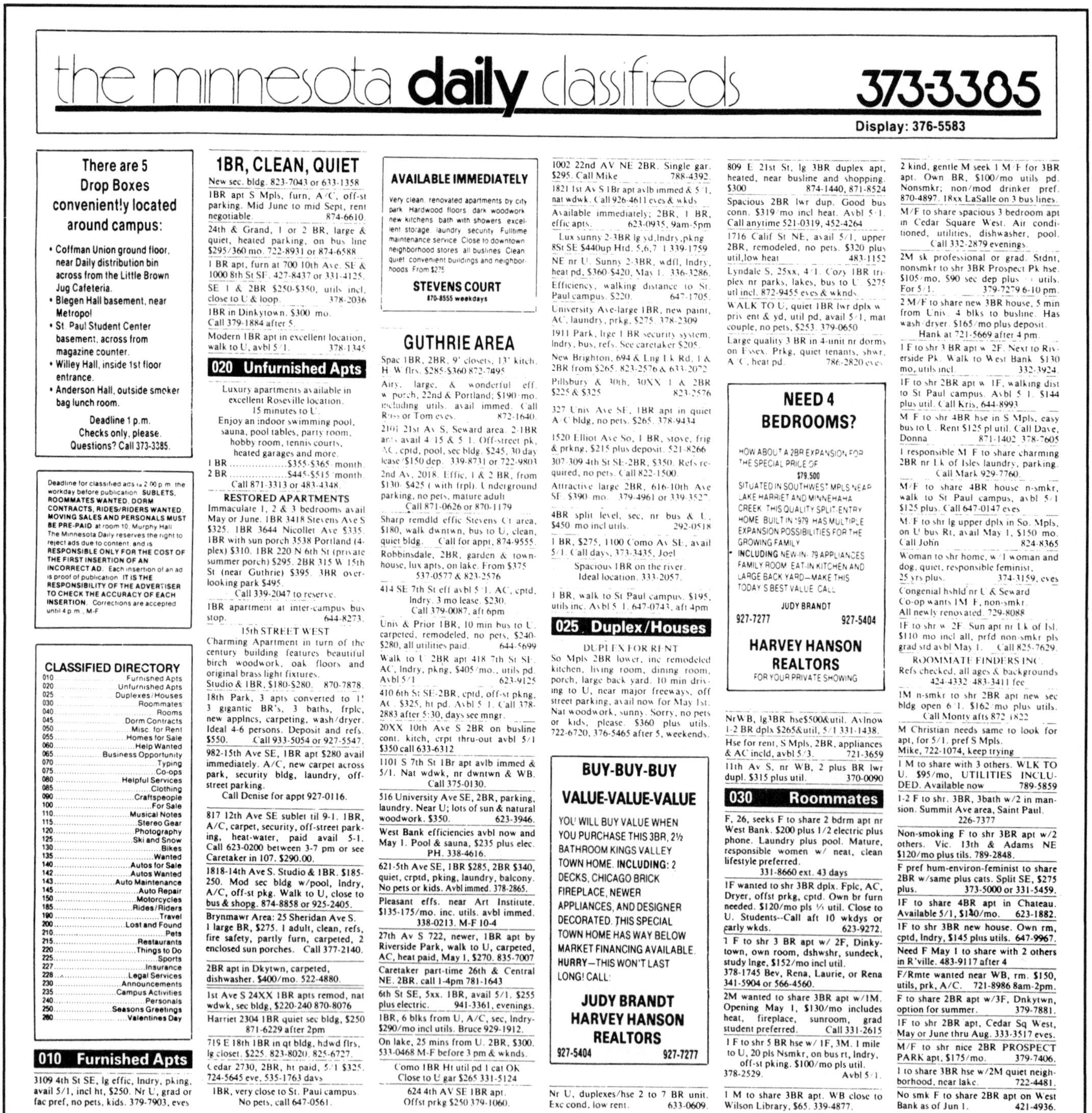

the minnesota **daily** classifieds 373-3385
Display: 376-5583

There are 5 Drop Boxes conveniently located around campus:

- Coffman Union ground floor, near Daily distribution bin across from the Little Brown Jug Cafeteria.
- Blegen Hall basement, near Metropol
- St. Paul Student Center basement, across from magazine counter.
- Willey Hall, inside 1st floor entrance.
- Anderson Hall, outside smoker bag lunch room.

Deadline 1 p.m.
Checks only, please.
Questions? Call 373-3385.

Deadline for classified ads is 2:00 p.m. the workday before publication. SUBLETS, ROOMMATES WANTED, DORM CONTRACTS, RIDES/RIDERS WANTED, MOVING SALES AND PERSONALS MUST BE PRE-PAID at room 10, Murphy Hall. The Minnesota Daily reserves the right to reject ads due to content, and is RESPONSIBLE ONLY FOR THE COST OF THE FIRST INSERTION OF AN INCORRECT AD. Each insertion of an ad is proof of publication. IT IS THE RESPONSIBILITY OF THE ADVERTISER TO CHECK THE ACCURACY OF EACH INSERTION. Corrections are accepted until 4 p.m., M-F

CLASSIFIED DIRECTORY

010	Furnished Apts
020	Unfurnished Apts
025	Duplexes/Houses
030	Roommates
040	Rooms
045	Dorm Contracts
050	Misc. for Rent
055	Homes for Sale
060	Help Wanted
065	Business Opportunity
070	Typing
075	Co-ops
080	Helpful Services
085	Clothing
090	Craftspeople
100	For Sale
110	Musical Notes
115	Stereo Gear
120	Photography
125	Ski and Snow
130	Bikes
135	Wanted
140	Autos for Sale
142	Autos Wanted
143	Auto Maintenance
145	Auto Repair
150	Motorcycles
185	Rides/Riders
190	Travel
200	Lost and Found
210	Pets
215	Restaurants
220	Things to Do
225	Sports
227	Insurance
228	Legal Services
230	Announcements
235	Campus Activities
240	Personals
250	Seasons Greetings
260	Valentines Day

010 Furnished Apts

3109 4th St SE, lg effic, lndry, pking, avail 5/1, incl ht, $250. Nr U, grad or fac pref, no pets, kids. 379-7903, eves

1BR, CLEAN, QUIET
New sec. bldg. 823-7043 or 633-1358

1BR apt S Mpls, furn, A/C, off-st parking. Mid June to mid Sept, rent negotiable. 874-6610.

24th & Grand, 1 or 2 BR, large & quiet, heated parking, on bus line $295/360 mo. 722-8931 or 874-6588

1 BR apt, furn at 700 10th Ave. SE & 1000 8th St SE. 427-8437 or 331-4125.

SE 1 & 2BR $250-$350, utils incl, close to U & loop. 378-2036

1BR in Dinkytown. $300 mo. Call 379-1884 after 5.

Modern 1BR apt in excellent location, walk to U, avbl 5/1. 378-1345

020 Unfurnished Apts

Luxury apartments available in excellent Roseville location. 15 minutes to U. Enjoy an indoor swimming pool, sauna, pool tables, party room, hobby room, tennis courts, heated garages and more.
1 BR ....$355-$365/month.
2 BR ....$445-$515/month.
Call 871-3313 or 483-4348.

RESTORED APARTMENTS
Immaculate 1, 2 & 3 bedrooms avail May or June. 1BR 3418 Stevens Ave S $325. 1BR 3644 Nicollet Ave $335. 1BR with sun porch 3538 Portland (4-plex) $310. 1BR 220 N 6th St (private summer porch) $295. 2BR 315 W 15th St (near Guthrie) $395. 3BR overlooking park $495.
Call 339-2047 to reserve.

1BR apartment at inter-campus bus stop. 644-8273.

15th STREET WEST
Charming Apartment in turn of the century building features beautiful birch woodwork, oak floors and original brass light fixtures.
Studio & 1BR, $180-$280. 870-7878.

18th Park, 3 apts converted to 1! 3 gigantic BR's, 3 baths, frplc, new applncs, carpeting, wash/dryer. Ideal 4-6 persons. Deposit and refs. $550. Call 933-5054 or 927-5547.

982-15th Ave SE, 1BR apt $280 avail immediately. A/C, new carpet across park, security bldg, laundry, off-street parking.
Call Denise for appt 927-0116.

817 12th Ave SE sublet til 9-1. 1BR, A/C, carpet, security, off-street parking, heat-water, paid avail 5-1. Call 623-0200 between 3-7 pm or see Caretaker in 107. $290.00.

1818-14th Ave S. Studio & 1BR. $185-250. Mod sec bldg w/pool, lndry, A/C, off-st pkg. Walk to U, close to bus & shopg. 874-8858 or 925-2405.

Brynmawr Area: 25 Sheridan Ave S. 1 large BR, $275. 1 adult, clean, refs, fire safety, partly furn, carpeted, 2 enclosed sun porches. Call 377-2140.

2BR apt in Dkytwn, carpeted, dishwasher. $400/mo. 522-4880.

1st Ave S 24XX 1BR apts remod, nat wdwk, sec bldg, $220-240 870-8076

Harriet 2304 1BR quiet sec bldg, $250 871-6229 after 2pm

719 E 18th 1BR in qt bldg, hdwd flrs, lg closet. $225. 823-8020. 825-6727.

Cedar 2730, 2BR, ht paid, 5/1 $325. 724-5645 eve, 535-1763 days

1BR, very close to St. Paul campus. No pets, call 647-0561.

AVAILABLE IMMEDIATELY
Very clean, renovated apartments by city park. Hardwood floors, dark woodwork, new kitchens, bath with showers, excellent storage, laundry, security. Fulltime maintenance service. Close to downtown neighborhood stores, all buslines. Clean, quiet, convenient buildings and neighborhoods. From $275
STEVENS COURT
870-8555 weekdays

GUTHRIE AREA
Spac 1BR, 2BR, 9' closets, 13' kitch. H/W flrs. $285-$360 872-7495

Airy, large, & wonderful eff. w/porch, 22nd & Portland; $190/mo. including utils. avail immed. Call Russ or Tom eves. 872-1640.

2101 21st Av S, Seward area. 2-1BR apts avail 4/15 & 5/1. Off-street pk, AC, cptd, pool, sec bldg. $245, 30 day lease/$150 dep. 339-8731 or 722-9803

2nd Av, 2018. Effic, 1 & 2 BR, from $130-$425 (with frpl). Underground parking, no pets, mature adult
Call 871-0626 or 870-1179

Sharp remdld effic Stevens Ct area, $180, walk dwntwn, bus to U, clean, quiet bldg. Call for appt, 874-9555.

Robbinsdale, 2BR, garden & townhouse, lux apts, on lake. From $375
537-0577 & 823-2576

414 SE 7th St eff avbl 5/1. AC, cptd, lndry. 3 mo lease. $230.
Call 379-0087, aft 6pm

Univ & Prior 1BR, 10 min bus to U, carpeted, remodeled, no pets, $240-$280, all utilities paid. 644-5699

Walk to U 2BR apt 418 7th St SE. AC, lndry, pkng, $405/mo., utils pd. Avbl 5/1 623-9125

410 6th St SE-2BR, cptd, off-st pkng, AC. $325, ht pd. Avbl 5/1. Call 378-2883 after 5:30, days see mngr.

20XX 10th Ave S 2BR on busline cont. kitch, crpt thru-out avbl 5/1 $350 call 633-6312

1101 S 7th St 1Br apt avlb immed & 5/1. Nat wdwk, nr dwntwn & WB. Call 375-0130.

516 University Ave SE, 2BR, parking, laundry. Near U; lots of sun & natural woodwork. $350. 623-3946.

West Bank efficiencies avbl now and May 1. Pool & sauna, $235 plus elec. PH. 338-4616.

621-5th Ave SE, 1BR $285, 2BR $340, quiet, crptd, pking, laundry, balcony. No pets or kids. Avbl immed. 378-2865.

Pleasant effs. near Art Institute. $135-175/mo. inc. utils. avbl immed. 338-0213. M-F 10-4

27th Av S 722, newer, 1BR apt by Riverside Park, walk to U, carpeted, AC, heat paid, May 1, $270. 835-7007

Caretaker part-time 26th & Central NE. 2BR. call 1-4pm 781-1643

6th St SE, 5xx. 1BR, avail 5/1. $255 plus electric. 941-3361, evenings.

1BR, 6 blks from U, A/C, sec, lndry-$290/mo incl utils. Bruce 929-1912.

On lake, 25 mins from U. 2BR, $300. 533-0468 M-F before 3 pm & wknds.

Como 1BR Ht util pd 1 cat OK
Close to U gar $265 331-5124

624 4th AV SE 1BR apt.
Offst prkg $250 379-1060.

1002 22nd AV NE 2BR. Single gar. $295. Call Mike 788-4392.

1821 1st Av S 1Br apt avlb immed & 5/1, nat wdwk. Call 926-4611 eves & wkds

Available immediately; 2BR, 1 BR, effic apts. 623-0935, 9am-5pm

Lux sunny 2-3BR lg yd, lndry, pkng 8St SE $440up Htd. 5,6,7/1 339-1759

NE nr U. Sunny 2-3BR, wdfl, lndry, heat pd, $360-$420, May 1. 336-3286.

Efficiency, walking distance to St. Paul campus. $220. 647-1705.

University Ave-large 1BR, new paint, AC, laundry, prkg, $275. 378-2309

1911 Park, lrge 1 BR security system, lndry, bus, refs. See caretaker $205.

New Brighton, 694 & Lng Lk Rd. 1 & 2BR from $265. 823-2576 & 633-2072

Pillsbury & 30th, 30XX 1 & 2BR $225 & $325 823-2576

327 Univ Ave SE, 1BR apt in quiet A/C bldg, no pets. $265. 378-9434

1520 Elliot Ave So, 1 BR, stove, frig & prkng, $215 plus deposit. 521-8266

307-309 4th St SE-2BR, $350. Refs required, no pets. Call 822-1500.

Attractive large 2BR, 616-10th Ave SE. $390/mo. 379-4961 or 339-3527.

4BR split level, sec, nr bus & U, $450/mo incl utils. 292-0518

1 BR, $275, 1100 Como Av SE, avail 5/1. Call days, 373-3435, Joel

Spacious 1BR on the river.
Ideal location. 333-2057.

1 BR, walk to St Paul campus. $195, utils inc. Avbl 5/1. 647-0743, aft 4pm

025 Duplex/Houses

DUPLEX FOR RENT
So Mpls 2BR lower, inc remodeled kitchen, living room, dining room, porch, large back yard. 10 min driving to U, near major freeways, off street parking, avail now for May 1st. Nat woodwork, sunny. Sorry, no pets or kids, please. $360 plus utils. 722-6720, 376-5465 after 5, weekends.

BUY-BUY-BUY
VALUE-VALUE-VALUE
YOU WILL BUY VALUE WHEN YOU PURCHASE THIS 3BR, 2½ BATHROOM KINGS VALLEY TOWN HOME. INCLUDING: 2 DECKS, CHICAGO BRICK FIREPLACE, NEWER APPLIANCES, AND DESIGNER DECORATED. THIS SPECIAL TOWN HOME HAS WAY BELOW MARKET FINANCING AVAILABLE. HURRY—THIS WON'T LAST LONG! CALL:
JUDY BRANDT
HARVEY HANSON
REALTORS
927-5404 927-7277

Nr U, duplexes/hse 2 to 7 BR unit. Exc cond, low rent. 633-0609.

809 E 21st St, lg 3BR duplex apt, heated, near busline and shopping. $300 874-1440, 871-8524

Spacious 2BR lwr dup. Good bus conn. $319/mo incl heat. Avbl 5/1. Call anytime 521-0319, 452-4264

1716 Calif St NE, avail 5/1, upper 2BR, remodeled, no pets. $320 plus util, low heat 483-1152

Lyndale S, 25xx, 4/1. Cozy 1BR triplex nr parks, lakes, bus to U. $275 utl incl. 872-9455 eves & wknds.

WALK TO U, quiet 1BR lwr dplx w/priv ent & yd, util pd, avail 5/1, mat couple, no pets, $253. 379-0650

Large quality 3 BR in 4-unit nr dorms on Essex. Prkg, quiet tenants, shwr, A/C, heat pd. 786-2820 eves

NEED 4 BEDROOMS?
HOW ABOUT A 2BR EXPANSION FOR THE SPECIAL PRICE OF
$79,500
SITUATED IN SOUTHWEST MPLS NEAR LAKE HARRIET AND MINNEHAHA CREEK. THIS QUALITY SPLIT-ENTRY HOME BUILT IN 1979 HAS MULTIPLE EXPANSION POSSIBILITIES FOR THE GROWING FAMILY
- INCLUDING NEW-IN-'79 APPLIANCES FAMILY ROOM, EAT-IN KITCHEN AND LARGE BACK YARD—MAKE THIS TODAY'S BEST VALUE. CALL

JUDY BRANDT
927-7277 927-5404
HARVEY HANSON
REALTORS
FOR YOUR PRIVATE SHOWING

NrWB, lg3BR hse$500&util. Avlnow 1-2 BR dplx $265&util, 5/1 331-1438.

Hse for rent, S Mpls, 2BR, appliances & AC incld, avbl 5/3. 721-3659

11th Av S, nr WB, 2 plus BR lwr dupl. $315 plus util. 370-0090

030 Roommates

F, 26, seeks F to share 2 bdrm apt nr West Bank. $200 plus 1/2 electric plus phone. Laundry plus pool. Mature, responsible women w/ neat, clean lifestyle preferred.
331-8660 ext. 43 days

1F wanted to shr 3BR dplx. Fplc, AC, Dryer, offst prkg, cptd. Own br furn needed. $120/mo pls ⅓ util. Close to U. Students--Call aft 10 wkdys or early wkds. 623-9272.

1 F to shr 3 BR apt w/ 2F, Dinkytown, own room, dshwshr, sundeck, study lnge, $152/mo incl util.
378-1745 Bev, Rena, Laurie, or Rena 341-5904 or 566-4560.

2M wanted to share 3BR apt w/1M. Opening May 1, $130/mo includes heat, fireplace, sunroom, grad student preferred. Call 331-2615

1 F to shr 5 BR hse w/ 1F, 3M. 1 mile to U, 20 pls Nsmkr, on bus rt, lndry, off-st pking. $100/mo pls util.
378-2529. Avbl 5/1.

1 M to share 3BR apt. WB close to Wilson Library, $65. 339-4877.

2 kind, gentle M seek 1 M/F for 3BR apt. Own BR, $100/mo utils pd. Nonsmkr; non/mod drinker pref. 870-4897. 18xx LaSalle on 3 bus lines.

M/F to share spacious 3 bedroom apt in Cedar Square West. Air conditioned, utilities, dishwasher, pool.
Call 332-2879 evenings.

2M sk professional or grad. Stdnt, nonsmkr to shr 3BR Prospect Pk hse. $105/mo, $90 sec dep plus utils. For 5/1. 379-7279 6-10 pm.

2 M/F to share new 3BR house, 5 min from Univ. 4 blks to busline. Has wash/dryer. $165/mo plus deposit.
Hank at 721-5669 after 4 pm.

1 F to shr 3 BR apt w/2F. Next to Riverside Pk. Walk to West Bank. $130 mo, utils incl. 332-3924.

1F to shr 2BR apt w/1F, walking dist to St Paul campus. Avbl 5/1. $144 plus util. Call Kris, 644-8993

M/F to shr 4BR hse in S Mpls, easy bus to U. Rent $125 pl util. Call Dave, Donna 871-1402 378-7605

1 responsible M/F to share charming 2BR nr Lk of Isles laundry, parking.
Call Mark 929-7760.

M/F to share 4BR house n-smkr, walk to St Paul campus, avbl 5/1 $125 plus. Call 647-0147 eves

M/F to shr lg upper dplx in So. Mpls, on U bus Rt, avail May 1, $150/mo. Call John 824-8365

Woman to shr home, w/1 woman and dog, quiet, responsible feminist, 25 yrs plus. 374-3159, eves

Congenial hshld nr U & Seward Co-op wants 1M/F, non-smkr. All newly renovated. 729-8088

1F to shr w/2F. Sun apt nr Lk of Isl. $110 mo incl all, prfd non-smkr pls grad std avbl May 1. Call 825-7629.

ROOMMATE FINDERS INC.
Refs checked, all ages & backgrounds
424-4332 483-3411 fee

1M n-smkr to shr 2BR apt new sec bldg open 6/1. $162/mo plus utils.
Call Monty afts 872-1822

M Christian needs same to look for apt, for 5/1. pref S Mpls.
Mike, 722-1074, keep trying

1 M to share with 3 others. WLK TO U. $95/mo, UTILITIES INCLUDED. Available now 789-5859

1-2 F to shr. 3BR, 3bath w/2 in mansion. Summit Ave area, Saint Paul.
226-7377

Non-smoking F to shr 3BR apt w/2 others. Vic. 13th & Adams NE $120/mo plus tils. 789-2848.

F pref hum-environ-feminist to share 2BR w/same plus cats. Split SE, $275 plus. 373-5000 or 331-5459.

1F to share 4BR apt in Chateau. Available 5/1, $140/mo. 623-1882.

1F to shr 3BR new house. Own rm, cptd, lndry, $145 plus utils. 647-9967.

Need F May 1 to share with 2 others in R'ville. 483-9117 after 4

F/Rmte wanted near WB, rm. $150, utils, prk, A/C. 721-8986 8am-2pm.

F to share 2BR apt w/3F, Dnkytwn, option for summer. 379-7881.

1F to shr 2BR apt, Cedar Sq West, May or June thru Aug. 333-3517 eves.

M/F to shr nice 2BR PROSPECT PARK apt, $175/mo. 379-7406.

1 to share 3BR hse w/2M quiet neighborhood, near lake. 722-4481.

No smk F to share 2BR apt on West Bank as of Jun 1. 421-4936.

Page 17

Figure 16–2. Classified ads usually run together in a section by themselves. Boxed ads ("Need 4 Bedrooms?" on the *right*) are called classified display ads. (From *Minnesota Daily,* University of Minnesota)

a local car company may buy ad space to try to convince buyers to come to its showroom instead.

School Advertising Programs

Advertising programs at school papers vary in size as much as the papers themselves. Large university papers may run many local and national display ads and several pages of classified every day. Some have operating budgets of more than a million dollars and therefore need large ad staffs to match that in advertising revenue.

Even small college newspapers, with operating budgets closer to $1,000, should set up an effective business and advertising program. On small papers the advertising manager can double as the business manager and help the adviser keep track of revenue and expenses.

The first step in setting up an advertising program is to hire or appoint a person to be in charge of the advertising and/or business end of the paper. This person should be selected early, preferably at the end of the prior school year, to allow enough time for the ad manager and the adviser to budget for the following year.

Publication Budget

The budget need not be a complicated one. But it needs to be worked out before the publication schedule can be set and ad rates decided. The ad manager and the adviser should calculate approximate expenses for the year, including printing costs, student salaries, photo supplies, and paste-up supplies. Then they should divide this figure into a per-issue cost.

The same calculations should then be made for income. Add together all expected income—school subsidy, student-government or activities-fees subsidies, advertising income—and figure the approximate income per issue. Use the previous year's ad rates, and average the number of advertising column inches per issue. If the estimated expense and income figures per issue are far apart, either fewer issues have to be published or ad rates have to be raised.

Final decisions on ad rates can be worked out later. A rough working budget gives the ad manager, editor, and adviser an idea of what the publication schedule should be. If a choice has to be made between more but smaller issues versus fewer, thicker issues, the former is the better choice. Publishing as frequently as possible provides more information to the reader.

It is important that the publication schedule be followed to the letter. Careful budget planning can prevent the all-too-common problem of nearing the end of the year without money to publish the last few issues. This situation irritates advertisers, who may have planned major ads in those issues. It also disappoints readers and breaks down staff morale.

Rate Cards

Once the publication schedule is completed, the advertising *rate cards* can be printed. Rate cards specify deadlines, publication dates, ad policies, charges for various sizes and frequencies of ads, and possibly demographic information on readers (Fig. 16–3).

Setting ad rates is a difficult but important task. If the rates are too high, advertisers will not buy space in your paper. If they are too low, the paper may not get the income needed to operate professionally.

Set your rates after carefully studying such competing media as the local daily paper, local shoppers or free weekly papers, and papers from other schools in similar markets. Make sure you also take into account their audiences and their

Summer ids

The summer ids is published Mondays, Wednesdays, and Fridays during both summer school sessions. The circulation averages 7,000, and is free on campus. The format for the summer is a 4 column x 14 inch tabloid size paper. The summer ids reaches over 10,000 students and 3,000 faculty and staff members who reside in the Bloomington area during the summer.

Credit Policy

1. The Daily Student will extend credit (deferred billing privileges) upon request under the following terms and conditions:
   a) A "New Account Application" has been completed and placed on file with the Daily Student Business Office by the advertiser.
   b) The advertiser has an established history of satisfactory credit purchase.
   c) The advertiser keeps his account "current" with the Daily Student.
2. The Daily Student Business Office will handle requests for credit in the following manner:
   a) Upon receipt of a "New Account Application." The Business Office will mail the advertiser a letter acknowledging the application and promising to respond within 30 days. (While the application is being processed, the advertiser will be required to pay cash prior to insertion).
   b) The Daily Student Business Office will evaluate the application based upon credit sources listed by the advertiser and other sources. (At that time, the ids also will ask for the salesperson's subjective judgement of the particular account).
   c) Within 30 days, the Business Office will send the advertiser either an acceptance or rejection of the credit application. If the application has been approved, the Business Office will then provide the advertiser with a detailed explanation of the invoice and ids billing practices. Copies of the letter will be provided to the Advertising Manager and placed on file.

Billing Procedure

1. Provided credit has been established, space used in any calendar month will be billed at the beginning of the following month and is payable at once. Special billing (more than once per month) is subject to a $1 service charge for each special bill.
2. Tearsheets will be provided in limited numbers as proof of advertising run in the ids when requested. The ids reserves the right to charge $.05 per paper for large numbers of tearsheets.
3. Charges appearing on ids invoices shall be considered correct and will constitute an account stated unless written objection is received by the ids within 30 days of the rendering of the invoice.

Advertising Policy

1. **Layout and content** of all advertising submitted for publication is subject to the approval of the ids. The ids reserves the right to revise or reject at its option, any advertisement it deems objectionable.
2. Proof arrangements:
   a) **Copy deadline** for advertisers who want to see a proof copy of their ad before publication 3 working days before publication.
   b) **Errors made by the ids** will be corrected at no charge provided proof copy is submitted to the production dept. by 3 p.m. the day before publication. Between 3 p.m. and 5 p.m. the advertiser will be charged $10.50 per hour ($3 minimum).
   c) **Errors made by the advertiser** may be corrected at a charge $10.50 per hour if submitted before the 3 p.m. deadline ($3 minimum). Between 3 p.m. and 5 p.m. the charge will be $21.00 per hour.
   d) **Ads submitted after the proof deadline** may be proofread by the advertiser in the ids production room subject to the charges explained above.
3. Ad Cancellation provision:
   a) **Advertisers may cancel space reserved** for the regular paper by 10 a.m. the day before publication at no charge. (Ads that have been produced are subject to a production service charge). Between 10 a.m. and 2 p.m. one-half of the space reserved will be charged. Ads cannot be cancelled after 2 p.m.
   b) **For ids publication with special deadlines:** space reservations cancelled by 10 a.m. three working days before publication will be charged at ½ space reserved. After 10 a.m. the full space will be charged.
4. Policy on errors made by the ids:
   a) The ids assumes no responsibility for ad errors beyond the cost of space occupied by the ad in which the error occurred. "Make goods" or "correction" ads will run, when appropriate, before billing adjustments are made.
   b) Billing adjustments or "make good" will be determined based on what percentage an error detracts from the effectiveness of the total advertising message, as determined by the ids publisher.
   c) The advertiser must notify the ids Advertising Manager or Business Manager within 5 days after the error occurs for adjustments or a "make good" ad to be considered.
5. **Page position requests** will be honored when possible but never guaranteed.
6. **All out-of-town and political advertising** is accepted cash-in-advance only.
7. **Political ads** are accepted as Paid Political Advertising, i.e. "Pd. Political Adv. by Committee for John Doe, Jane Doe, Treasurer."

Advertising Policy (cont'd)

8. **Advertisements having the appearance of editorial** material must be identified as "Paid Advertisements" at the top of the ad.
9. **Ads over ½ reverse** (white type on black background) will be charged $60 in addition to cost of ad space.
10. The ids must have a **signed model release** from persons pictured in photos submitted for publication.
11. The ids must have a **signed signature release** from persons whose names are being used in an ad to endorse a product or cause.
12. The ids is not responsible for materials submitted for use in ad production unless given instructions for return delivery within 30 days.
13. The advertiser assigns to the ids all right, title, and interest to all pasteups and original art produced by the ids.

1979-'80 Awards

1979-Society of Professional Journalists, Sigma Delta Chi National Mark of Excellence Award for Best College Daily Newspaper.
1980-The Inland Daily Press Association Honorable Mention for layout and design.
1980-Indiana Collegiate Press Association Newspaper of the Year Award.
1980-Indiana Collegiate Press Association Advertising Newspaper of the Year Award

Affiliations

News Affiliations:
Associated Press (AP)
United Press International (UPI)
Associated College Press
Hoosier State Press Association
Indiana Collegiate Press Assoc.

Business Affiliations:
American Newspaper Publishers Assoc.
Newspaper Advertising Bureau
International Newspaper Adv. Exec.
Inland Daily Press Assoc.
Advertising Checking Bureau
College Newspaper Bus. and Adv. Mgrs.
Western Assoc. of Univ. Pub. and Managers

Publisher, Pat Siddons
Business Manager, Don Cross
Advertising Manager, Matt Danielson
Sales Manager, Gail Rissler

ids

rates and data
effective August 24 1980

Indiana Daily Student
Ernie Pyle Hall
Bloomington, Indiana 4740·
(812) 337-0763

Indiana U. Market Facts:

(Estimates for Fall 1980)
1. Total Students: 31,834
- Men ... 16,421
- Women ... 15,413
- Blacks ... 1,381
- Married ... 4,423
- Foreign ... 1,800
- 56% are 21 or older
- Disposable income: $50 million
- Live on campus: 17,566
- Live off campus: 14,052
- 8,351 car registrations

2. Total Faculty: 1,711
- Men: 1,403
- Women: 323
- Married: 1,197
- Ave. per Household: 3
- Ave. income: $16,500-$22,000

3. Staff: 4,353 (does not include hourly employees)
4. The I.U. Community (37,898 persons)
Comprises 52% of the Bloomington Metropolitan area population.

Market Penetration

The ids' current paid circulation of 15,000 serves the entire Indiana University Community:
- 90.6% Student readership
- 79% Faculty readership
- 60% Staff Readership*

*Source: Beldon Assoc. Market Study. Studies also show that on the average 2.14 persons read each issue of the ids.

Advertiser's Questions:

1. **Question:** When will my ad hit the streets?
Answer: The ids is Bloomington's only morning newspaper with carrier delivery by 7:30 a.m. each morning Monday thru Friday.
2. **Question:** What will my ad look like?
Answer: The ids is printed by offset process which is noted for its clean, crisp photo, art, & copy reproduction. ids account representatives are trained in layout technique and have a complete art service available to help them create ad layouts that sell your product. The ids has won numerous awards for typographical excellence.
3. **Question:** The campus paper at the college I went to was a weekly tabloid that nobody read. How big is the ids and how does it rate editorially?
Answer: The ids averages 19 broadsheet pages Monday thru Friday. It is one of the five largest college papers in the country and is larger than most papers in Indiana. Bill Ward, a writer for "Scholastic Editor" magazine, called the ids "the best all-around college paper in the country." The paper has earned the Associated Collegiate Press "All-American" rating for editorial excellence each of the past nine years.
4. **Question:** Why does the ids have a 6 column format instead of 8 or 9 like most papers?
Answer: Because it's easier to read and more attractive visually. Readership studies have proven that a story with lines 2 ¼" wide can be read much quicker and with less eye strain than the same story with 1 ⅝" lines. This means better readership of the entire paper including advertising. Many other newspapers have switched to the 6 column format in the past ten years including the Louisville Courier-Journal.

Display Rates

Effective August 24, 1980

Reduce ids rates 30% for comparison with 8-column newspaper rates (see mechanical information).

Open rate ... $5.64 per column inch ($.40 per line) (commissionable to recognized agencies)

Cash-in-advance discount rate ... $4.66 per column inch (cash-with-copy necessary if credit hasn't been established)

Contract Discount Rates

(one calendar year minimum contract period)

Contract	Rate	Minimum
1. **Daily****	2.98 per col. inch	**2"** per day
2. **Weekly****	3.35 per col. inch	**4"** per week
3. **Monthly****	3.95 per col. inch	**4"** per month

****Monthly Volume Discount Schedule**
Advertisers on a daily, weekly, or monthly contract may earn a lower rate on all inches run in a month as listed in the schedule below.

Total inches for month	Daily/Weekly Contract	Monthly Contract
31-63	3.20	3.60
64-125	3.10	3.45
126-251	2.95	3.30
252-377	2.85	3.16
378-503	2.75	3.01
503-1008	2.65	2.95
1009 or more	2.60	2.91

4. **Yearly** ... $4.20 per col. inch .... **126"** per year (must run a least one ad each semester)

The advantages of a contract: In addition to the significant reduction in rates, a contract motivates the advertiser to budget advertising dollars and plan advertising strategy in advance which reduces the risk of needless spending and wasted effort.

Your contract is ________________

Color Rates*

Spot and process color are available run-of-paper at the following rates:

1 color and black	$85
2 colors and black	$163
3 colors and black	$239
Process (3 colors and black)	$356

*Color split option: When two advertisers agree to share one or more colors in one day's paper these discount rates are available: one color $55, two colors $101, 3 colors $150, process color $262.

Advantages of color: Readership studies indicate a 40-70% increase in ad readership with the addition of one color. Full (Process) color almost doubles readership.

Insert Rates

(Preprinted inserts, single advertiser only)

Tabloid pages	Contracted Advertisers	Non-contract
2-4	**$30/thou.** (3.0¢ per insert)	**$35/thou.** (3.5¢)
5-8	**$35/thou.** (3.5¢ per insert)	**$40/thou.** (4.0¢)
9-12	**$40/thou.** (4.0¢ per insert)	**$45/thou.** (4.5¢)
13-16	**$45/thou.** (4.5¢ per insert)	**$50/thou.** (5.0¢)
17 or more	**$50/thou.** (5.0¢ per insert)	**$55/thou.** (5.5¢)

Volume Discount: If advertiser runs 12 or more inserts in a year reduce rates above $5 per thousand.

Please Note: (1)Insert service available for non-U.S. mail circulatiion only which is 13,500 copies (2) For inserting less than 13,500 copies: 9,000-13,000 ... add $5/thou., 5,000-8,900 ... add $10/thou. Minimum: 5000 inserts (3) The ids Advertising Manager must receive a sample copy of the proposed insert for review of acceptability, before shipment.

Deadlines

Publication Date	Copy Deadline
Monday	5 p.m. Thursday
Tuesday	5 p.m. Friday
Wednesday	5 p.m. Monday
Thursday	5 p.m. Tuesday
Friday	5 p.m. Wednesday

Proof deadline: three weekdays in advance of publication (i.e. Thursday proof deadline: 5 p.m. Monday).

Insert deadline: three weekdays in advance

Process color deadline: 7 weekdays in advance

Mechanical Information

(6-column format, offset printing, cold type makeup)

8-column paper column width 1 ⅝"

ids column width 2 ¼"

- Depth: 21
- Column widths:
  1 col. 2 ¼"
  2 col. 4 ⅝"
  3 col. 7"
  4 col. 9 ⅜"
  5 col. 11"
  6 col. 14 ¼"

Minimum sizes:
1 column width must be 1 ½ inches deep
2 column width must be 2 inches deep
3 column width must be 3 ½ deep
4 column width must be 5 inches deep
5 column width must be 6 ½ deep
6 column width must be 8 inches deep
- Advertising exceeding 18" in depth will be billed as 21" deep advertisements.
- Double trucks must be at least 8 columns by 16"
- Advertising for a tabloid page exceeding 12" in depth will be billed as 14" deep advertising.

Publication Calendar

(Publication days shaded)

AUGUST 80

S	M	T	W	T	F	S
					1	2
3	4	5	6	7	8	9
10	11	12	13	14	15	16
17	18	19	20	21	22	23
24	25	26	27	28	29	30
31						

SEPTEMBER 80

S	M	T	W	T	F	S
	1	2	3	4	5	6
7	8	9	10	11	12	13
14	15	16	17	18	19	20
21	22	23	24	25	26	27
28	29	30				

OCTOBER 80

S	M	T	W	T	F	S
			1	2	3	4
5	6	7	8	9	10	11
12	13	14	15	16	17	18
19	20	21	22	23	24	25
26	27	28	29	30	31	

NOVEMBER 80

S	M	T	W	T	F	S
						1
2	3	4	5	6	7	8
9	10	11	12	13	14	15
16	17	18	19	20	21	22
23	24	25	26	27	28	29
30						

DECEMBER 80

S	M	T	W	T	F	S
	1	2	3	4	5	6
7	8	9	10	11	12	13
14	15	16	17	18	19	20
21	22	23	24	25	26	27
28	29	30	31			

JANUARY 81

S	M	T	W	T	F	S
				1	2	3
4	5	6	7	8	9	10
11	12	13	14	15	16	17
18	19	20	21	22	23	24
25	26	27	28	29	30	31

FEBRUARY 81

S	M	T	W	T	F	S
1	2	3	4	5	6	7
8	9	10	11	12	13	14
15	16	17	18	19	20	21
22	23	24	25	26	27	28

MARCH 81

S	M	T	W	T	F	S
1	2	3	4	5	6	7
8	9	10	11	12	13	14
15	16	17	18	19	20	21
22	23	24	25	26	27	28
29	30	31				

APRIL 81

S	M	T	W	T	F	S
			1	2	3	4
5	6	7	8	9	10	11
12	13	14	15	16	17	18
19	20	21	22	23	24	25
26	27	28	29	30		

MAY 81

S	M	T	W	T	F	S
					1	2
3	4	5	6	7	8	9
10	11	12	13	14	15	16
17	18	19	20	21	22	23
24	25	26	27	28	29	30
31						

JUNE 81

S	M	T	W	T	F	S
	1	2	3	4	5	6
7	8	9	10	11	12	13
14	15	16	17	18	19	20
21	22	23	24	25	26	27
28	29	30				

JULY 81

S	M	T	W	T	F	S
			1	2	3	4
5	6	7	8	9	10	11
12	13	14	15	16	17	18
19	20	21	22	23	24	25
26	27	28	29	30	31	

Special Publications Schedule

- **Welcome Back Edition** Aug. 24
- **Football Contest** begins Sept. 9
- **Fall Fashion Edition** Sept. 30
- **Special Car Care Supplement** Nov. 5
- **Bahamas Promotion** begins Jan. 19
- **Valentine's Day Special** Feb. 10
- **Apartment Living Guide** March 3
- **Spring Fashion Edition** March 10
- **Little 500 Special Edition** April 21
- **New Student Orienter** June 29

Phone Number 337-0763

Advertising • News • Circulation • Bookkeeping

circulation area. Then, by comparing your newspaper's audience and the market it offers advertisers, you can set your ad rates at a competitive level. See the sidebar to this chapter for more information on setting ad rates.

Display-ad rates are set up differently for local ads and for national ads. Local ads are normally charged by the *column inch*—a space one column wide by one-inch deep. Thus a two-column ad that is five inches deep would consist of 10 column inches. Column-inch rates run on a sliding scale, giving price reductions to businesses that buy very large ads or run smaller ads frequently.

The rate that a one-time advertiser pays for a small ad is called the *open rate*, usually the highest ad rate in the paper. Advertisers usually get a price break below the open rate if the ad is very large, say a half-page or more. Newspapers also offer reduced *contract rates* when a business signs a contract to run a certain number of column inches so many times a month, a semester, or a school year. These rates go down as numbers of column inches rise.

National display-ad rates are usually set up on a per-*line* (14 to an inch) basis. (A 14-line ad would be the same as a one-column-inch ad, that is, one column wide and one inch deep.) National rates are nearly always higher than local column-inch rates because the advertising agencies that land most national ads for newspapers take a percentage from the paper's revenues. Papers should set national ad rates high enough to compensate for agency fees.

Classified-ad rates are charged on a per-line or per-word basis. Because of the high volume of classified ads, the rates should reflect only a slight percentage profit above the cost of setting the ad. A little money made on many ads will result in a good income for the paper. In a student paper, classified rates are generally substantially lower than local professional classified rates, and student use of the space is often heavy.

The publication schedule on the rate card should be clear and easy to read. School holidays, special events, vacation periods, and examination periods should be marked. Advertisers use this schedule to plan their budget. An advertiser may decide today to run an ad in an issue three months from now, so the schedule must be accurate.

The advertiser should also understand the ad policies of your paper. Include important policies in the rate card. If you have a *make-good policy* covering late papers or ad reruns caused by mistakes, get it to the advertiser in writing *before* a problem develops. Remember that advertisers expect something for their money and they expect to be treated professionally. Other policies that you may include are the kinds of ads you do not accept (such as ads for X-rated movies or for professional term-paper-writing), as well as ad deadlines, credit availability, billing procedures, late payment charges, availability of color, and use of inserts in the paper.

Many rate cards also include demographics information about readers (such as age, faculty and staff readership, money spent on fast foods and clothes, and other information that would be pertinent to prospective advertisers (Fig. 16–4). The ad staff can put together a simple demographics sheet from information from the registrar and financial aids offices on campus. More detailed studies can be furnished by professional market research firms. This information is invaluable in showing advertisers how much money your readers have to spend and how to reach them through ads in your paper.

For instance, studies have shown that college students read college newspapers more than they read professional papers. So an advertiser who wants to

Figure 16–3. (*Opposite*) This *IDS* (Indiana University) rate card includes rates, ad size, and a publication calendar. Included on the back are policy and billing information.

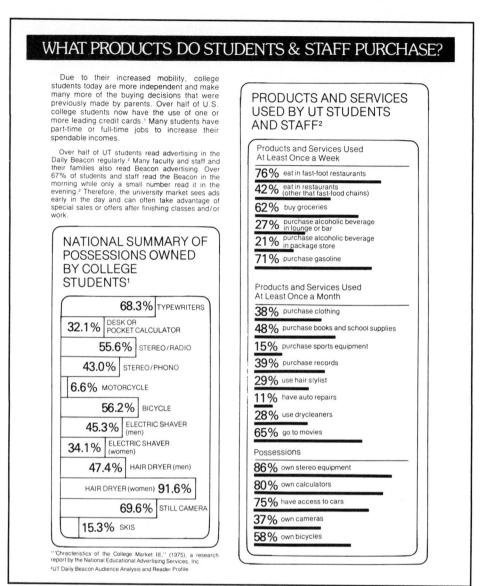

WHAT PRODUCTS DO STUDENTS & STAFF PURCHASE?

Due to their increased mobility, college students today are more independent and make many more of the buying decisions that were previously made by parents. Over half of U.S. college students now have the use of one or more leading credit cards.[1] Many students have part-time or full-time jobs to increase their spendable incomes.

Over half of UT students read advertising in the Daily Beacon regularly.[2] Many faculty and staff and their families also read Beacon advertising. Over 67% of students and staff read the Beacon in the morning while only a small number read it in the evening.[2] Therefore, the university market sees ads early in the day and can often take advantage of special sales or offers after finishing classes and/or work.

NATIONAL SUMMARY OF POSSESSIONS OWNED BY COLLEGE STUDENTS[1]

68.3% TYPEWRITERS
32.1% DESK OR POCKET CALCULATOR
55.6% STEREO/RADIO
43.0% STEREO/PHONO
6.6% MOTORCYCLE
56.2% BICYCLE
45.3% ELECTRIC SHAVER (men)
34.1% ELECTRIC SHAVER (women)
47.4% HAIR DRYER (men)
HAIR DRYER (women) 91.6%
69.6% STILL CAMERA
15.3% SKIS

"Chracteristics of the College Market III," (1975), a research report by the National Educational Advertising Services, Inc.
[2]UT Daily Beacon Audience Analysis and Reader Profile.

PRODUCTS AND SERVICES USED BY UT STUDENTS AND STAFF[2]

Products and Services Used At Least Once a Week
76% eat in fast-foot restaurants
42% eat in restaurants (other that fast-food chains)
62% buy groceries
27% purchase alcoholic beverage in lounge or bar
21% purchase alcoholic beverage in package store
71% purchase gasoline

Products and Services Used At Least Once a Month
38% purchase clothing
48% purchase books and school supplies
15% purchase sports equipment
39% purchase records
29% use hair stylist
11% have auto repairs
28% use drycleaners
65% go to movies

Possessions
86% own stereo equipment
80% own calculators
75% have access to cars
37% own cameras
58% own bicycles

Figure 16–4. This page from the University of Tennessee's *The Daily Beacon* advertising information booklet is a good visual presentation of spending habits of UT students and staff. (From *The Daily Beacon*, University of Tennessee)

focus on the college market would be better off spending money on the college paper, not the local professional paper. Advertisers should be shown these facts.

Other useful general information about the college market: Students spend most of their income—about $250 per month—on themselves; between 85 and 90 percent of college students read their college paper weekly; college students listen to radio less than their noncollege peers; and students trust their student newspaper, which they believe is the most honest medium available to them, more than they trust television.

More current information can be gathered from reference books in the library and from national advertising agency statistical surveys. A national agency, Communications and Advertising Services to Students (CASS), can supply this kind of demographics information (see the appendix).

The rate card and demographics information should be part of a sales kit utilized by every ad rep on the staff. This kit could also include sample copies of the paper that can be left with prospective advertisers, sample ad sizes, examples of special printing effects you can offer, contracts, and business card (see Fig. 16–3).

Displaying all this material in a neat folder or portfolio makes a good impression on prospective clients. Many advertisers wrongly believe that buying an ad in a school paper is a "token," a way of showing community support for the school. A professional approach, including a sales kit, will convince the advertisers that they are definitely getting something in return for their money.

Ad-Staff Organization

An advertising staff of more than one person should have a competent ad manager. The ad manager works with the adviser on the budget as well as on other advertising and business matters throughout the year, such as billing. The ad manager also works with the adviser and editor to set up the publication schedule and plan special issues. The most important duty of the ad manager, however, is to coordinate and supervise the ad staff.

The advertising manager should be in charge of organizing account lists—or lists of businesses to contact—for the ad reps at the beginning of the year. When an ad rep gets a new account, the ad manager adds it to the rep's list. New accounts that come in over the phone are assigned fairly and equally to the ad staff by the ad manager.

The ad manager can organize the account lists by (1) grouping the businesses geographically so that each rep can concentrate on one part of town or (2) giving each rep a cross section of advertisers so that each rep starts out the year with nearly the same expected revenue from advertisers. From then on, each rep should try to add as many new accounts as possible to the list.

Some ad staffs have weekly meetings in which reps report to the manager what contacts they made, what new accounts they brought in, what accounts were canceled and why, and what problems they are encountering in the ad-gathering process. Large ad staffs often utilize forms for new accounts and contacts during the week and require a certain minimum number of the contacts from each rep.

Selling

In many ways ad reps for a college paper have little problem selling ads because local merchants may have ties with the school (as alumni or parents of students) and because the audience for a school newspaper is demographically much narrower than that for a professional newspaper. It is actually easier to sell certain types of ads in school papers than in professional ones because students spend on certain easily defined items, such as clothes, fast food, records, and books. So the ad rep is selling ad space to the merchant for a specific market.

Good organization and preparation are keys to a successful individual sales effort. Ad reps, especially student reps who have only nonclass hours to do their selling, should plan sales trips ahead of time to minimize time lost calling on merchants who are not there and to cut down on travel expenses.

Select an area in which you have several merchants to call on. Phone ahead to be sure that they will indeed be there when you visit. Most merchants appreciate knowing that a salesperson will be coming by.

Then the key becomes preparation. A good ad rep will always have enough materials on hand to give the merchant something with the paper's name on it, such as a business card or rate card. Good preparation for a call also includes research into how much the merchant spent last year in your paper, how much his or her competitors are spending, and what average percentage of gross income is spent by similar businesses on advertising. This information is easily gathered from advertising trade publications and books. Having this kind of information at hand will help you make a good sales presentation. It is not enough to walk in, sell merchants space, and then walk out without helping them fill that space effectively. You should be able to plan an advertising campaign as well as help with specific ad copy and design.

In your approach to selling, remember that buying advertisement space is not *spending* money, it is *investing* money. Your job is to help that merchant plan an advertising investment wisely. Part of a good campaign, for instance, includes not only big ads during the merchant's heavy sales months but also constant advertising in smaller amounts throughout the year. If the largest sales month for widgets is October, then certainly the merchant should advertise heavily during that month. But because someone probably wants to buy a widget every month, some advertising should appear regularly. Research has shown that a message must be repeated regularly to be effective.

If you are courteous and considerate when merchants refuse to buy ad space (as almost all do once in a while), if you are prepared with information and a complete sales kit, and if you are knowledgeable about effective advertising, *you will sell ads*. The college paper is too good a market for many advertisers to pass up.

Co-ops and Coupons

Two good sales tools are co-op ads and coupons. With co-op ads, local merchants are partially reimbursed by national concerns for ads run in local papers. Many companies have co-op funds available, and surprisingly, many local merchants either don't know about them or have forgotten about them. Because it is such a good way for the local merchant to drastically reduce ad costs (the majority of co-op plans are a 50–50 split between retailer and company), the ad rep should be aware of and mention co-op advertising. Co-op ads are good for small businesses because the national company can supply slick and professionally produced ads that help connect a local store with a national brand and logo.

National businesses dealing with clothes (especially designer jeans and other specialty apparel), fast food, cosmetics, CDs and tapes, appliances, automotive accessories, jewelry, and hardware are the ones most likely to have co-op plans. Ad reps should always suggest co-op advertising to local department stores, discount stores, and drug stores.

Coupons can be used effectively in school newspapers. Many merchants use coupons to count the number of people who read the ad. This, however, is not always a valid measure of response. Many persons who see ads may forget to redeem the coupon when they purchase something or may purchase an item after the time limit of the coupon has expired.

Suggesting a trial coupon ad often is enough to push a hesitant advertiser over the line for a sale. Two important points should be remembered about coupon ads: First, the merchant needs to make the coupon offer a real bargain. Giving 10 percent off a minor item will not draw many coupon-holders to the store. Second, the coupon needs to be displayed prominently on the outside edge of a page to give it high visibility and make it easy to cut out. A coupon should not be back to back with a coupon on the next page.

Ad Design

Ads should be simple both in writing and in graphic design. The object is to sell a product, not to impress readers with clever heads, snappy writing, or innovative illustrations. No matter how attractive an ad may be, if it doesn't "sell" the product or service, it is simply not a good ad.

The principles of design mentioned in Chapter 13 apply to ads as well. The three important principles for ads are balance, pleasing proportion, and a point of focus. An ad may have formal or informal balance. Its proportions—that is, the headline, copy block, and illustration(s)—should be pleasing. One item, however, should be the point of focus or emphasis: the place you want the reader to look at first (usually the headline or illustration). Most ads should employ a simple illustration or photo, especially if the store's logo isn't artistically pleasing to the eye and worthy of emphasis.

The rules for copy writing are the same as for good newswriting. Because the best copy block is usually short (readers of ads don't want to read much more than the basic information on a product), make each word count. Ads occasionally may break traditional rules of grammar—such as using sentence fragments—for emphasis, but only occasionally.

Headlines for ads should be short. One line is preferable to two, and two to three. The headline should set the tone or theme for the ad, grab the reader's attention, and sell the product. Writing copy and heads for ads demands hard work and creativity.

Layout

After the ads themselves have been designed, the ad manager must lay out those ads on the pages before delivering the dummies to the editor. This task is not as easy as it may seem. The ad manager must (1) be aware of specific page requests from certain advertisers, (2) place ads for competing businesses on different pages if possible, (3) make sure that coupons are on the outside edge of the page and that they do not back up to another coupon on the next page, (4) try not to overload one section of the paper with ads, (5) follow appropriate guidelines for pyramid- or modular-ad layout, and (6) leave a news hole shaped so that the editor can effectively use design principles in laying out the page.

Many advertisers will request a spot on a right-hand page for their ad because right-hand pages get more eye travel than left-hand pages. More eye travel means better possible sales. But not everyone can have that space. A good ad manager, however, will try to honor all specific requests. Some advertisers request that their ads appear in a specific section, for obvious reasons. Theaters prefer the entertainment section to business pages and sporting goods stores prefer the sports section to features.

The rule in ad layout has been to make sure that every ad on the page touches editorial matter. Many advertisers believe that an ad will get more visual traffic if it is not buried beneath a stack of other ads. Trying to get all ads to touch copy led to the pyramid-shaped ad hole, which chops the page into awkward sections for the page designer to deal with. Most newspapers no longer worry about burying large ads. Research has shown that well-designed ads will get good eye traffic, even when they are buried. So some newspapers have gone to a modular design for the ad hole. Modular design (Fig. 16–5) places all the ads into a rectangle, leaving another rectangle for the page designer. This system works more easily if the paper has adopted *Standard Advertising Units* (SAUs). SAUs are standardized ad sizes that may eventually be adopted by a majority of newspapers (Fig. 16–6).

The trick in laying out ads on a page, whatever the shape, is to place a large ad in the lower right corner. Because of its large size, its visual weight will draw the reader's eye, even if the ad is buried beneath other ads.

Newspaper designer Michael Keegan believes that the ad itself, and not the placement, should draw the reader's eye. "I think it's an old wives' tale about sticking an ad next to copy," he said.

When a page cannot be laid out in modules, the ad manager should try to leave as few steps as possible on the pyramid. The steps should be at least four inches deep so the designer can use them as break-off points for story rectangles (Fig. 16–7).

Figure 16–5. Modular ad holes can be used either horizontally or vertically in tabloid- or magazine-sized papers. Full-sized papers rarely use vertical ad modules. (From *The Daily Illini,* Illini Publishing Company, Champaign, IL)

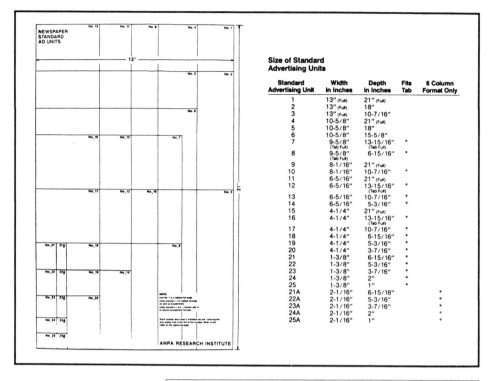

Size of Standard Advertising Units

Standard Advertising Unit	Width in Inches	Depth in Inches	Fits Tab	6 Column Format Only
1	13" (Full)	21" (Full)		
2	13" (Full)	18"		
3	13" (Full)	10-7/16"		
4	10-5/8"	21" (Full)		
5	10-5/8"	18"		
6	10-5/8"	15-5/8"		
7	9-5/8" (Tab Full)	13-15/16" (Tab Full)	°	
8	9-5/8" (Tab Full)	6-15/16"	°	
9	8-1/16"	21" (Full)		
10	8-1/16"	10-7/16"	°	
11	6-5/16"	21" (Full)		
12	6-5/16"	13-15/16" (Tab Full)	°	
13	6-5/16"	10-7/16"	°	
14	6-5/16"	5-3/16"	°	
15	4-1/4"	21" (Full)		
16	4-1/4"	13-15/16" (Tab Full)	°	
17	4-1/4"	10-7/16"	°	
18	4-1/4"	6-15/16"	°	
19	4-1/4"	5-3/16"	°	
20	4-1/4"	3-7/16"	°	
21	1-3/8"	6-15/16"	°	
22	1-3/8"	5-3/16"	°	
23	1-3/8"	3-7/16"	°	
24	1-3/8"	2"	°	
25	1-3/8"	1"	°	
21A	2-1/16"	6-15/16"		°
22A	2-1/16"	5-3/16"		°
23A	2-1/16"	3-7/16"		°
24A	2-1/16"	2"		°
25A	2-1/16"	1"		°

Figure 16–6. SAUs are gaining popularity with professional papers. Student papers would do well to adopt these standard sizes.

Figure 16–7. Even if the ads are not laid out in modules, a clever page designer can create modules by using ad steps as breaks on the page. The ads must be laid out in steps at least four inches deep so the designer can do this.

STORY MODULE

STORY MODULE   AD

STORY MODULE   AD

AD

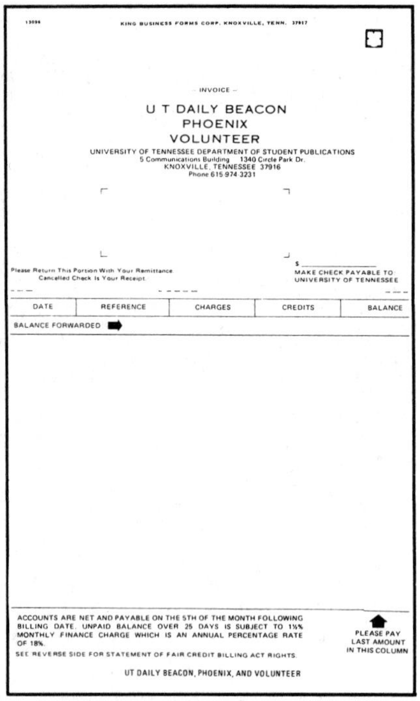

13098 KING BUSINESS FORMS CORP. KNOXVILLE, TENN. 37917

– INVOICE –

U T DAILY BEACON
PHOENIX
VOLUNTEER

UNIVERSITY OF TENNESSEE DEPARTMENT OF STUDENT PUBLICATIONS
5 Communications Building 1340 Circle Park Dr.
KNOXVILLE, TENNESSEE 37916
Phone 615 974 3231

Please Return This Portion With Your Remittance.
Cancelled Check Is Your Receipt.

$ ______
MAKE CHECK PAYABLE TO:
UNIVERSITY OF TENNESSEE

DATE	REFERENCE	CHARGES	CREDITS	BALANCE
BALANCE FORWARDED				

ACCOUNTS ARE NET AND PAYABLE ON THE 5TH OF THE MONTH FOLLOWING BILLING DATE. UNPAID BALANCE OVER 25 DAYS IS SUBJECT TO 1½% MONTHLY FINANCE CHARGE WHICH IS AN ANNUAL PERCENTAGE RATE OF 18%.

SEE REVERSE SIDE FOR STATEMENT OF FAIR CREDIT BILLING ACT RIGHTS.

PLEASE PAY LAST AMOUNT IN THIS COLUMN

UT DAILY BEACON, PHOENIX, AND VOLUNTEER

Figure 16–8. A bill should be easy to read and should include policies. This bill from *The Daily Beacon* also includes a summary of the federal Fair Billing Act on the back side. (From *The Daily Beacon,* University of Tennessee)

Billing and Collection

Selling ads will do the paper no good if the money cannot be collected from advertisers. Billing should be done regularly and professionally, according to rules and procedures agreed upon by the newspaper and the advertiser. These policies are usually explained in the rate card or contract.

Billing for ads is normally done once a month or sometimes after every issue of semi-monthly papers. A bill includes the actual invoice (Fig. 16–8), which is made out in duplicate or triplicate (one copy for office records), and a *tear sheet* (the actual page the ad appeared on). The tear sheet verifies that the ad was published. Advertisers who run co-op ads require extra copies of both invoice and tear sheet to send on to the national company. One of the main reasons for folios on inside pages is to date tear sheets and provide proof to advertisers that ads did indeed run on the dates requested.

Many school papers offer a discount to advertisers who pay in advance. A cash-with-copy discount of 5 percent, for instance, should interest enough advertisers to save the paper billing time. A cash-with-copy rule is also recommended for out-of-town advertisers or for advertisers who have not established credit with your paper. Limiting credit only to local merchants who have done business with you minimizes possible collection problems later.

The ad contract should specify the paper's procedure for past-due accounts and include information on any additional billing penalties and collection agency policy. Many school papers specify that they will *always* use a collection agency, no matter how small the amount owed, to discourage foot-dragging by slow-paying businesses. A common penalty is 1½ percent per month (or 18 percent per year) of the outstanding balance, charged after the account is 60 days past due.

Ad reps should help collect money from past-due accounts. After the ad manager notifies an account that it is 45 days or so past due, the rep should stop by and try to get complete payment on the spot. The rep should not be paid a commission for unpaid ads.

Commissions

On papers with small budgets, advertising reps may get only credit in a newspaper course as compensation. On most papers, however, ad reps are paid a commission on the ads they sell. The commission may be paid in many different ways. A flat commission of 15 percent, and sometimes a per-diem or per-publication amount for expenses, is a common rate. Many large newspapers also increase commission percentages as the total number of column inches goes up in a given month. The paper, for instance, may pay 15 percent for the first 300 column inches per month and 20 percent for every additional column inch. This 5 percent bonus is an incentive for ad reps to make more money for themselves—and for the paper.

Commissions are paid to reps at the University of Tennessee's *The Daily Beacon* only if all deadlines have been met and correct procedures followed for turning in the ads. These requirements help ensure that ad deadlines are met. *The Daily Beacon* also has "Rep of the Month" and "Rep of the Quarter" awards and "Sales Achiever of the Month" gift certificates from the university bookstore. Bonuses are paid for color ads and for new ad contracts.

Classified Advertising

Classified ads are big money makers for professional papers, and they can be for college papers as well. Classifieds bring in more money per square inch than any other kind of advertising. A classified section provides a service to the campus community that can be invaluable.

One way to begin a classified section is to solicit ads right on campus. Many campus offices, such as financial aids, housing, and job placement, would like an opportunity to advertise. You could either offer on-campus offices an initial price break to get the section started or set up a permanent price break for all on-campus groups, clubs, and service organizations.

Another way to initiate the classified section is to start with a special promotion. For instance, publishing St. Valentine's Day messages at cost can draw a large response and get people thinking about using your paper to advertise (Fig. 16–9). Or you could run a half-price offer to holders of student-body cards during the start-up period. Make the section visible enough so that potential advertisers see it as an effective advertising tool.

The ad manager can contact businesses that place display ads in the paper. Many businesses like to run display ads in the classified section (see Fig. 16–2) because readers who want to buy a specific item will look there first. A used-car dealer is assured that his display ad next to "Used Cars for Sale" in the classified section will be seen by used-car buyers. The high visibility of ads in the classified section justifies the slightly higher rate per column inch the advertiser pays.

Classified ads are usually billed by the word or by the line. "Billed" is used loosely because most classifieds are set up on a cash-with-order basis, except for regular display advertisers who also run classifieds or classified display ads. Cash up front is always a good idea and it simplifies bookkeeping and billing, which can be complex enough with display ads.

Special forms for classified ads minimize time spent with clients who walk in the office to purchase advertising. The forms should include all the necessary information about rates, insertion deadlines for pulling the ad, refund policies, and so on. Use a receipt book to give the buyer a record of the purchase.

As with display-ad contracts, price breaks can be given for ads that run more than one day. Once the ad has been keyboarded, it is easy to reuse it in the next issue, so the profit on that small space increases tremendously on multiple-day runs. For PC-based publishing systems, special software packages for classified ads are available.

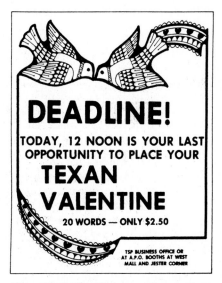

Figure 16–9. Classified promotions, such as this Valentine's Day ad, can be used to make money for the newspaper. (From *The Daily Texan,* University of Texas)

Advertising Agencies

Several national ad agencies cater exclusively to school newspapers. The largest is Communications and Advertising Services to Students (CASS). These agencies can bring extra income to papers. Their ads are already designed and ready for the page with little if any typesetting needed. Billing is easy because the agency usually wants no invoice, only several copies of the issue the ad ran in *immediately* upon publication, not at the end of the month.

The two drawbacks to these agencies are the considerable lag between the publication date and the date they pay you (90 to 120 days) and the large agency commissions and fees they deduct from the gross cost of the ad to the advertiser. Set your national ad rates high enough so that after deductions, you are left with a large enough net amount to make running the ad worthwhile (see sidebar). But don't set your national rates so high that you lose prospective advertisers. Because your paper doesn't have to spend ad-rep time or expense getting the ads, lower net revenue will still be profitable for the paper.

A newspaper is a business first

Nancy Green became general manager of Texas Student Publications (University of Texas, Austin) in August 1982. Before that she was the student-publications adviser at the University of Kentucky for 11 years. She is now publisher of Gannett's Springfield (Mo.) News-Leader.

Q: Should even small student newspapers be set up as "businesses"? Aren't they more properly learning tools for student journalists?

A: *Any* student newspaper, whether it is at a two-year or a four-year institution, ought to be organized on a professional basis. Many administrators are only concerned with the editorial side of the newspaper, not the business or advertising side. They have little concern for a well-organized and professional business and advertising operation. This is extremely unfortunate because it does not provide the students with a good educational experience. In order to have a good image in the community, your business and advertising operation must be well run, professionally run.

Q: Specifically, what should a good business operation include?

A: A good business operation should include good letterhead stationery and envelopes, preprinted billing statements, and business cards for sales representatives. You should have an organization that includes insertion orders for each ad that is placed and a system to pull tear sheets. Advertising should be billed at the end of every month, there should be credit procedures so that an advertiser is not allowed to run for months and months without paying on his bill, and the school should work with the adviser and the staff on an "aging-of-accounts" procedure so that the ad reps will know if advertisers have paid their bills.

There should be running information on the number of inches sold to each advertiser so at the end of the year advertisers can plan for additional sales or follow-up sales. There should be an account of the money collected so you have a running total of dollars that have been spent.

You should have a collection procedure so that 45 or 60 days after the billing you cut off an advertiser and accept only cash-in-advance for subsequent advertising. You should work with the legal department of the institution to enforce collection because *you are running a business*. If the college doesn't support the business staff on the collection process, the college—as well as the paper—has to look like a pretty slipshod operation out in the community. The adviser should work with students on all this so that procedures are followed, there is an orderly routine, files are kept, and rates and contracts are adhered to day after day after day.

Q: Many school newspapers are not allowed to keep their advertising revenues in an account separate from the college's general fund. Is it better to allow the newspaper to keep its own ad revenues?

A: First of all, many institutions are faced with money problems these days. It's far more realistic for the institution to look at the advertising operation as a business and revenue operation and allow the publication to generate funds on a long-term basis. As it brings in more and more advertising revenue, college support for the publication can be withdrawn as the ad revenue goes up. This will make the publication more self-sufficient.

Also, any publication ought to be allowed to keep at least some portion of the revenues for the following year because business cycles are very different from state-funding cycles. In some years the sales operation isn't as successful as in others, and the publication needs some backlog of funds to accommodate those dips in the economy.

Finally, these self-generated reserves can be used to purchase equipment, provide seminars, and let students travel for educational purposes.

Q: How should a newspaper staff set its ad rates?

A: The appropriate way to do that is to look at the cost of generating an issue of the publication. Then decide on the percentage of the publication you want to be advertising. Most school papers operate at 48 to 60 percent advertising. Add up the total number of column inches available for advertising, divide the total cost for that issue by the total number of inches you can use for advertising, and you'll have a basic rate per inch. You'll need to adjust that up or down depending on what the local economy is like and what the funding pattern is at your institution.

Then you can build a rate structure from that. You'll need an open rate for the transient advertiser, and for a small publication three or four contract rates, depending on the amount of advertising you can sell—say, 100, 300, 500, and 700 column inches. The rates should have equal distance steps. For instance, if one rate is $4 and the one below it is $3.80, then all steps should have a 20-cent difference in price.

Your national line rate can be determined in three ways: First, you can take your lowest contract rate and add on to that the percentage of commissions you are paying to the national representative firm. Second, you can take the average rate for a column inch and add the commissions to it. Third, you can take your open rate and add the commissions to it. You should look at your circulation and decide which way is best. A 1,500-circulation paper, for instance, shouldn't charge as much as a 39,000-circulation paper.

It's important to realize that your national line rate should reflect what you wish to earn in income and the very high cost of dealing with a national representative. The firms charge 15 percent for the company that places the ad, 2 percent for that company's fast payment, and then 25 to 30 percent—depending on the firm—for handling the account.

The way to calculate this is to take 100 percent, deduct the 15 percent agency commission, and then deduct 2 percent of that for fast payment to the agency. Now you have 83 percent. Deduct the firm's commission, say 30 percent, which leaves you with 53 percent—your income from the ad.

Q: What's the best way to determine the size of an issue?

A: It should be governed by the amount of advertising sold. If you have a percentage set for the amount of ad space in an issue, let's say 50 percent, then the size of the issue should be determined by the number of column inches of advertising sold. If it's 50 percent ads, then the editorial department knows it has the remaining 50 percent of the pages to fill. If you limit the number of pages in an issue, you are eventually going to be limiting the advertising revenue as well.

To give the editorial department the time to fill the issue, the advertising-space deadline should be at least three working days before publication. The page dummies should be available ahead of time so that the editorial department knows how much space is available and can compensate for large papers.

Q: What kind of relationship should the advertising and editorial staffs of a student newspaper have?

A: Occasionally there is animosity between the two because the advertising staff earns commissions; they are paid on the basis of how well they sell. The editorial department gets a flat rate if they get paid at all. The advertising staff usually takes home more money than the editorial staff does. But you have to under-

stand that the ad rep is responsible for gas, better clothes, and other expenses involved in the selling process that a reporter or editor doesn't have to worry about.

In addition, the editorial staff may not like the kind of advertising that is sold in the publication. The ad staff may not like the editorial product because they say it makes it hard to sell. The best attitude is that there *will* be differences; the two staffs have different roles to perform. The advertising department is running a business. They are selling a product. The editorial department is creating the product. Their goals are different. They should *not* be joined. Still, they need to work together for the best possible product.

Ads and the Law

Sometimes you have to say no to an advertiser who wants to buy space in your paper. There are certain legal requirements and First Amendment rights concerning advertising that all newspaper staffs should be aware of. These requirements and rights are not easily delineated because laws regarding advertising vary by state. They are further complicated by unclear court decisions regarding the status of school papers versus privately owned papers and product advertising versus "editorial" advertising. (Editorial ads are those that espouse an idea—such as abortion rights—rather than sell a product.)

Privately owned newspapers are not required to accept advertising. Many no longer accept ads for theaters that show X-rated movies, for instance. But because school newspapers are set up as public forums for free expression, some courts have found that they must accept *editorial* ads. The courts argue that advertising columns are the only access to free forum some members of the public have.

The courts have been unclear on whether a student newspaper can reject commercial advertising. Many college papers do not accept ads for cigarettes, alcohol, contraceptive devices, or term-paper-writing services. But if a merchant decides to challenge an ad rejection in court, the school paper may have to publish these ads because of the open-forum concept.

The one area that is clearly defined is fraud. Fraudulent ads are basically the responsibility of the advertiser and not of the paper, and law-enforcement officials will focus their efforts on the advertiser. A paper that *knowingly* publishes a fraudulent ad, however, can be liable. Therefore, many papers do not accept ads from term-paper-writing firms or $10 diploma mills. These ads constitute possible fraudulent academic practices, even if the ads themselves deliver what they claim.

Because the law is not always clear, each staff should find out about state and local laws and college regulations concerning advertising. Be sure that the school rules reflect recent court decisions, that advertising policies are also up-to-date and clearly written, and that the policies outline what will be accepted or rejected as advertising. Even if the courts are unclear about regulations for school papers, you should clearly state what rules you will follow. Legal problems with advertising rarely crop up. But be prepared. Avoid problems by knowing your rights and what you are legally required to do as a publisher.

For a professional paper, a budget must be set up and ads must be gathered before the paper can send out reporters. But because most school newspapers are subsidized, advertising revenue is not nearly as crucial as it is to professional papers. The advertising program should not be an afterthought, however. Selling ads for a school paper can be an invaluable experience for an advertising student. Prospective journalists and advertising sales reps can both benefit from working in a professional setting to acquire the best possible education for a newspaper career.

Suggested Projects

Vocabulary

column inch
contract rate
co-op ad
display advertising
line
make-good policy
open rate
rate card
SAU
tear sheet

1. Do a demographics and spending-habits study of your readers. The questionnaire should include questions about how much spending money the student has, what it is spent on (clothes, food, entertainment, movies, tapes or CDs, transportation), what media students read or watch, what local stores or restaurants they frequent, and what specific products or line of products they buy or use regularly. Also gather information from the financial aids office and the registrar. Then design and print a brochure to include in your sales kit. Update it regularly.

2. Ask an art student, an art instructor, or an artist from the local paper to work with the ad staff designing ads. Have a list of typefaces used by your print shop available for this person.

3. Cut out an ad and redesign it to make it a more effective selling tool.

4. Check with a local paper that might be discarding its old clip art books. You could use these for practice ads between issues. You may also want to contact the company to see if you can use the "old" art in your ads for free or for a small fee.

distribution and promotion 17

Unless the newspaper is just a classroom exercise, it must be delivered to the public. Professional papers and large university papers are distributed through regular and paid-mail subscription and through newsracks in the community or on campus. Colleges that publish less often than daily usually focus their distribution on campus. No matter how large or small the paper is, however, it can serve its public only if that public can easily pick up the paper and read it.

The specific publication day for a nondaily paper can, to a considerable extent, determine the paper's success. The wrong day for your campus may mean fewer readers and, therefore, less advertising revenue and may eventually put you out of business. If the paper comes out on Monday, for instance, it can't cover weekend sports unless the staff works weekends; coverage would have to be in next week's issue, when the game would be 10 days old. Tuesdays are not much of an improvement.

Wednesdays are popular days for distribution for several reasons. First, on many college campuses, more students go to classes on Wednesdays than any other day (with Tuesdays a close second). More students have the opportunity to see the paper on that day, so circulation will probably be the optimum. A Wednesday release also allows the weekly paper to cover the previous weekend's sports events and late-breaking news from early in the week, yet it can preview upcoming events without being too far ahead of time.

Many papers publish on Thursdays because the later-in-the-week timing gives the staff more time to put the paper together but still avoids putting out a Friday paper. Fridays are very popular publication days for weekly papers because the staff has the entire week to work on the issue and can publish an end-of-the-week wrap-up. It is also effective timing for previewing weekend sports. But Fridays are a problem on many campuses because students tend to cut Friday classes, and unless the paper comes out very early in the morning, it doesn't reach the students until Monday and ruins your weekend preview of entertainment and sports events.

Each staff ought to study printer and staff deadline schedules, the high attendance days of students at the school, and the coverage goals of the paper. After weighing all sides of the situation, the staff should select a publication day that will best serve both its capabilities and the needs of its readers.

The time-of-day distribution is also important. At many commuter colleges, afternoons may be relatively dead times, when students leave for jobs or sports activities. Papers may sit in the newsracks overnight.

Early mornings are usually good for distribution. The papers could be picked up from the printer and distributed late in the afternoon preceding publication day. Even the earliest student on campus could then pick up a paper on publication day and read it while waiting for classes to start.

233

Distribution Systems

No matter what time the paper comes out, readers still have to be able to find its distribution centers quickly and pick up a paper easily. Using newsracks is better than just dumping stacks of papers at high traffic points on campus. Newsracks add an air of professionalism to the paper, especially if the racks are of professional quality. Local newspaper distributors often place a long line of newsracks on campus with several local papers in them. You probably could get the distributor to put one more rack in the line for your paper for a small fee. By altering it to work without coins or by taking out the Plexiglas front (if your paper is free), you make it easy for readers to find and pick up your paper.

As an alternative, a staff could purchase its own racks, build some, or have the campus wood or welding shop construct them. At College of the Sequoias in Visalia, California, students in an architectural-design course submitted newsrack designs to a committee of instructors and students, and one design was selected. Then the college welding shop made the racks (Fig. 17–1).

The newsrack should be highly visible and should release one issue at a time without disturbing the other issues. Other than these requisites, the rack may take any design. A newsrack doesn't have to look like every other one.

Naturally, newsracks should be placed in areas of highest student traffic on campus. Evaluate the traffic flow in these areas regularly, especially if the newsracks are new on campus. Discover which racks get the highest use and which the lowest; distribute papers to these racks in that ratio. If a rack gets little usage, find a better position for it.

You shouldn't forget night-school students when you distribute the paper. Make sure the racks are full late in the day so that students who attend only at night can get a paper. These night-school students can increase your ad revenue through expanded circulation and better demographics.

The faculty and administration should also get special consideration when it comes to distribution. At small schools, papers can be placed in or near faculty mailboxes; some faculty members don't get out on campus as frequently as students, and if they have a special parking area, will miss the newsracks by the student parking lots. Administration officials will appreciate getting the paper

Figure 17–1. Newsracks can take any form as long as they clearly display papers and easily release one at a time.

Figure 17–2. One way to increase circulation is to get alumni to subscribe. The fee can cover the cost of mailing. (From *The Daily Pennsylvanian,* University of Pennsylvania)

delivered early and right to them. It's not a matter of playing up to them; it's good public relations to help administrators think highly of the newspaper staff.

To increase circulation, distribute the paper to at least a few places in the community, including businesses, restaurants, the YMCA, and the community center. Many advertisers will allow you to place stacks on their counters by cash registers so that customers can pick up copies when they pay for their purchases. Also, many persons in your community—perhaps alumni, parents of current students, or those whose children will attend the following year—would like to read your paper to find out what's happening on campus.

It is easy to see why professional papers have people in charge of circulation. There are many aspects to the job, even on a campus with a weekly paper: delivering the pages to the printer and picking up the papers, getting the papers out on campus, keeping the newsracks stocked, getting papers out to community distribution centers, mailing papers to subscribers (such as interested alumni who have moved away) (Fig. 17–2), and sending papers to other schools on the exchange-paper list. A responsible person should be selected as circulation manager. This person should work closely with the business department as well as the editorial department.

Promotion

Many times, for reasons the present staff is not responsible for, a newspaper has a bad reputation on campus. Students don't read it much, and when they do, they read it just for laughs. Circulation figures are low, potential advertisers are just not interested, and students don't want to be on the staff. The situation is the same as a coach trying to get athletes to enroll in a college with a history of losing teams. Promoting the paper to increase its popularity—and its circulation—then becomes a major hurdle for the newspaper staff.

Successful papers also engage in promotional activities. Professional papers promote themselves because they want to make money. They run promotions to increase circulation, and they run special promotional sections, largely advertising based, around a certain theme: summer vacation, weddings, Christmas. School papers can also benefit from promotions and for the same reasons: There's nothing wrong with the paper making money (Fig. 17–3). Promotions remind the ever changing readership group of the value of reading the paper.

Many promotional ideas have worked for school newspapers; you can devise several more that fit the special needs of your school, community, and readers. Many advertisers like to run coupons in the paper. With these coupons your readers can save money during the course of a semester or year. Posters advertising the money that can be saved by using the coupons will help draw attention to both the paper and the ads. The more coupons used, the happier the advertiser. If students are convinced that they can save money by reading your paper, you'll have more readers and probably more advertisers.

Figure 17–3. Creating a special section with a central theme is a great way to sell space to specific advertisers, as well as provide a valuable service for your readers. (Courtesy of the *Daily Bruin*)

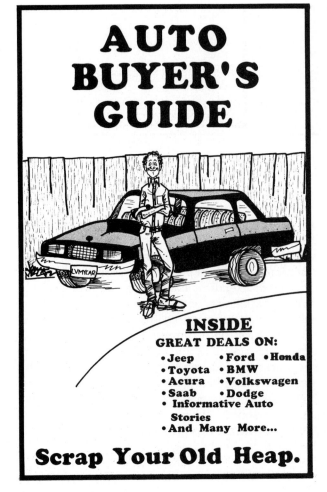

Hiding a student's name or ID number in an ad each issue and awarding a prize or cash if he or she finds it can also draw readers. Advertisers will like the virtual guarantee of heavy readership of the ads, and students will like the opportunity to win something. An advertiser will often provide the prize—a special discount or a free item—so the newspaper itself does not have to pay for the promotion.

Various contests can also be run in the paper—perhaps a treasure hunt with clues hidden in the ad hole or classified ads—again with advertisers providing the prizes in exchange for free advertising. The sports department can run a pick-a-winner contest every week, though this may be illegal in some states. Many other game possibilities will draw readers and please advertisers at the same time.

Another promotional idea is to sponsor fun or entertaining events on campus, such as a paper-airplane-flying contest or a band or film series. By sponsoring a popular event, the paper gains visibility, readership, and perhaps even a few new staff members. These events have to be run smoothly; this professionalism will then carry over in readers' attitudes toward the paper.

The newspaper staff can also participate in campus events such as blood drives, campus carnivals, or food drives at Christmas. Again, high visibility is the goal for the paper, so doing well in these events is helpful, naturally. The newspaper can promote these community-service events while the participation of the staff promotes the paper.

After the newspaper has promoted itself into a position of high esteem on campus, it is time to approach the student government or the administration about retaining advertising funds for newspaper equipment or supplies or increasing student-activities fees to go directly to support the paper. The paper can only improve with better equipment and supplies. If the paper is looked upon favorably through all its positive promotional activity on campus and through its professional-quality work, these increases in funding are not that hard to get. You are glad to have a good image on campus when you face the person or committee who holds the purse strings.

The most important way to promote the paper on campus, however, has nothing to do with posters, games, or film series. The best promotional gimmick is no gimmick at all: It is publishing a good newspaper issue after issue after issue. If, behind all the camouflage of the promotional campaigns, the newspaper is still a prime example of shoddy workmanship and lackadaisical staff attitudes, the best promotional campaign in the country will not improve its image. Most readers expect and appreciate a professional approach to reporting at their school. If you give them that above all else, the paper will be popular, read, and respected.

Another major promotion campaign probably has more to do with the instructor and/or adviser to the paper than with the staff. Nevertheless, the staff should be aware of this campaign: promoting the journalism department to prospective students. The staff and the adviser can work together in this area. If the best prospective journalism students refuse to sign up for your journalism program or decide to attend another school, you have a major problem in staffing your paper. The journalism department should actively recruit talented prospects to make sure they sign up for the paper. Recruiting is the best way to ensure quality.

There are many ways to recruit good students. Although the adviser has to do the majority of the work, the staff can help, too. For instance, college journalists can visit local high schools and sell the program to the top journalism students there. The staff can host open houses and give tours of the department to prospective students. These activities increase the visibility and respectability of your journalism program.

Other recruiting aids you might use are departmental brochures; slide presentations to illustrate why students should study journalism; a journalism scholarship program; regular critiquing by state and national scholastic journalism associations; the support of admissions counselors; letters to students who score well on language/communication entrance examinations; awards banquets every term or year to honor top students in the program; and most important of all, a good newspaper.

Departmental brochures (Figs. 17–4 and 17–5) are helpful in several ways. They can be mailed directly to local high school journalism departments, to admissions counselors, or to the students themselves if you can get lists from journalism teachers. Give students something to read at a later date when they visit the school. The brochures can be sent out by counseling services at your own school. The brochures should provide information on the program itself—how to enroll, what courses it offers the prospective journalism major.

Visits to other schools are good because they offer the adviser and staff an opportunity to meet prospective students face-to-face and answer questions. Organize a slide show (which could even be humorous) to show highlights of your program and how your system works. Then after your discussion and question-and-answer period, hand out the brochures.

Because finances are such an important problem for students today, developing a scholarship program is a real plus for a program. A small scholarship could be funded through bake sales and car washes. The money could be given at

Figure 17–4. A brochure that can be mailed or given out to prospective students is a good way to promote the journalism department and the paper. (From *Skyline Press,* Skyline College)

Welcome to Skyline College . . . . the community college serving the students and residents of North San Mateo County.

Skyline College established in 1969 is one of the three two-year institutions in the San Mateo County Community College District. It is an accredited community college by the Western Association of Schools and Colleges and is approved for veterans training under California and federal laws.

Skyline College overlooks the Pacific Ocean and is situated near Skyline Boulevard between Sneath Lane and Westborough Boulevard at 3300 College Drive in San Bruno, California. The administration and faculty in both the day and evening programs primarily serve students from the communities of Daly City, South San Francisco, Brisbane, Colma, Pacifica, San Bruno, and Millbrae.

The college's curriculum includes courses which lead to the Associate in Arts Degree, two-year vocational-technical certificates and terminal programs, and two-year programs for transfer to the four-year college or university.

Admission to Skyline College . . . Any high school graduate or person over 18 years of age who is a resident of San Mateo County is eligible to enroll and register at Skyline College.

A legal resident from another community college district can apply for admission to Skyline College. However, such an individual seeking admission must be a graduate of a high school or must be 18 years of age or older and must submit a release from the community college district of his residence.

Official Skyline College admission forms are available at local high schools or may be obtained from the college at the Office of Admissions-Records. These forms may be completed during the student's senior year in high school. Forms must be filed with the admissions office by all students who wish to enroll at Skyline College.

Along with the admissions form, students must submit two complete official transcripts of records from their high school of graduation (or the last high school they attended) and from each college previously attended.

Veterans also should file copies of their military record, special training courses, and discharge certificate in order to receive proper college credit.

Registration – Tests – Costs . . . Students are required to complete a placement test. The purpose of this placement test is not to bar anyone from attending the college. Test results are used only as guidelines for the student and the counselor in helping to determine the level of instruction which will be best for the student. The application form will contain a list of test places, dates, and deadlines.

Students who have taken other kinds of tests (see other kinds of tests listed on the admissions form) at their high school or other collegiate institution need not take the placement test. However, these other test results must be included with transcripts.

After completing the admission procedures and requirements (filing application form, submitting transcripts, taking placement test), the student will be given a counseling-registration appointment. Both the college counselor and the journalism instructor are available to assist the student in planning the semester schedule and future programs.

There is no tuition fee at Skyline College (except for out-of-state resident and foreign students). The cost of attending Skyline College is minimal with a $4.00 health fee being the lone required fee. The average cost per semester for books and supplies is about $65 The college has financial aid and scholarship programs, a job placement office, federal work-study opportunities, and loan funds for students enrolled at Skyline College.

Welcome to the Skyline College Journalism Department . . . which offers courses that are designed to introduce the student to the mass media and to aid individuals in a pre-professional career experience, leading to an Associate-in-Arts degree and transfer to a four year college or university.

The Skyline College journalism program includes both the liberal arts and academic studies and practical vocational training courses.

Student journalists are involved in the exciting, active world of mass media communication which includes a variety of group and individual lessons. They include learning the skills, responsibilities of the journalist, introduction to mass media and communications, reporting and newswriting, advance newswriting and indepth reporting, newspaper production and editing,

the end of the year to the top student leaving the program and continuing studies in communications.

A larger scholarship fund could be financed through the donations of local papers and alumni who are now working as journalists. Many would be happy to donate a small amount to begin a revolving journalism-scholarship fund at their alma mater. By advertising the availability of these scholarships to prospective students, you may be able to get a few more good journalists to join your program. An active adviser can also inform staff members about scholarship opportunities on campus and from local and national organizations.

"Journalism days"—with contests or without—are good ways to promote the program, especially if you can arrange for good speakers. Whether the event is

Figure 17–5. This brochure publicizes the various mass media that are part of the Illini Publishing Company. (From *The Daily Illini*, Illini Publishing Company, Champaign, IL)

the daily illini

The Daily Illini is a newspaper started solely by students for the University community in Champaign-Urbana, with a circulation of over 14,000 and a readership of more than twice that number.

Traditionally, the paper has been in the vanguard of college journalism, employing the latest technology available to print media. The Daily Illini is a recent winner of the Society For Professional Journalism's Mark of Excellence, Best Student Newspaper award, and has won the Inland Daily Press' College Makeup and Typography Award the last three years.

The paper publishes five days a week during the school year, Tuesday through Saturday. Regular news, opinions, features and sports appear daily; and a 20-page magazine, Spectrum, appears on Saturday. Local stories are supplemented with The Associated Press and the Field News Service, as well as columnists Mike Royko, Roger Simon, Richard Reeves, Mary McGrory and James Kilpatrick, and sports columnists Ray Sons, Ron Rapaport and John Schulian.

The Daily Illini also has separate photo and graphics departments, and purchases United Press International's Unifax photos.

illio

The Illio is the magazine-style yearbook at the University. Published by the Illini Publishing Company and run entirely by students, the Illio reflects the highlights of the University year. News, sports, concerts, features, organizations and seniors are all a part of the 432-page hardbound book.

The Illio is for every student at the University as it captures the flavor of the school year with diverse stories that will inform and entertain you today and ten years from now when you're looking back on your college days.

The entertainment section highlights the year's best talents, offering students everything from operas and stage plays to the vibrant concert sounds of Billy Joel, Santana and George Benson. The lifestyles section covers controversial issues like single parent students and rape to campus health food crazes and dormitory apartment life; while the news in Illio highlights both local and national events that shaped the year. Big Ten sports, the Fighting Illini, the Greek System, residence halls, campus groups and seniors are all a part of Illio.

Diverse. Entertaining. Informative. ILLIO 80. Capturing the year today .. so you can relive it tomorrow.

held on a weekday or on a Saturday, a well-run program will be well worth the cost because of the good journalists you will attract. Because you can often hold this event on campus and get local professionals to donate their time, the only cost to you is your time and perhaps a lunch for guest speakers.

Statewide journalism organizations and several good national organizations are open to students (see the appendix). These organizations provide student newspapers with many services, ranging from national student news and features to critique services. The critique services are especially good when you have a staff that is working hard to improve the paper. Knowing that the newspaper will be critiqued by a professional can be a great incentive to a staff to work harder to win more awards or score more points than the previous semester's staff. This positive competitive spirit is good both for the present staff and for prospective staff members. People like to sign up for a winner. No matter what the relative quality of the paper, comments from experts can only improve staff members' education. Memberships in these organizations are definitely worth the cost to the department.

Sometimes even the admissions counselors or advisers on your own campus have little idea of what the journalism department has to offer, especially if the program has changed in recent months. Meet with the counselors regularly, give them copies of the most recent brochure, and ask that they suggest the introductory journalism course to students with good communication skills. Many good students who think they wouldn't be interested in newspaper work will join the staff with just a little encouragement from those who help them select courses.

The counseling department may be able to provide a computer listing of students who scored high in the language-skills area of the entrance examination. Send a letter to these students telling them that their scores indicate communication skills at high enough levels to be members of the newspaper staff. You'll flatter them by noticing their language skills, and maybe you'll make them interested enough to at least come by and take a look. Then if they do sign up, you can be assured that you are getting people who can write well.

Staff-awards banquets at the end of every term or at the end of the year can be great ways to promote the program. If you keep the present staff happy, the word will filter down to incoming students. The awards banquet can be a time to honor those students who have done an outstanding job on the paper and maybe even to give out a scholarship or two. These banquets, which are usually planned by staff members, can also include some humorous awards and trophies. The staff that can play and laugh together can also work well together and produce a good newspaper.

If the paper is good, if the readers respect and enjoy it, if the staff is happy, other students are going to want to get in on the action. The student grapevine can make or break many classes or programs. Excellence in teaching and in the newspaper will bring in students, even if the financial situation is a little tight. Dedication to that excellence, from the adviser as well as from staff members, will keep the keyboards and cameras active year after year.

Suggested Projects

1. If your newspaper does not have good newsracks, begin a study to see if newsracks would help the image and circulation of the paper on campus. Ask readers what changes are needed to make it easier to get a paper. Have several designs worked up, look at places on campus where the racks might be placed, and begin a circulation plan that includes on-campus, off-campus, and subscription circulation.

2. Write to the editors and advisers of the best newspapers in your area or in your state. You could also write the award-winning papers used as illustrations in this book. Find out how they promote their journalism classes and what kinds of events (such as journalism days and awards banquets) they plan during the year. What kinds of on-campus promotional campaigns do they engage in? Which ideas can you use on your campus?

journalism organizations

The following student and faculty journalism organizations and national advertising agencies can provide important information to any newspaper staff and adviser. The faculty organizations are especially helpful for advisers without previous practical experience. The student organizations provide critique services and contests and sometimes offer journalism scholarships.

American Council on Education for Journalism and Mass Communications

ACEJMC is basically an accrediting agency for professional education in journalism. An ACEJMC accreditation team will visit a campus on request and evaluate the journalism program(s). ACEJMC also has begun accrediting graduate programs. Included under the ACEJMC umbrella are the Association for Education in Journalism and Mass Communication (AEJMC), the American Association of Schools and Departments of Journalism (AASDJ), and the American Society of Journalism School Administrators (ASJSA), all to be discussed in more detail.

Address: See AEJMC.

Associated Collegiate Press

ACP began in 1933 as an offshoot of the National Scholastic Press Association, a high school press service. ACP members, both two- and four-year colleges, receive critiques each semester. ACP also offers individual publications critique services, annual conferences, *Scholastic Editor* magazine, access to the ACP Bookstore, periodic information bulletins, and a loan service of award-winning publications.

Critiqued publications received point totals in five categories based upon national standards. Overall point totals decide the final ranking of the publication, from all-American to third class. All-American papers are those that receive marks of distinction in at least four of the five categories. Five-star all-American papers from the spring semester are eligible for the following fall's Pacemaker Award, the highest award given by ACP. Judges also record comments throughout the guidebook on specific strengths and weaknesses in a semester's issues.

Address: ACP, 620 Rarig Center, 330 21st Ave. South, University of Minnesota, Minneapolis, MN 55455.

Association for Education in Journalism and Mass Communication

AEJMC, which also includes AASDJ and ASJSA, has approximately 1,700 members. AASDJ works with media practitioners to raise educational standards. ASJSA helps journalism departments work toward accreditation and discusses administrative and teaching problems through its internal publication, *The Roundtable.* AEJMC also publishes *Journalism Educator* (the January issue contains valuable information about journalism programs and organizations), *Journalism Quarterly,* and *Journalism Monographs.*

Address: AEJMC, College of Journalism, University of South Carolina, Columbia, SC 29208.

College Media Advisers, Inc.

CMA (formerly the National Council of College Publications Advisers) members are largely advisers and business managers of two- and four-year college newspapers. Other persons interested in the student press may also be members. CMA holds conferences every March and October and an adviser workshop in June. The organization honors teachers and advisers every year and sponsors an annual student cartoon contest.

CMA publishes a monthly newsletter and a quarterly, *College Press Review.* It is also working on a multivolume college-student-press series. Already published are *College Student Press Law* and *Ethics and Responsibilities of Advising Student Publications,* both valuable publications.

Address: CMA, Journalism Department, Memphis State University, Memphis, TN 38152.

College Media Placement Service

CMPS is a national advertising representative, although it also is a leader nationwide in on-campus employee recruitment for major companies. It publishes a four-color magazine supplement to college newspapers, *Ampersand.* CMPS focuses on junior and senior colleges with more than 13,000 students.

Address: CMPS, 1680 N. Vine, Suite 209, Hollywood, CA 90028.

Columbia Scholastic Press Association

CSPA, founded in 1924, provides critique and rating services for high school and college student newspapers, magazines, and yearbooks. The best in each category every year are given Medalist Awards. Judges comment on specific strengths and weaknesses in a guidebook mailed to the paper's adviser. CSPA publishes *School Press Review*, a monthly magazine during the school year, and *The School Journalist*, a newsletter.

Address: CSPA, Box 11, Central Mail Room, Columbia University, New York, NY 10027.

Communications and Advertising Services to Students

Begun in 1968, CASS is a national advertising agency for college newspapers. Besides lining up national ads for college papers, CASS also provides other services for prospective college newspaper advertisers, including college market research, special merchandising programs, and consulting. CASS publishes a quarterly newsletter, *College Market Report*, and offers press-release services to colleges.

Address: CASS, 1633 Central Street, Evanston, IL 60201. CASS also has a toll-free telephone number, (800) 323–4044, for calls from out of state.

Community College Journalism Association

This national association began in 1968 as the Junior College Journalism Association and was renamed in 1974. CCJA is now a recognized affiliate of AEJMC.

CCJA publishes the CCJA *Newsletter* and the *Community College Journalist*, a quarterly magazine. Both are included in the membership fee.

Address: CCJA, Journalism Department, Midland College, 3600 N. Garfield, Midland, TX 79701.

Journalism Education Association

JEA is a professional organization for journalism and mass media teachers whose specialty is television. Advisers to student publications are also members. JEA holds two conferences yearly, one of which is on the West Coast, the other on the East Coast or in the Midwest. Students are honored in annual contests. Outstanding teachers and advisers are honored as well. JEA publishes *Newswire* and *Communication: Journalism Education Today*.

Address: JEA, 4933 17th Pl., Lubbock, TX 79416.

Major College Newspapers, Inc.

MCN is the newest of the college national-advertising representatives. MCN is affiliated with Branham Newspaper Sales, a Chicago sales agency for professional papers. As with the other national agencies, MCN takes care of soliciting and billing for all ads it gets for the paper.

Address: MCN, 444 N. Michigan Ave., Chicago, IL 60611.

The Newspaper Fund, Inc.

The goal of this organization is to encourage students to consider careers in journalism. TNF offers 50 internships every year, 40 to undergraduate students and 10 to minority graduate students. It also sponsors summer workshops for inner-city journalism students and for high school journalism teachers with no previous experience.

The organization has two valuable publications, *The Journalism Career and Scholarship Guide* and a monthly newsletter.

Address: TNF, P. O. Box 300, Princeton, NJ 08540.

Student Press Law Center

A project of the Robert F. Kennedy Memorial, SPLC serves as a clearinghouse of information for student journalists and advisers interested in preserving press freedom in colleges and high schools. The center publishes a quarterly *Report*, which discusses student press issues and current cases; it also provides regular background information on press issues through the SPLC News Service. SPLC is an especially helpful center of information about student press rights.

Address: SPLC, 800 18th Street N.W., Washington, DC 20006.

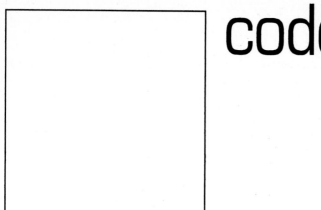

codes

Associated Press Managing Editors

This code is a model against which newspaper men and women can measure their performance. It is meant to apply to news and editorial staff members, and others who are involved in, or who influence, news coverage and editorial policy. It has been formulated in the belief that newspapers and the people who produce them should adhere to the highest standards of ethical and professional conduct.

Responsibility

A good newspaper is fair, accurate, honest, responsible, independent and decent. Truth is its guiding principle.

It avoids practices that would conflict with the ability to report and present news in a fair and unbiased manner.

The newspaper should serve as a constructive critic of all segments of society. Editorially, it should advocate needed reform or innovations in the public interest. It should expose wrongdoing or misuse of power, public or private.

News sources should be disclosed unless there is clear reason not to do so. When it is necessary to protect the confidentiality of a source the reason should be explained.

The newspaper should background, with the facts, public statements that it knows to be inaccurate or misleading. It should uphold the right of free speech and freedom of the press and should respect the individual's right of privacy.

The public's right to know about matters of importance is paramount, and the newspaper should fight vigorously for public access to news of government through open meetings and open records.

Accuracy

The newspaper should guard against inaccuracies, carelessness, bias or distortion through either emphasis or omission.

It should admit all substantive errors and correct them promptly and prominently.

Integrity

The newspaper should strive for impartial treatment of issues and dispassionate handling of controversial subjects. It should provide a forum for the exchange of comment and criticism, especially when such comment is opposed to its editorial positions. Editorials and other expressions of opinion by reporters and editors should be clearly labeled.

The newspaper should report the news without regard for its own interests. It should not give favored news treatment to advertisers or special interest groups. It should report matters regarding itself or its personnel with the same vigor and candor as it would other institutions or individuals.

Concern for community, business or personal interests should not cause a newspaper to distort or misrepresent the facts.

Conflicts of Interest

The newspaper and its staff should be free of obligations to news sources and special interests. Even the appearance of obligation or conflict of interest should be avoided.

Newspapers should accept nothing of value from news sources or others outside the profession. Gifts and free or reduced-rate travel, entertainment, products and lodging should not be accepted. Expenses in connection with news reporting should be paid by the newspaper. Special favors and special treatment for members of the press should be avoided.

Involvement in such things as politics, community affairs, demonstrations and social causes that could cause a conflict of interest, or the appearance of such conflict, should be avoided.

Outside employment by news sources is an obvious conflict of interest, and employment by potential news sources also should be avoided.

Financial investments by staff members or other outside business interests that could conflict with the newspaper's ability to report the news or that would create the impression of such conflict should be avoided.

Stories should not be written or edited primarily for the purpose of winning awards and prizes. Blatantly commercial journalism contests, or others that reflect unfavorably on the newspaper or the profession, should be avoided.

No code of ethics can prejudge every situation. Common sense and good judgment are required in applying ethical principles to newspaper realities. Individual newspapers are encouraged to augment these guidelines with locally produced codes that apply more specifically to their own situations.

THE SOCIETY OF PROFESSIONAL JOURNALISTS

Code
OF Ethics

THE SOCIETY of Professional Journalists, Sigma Delta Chi believes the duty of journalists is to serve the truth.

WE BELIEVE the agencies of mass communication are carriers of public discussion and information, acting on their Constitutional mandate and freedom to learn and report the facts.

WE BELIEVE in public enlightenment as the forerunner of justice, and in our Constitutional role to seek the truth as part of the public's right to know the truth.

WE BELIEVE those responsibilities carry obligations that require journalists to perform with intelligence, objectivity, accuracy and fairness.

To these ends, we declare acceptance of the standards of practice here set forth:

RESPONSIBILITY:

The public's right to know of events of public importance and interest is the overriding mission of the mass media. The purpose of distributing news and enlightened opinion is to serve the general welfare. Journalists who use their professional status as representatives of the public for selfish or other unworthy motives violate a high trust.

FREEDOM OF THE PRESS:

Freedom of the press is to be guarded as an inalienable right of people in a free society. It carries with it the freedom and the responsibility to discuss, question and challenge actions and utterances of our government and of our public and private institutions. Journalists uphold the right to speak unpopular opinions and the privilege to agree with the majority.

ETHICS:

Journalists must be free of obligation to any interest other than the public's right to know the truth.

1. Gifts, favors, free travel, special treatment or privileges can compromise the integrity of journalists and their employers. Nothing of value should be accepted.

2. Secondary employment, political involvement, holding public office and service in community organizations should be avoided if it compromises the integrity of journalists and their employers. Journalists and their employers should conduct their personal lives in a manner which protects them from conflict of interest, real or apparent. Their responsibilities to the public are paramount. That is the nature of their profession.

3. So-called news communications from private sources should not be published or broadcast without substantiation of their claims to news value.

4. Journalists will seek news that serves the public interest, despite the obstacles. They will make constant efforts to assure that the public's business is conducted in public and that public records are open to public inspection.

5. Journalists acknowledge the newsman's ethic of protecting confidential sources of information.

ACCURACY AND OBJECTIVITY:

Good faith with the public is the foundation of all worthy journalism.

1. Truth is our ultimate goal.

2. Objectivity in reporting the news is another goal, which serves as the mark of an experienced professional. It is a standard of performance toward which we strive. We honor those who achieve it.

3. There is no excuse for inaccuracies or lack of thoroughness.

4. Newspaper headlines should be fully warranted by the contents of the articles they accompany. Photographs and telecasts should give an accurate picture of an event and not highlight a minor incident out of context.

5. Sound practice makes clear distinction between news reports and expressions of opinion. News reports should be free of opinion or bias and represent all sides of an issue.

6. Partisanship in editorial comment which knowingly departs from the truth violates the spirit of American journalism.

7. Journalists recognize their responsibility for offering informed analysis, comment and editorial opinion on public events and issues. They accept the obligation to present such material by individuals whose competence, experience and judgment qualify them for it.

8. Special articles or presentations devoted to advocacy or the writer's own conclusions and interpretations should be labeled as such.

FAIR PLAY:

Journalists at all times will show respect for the dignity, privacy, rights and well-being of people encountered in the course of gathering and presenting the news.

1. The news media should not communicate unofficial charges affecting reputation or moral character without giving the accused a chance to reply.

2. The news media must guard against invading a person's right to privacy.

3. The media should not pander to morbid curiosity about details of vice and crime.

4. It is the duty of news media to make prompt and complete correction of their errors.

5. Journalists should be accountable to the public for their reports and the public should be encouraged to voice its grievances against the media. Open dialogue with our readers, viewers and listeners should be fostered.

PLEDGE:

Journalists should actively censure and try to prevent violations of these standards, and they should encourage their observance by all newspeople. Adherence to this code of ethics is intended to preserve the bond of mutual trust and respect between American journalists and the American people.

Adopted 1926, Revised 1973

American Society of Newspaper Editors

A Statement of Principles.

PREAMBLE

The First Amendment, protecting freedom of expression from abridgment by any law, guarantees to the people through their press a constitutional right, and thereby places on newspaper people a particular responsibility.

Thus journalism demands of its practitioners not only industry and knowledge but also the pursuit of a standard of integrity proportionate to the journalist's singular obligation.

To this end the American Society of Newspaper Editors sets forth this Statement of Principles as a standard encouraging the highest ethical and professional performance.

ARTICLE I - Responsibility

The primary purpose of gathering and distributing news and opinion is to serve the general welfare by informing the people and enabling them to make judgments on the issues of the time. Newspapermen and women who abuse the power of their professional role for selfish motives or unworthy purposes are faithless to that public trust.

The American press was made free not just to inform or just to serve as a forum for debate but also to bring an independent scrutiny to bear on the forces of power in the society, including the conduct of official power at all levels of government.

ARTICLE II - Freedom of the Press

Freedom of the press belongs to the people. It must be defended against encroachment or assault from any quarter, public or private.

Journalists must be constantly alert to see that the public's business is conducted in public. They must be vigilant against all who would exploit the press for selfish purposes.

ARTICLE III - Independence

Journalists must avoid impropriety and the appearance of impropriety as well as any conflict of interest or the appearance of conflict. They should neither accept anything nor pursue any activity that might compromise or seem to compromise their integrity.

ARTICLE IV - Truth and Accuracy

Good faith with the reader is the foundation of good journalism. Every effort must be made to assure that the news content is accurate, free from bias and in context, and that all sides are presented fairly. Editorials, analytical articles and commentary should be held to the same standards of accuracy with respect to facts as news reports.

Significant errors of fact, as well as errors of omission, should be corrected promptly and prominently.

ARTICLE V - Impartiality

To be impartial does not require the press to be unquestioning or to refrain from editorial expression. Sound practice, however, demands a clear distinction for the reader between news reports and opinion. Articles that contain opinion or personal interpretation should be clearly identified.

ARTICLE VI - Fair Play

Journalists should respect the rights of people involved in the news, observe the common standards of decency and stand accountable to the public for the fairness and accuracy of their news reports.

Persons publicly accused should be given the earliest opportunity to respond.

Pledges of confidentiality to news sources must be honored at all costs, and therefore should not be given lightly. Unless there is clear and pressing need to maintain confidences, sources of information should be identified.

These principles are intended to preserve, protect and strengthen the bond of trust and respect between American journalists and the American people, a bond that is essential to sustain the grant of freedom entrusted to both by the nation's founders.

—adopted by the ASNE board of directors, Oct. 23, 1975.

stylebook

Most of the following rules are based on the *Associated Press Stylebook*. Staffs would do well to have several copies in the newsroom. Major newspapers, such as the *Washington Post* and the *Los Angeles Times*, have developed their own stylebooks. This stylebook includes only a few common examples of newspaper style and a few suggestions for covering campus news that professional journalism stylebooks don't cover. Add style citations that are unique to your campus in the space at the end of the stylebook.

Abbreviation

1. Abbreviate titles when used before a full name on first reference (Dr., Gov., Mrs., Sen., Prof., and so on). On second reference, drop the title and use the last name only. When a title follows a name ("Jean Kaye, senator, said that . . . "), write it out.

2. Abbreviate *Street* (St.), *Avenue* (Ave.), and *Boulevard* (Blvd.) when used in numbered addresses (3839 Sequoyah Ave.). Spell out when used without numbers (on Sequoyah Avenue). All other street references are written out (*Road, Terrace, Lane, Circle,* and so on).

3. Abbreviate months of the year when used with numerals (*Oct. 14, 1953*). Spell them out when they stand alone (*October 1953*). Never abbreviate *March, April, May, June, July*. The standard abbreviations are *Jan., Feb., Aug., Sept., Oct., Nov.,* and *Dec.*

4. Commonly recognized groups may be abbreviated on first reference without explanation (*FBI, NATO, GRE*). When citing a group not commonly known, do not use initials after it unless the reader cannot easily make the connection (in "Student Government Association [SGA]," the [SGA] is not necessary).

5. Abbreviate state names when used with the name of a city or town (*Mulberry, FL*). Spell them out when they stand alone (*Florida*). Do not use states at all with commonly known cities (for example, *Chicago, Denver, New York*). Never abbreviate *Alaska, Hawaii, Idaho, Iowa, Maine, Ohio, Texas,* and *Utah*. Standard abbreviations for states are listed below with the U.S. Postal Service's two-letter designation for each state. Many papers are beginning to use these as the standard abbreviation.

Ala. (AL)	Ind. (IN)	Neb. (NE)	S.C. (SC)
Alaska (AK)	Iowa (IA)	Nev. (NV)	S.D. (SD)
Ariz. (AZ)	Kan. (KS)	N.C. (NC)	Tenn. (TN)
Ark. (AR)	Ky. (KY)	N.D. (ND)	Texas (TX)
Calif. (CA)	La. (LA)	N.H. (NH)	Utah (UT)
Colo. (CO)	Maine (ME)	N.J. (NJ)	Va. (VA)
Conn. (CT)	Md. (MD)	N.M. (NM)	Vt. (VT)
Del. (DE)	Mass. (MA)	N.Y. (NY)	Wash. (WA)
Fla. (FL)	Mich. (MI)	Ohio (OH)	Wis. (WI)
Ga. (GA)	Minn. (MN)	Okla. (OK)	W. Va. (WV)
Hawaii (HI)	Miss. (MS)	Ore. (OR)	Wyo. (WY)
Idaho (ID)	Mo. (MO)	Pa. (PA)	
Ill. (IL)	Mont. (MT)	R.I. (RI)	

6. Do not abbreviate days of the week except in tabular material.

7. Abbreviate degrees when they follow names. Otherwise spell them out. ("John Doe, B.A. in art." "She has a master's degree in electrical engineering.") Use an apostrophe in *bachelor's* and *master's*.

Capitalization

1. Capitalize formal titles when used before a name (see 1 under "Abbreviations"). Lowercase when used after a name.

2. Capitalize names of schools, departments, or divisions within an institution if they are proper names (*English department*). Lowercase names that are not proper names (*biology department*).

3. Capitalize names that are trademarks (*Coke, Kleenex*). Do not use these names to indicate the generic product (*cola drink, facial tissue*).

4. Capitalize the names of buildings on campus (*Music Building, Stanton Hall*).

Numerals

1. Spell out numerals below 10 except when referring to time, an amount of money, age, or measurement ("*four* days to go," but "She is 4 years old"). This rule also applies to ordinal numbers (*first, seventh, 13th*).

2. Spell out a numeral at the beginning of a sentence. If the numeral is large, write around it by approximating. ("More than 100,000 cadets were trained.")

3. In street names, spell out numerals under 10 and use numerals above (*First Street, 10th Street*).

4. When spelling out large numbers, use a hyphen only when the first word ends in *y* (*twenty-six, one hundred and sixty*).

5. Always use numbers in percentages. For amounts less than 1 percent, add a zero before the decimal (*0.3 percent*).

6. Fractions standing alone are written out (*one half*). Use numerals when the fraction is a modifier (*1/2-inch margin*).

7. In a series of three or more numbers, all should be numerals (*13 rabbits, 10 dogs and 3 cats*). When just two items are listed, follow the rule in 1 (*10 dogs and three cats*).

8. Always use numerals with dates (*Dec. 1, 1983*). Never use ordinal numbers. No comma is necessary between the month when used alone and year (*August 1978*).

9. Centuries follow rule 1 (*ninth century, 20th century*).

10. Plurals of years do not contain an apostrophe (*1960s, 1990s*).

Punctuation

1. Use commas to separate elements in a series, but do not use a comma before the words *and, or, nor* and *but* when they introduce the final element in the series ("We went here, there and everywhere"). When an element in a series is itself punctuated with a comma, use semicolons to divide elements ("Attending were Jane Doe, president; John Doe, vice-president; and Mary Edwards, treasurer").

2. Quotation marks are placed outside commas and periods ("On the other hand," he said, "the second part is unimportant."). Quotation marks are placed inside colons and semicolons. Although question marks and exclamation points may be placed either inside or outside quotation marks, depending on usage, commonly they are inside quotation marks in newspaper style. If you quote a declarative quote within a question, for instance, the question mark may fall outside the quotation marks ("Is he really part of a 'band on the run?'"). Set off a quote within quotes with single quotation marks ("As Alexander Pope put it, 'Whatever is, is right.'").

3. When a direct quote runs more than one paragraph, end quote marks are not used at the end of the first paragraph. The second paragraph, however, should begin with opening quotes.

4. Use quotation marks around books, plays, poems, songs, speeches, and newspaper stories. Do not use them around names of newspapers or magazines.

5. No comma is used before *Jr.* or numeral designations following a name (*H. Allen James Jr.* or *Patrick Peterson IV*).

6. Hyphenate compound adjectives that precede a noun (*five-yard run, 5-year-old child, two-day meeting*).

7. Use commas in four-digit numbers except in years ("He had 1,992 cars," but "1992 is the copyright date of this book"): Figures of 1,000,000 or larger may be stated as *one million, 10 million*. For money, use *$1 million, $27.5 million*.

8. Use a comma in a date only when it includes day of the month (*Aug. 5, 1966, August 1966*).

Miscellaneous

1. *Percent* is not hyphenated.

2. *Adviser* is correct, not *advisor*.

3. Use *a.m.* and *p.m. Noon* and *midnight* are used alone without numerals. Avoid redundancies such as *8 p.m. tonight*. Do not use *yesterday* and *tomorrow*; use the name of the day instead. Do not use dates when referring to days within one week of publication (*last Wednesday, next Friday*). Use dates when the event is more than a week away ("It will happen Friday, Nov. 23").

4. In general, use last names only on second reference (*Melissa Reid*, then use *Reid*). With a married woman, use *Mrs.* on second reference only if she requests that you use her husband's name (*Mrs. Robert Reid*). With an unmarried woman, use her choice of *Miss* or *Ms.* on second reference or nothing at all.

5. Identify faculty by department and rank ("Attending was Mary James, assistant professor, English"). Identify students by class and hometown ("He is Mike Kramer, sophomore, Austin") or by major if the majority of students are from the same town.

6. Avoid sexism wherever possible. Most newspapers use the male pronoun to refer to both males and females. By using a plural (*they, their*) or by restructuring the sentence, the problem can often be avoided.

Additions

Add to this section any style items unique to your campus.

Add your comments here

glossary

ad—abbreviation for "advertisement."

add—an additional page after the first page of a story.

advance—a story written before an event takes place.

agate—five and one-half point type. Used in sports summaries and other tabular material.

all caps—headline or other editorial material in all uppercase letters.

angle—the major focus of a story. A story about fee increases, for example, can take the angle of its effect on students or on the budget problems that caused the increase.

armpit—unattractive layout pattern in which the story has both a long and a short column in the shape of an upside-down L.

art—a photo, illustration, map, graph, chart, drawing.

ascender—portion of a letter that extends above the x-height, such as in *b, d, h.*

attribution—reference to the source of information in a story.

background—information used by the reporter to better understand a news issue or event.

banner—headline, usually the largest on the page, that extends across the width of the page.

baseline—imaginary line along the base of capital letters in a line of type.

basement—bottom half of the front page.

beat—a person or place checked regularly for news by a reporter.

beat reporter—a reporter who covers a beat, as opposed to a general-assignment reporter.

blanket roller—in offset printing, the roller that takes the inked impression from the printing plate and transfers it to the paper.

blind lead—a lead that describes someone instead of naming him or her.

block paragraph—a journalistic device used to make editing and cutting easier. Because block grafs use no obvious transitions, they can be easily deleted from a story.

body type—type used for stories in the newspaper.

boldface—a typeface with thick strokes that make the letter darker in the paper. Occasionally used for typographical emphasis in a story or for an all-caps caption. Subheads are also usually set in boldface type.

box—a border around a story or photo.

bright—a short, often humorous news story. Many papers try for at least one bright on a front page.

broadsheet—full size, the size of standard newspapers, such as the *New York Times.*

budget—a listing of all editorial matter for a page (page budget) or an entire issue (master budget).

bullet—an oversized period that precedes items in a list, used for emphasis in design.

bumping heads—two heads that fall together on a page so that they may be read as one. Also called tombstoning.

by-line—the name of the writer of the story, usually at the top of the first column, but sometimes used elsewhere for design purposes.

camera ready—the final status of the flat when it is ready to be sent to the camera for a page negative to be made.

cap—short for "capital" letter.

caption—brief, descriptive information for a photo. Usually short and above, or leading into, the cutline.

catchline—larger type used with a cutline (also a *caption*). Catchlines can also be used above a photo, when it is an *overline.*

cathode ray tube (CRT)—another term for a VDT.

classified advertising—ads run in small type in a separate section apart from the editorial content. Ads are *classified* into categories, such as homes for sale, autos, help wanted.

clean copy—a story with few editing corrections.

clip—a story cut out of a paper; sometimes used in job interviews.

clip file—a subject-by-subject file of clips cut from the paper or a reporter's personal clips.

COB—cut out background. Either by knife or by Liquid White-out, taking away the background from the main subject in a velox or photo. Also called silhouette, outline.

cold type—type set by a phototypesetter.

column inch—a measurement of advertisements and stories. A column inch is one column wide (whatever the column width) and one inch deep.

combination head—a headline that covers two related stories although each story has a drop or readout head.

composing room—area where paper is pasted up.

contact sheet—*see* proof sheet.

contract rate—a lower advertising rate than the *open rate*. An advertiser must sign a contract guaranteeing a certain number of column inches of ads to get a contract rate.

co-op ad—an ad paid for jointly by a local business and a national manufacturer or chain.

copy—a story or article written for a newspaper.

copy block—a brief story accompanying a photo story or essay.

copy editor—a person whose primary job is to read copy for errors, write headlines, and lay out pages.

copy flow—the system in which a story moves from reporter through editor to the typesetter.

copy-read—another term for editing a story.

copyright—legal procedure for protecting a story or photo from use by others.

copy wrap—fitting lines of type around an irregular shape, a silhouetted photo for instance.

crop—eliminating unwanted areas from a photo or cutting a photo down to publication size.

curmudgeon—a surly, cantankerous person, usually an editor (at least that is what reporters think).

cursive—type that has visually connecting lines, although lines do not actually touch.

cursor—square or underline on a computer monitor that indicates where new information will be added.

cut—a hot-type term for a photo (thus *cut*lines).

cutline—explanatory material that runs with a photo, either beneath it or, in the case of some photo essays and stories, in a separate block.

cut-off rule—a border beneath a cutline to visually separate the photo from a story it does not illustrate.

deadline—*not* when a story or photo should be turned in, but the last possible moment it can be accepted for publication.

deck—a second, smaller headline beneath a larger main headline.

delayed-identification lead—a lead for a story that uses someone's name but no other descriptive material.

descender—portion of a letter that descends below the baseline, such as in *g*, *p*, *q*.

dingbat—a typographical gimmick, such as a bullet or a star. Often used before a jump headline.

direct quote—set inside quotation marks, it represents a nearly exact replication of the source's words.

display advertising—ads which appear throughout the news paper from local and national businesses and stores.

display type—type larger than body type that is used to attract attention. Includes headlines.

double truck—the middle two pages of a paper, separated only by the fold. Often used for special spreads that display type or photos across the fold.

down style—a headline style that capitalizes only the first word in the headline and all proper nouns.

drop head—a smaller head beneath a combination head. Also called a readout.

dropout—a special effect on a photograph in which white letters of a head (or another second image) show in a black or dark area of the photo. The opposite of an *overprint*, in which black letters appear over a light area of the photo. *See also* reverse.

duotone—printing process in which a light and dark color are mixed to produce a third color in a photo. A "fake" duotone photo is one in which the colored ink is merely placed on top of the normal screened photo.

edit—checking over a story or photo for mechanical and factual errors. Also, the processing of stories and photographs after they are turned in by the reporter or photographer.

editor—staff member who reviews the work of others. In this book, *editor* also refers to the head of the paper or section. *See also* page editor, section editor.

editorialize—to inject opinion in what should be an objective news report, something that should be avoided in good journalism.

editorial page—page in paper that carries editorial comments, letters to the editor, the masthead, editorial cartoons, and so on.

em space—a space equal to the width of the letter M in a given alphabet, which is usually the same as the point size of the letter.

en space—one half an em space.

exchange editor—a staff member who mails out copies of the paper to other schools and files copies that are received.

expository editorial—an editorial that explains a complex issue rather than takes a stand on it.

feature—story in which the entertainment angle is as important as (or more so than) the news angle.

feature photo—*see* stand-alone photo.

fillers—short news stories used to fill small gaps in the page during paste-up.

fit—an instruction to paste-up personnel to adjust the page as necessary to include the entire story.

flag—the name of the newspaper on page 1 (*see also* nameplate), and section names inside the paper. Also called logos.

flat—paste-up sheet.

flexography—a printing method using a resilient letterpress-type plate and water-borne ink (instead of the normal oil base). Very high-quality method.

flush left—all material is aligned along the left margin.

flush right—all material is aligned along the right margin.

folio—small lines of type that include the page number and date of publication.

follow copy—an instruction to the typesetter to set copy exactly as written, even if misspellings or unusual type specifications are requested.

formal balance—balance achieved through duplication of design elements on both halves of a page; the halves are mirror-images of each other.

format—size and general design appearance of a newspaper.

four-color process—the process by which color photographs are reproduced in the paper. Four separate printing plates are used.

full frame—the photo print when the entire negative is reproduced.

full size—the size of standard newspapers, such as the *New York Times. See also* broadsheet.

galley—long column of type that is to be proofread.

gaze motion—*see* leading lines.

golden mean—a ratio of .62 to 1 that represents the most pleasing visual proportion. It should be used whenever possible in page design and photo cropping.

graf—short for "paragraph."

gutter—the narrow strip of white space that separates columns of type on a page.

hairline—the narrowest size line that can be used on the page as a box, cutoff rule, and rule.

halftone—a continuous-tone photo that has been converted into a dot pattern to represent shades of gray in a printed photograph.

hammer head—the opposite of a kicker. A large head of only one or two words, with a longer and smaller headline underneath. Also called reverse kicker.

hanging indent—the indented lines following the flush-left first line of a multiline head.

hard news—news that is timely or event-oriented.

head count—a method of estimating the length of a headline to be sure it fits in the space allowed.

headline—display type above or to the side of a story.

headline schedule—list of all heads used in the paper and the unit counts for various column widths.

horizontal layout—design technique that displays stories and story/photo combinations across the width of the page.

hot type—old typesetting method using hot lead and linotype machines.

indirect quote—a summary or paraphrase of what a source said. Because the words are not precisely what the source said, quotation marks are not used. *See also* direct quote.

informal balance—a method of designing a page so that the two sides are balanced by means other than exact replication, as in *formal balance.*

initial letter or cap—a large display-type letter that starts off a paragraph. Initial letters may be set within the graf or they may stick up above the first line of type. Use them to break up long columns of type.

insert—an ad supplement inserted mechanically or by hand in a newspaper.

inverted pyramid—a method of structuring a story by giving the most important facts first and using the remaining facts in descending order of importance.

investigative reporting—reporting that requires much research and behind-the-scenes interviewing. Probably a misnomer because *all* stories need to be "investigated" until the entire story is known by the reporter and transmitted to the reader.

italic—a typeface designed to slant to the right. *See also* oblique.

kern—taking out space between letters in a line of type to make the line fit within a certain space.

kicker—a small headline used above a larger main headline.

label head—a head without a verb; to be avoided.

layout, lay out—*(n)* the design of a page; *(v)* the process of making a layout.

lead—pronounced lēēd, this is the beginning section of a story, however many grafs that is; sometimes just the first graf.

leading—the amount of white space between lines.

leading lines—lines within a photograph that force the eye to move in the direction the lines point. These lines should not lead the eye away from the story the photo illustrates or off the page.

letterpress—a method of printing in which the inked printing plate is literally pressed on the paper.

libel—falsely defaming or ruining someone's reputation in print.

light table—a paste-up table from which light shines. When a flat is placed over the translucent glass cover, the light shows whether a column of type has been pasted down properly.

line—one line of a multiline headline; $1/14$ inch, a measurement used in place of column inches in national advertising.

line art, line shot—an illustration with no shades of gray, such as a cartoon. May be reproduced without screening.

linespacing—same as *leading.*

localize—writing a story about a statewide or national event with a local angle.

lowercase—small, noncapital letters.

make-good policy—in advertising, policy that states what the paper should do with an ad that cannot be used in the specific issue of the paper desired by the advertiser.

make-up—*layout* in hot-type printing method.

master budget—listing of all editorial material for an issue of the paper.

masthead—box listing the publisher, editors, and other staff members that appears nearly always on the editorial page. Sometimes called staff box.

measure—term referring to the horizontal length of a line of type.

modular system—page-design system in which all elements on the page fit into rectangular modules.

morgue—old newspaper term referring to the library or clip file of the paper. Many papers simply use *library* today.

mortice—area removed from a photograph so another photo or copy block can fit into the space.

mug—a face or a head-and-shoulders shot of a person.

naked wrap—a column of type outside the columns covered by the headline for the story; to be avoided.

nameplate—the name of the paper and other information that goes with it on page 1.

national ad—an ad that refers to a national business or chain, not a local business, and usually placed through advertising agencies.

news hole—the space left in the paper after the ads have been dummied onto the pages.

news issue—a set of situations or ideas that come together at a point to become a news event. News issues exist behind every news event, which is much easier to find.

news peg—a news event that an issue, feature story, or editorial is tied to.

news side—the newsroom, as opposed to the sports or photo departments.

news values—attributes of a newsworthy event or issue, such as proximity, timeliness, consequence.

objectivity—a method of approaching and writing a story that excludes the reporter's opinion.

obscenity—basically, whatever a local jury decides it means. Not to be confused with vulgar or coarse language.

offset—a printing method of higher quality than letterpress in which the printing plate transfers an image to a blanket roller and from the roller to the paper.

off the record—information given to a reporter that is not to be used in print.

op-ed—means Opposite Editorial. A page opposite the editorial page devoted to opinions from staff members and members of the public.

open rate—the highest rate for an ad. One-time advertisers, unless their ads are very large, are charged the open rate.

optical weight—the relative ability of a design element to draw the reader's eye. Dark or unusually shaped elements have heavier optical weights than light or usual elements.

overlay—clear acetate or tracing tissue laid over the page on which material to be overprinted is pasted up or drawn in.

overline—a headline above a stand-alone or wild photo.

overprint—a second printing impression directly on top of the first.

overset—copy that is set in type, but not used in the issue.

padding—adding unnecessary material to a story to make it longer.

page budget—listing of all editorial material on a page.

page dummy—a scaled-down "map" of a page used by an editor to lay out the paper.

page editor—newsroom person in charge of seeing a page through the paste-up process.

page proof—checking the pasted-up flat for errors.

pagination—a computer-based system of laying out a page inside a computer terminal. Simple programs are available for PCs.

paste-up, paste up—(n) the page with all material positioned in place; (v) the process of positioning ads, copy, and such on the final page.

photo-blue—light color used in proofreading pens and on paste-up sheets that is "invisible" to the negative-making camera.

photo credit—name of the photographer who shot a photograph.

photo editor—person in charge of photo staff, photo flow, and photo-filing systems.

photo mechanical transfer—PMT for short, another term for producing a halftone.

photo release—form used by photographers for persons in photos not taken at a news event. It gives the photographer and publication the right to print the photo.

phototypesetting—sometimes called cold type, this method of setting type involves light and light-sensitive paper.

pica—1/6-inch printing measurement.

play—prominence in either placement or size of a story or photo.

point—1/72-inch printing measurement.

process color—standard ink colors used in four-color printing process.

profile—feature story about a person; personality sketch.

proofread—make corrections on a galley of type.

proof sheet—unenlarged prints directly from negative. Also called contact sheet.

proportional scale—device used to calculate dimensions of a photo for enlargement or reduction.

pullquote—same as quoteout.

quoteout—quote from a news source that is set in larger type and narrower measure than body type and inserted in a column of type to break up the gray and add visual interest to the page.

ragged right—unjustified type set flush left.

rate card—includes publication schedule, ad rates, ad policies, and other information for advertisers.

readout—second, smaller head beneath a combination head.

registration marks—usually crosses within circles that line up multiple printings from different plates.

retraction—a correction used when the paper has printed an error in an earlier issue.

reverse—*see* dropout.

reverse kicker—*see* hammer head.

rim—outside of U-shaped copy desk where stories are edited and headlines written. Term not used much anymore because VDTs have made the U-shape obsolete.

roman—type with thick-and-thin strokes and serifs.

rule—line that separates columns of type or surrounds a design element to make a *box*. Made with a roll of border tape in photocomposition. Sometimes just called *tape*.

rule of thirds—concept in photography that the center of interest should fall on one of the lines that divides a photo into thirds, not in the exact center.

sans serif—type with no serifs.

SAU—Standard Advertising Units. Standard sizes for ads to minimize problems advertisers have because of varying column widths of papers across the country.

screen—a process that makes shades of gray from black ink by using various dot patterns.

script—type with connecting lines between letters, like hand-writing.

section editor—editor of news, features, sports, or any other named section of the paper.

serif—small decorative hook on the main stroke of a letter.

set solid—type set with leading the same size as the point size of the type.

shotgun head—*see* combination.

sidebar—a story, usually with a feature approach, that accompanies another story.

silhouette—*see* COB.

size—to enlarge or reduce a photo for reproduction in the newspaper. Also called scale.

skyline—head at top of the page that runs the width of the page.

slant—editorialize. Also used to mean major focus of story (*see* angle).

slot—person who manages the copy desk, edits, assigns heads to be written to rim persons, and lays out pages.

slug—one or two words that describe a story. Typed in upper left corner of every page of a story. All information in upper left is sometimes referred to as the slug.

slugline—the one or two words that specifically describe the story in the upper left corner of page.

soft news—news that is timeless or not tied to a specific news event or issue.

spot color—one additional color besides black used for special design effects.

square serif—type with rectangular serifs. Also called slab serif.

staff box—*see* masthead.

stand-alone photo—photo that does not illustrate or accompany a story. Also called a feature photo, wild photo.

standing head—used over a regular column in every issue.

stet—copy-editing instruction meaning "let it stand."

streamer—*see* banner.

stringer—someone who works for a paper on a piece-by-piece basis.

strip in—printing process in which halftone negatives are taped into place on the page negative. *Windows* are used on the flat instead of *veloxes.*

style—rules regarding abbreviation, punctuation, capitalization, spelling, and use of numerals.

style book—compilation of style rules for a newspaper.

subhead—a boldface line of type used to break up columns of gray.

summary lead—short rundown of important points of a news story; used with the inverted pyramid.

swipe file—collection of design, photo, and story ideas from other publications.

syndicate—service that mails features, columns, cartoons, and other entertainment packages to newspapers.

tabloid—newspaper format that is half the size of a standard broadsheet page, as in *Rolling Stone, The Sporting News.*

take—one page of a typed story.

tear sheet—a page cut out of the paper and mailed to an advertiser as proof of publication.

30—symbol meaning the end. Also, #.

timeless story—story without a specific news peg and thus may be held for another issue. Also called time copy.

tombstone heads—*see* bumping heads.

transition—a device used in writing to get a reader quickly and clearly from one idea to the next.

trim—slightly cutting down a story (as opposed to "cut," which is a major reduction in length, and "boil down," which is reduction achieved by deleting excess verbiage rather than paragraphs).

type font—the alphabet, numbers, and symbols in one typeface. Also used to mean an entire negative of alphabets for a phototypesetter.

typo—typographical error, either by reporter or typesetter.

unit count—method of counting headline length.

up style—headline in which all words are capped.

velox—screened version of a photo that is pasted down on the page. Also called *PMT,* for photo mechanical transfer.

video display terminal (VDT)—a keyboard and "television" screen hooked to a computer that reporters, editors, and designers use to put the paper together.

walkoff—a partial COB in which part of the photo extends beyond the normal rectangular shape.

Wall Street Journal **formula**—a method of writing a story that lead, and ends, with a specific incident to illustrate the main point of the story.

web press—a press that uses a continuous roll of paper rather than individual sheets.

weight—*see* optical weight.

widow—a short line of type at the top of a column.

wild photo—*see* stand-alone photo.

x-height—height of lowercase letters, excluding ascenders and descenders.

bibliography

The following is only a brief list. Many more good books and periodicals are available in each category. Only those publications that would be most helpful, given the approach to newspapers in this book, have been included. A few entries have been annotated. Other helpful publications are listed in the appendix under Journalism Organizations. (P) indicates a periodical.

Chapter 1: Introduction to newspapering

MOTT, FRANK LUTHER, *American Journalism: A History of Newspapers in the United States through 270 Years, 1690–1960.* New York: Macmillan, Inc., 1962. A good book for any historical question about newspapers. No longer in print, but certainly in most libraries.

Chapter 3: Staff organization and copy flow

WILLIAMS, HERBERT L., *Newspaper Organization and Management* (5th ed.). Ames: Iowa State University Press, 1978.

Chapter 4: Gathering the news

METZLER, KEN, *Creative Interviewing* (2nd ed.). Englewood Cliffs, N.J.: Prentice-Hall, Inc., 1989.

Chapter 5: Legal and ethical issues

PEMBER, DON R., *Mass Media Law.* Dubuque, Iowa: Wm. C. Brown, 1984. *Student Press Law Center Report* (P). Student Press Law Center, 800 18th Street N.W., Washington, D.C. 20001. This quarterly is the best place to look for pertinent information about student (and adviser) legal problems.

TRAGER, ROBERT, AND DONNA L. DICKERSON, *College Student Press Law.* Terra Haute, Ind.: National Council of College Publications Advisers, 1979. Excellent book, even for high school papers. Be aware, however, that the laws and rulings have changed since publication.

Chapter 6: Newswriting

Associated Press Stylebook. New York: The Associated Press, 1989.

BERNSTEIN, THEODORE M., *The Careful Writer: A Modern Guide to English Usage.* New York: Atheneum Publishers, 1965.

BROOKS, BRIAN, AND JAMES PINSON, *Working with Words: A Concise Handbook for Media Writers and Editors.* New York: St. Martin's Press, Inc., 1989. Short and sweet.

FLESCH, RUDOLF, *The Art of Readable Writing.* New York: Harper & Row, Publishers, Inc., 1974.

KESSLER, LAUREN, AND DUNCAN MCDONALD, *Uncovering the News: A Journalist's Search for Information.* Belmont, Calif.: Wadsworth Publishing Co., 1987.

KESSLER, LAUREN, AND DUNCAN MCDONALD, *When Words Collide: A Journalist's Guide to Grammar and Style.* Belmont, Calif.: Wadsworth Publishing Co., 1987. Another short and sweet one.

MACDOUGALL, CURTIS D., AND ROBERT D. REID, *Interpretative Reporting* (9th ed.). New York: Macmillan, Inc., 1987.

MEYER, PHILIP, *Precision Journalism: A Reporter's Introduction to Social Science Methods* (2nd ed.). University Microfilm International (U. of Michigan), 1990. Though out of print, you may get a reprint this way.

PREJEAN, BLANCHE, AND WAYNE A. DANIELSON, *Programed News Style.* Englewood Cliffs, N.J.: Prentice-Hall, Inc., 1988. A good way to learn style.

STRUNK, WILLIAM, JR., AND E. B. WHITE, *The Elements of Style.* (3rd ed.) New York: Macmillan, Inc., 1979.

ZINSSER, WILLIAM, *On Writing Well* (3rd ed.). New York: Harper & Row, Publishers, Inc., 1985.

Chapter 7: Features and reviews

BROOKS, BRIAN S., AND OTHERS, *News Reporting and Writing.* New York: St. Martin's Press, Inc., 1980.

RUEHLMANN, WILLIAM, *Stalking the Feature Story.* New York: Random House, 1979. Highly recommended to all writers, not just feature writers.

Chapter 8: Editorials and opinion columns

BETTINGHAUS, ERWIN PAUL, *Persuasive Communication.* New York: Holt, Rinehart & Winston, 1987.

MACDOUGALL, CURTIS D. *The Principles of Editorial Writing.* Dubuque, IA: Wm. C. Brown, 1973.

Chapter 9: Sports

Sports Illustrated (P). Time-Life Building, New York, N.Y. 10020. Follow the leader.

Chapter 10: Photo production

CRAVEN, GEORGE M., *Object and Image: An Introduction to Photography* (3rd ed.). Englewood Cliffs, N.J.: Prentice-Hall, Inc., 1989.

EVANS, HAROLD, *Pictures on a Page: Photojournalism and Picture Editing*. Belmont, Calif.: Wadsworth Publishing Co., 1979.

KERNS, ROBERT L., *Photojournalism: Photography with a Purpose*. Englewood Cliffs, N.J.: Prentice-Hall, Inc., 1980.

Chapter 11: Editing

RIBLET, CARL, JR., *The Solid Gold Copy Editor*. Dubuque, Iowa: Kendall/Hunt Publishing Co., 1983. See also books listed in Chapter 6.

Chapter 12: Typography and printing

ARNOLD, EDMUND, *Ink on Paper 2*. New York: Harper & Row, Publishers, Inc., 1972. Out of print, but good.

CONOVER, THEODORE, *Graphic Communications Today* (2nd ed.). Minneapolis: West Publishing, 1990.

Pocket Pal. International Paper Company (most recent ed.). A must for all newspaper staffs that do their own paste-up or have a print shop on campus.

SOLOMON, MARTIN, *The Art of Typography*. New York: Watson-Guptill Publications, 1986.

Chapter 13: Page design

BOHLE, ROBERT, *Publication Design for Editors*. Englewood Cliffs, N.J.: Prentice-Hall, Inc., 1990. Good explanation of design principles and concepts behind integrated editing.

Design: The Journal of the Society of Newspaper Design (P). The Newspaper Center, Box 17290, Dulles International Airport, Washington, D.C. 20041.

GARCIA, MARIO, *Contemporary Newspaper Design: A Structural Approach* (2nd ed.). Englewood Cliffs, N.J.: Prentice-Hall, Inc., 1987.

HARROWER, TIM, *Newspaper Designer's Handbook*. Dubuque, Iowa: Wm. C. Brown, 1989. Good examples of all design principles with "good" versus "weak" layouts and pages shown.

MOEN, DARYL R., *Newspaper Layout and Design* (2nd ed.). Ames: Iowa State University Press, 1989. Comes with workbook and teacher's manual.

NELSON, ROY PAUL, *Publication Design* (5th ed.). Dubuque, Iowa: Wm. C. Brown, 1982.

PARKER, ROGER, *Looking Good in Print* (2nd ed.). New York: Ventana Press, 1989. Good tips for desktop design.

Chapter 14: Headlines

See Chapter 11.

Chapter 15: Production

BEACH, MARK, STEVE SHEPRO, AND KEN RUSSON, *Getting It Printed*. Portland, Ore.: Coast to Coast Books, 1986. Not as technical as *Pocket Pal*, but very good.

See *Pocket Pal*, listed for Chapter 12.

Chapter 16: Advertising

BURTON, PHILIP WARD, *Advertising Copywriting* (5th ed.). New York: John Wiley & Sons, 1984.

NELSON, ROY PAUL, *The Design of Advertising* (5th ed.). Dubuque, Iowa: Wm. C. Brown, 1989.

WATKINS, DON, *Newspaper Advertising Handbook*. Wheaton, IL: Dynamo, Inc., 1980.

index